THE VATICAN COUNCIL
AND CHRISTIAN UNITY

THE VATICAN COUNCIL AND CHRISTIAN UNITY

A Commentary on the Decree on Ecumenism of the Second Vatican Council, together with a translation of the text

BERNARD LEEMING S.J.

*Newman Professor of Ecumenical Theology,
The Heythrop Pontifical Athenaeum,
Oxon., England*

HARPER & ROW, PUBLISHERS
NEW YORK

FIRST EDITION

LIBRARY OF CONGRESS CATALOG CARD NUMBER: 66-15863

CONTENTS

v

CHAPTER THREE

CHURCHES AND ECCLESIASTICAL COMMUNITIES
SEPARATED FROM THE ROMAN APOSTOLIC SEE

SECTION I

Special Consideration of the Eastern Orthodox Churches

SECTION II

Separated Churches and Ecclesiastical Communities
in the West

APPENDICES

FOREWORD

I now wonder if it was not rash to have accepted the invitation of the publishers of this book to write a commentary on the Decree of the Second Vatican Council on Ecumenism. Both they and I had imagined that a commentary could be written in a comparatively short time. But I became more and more disillusioned of this idea. The Decree is, indeed, simple and clear. But behind its simplicity and clarity lie very complex situations and complicated issues. The Decree itself took more than three years to compose, and into it went the combined knowledge and wisdom of bishops and scholars, both clerical and lay, who had had experience in many parts of the world. Every single sentence in the document was discussed exhaustively and often exhaustingly at full sessions of the Secretariat, and the Fathers of the Council made suggestions, some at the public sessions of the Council, some in writing, for modifications, not seldom about the choice of a single word. There are three small volumes of *Modi*, or suggested modifications proposed by the Fathers of the Council, some of which were accepted by the Secretariat, some rejected and the reasons for rejection given.

The evident aim of the Secretariat for the Promotion of Christian Unity was to write in a 'pastoral' way, to keep the large-heartedness of Pope John XXIII and the humble spirit of Pope Paul VI when he asked forgiveness. But it was also the duty of the Secretariat to represent faithfully the mind of the Council, which numbered over two thousand members, as far as this was possible. The Decree succeeds, I think, in all these aims, and very manifestly in the last, since the Decree was approved with only eleven votes against and over two thousand in favour.

The Decree, however, does not stand alone but is part of the whole effort of the Second Vatican Council at reform and renewal of the Catholic Church; and hence it must be taken in conjunction with the pronouncements of the Church, on the

Liturgy, on the Eastern Catholic Churches, as, also, on religious liberty. None of these matters, of course, affects the substance of the Decree on Ecumenism, but they may serve, so to speak, as background material in which the ecumenical document stands out.

The Decree forms part, also, of the general Christian movement towards the fulness of the unity which Christ wills for his Church; for it arose out of that movement and may in turn affect that movement. Separated brethren, I think, received the document favourably, on the whole. Some, indeed, expressed doubts on the ground that the Decree appeared to make Rome the 'centre' of the ecumenical movement. Such fears should, one may think, be modified by the fact that the Decree is not dealing with ecumenism in general but is a directive to Catholics, giving the principles which should guide them in their participation in the efforts of all Christians. Among those principles is sincere esteem for others and humility about ourselves.

It has been my privilege during these last few years to have had contact with members of many different Communions. It is impossible to exaggerate my sense of their integrity and dedication. I feel one in heart and spirit with them, and can attribute our divisions only to some diabolic spirit of evil which opposes the Holy Spirit of God who is moving us all to greater unity.

If this inadequate account of Catholic principles of ecumenism can in any way help towards the fulness of unity, I should be most grateful to the Holy Spirit. But I am acutely conscious of deficiencies, and if any feel that I have misrepresented anything, I apologize beforehand and express complete willingness to accept correction.

By the time this book appears, the Second Vatican Council will have concluded its sessions and will have issued sixteen main documents. Is it possible to make a general division and to say that half of these refer to the internal life of the Church and half to its relations with others?

On such a division, to the internal life of the Church belong the documents on the Liturgy, the Church, the Lay Apostolate,

the Pastoral Office of Bishops, Religious Orders and Congregations, the Training of Priests, the Priestly Life and Ministry,
and Christian Education. To the relations of the Church with
others belong the documents on Media of Communication,
Ecumenism, Religious Liberty, Missions, the Church and the
World, the Church and non-Christian Religions, Revelation,
and—because of their special position and vocation—the
Eastern Catholic Churches. These are, of course, part, even an
essential part, of the Church's catholicity; yet their affinity with
their Orthodox brethren gives them a very special place.

The very attempt, however, to make such a division reveals
its inadequacy, because the essential mission of the Church is to
bring all men to Christ, and hence nothing is so 'internal' to the
Church that it has not a relation to those who are not within the
unity which Christ wills.

A synod of bishops, foreshadowed by Pope Paul VI in the
second and third sessions (cf. *below* pp. 122 and 224), was set up
by him on 15th September 1965 (text in *Osservatore Romano*,
16: IX: 65). Its general functions are 'to encourage close union
and collaboration between the Pope and the bishops of the
entire world; to ensure that direct and real information is provided on situations and questions touching upon the internal
action of the Church and its necessary action in the world of
today; and to facilitate agreement on essential matters of doctrine and on methods of procedure in the life of the Church.'
General, extraordinary and special assemblies are planned: the
general, consisting of patriarchs, major archbishops, and representatives elected by national conferences of bishops, on the
general basis of one representative for twenty-five members,
together with religious elected by the Roman union of clerical
religious institutes; at the extraordinary assemblies the presidents of the national or regional conferences take the place of
elected representatives; and at the special assemblies, which
deal with matters of regional interest, representation is the
same as for general assemblies, account taken of the limited
number of national or regional conferences involved.

The time and place of the meetings of the Synod are left to
the determination of the Pope, who also appoints a permanent
Secretary. It is clear that the Synod of bishops will depend

upon the more exact definition of procedures in the various Bishops' Conferences, whether national or regional.

This measure, together with the reforms in the Curia (*below*, p. 122), and the continuance of some, at least, of the Council's Commissions and Secretariats, indicate a real decentralization. It may be anticipated that more and more the laity will play its part in the decision-making of the Church; the Special Commission set up by Pope Paul to advise him about methods of responsible parenthood contained a number of lay men and women.

It would be premature to attempt here any estimate of the effect of the Council in the life of the Church and in relations with separated brethren; the Council is rather a beginning than an end, since its insights must be assimilated by the whole body of the faithful, and since, as the Decree on Ecumenism says, 'no obstacle must be placed to the ways of divine providence nor any limit set to the future inspirations of the Holy Spirit' (n. 24). The Decree, though directed only to Catholics, forms part of a great movement of the Holy Spirit in the minds and hearts of men, making them aware of their interdependencies, and causing them to seek for a unity which will truly be a sign to the world that Christ is sent by God. Many member Churches of the British Council of Churches have covenanted together for unity by Easter Day 1980: which may be, as Dr Norman Goodall said, 'a splendidly irrational symbol', but yet a clear manifestation of a certain holy impatience, felt even by those who have doubts and misgivings. The official Catholic observers at the British Council of Churches, if they share some of the misgivings, share also the hopes and the exhilaration of a great enterprise. The words of Dr Douglas Horton, an observer at the Vatican Council, may well be re-echoed:

'Because you have made us your friends, nothing important to you can be unimportant to us. We shall never again be indifferent, however we may disagree, with anything in your theology, your polity, your liturgy. Let this relationship of simple human friendship be carried from the centre you have created here to the boundaries of Christendom and we have at least the beginning of ecumenism.' (*Tablet*, 2: x: 65, p. 1102.)

ACKNOWLEDGEMENTS

Grateful acknowledgement of permission to quote extracts of copyright material is made to the following:

The Right Rev O. S. Tomkins, Bishop of Bristol; Dr W. A. Visser 't Hooft, World Council of Churches publications, including the *Ecumenical Review*; the S.C.M. Press Ltd: *Faith and Order*, Proceedings of the World Conference at Lausanne 1927, ed H. N. Bate; *The First Assembly of the World Council of Churches* (Amsterdam, 1948), ed W. A. Visser 't Hooft, 1962; *The Fourth World Conference on Faith and Order*, (Report from Montreal), eds P. C. Rodger and L. Vischer, 1964; *Unity Begins at Home* (First British Conference on Faith and Order, Nottingham) 1964; *The Reunion of the Church* (2nd ed) Lesslie Newbigin, 1960; *A Future for the Free Churches?* Christopher Driver, 1962; The Marcham Manor Press Ltd: *Priesthood and Sacraments*, R. T. Beckwith, 1965; The McGraw-Hill Book Company: *Challenge to Reunion*, eds R. M. Brown and D. H. Scott, 1963; George Allen and Unwin Ltd: *The Pentecostal Movement*, Nils Bloch-Hoell, 1965; Thomas Nelson and Sons Ltd: *The Eastern Churches and Catholic Unity*, ed Patriarch Maximos, 1964; Hodder and Stoughton Ltd: *The Riddle of Roman Catholicism*, J. Pelikan, 1960; Geoffrey Chapman Ltd: *The Christian Churches of the East*, D. Attwater, 1963; Harper and Row Inc: *On the Road to Christian Unity*, S. McC. Cavert; United Church Press: *A Vatican Diary*, D. Horton.

My thanks are due to the Rt Rev Thomas Holland, Bishop of Salford, who read part of this manuscript and gave me some most useful advice; and likewise to the Rev Maurice Bévenot, S.J., who helped greatly with translation and put at my disposal his specialized knowledge of the progress of the various *Schemata* through diverse stages to the final Decree. Neither is, of course, in any way responsible for the judgments or opinions expressed. I thank, also, the Rev G. Walkerlwy, B. Hall, and M. Keane, who helped in the correction of proofs, and, last but not least, the Rev C. Charlier, who most kindly compiled the Index.

THE DECREE ON ECUMENISM
BY THE SECOND VATICAN COUNCIL
PROMULGATED BY POPE PAUL VI ON
NOVEMBER 21, 1964

INTRODUCTION

1. THE RESTORATION OF UNITY among all Christians is one of the principal concerns of the Second Vatican Council. Christ the Lord founded one Church and one Church only. Nevertheless, many Christian Communions claim to be the true inheritors of Jesus Christ. All, indeed, avow that they are followers of the Lord, but they are divided in their convictions and go their different ways, as if Christ himself were divided.[1] Such division is clearly contrary to Christ's will. It is a scandal to the world and a hindrance to the sacred task of preaching the Gospel to every creature.

But the Lord of the ages works out with patience and wisdom the plan of his grace on our behalf, sinners though we are. In recent times more than ever before he has been rousing divided Christians to repentance over their divisions and to a longing for unity. Everywhere large numbers have felt the impulse of this grace; and among our separated brethren likewise, through the inspiration of the Holy Spirit, a movement has grown and developed, whose aim is the restoration of the unity of all Christians. Those who take part in this movement, called 'ecumenical', invoke the triune God and confess Jesus Christ as Lord and Saviour. This they do not merely as individuals but also as corporate bodies, everyone regarding the body in which he heard the Gospel as his Church and as God's Church. Yet almost all, though in different ways, long for the one visible Church of God, that truly universal Church whose mission is to convert the whole world to the Gospel, so that the world may be saved, to the glory of God.

It is with joy of spirit that this sacred Council has given its attention to all these aspirations. It has already declared its teaching about the Church, and now, moved by desire for the restoration of unity among all the followers of Christ, it wishes to set before all Catholics the ways and the means by which they can respond to the grace of this divine call.

[1] I Cor 1: 13.

Chapter 1

CATHOLIC PRINCIPLES OF ECUMENISM

2. In this the love of God was made manifest among us, that the Father sent his only-begotten Son into the world so that, being made man, he might by his redemption give new life and unity to the entire human race.[1] Before offering himself up as a spotless victim upon the altar of the cross, Christ prayed to his Father for all who believe in him: 'that they may all be one; even as thou, Father, art in me, and I in thee, that they also may be one in us, so that the world may believe that thou has sent me' (Jn 17: 21). In his Church he instituted the wonderful sacrament of the Eucharist by which the unity of his Church is both signified and made a reality. He gave his followers a new commandment to love one another,[2] and promised the Spirit, their Advocate[3] who, as Lord and life-giver, should remain with them forever.

After being lifted up on the cross and glorified, the Lord Jesus poured forth his Spirit as he had promised, and through the Spirit he has called and gathered together the people of the New Covenant, who are the Church, into a unity of faith, hope and charity, as the Apostle teaches us: 'There is one body and one Spirit, just as you were called to the one hope of your calling; one Lord, one faith, one baptism' (Eph 4: 4–5). For 'all you who have been baptized into Christ have put on Christ . . . for you are all one in Christ Jesus' (Gal 3: 27–8). It is the Holy Spirit, dwelling in those who believe and filling and ruling over the Church as a whole, who brings about that wonderful communion of the faithful. He brings them into intimate union with Christ, so that he is the principle of the Church's unity. The distribution of graces and offices is his work too,[4] enriching the Church of Jesus Christ with different functions 'in order to equip the saints for the work of service, so as to build up the body of Christ' (Eph 4: 12).

In order to establish this his holy Church everywhere in the world till the end of time, Christ entrusted to the College of the Twelve the task of teaching, ruling and sanctifying.[5] Among their number he selected Peter, and after his confession of faith determined that on

---

[1] 1 Jn 4: 9; Col 1: 18–20; Jn 11: 52.   [2] Jn 13: 34.   [3] Jn 16: 7.
[4] 1 Cor 12: 4–11.   [5] Mt 28: 18–20; cf. Jn 20: 21–3.

him he would build his Church. To Peter also he promised the keys of the kingdom of heaven,[1] and after his profession of love, entrusted all his sheep to him to be confirmed in faith[2] and shepherded in perfect unity.[3] Christ Jesus himself was forever to remain the chief cornerstone[4] and shepherd of our souls.[5]

Jesus Christ, then, willed that the Apostles and their successors—the bishops with Peter's successor at their head—should preach the Gospel faithfully, administer the sacraments, and rule the Church in love. It is thus, under the action of the Holy Spirit, that Christ wills his people to increase, and he perfects his people's fellowship in unity: in their confessing the one faith, celebrating divine worship in common, and keeping the fraternal harmony of the family of God.

The Church, then, is God's only flock; it is like a standard lifted high for the nations to see it:[6] for it serves all mankind through the Gospel of peace[7] as it makes its pilgrim way in hope towards its home in heaven.[8]

This is the sacred mystery of the unity of the Church, in Christ and through Christ, the Holy Spirit enriching this unity with a variety of gifts. It is a mystery that finds its highest model and source in the unity of the Persons of the Trinity: the Father and the Son in the Holy Spirit, one God.

3. Even in the beginnings of this one and only Church of God there arose certain rifts,[9] which the Apostle strongly condemned.[10] But in subsequent centuries much more extensive dissensions made their appearance and large communities came to be separated from full communion with the Catholic Church—for which, often enough, men of both sides were to blame. The children who are born into these communities and who grow up believing in Christ cannot be accused of the sin involved in the separation, and the Catholic Church looks upon them as brothers, with respect and affection. For men who believe in Christ and have been truly baptized are in real communion with the Catholic Church even though this communion is imperfect. The differences that exist in varying degrees between them and the Catholic Church—whether in doctrine and sometimes in discipline, or concerning the structure of the Church—do indeed create many obstacles, sometimes serious ones, to full ecclesiastical communion. The ecumenical movement is striving to

---

[1] Mt 16: 18; cf. Mt 18: 18.   [2] Lk 22: 32.
[3] Jn 21: 15–18.   [4] Eph 2: 20.
[5] 1 Pet 2: 25; Vat. Council I, Sess. IV (1870) Constitutio *Pastor Aeternus*: Coll. Lac. 7, 482 a.
[6] Is 11: 10–12.   [7] Eph 2: 17–18; cf. Mk 16: 15.
[8] 1 Pet 1: 3–9.   [9] 1 Cor 11: 18–19; Gal 1: 6–9; 1 Jn 2: 18–19.
[10] 1 Cor 1: 11 ff.; 11: 22.

overcome these obstacles. But even in spite of them it remains true that all who have been justified by faith in baptism are members of Christ's Body,[1] and have a right to be called Christian, and so are with solid reason recognized as brothers by the children of the Catholic Church.[2]

Moreover, some, and even most, of the significant elements and endowments which together go to build up and give life to the Church itself, can exist outside the visible boundaries of the Catholic Church: the written word of God; the life of grace; faith, hope and charity, with the other interior gifts of the Holy Spirit, and visible elements too. All of these, coming from Christ and leading back to Christ, properly belong to the one Church of Christ.

The brethren divided from us also celebrate many liturgical actions of the Christian religion. These most certainly can truly engender a life of grace in ways that vary according to the condition of each Church or Community. These liturgical actions must be regarded as capable of giving access to that communion in which is salvation.

It follows that the separated Churches[3] and Communities as such, though we believe them to be deficient in some respects, have by no means been deprived of significance and importance in the mystery of salvation. For the Holy Spirit has not refrained from using them as means of salvation whose efficacy comes from that grace and truth which in all its fulness has been entrusted to the Catholic Church.

Nevertheless, our separated brethren, whether considered as individuals or as Communities and Churches, are not blessed with that unity which Jesus Christ wished to bestow on all those who through him were born again into one body, and with him quickened to newness of life—that unity which the Holy Scriptures and the ancient tradition of the Church proclaim. For it is only through Christ's Catholic Church, which is 'the all-embracing means of salvation', that they can benefit fully from the means of salvation. We believe that our Lord entrusted all the blessings of the New Covenant to none others than the apostolic college of which Peter is the head. They were to establish the one Body of Christ on earth into which all should be fully incorporated who belong in any way to the people of God. This people of God, though still in its members

---

[1] Council of Florence, Sess. VIII (1439), Decretum *Exultate Deo*: Mansi 31, 1055 A.
[2] St Augustine, *In Ps. 32, Enarr. II, 29*: PL 36, 299.
[3] Fourth Lateran Council (1215) Constitutio IVa: Mansi 22,990; Second Council of Lyons (1274), Professio fidei Michaelis Palaeologi: Mansi 24,71 E; Council of Florence, Sess. VI (1439), Definitio *Laetentur caeli*: Mansi 31,1026 E.

liable to sin, is ever growing in Christ during its pilgrimage on earth, and is guided by God's gentle wisdom, according to his hidden designs, until it shall happily arrive at the fulness of eternal glory in the heavenly Jerusalem.

4. Today, in many parts of the world, under the inspiring grace of the Holy Spirit, many efforts are being made in prayer, word and action to attain that fulness of unity which Jesus Christ desires. The sacred Council exhorts all the Catholic faithful to recognize the signs of the times and to take an active and intelligent part in the work of ecumenism.

The term 'ecumenical movement' indicates the measures and activities planned and undertaken, according to the various needs of the Church and as opportunities offer, to promote Christian unity. These are: first, every effort to avoid expressions, judgements and actions which do not represent the condition of our separated brethren with truth and fairness and so make mutual relations with them more difficult; then, 'dialogue' between competent experts from different Churches and Communities. At these meetings, which are organized in a religious spirit, each explains the teaching of his Communion in greater depth and brings out clearly its distinctive features. In such dialogue, everyone gains a truer knowledge and more just appreciation of the teaching and religious life of both Communions. In addition, the way is prepared for co-operation between them in the duties for the common good of humanity which are demanded by every Christian conscience; and, wherever this is allowed, there is prayer in common. Finally, all are led to examine their own faithfulness to Christ's will for the Church and accordingly to undertake with vigour the task of renewal and reform.

When such actions are undertaken prudently and patiently by the Catholic faithful, with the attentive guidance of their bishops, they promote justice and truth, concord and collaboration, as well as the spirit of brotherly love and unity. This is the way that, when the obstacles to perfect ecclesiastical communion have been gradually overcome, all Christians will at last, in a common celebration of the Eucharist, be gathered into a single Church in that unity which Christ bestowed on his Church from the beginning. We believe that this unity exists in the Catholic Church as something she can never lose, and we cherish the hope that it will go on increasing.

However, it should be evident that, when individuals wish for full Catholic communion, their preparation and reconciliation is an undertaking which of its nature is distinct from ecumenical action.

But there is no opposition between the two, since both proceed from the marvellous ways of God.

Catholics, in their ecumenical work, must assuredly be concerned for their separated brethren, praying for them, keeping them informed about the Church, making the first approaches towards them. But their primary duty is to make a careful and honest appraisal of whatever needs to be done or renewed in the Catholic household itself, in order that its life may bear witness more clearly and faithfully to the teachings and institutions which have come to it from Christ through the hands of the Apostles.

For although the Catholic Church has been endowed with all divinely revealed truth and with all means of grace, yet its members fail to live by them with all the fervour that they should, so that the radiance of the Church's image is less in the eyes of our separated brethren and of the world at large, and the growth of God's kingdom is delayed. All Catholics must therefore aim at Christian perfection[1] and, each according to his station, play his part that the Church may daily be more purified and renewed. For the Church must bear in her own body the humility and dying of Jesus,[2] against the day when Christ will present her to himself in all her glory without spot or wrinkle.[3]

All in the Church must preserve unity in essentials. But let all, according to the gifts they have received, enjoy a proper freedom, in their various forms of spiritual life and discipline, in their different liturgical rites, and even in their theological elaborations of revealed truth. In all things let charity prevail. If they are true to this course of action, they will be giving ever better expression to the authentic catholicity and apostolicity of the Church.

On the other hand, Catholics must gladly acknowledge and esteem the truly Christian endowments from our common heritage which are to be found among our separated brethren. There are those who bear witness to Christ, even at times to the shedding of their blood; and it is right and salutary to recognize such riches of Christ in the virtuous deeds and the lives of others. For God is always wonderful and his works too deserve our wonder.

Nor should we forget that anything wrought by the grace of the Holy Spirit in the hearts of our separated brethren can be a help to our own edification. Whatever is truly Christian is never contrary to what genuinely belongs to the faith; indeed, it can always bring a deeper realization of the mystery of Christ and the Church.

Nevertheless, the divisions among Christians prevent the Church

---

[1] Jas 1: 4; Rom 12: 1-2.   [2] 2 Cor 4: 10; Phil 2: 5-8.   [3] Eph 5: 27.

from attaining the fulness of catholicity proper to her, in those of her sons who, though attached to her by baptism, are yet separated from full communion with her. Furthermore, the Church herself finds it more difficult to express in actual life her full catholicity in all its bearings.

This sacred Council is gratified to note that the participation by the Catholic faithful in ecumenical work is growing daily. It commends this work to the bishops everywhere in the world to be vigorously stimulated by them and guided with prudence.

Chapter 2

THE PRACTICE OF ECUMENISM

5. The attainment of union is the concern of the whole Church, faithful and clergy alike. This concern extends to everyone, whatever his talent, whether it be exercised in ordinary Christian life or in theological and historical research. This very concern itself reveals to some extent the bond of brotherhood between all Christians and it helps towards that full and perfect unity which God in his kindness wills.

6. Every renewal of the Church[1] is essentially grounded in an increase of fidelity to her own calling. Undoubtedly this is the basis of the movement towards unity.

Christ summons the Church to continual reformation in her pilgrimage on earth. The Church is always in need of this, in so far as she is an institution of human beings here on earth. Thus if, in various times and circumstances, there have been deficiencies in moral conduct or in Church discipline, or even in the way that Church teaching has been formulated—to be carefully distinguished from the deposit of faith itself—these can and should be set right at the opportune moment.

Church renewal has therefore notable ecumenical importance. In various spheres of the Church's life, this renewal is already taking place. The biblical and liturgical movements, the preaching of the Word of God and the teaching of the catechism, the apostolate of the laity, new forms of religious life and the spiritualizing of married life, and the Church's social teaching and activity—all these should be considered as promises and guarantees for the future progress of ecumenism.

7. There can be no ecumenism worthy of the name without a change of heart. For it is from the renewal of the inner life of our minds,[2] from self-denial and an unstinted love that desires of unity take their rise and develop in a mature way. We should therefore pray to the Holy Spirit for the grace to be genuinely self-denying, humble, gentle in the service of others, and to have an attitude of brotherly generosity towards them. St Paul says: 'I, therefore, a prisoner for the Lord, beg you to lead a life worthy of the calling to

[1] Fifth Lateran Council, Sess. XII (15517). Constitutio *Constituti*: Mansi 32, 988 B–C.
[2] Eph 4: 24.

8

which you have been called, with all humility and meekness, with patience, forbearing one another in love, eager to maintain the unity of the spirit in the bond of peace' (Eph 4: 1–3). This exhortation is directed especially to those raised to sacred orders precisely that the work of Christ may be continued. He came among us 'not to be served but to serve' (Mt 20: 28).

The words of St John hold good about sins against unity: 'If we say we have not sinned, we make him a liar, and his word is not in us' (1 Jn 1: 10). So we humbly beg pardon of God and of our separated brethren, just as we forgive them that trespass against us.

The faithful should remember that the more effort they make to live holier lives according to the Gospel, the better will they further Christian unity and put it into practice. For the closer their union with the Father, the Word, and the Spirit, the more deeply and easily will they be able to grow in mutual brotherly love.

8. This change of heart and holiness of life, along with public and private prayer for the unity of Christians, should be regarded as the soul of the whole ecumenical movement, and merits the name 'spiritual ecumenism'.

It is a recognized custom for Catholics to have frequent recourse to that prayer for the unity of the Church in which the Saviour himself on the eve of his death so fervently appealed to his Father, 'that they may all be one' (Jn 17: 20).

In certain special circumstances, such as the prescribed prayers 'for unity', and during ecumenical gatherings, it is allowable, and indeed desirable that Catholics should join in prayer with their separated brethren. Such prayers in common are certainly an effective means of obtaining the grace of unity, and they are a true expression of the ties which still bind Catholics to their separated brethren. 'For where two or three are gathered together in my name, there am I in the midst of them' (Mt 18: 20).

Yet worship in common (*communicatio in sacris*) is not to be considered as a means to be used indiscriminately for the restoration of Christian unity. There are two main principles governing the practice of such common worship: first, the bearing witness to the unity of the Church, and second, the sharing in the means of grace. Witness to the unity of the Church very generally forbids common worship to Christians, but the grace to be had from it sometimes commends this practice. The course to be adopted, with due regard to all the circumstances of time, place, and persons, is to be decided by local episcopal authority, unless otherwise provided for by the Bishops' Conference according to its statutes, or by the Holy See.

9. We must get to know the outlook of our separated brethren. To achieve this purpose, study is of necessity required, and this must be pursued with a sense of realism and good will. Catholics, if they are to be properly equipped for the task, need to acquire a more adequate understanding of the respective doctrines of our separated brethren, their history, their spiritual and liturgical life, their religious psychology and general background. Most valuable for this purpose are meetings of the two sides—especially for discussion of theological problems—where each can treat with the other on an equal footing—provided that those who take part in them are truly competent and have the requisite approval. From such dialogue will emerge still more clearly what the situation of the Catholic Church really is. In this way too the outlook of our separated brethren will be better understood, and our own belief more aptly explained.

10. Sacred theology and other branches of knowledge, especially of an historical nature, must be taught with due regard for the ecumenical point of view, so that they may correspond more exactly with the facts.

It is most important that future pastors and priests should have mastered a theology that has been carefully worked out in this way and not controversially, especially with regard to those aspects which concern the relations of separated brethren with the Catholic Church.

This importance is the greater because the instruction and spiritual formation of the faithful and of religious depends so largely on the formation which their priests have received.

Moreover, Catholics engaged in missionary work in the same territories as other Christians ought, particularly in these times, to know the problems and the benefits in their apostolate which derive from the ecumenical movement.

11. The way in which the Catholic faith is expressed should never become an obstacle to dialogue with our brethren. It is, of course, essential that the doctrine should be clearly presented in its entirety. Nothing is so foreign to the spirit of ecumenism as a false irenicism, in which the purity of Catholic doctrine suffers loss and its assured genuine meaning is clouded.

At the same time, the Catholic faith must be explained more profoundly and precisely, in such a way and in such terms as our separated brethren can also really understand.

In ecumenical dialogue, when Catholic theologians join with separated brethren in common study of the divine mysteries, they should, while standing fast by the teaching of the Church, pursue the work with love for the truth, with charity, and with humility. When comparing doctrines with one another, they should remember that in Catholic doctrine there exists a 'hierarchy' of truths, since they vary in their relation to the fundamental Christian faith. Thus the way will be opened whereby this kind of 'fraternal emulation' will incite all to have a clearer awareness and a deeper realization of the unfathomable riches of Christ.[1]

12. Before the whole world let all Christians confess their faith in God, one and three, in the incarnate Son of God, our Redeemer and Lord. United in their efforts, and with mutual respect, let them bear witness to our common hope which does not play us false. In these days when co-operation in social matters is so widespread, all men without exception are called to work together. This applies with much greater reason to all those who believe in God, and most of all, to Christians in that they bear the name of Christ. Co-operation among Christians vividly expresses the relationship which in fact already unites them, and it sets in clearer relief the features of Christ the Servant. Such co-operation, which has already begun in many countries, should be developed more and more, particularly in regions where a social and technical evolution is taking place. It should contribute to a just evaluation of the dignity of the human person, to the establishment of the blessings of peace, the application of gospel principles to social life, and the advancement of the arts and sciences in a truly christian spirit. Co-operation among Christians should also employ every possible means to relieve the afflictions of our times such as famine and natural disasters, illiteracy and poverty, lack of housing and the unequal distribution of wealth. All believers in Christ can, through such co-operation, be led to acquire a better knowledge and appreciation of one another, and so the road which leads to Christian unity is made smooth.

[1] Eph 3: 8.

Chapter 3

CHURCHES AND ECCLESIASTICAL COMMUNITIES SEPARATED FROM THE ROMAN APOSTOLIC SEE

13. We now turn our attention to the two chief types of division as they affect the seamless robe of Christ.

The first divisions occurred in the East, when the dogmatic formulae of Ephesus and Chalcedon were challenged, and later when ecclesiastical communion between the Eastern Patriarchates and the Roman See was dissolved.

Other divisions arose more than four centuries later in the West, stemming from the events which are usually referred to as 'The Reformation'. As a result, many Communions, national or confessional, were separated from the Roman See. Among those in which Catholic traditions and institutions in part continue to exist, the Anglican Communion occupies a special place.

These various divisions differ greatly from one another not only by reason of their origins, place and time, but still more in the serious matters of belief and the structure of the Church. Therefore, without minimizing the differences between the various Christian bodies, and without overlooking the bonds between them which exist in spite of these differences, the Council proposes the following considerations for prudent ecumenical action.

I. *The Special Position of the Eastern Churches*

14. For many centuries the Churches of the East and of the West followed their several ways though linked in a brotherly union of faith and sacramental life; the Roman See by common consent acted as guide when disagreements arose between them over matters of faith or discipline. Among other matters of moment, it is a pleasure for this Council to remind everyone that there exist in the East many particular or local Churches, among which the Patriarchal Churches hold first place, and many of which are proud to trace their origins back to the Apostles themselves. Hence a matter of primary concern and care among the Easterns, in their local churches, has been, and still is, to preserve the family ties of common faith and charity which ought to exist between sister Churches.

Similarly it must not be forgotten that from the beginning the Churches of the East have had a treasury from which the Western Church has drawn extensively—in liturgical practice, spiritual tradition, and law. Nor must we undervalue the fact that it was the Ecumenical Councils held in the East that defined the basic dogmas of the Christian faith, on the Trinity, on the Word of God, who took flesh of the Virgin Mary. To preserve this faith these Churches have suffered and still suffer much.

However, the inheritance handed on by the Apostles was received with differences of form and manner, so that from the earliest times of the Church it was explained variously in different places, owing to diversities of character and condition of life. All this, quite apart from external causes, prepared the way for divisions arising also from a lack of charity and mutual understanding.

For this reason the Council urges all, but especially those who intend to devote themselves to the restoration of communion in all its desired fulness between the Churches of the East and the Catholic Church, to give due consideration to this special feature of the origin and growth of the Eastern Churches, and to the character of the relations which obtained between them and the Roman See before separation. They must take full account of all these factors and, where this is done, it will greatly contribute to the dialogue in view.

15. Everyone knows with what great love the Christians of the East celebrate the sacred liturgy, especially the eucharistic mystery, source of the Church's life and pledge of future glory. There the faithful, united with their bishop, have access to God the Father through the Son, the Word made flesh, suffering, and glorified, and so, in the outpouring of the Holy Spirit, they enter into communion with the most holy Trinity, being made 'partakers of the divine nature' (2 Pet 1: 4). Hence, through the celebration of the Holy Eucharist in each of these Churches, the Church of God is built up and grows in stature,[1] and through concelebration, their communion with one another is made manifest.

In their liturgical worship, the Christians of the East pay high tribute, in beautiful hymns of praise, to Mary ever Virgin, whom the ecumenical Synod of Ephesus solemnly proclaimed to be the holy Mother of God, so that Christ might be acknowledged as being truly Son of God and Son of Man, according to the Scriptures. Many also are the saints whose praise they sing, among them the Fathers of the universal Church.

These Churches, although separated from us, yet possess true

[1] St John Chrysostom, *In Ioannem Homelia XLVI*, PG 59, 260-2.

sacraments and above all, by apostolic succession, the priesthood and the Eucharist, whereby they are linked with us in closest intimacy. Therefore some worship in common (*communicatio in sacris*), given suitable circumstances and the approval of Church authority, is not merely possible but to be encouraged.

Moreover, in the East are to be found the riches of those spiritual traditions which are given expression especially in monastic life. From the glorious times of the holy Fathers, monastic spirituality flourished in the East, then later flowed over into the Western world, and there provided the source from which Latin monastic life took its rise and has drawn fresh vigour ever since. Catholics therefore are earnestly recommended to avail themselves still more of the spiritual riches of the Eastern Fathers which lift up the whole man to the contemplation of the divine.

The rich liturgical and spiritual heritage of the Eastern Churches should be known, venerated, preserved and cherished by all. They must recognize that this is of supreme importance for the faithful preservation of the fulness of Christian tradition, and for bringing about reconciliation between Eastern and Western Christians.

16. From the earliest times the Eastern Churches followed their own forms of ecclesiastical law and custom, which were sanctioned by the approval of the Fathers of the Church, of Synods, and even of Ecumenical Councils. Far from being an obstacle to the Church's unity, such diversity of customs and observances only adds to her seemliness, and is of great help in carrying out her mission, as has already been stated. To remove, then, all shadow of doubt, this holy Synod solemnly declares that the Churches of the East, while mindful of the necessary unity of the whole Church, have the right to govern themselves according to the disciplines proper to them, since these are better suited to the character of their faithful, and more for the good of their souls. The perfect observance of this principle which is sanctioned by long-standing tradition, but in fact has not always been followed, is one of the essential prerequisites for any restoration of unity.

17. What has just been said about the variety that can exist in the Church must also be taken to apply to the differences in theological expression of doctrine. In the study of revelation East and West have followed different methods, and have developed differently their understanding and confession of God's truth. It is hardly surprising, then, if from time to time one tradition has come nearer to a full appreciation of some aspects of a mystery of revelation than the other, or has expressed it to better advantage. In such cases, these

various theological expressions are often to be considered as mutually complementary rather than conflicting. Where the authentic theological traditions of the Eastern Church are concerned, we must recognize the admirable way in which they have their roots in Holy Scripture, and how they are nurtured and given expression in the life of the liturgy. They derive their strength too from the living tradition of the Apostles and from the works of the Fathers and spiritual writers of the Eastern Churches. Thus they promote the right ordering of christian life, and indeed, pave the way to a full vision of christian truth.

All this heritage of spirituality and liturgy, of discipline and theology, in its various traditions, this sacred Council declares to belong to the full catholic and apostolic character of the Church. We thank God that many Eastern children of the Catholic Church, who preserve this heritage, and wish to express it more faithfully and completely in their lives, are already living in full communion with their brethren who follow the tradition of the West.

18. After taking all these factors into consideration, this sacred Council solemnly repeats the declaration of previous Councils and Roman pontiffs, that for the restoration or the maintenance of unity and communion it is necessary 'to impose no burden beyond what is essential' (Acts 15: 28). It is the Council's urgent desire that, in the various organizations and living activities of the Church, every effort should be made towards the gradual realization of this unity, especially by prayer, and by brotherly discussions on points of doctrine and the more pressing pastoral problems of our time. Similarly, the Council commends to the pastors and faithful of the Catholic Church the development of closer relations with those who are no longer living in the East but are far from home, so that friendly collaboration with them may increase, in the spirit of love, to the exclusion of all feeling of rivalry or strife. If this cause is wholeheartedly promoted, the Council hopes that the barrier dividing the Church between East and West will be removed, and that at last there may be but the one dwelling, firmly established on Christ Jesus, the cornerstone, who will make both one.[1]

II. Separated Churches and ecclesial Communities in the West

19. In the great upheaval which began in the West towards the end of the Middle Ages, and in later times too, Churches and ecclesial communities came to be separated from the Apostolic See of Rome. Yet they have retained a particularly close affinity with the

[1] Council of Florence, Sess. VI (1439), Definitio *Laetentur caeli*: Mansi 31, 1026 E.

Catholic Church as a result of the long centuries in which all Christendom lived together in ecclesiastical communion.

However, these Churches and ecclesial communities have different origins, and different convictions in matters of doctrine and the spiritual life. Since they vary considerably not only with us, but also among themselves, the task of describing them at all adequately is extremely difficult; and we have no intention of making such an attempt here.

Although the ecumenical movement and the desire for peace with the Catholic Church have not yet taken hold everywhere, it is our hope that among all ecumenical feeling and mutual esteem may gradually increase.

It must however be admitted that in these Churches and ecclesial communities there exist important differences from the Catholic Church, not only of an historical, sociological, psychological and cultural character, but especially in the interpretation of revealed truth. To make easier the ecumenical dialogue in spite of these differences, we wish to set down some considerations which can, and indeed should, serve as a basis and encouragement for such dialogue.

20. Our thoughts turn first to those Christians who make open confession of Jesus Christ as God and Lord and as the one mediator between God and men, to the glory of the one God, Father, Son and Holy Spirit. We are aware indeed that there exist considerable divergences from the doctrine of the Catholic Church concerning Christ himself, the Word of God made flesh, the work of redemption, and, consequently, concerning the mystery and ministry of the Church, and the role of Mary in the plan of salvation. But we rejoice to see that our separated brethren look to Christ as the source and centre of Church unity. Their longing for union with Christ inspires them to seek an ever closer unity, and also to bear witness to their faith among all nations everywhere.

21. Love and reverence, almost a cult, for Holy Scripture leads our brethren to a constant and fruitful study of the sacred text. For the Gospel 'is the power of God for salvation to every one who has faith, to the Jew first and then to the Greek' (Rom 1 : 16).

Calling upon the Holy Spirit, they seek God in the Scriptures as speaking to them in Christ, the Word of God made flesh for us, whom the prophets foretold. They contemplate in the Scriptures the life of Christ and what the Divine Master taught and did for our salvation, especially the mysteries of his death and resurrection.

But while our separated Christian brethren hold strongly to the divine authority of the Sacred Books, they differ from us—some in one way, some in another—regarding the relationship between Scripture and the Church. For, according to Catholic belief, the authentic teaching of the Church has a special place in the interpretation and preaching of the written Word of God.

But Sacred Scriptures provide for the work of dialogue an instrument of the highest value in the mighty hand of God for the attainment of that unity which the Saviour holds out to all.

22. Whenever the Sacrament of Baptism is duly administered as our Lord instituted it, and is received with the right dispositions, a person is truly incorporated into the crucified and glorified Christ, and reborn to a sharing of the divine life, as the Apostle says: 'you were buried together with him in baptism, and in him also rose again—through faith in the working of God, who raised him from the dead' (Col 2: 12).[1]

Thus baptism establishes a sacramental bond of unity which links all who have been reborn by it. But of itself baptism is only a beginning, an inauguration wholly directed towards the fulness of life in Christ. Baptism, therefore, envisages a complete profession of faith, complete incorporation in the plan of salvation such as Christ willed it to be, and finally the completeness of unity which eucharistic communion gives.

Though the ecclesial communities which are separated from us lack the fulness of unity with us which should flow from baptism, and though we believe they have not retained the authentic and full reality of the eucharistic mystery, especially because of the absence of the sacrament of Orders, nevertheless when they commemorate his death and resurrection in the Lord's Supper, they profess that it signifies life in communion with Christ and look forward to his coming in glory. For these reasons dialogue should include among its subjects the Lord's Supper and other sacraments, worship and the Church's ministry.

23. The daily Christian lives of these brethren are nourished by their faith in Christ. They are strengthened by the grace of baptism and by hearing the words of God. This shows itself in their private prayer, their meditation on the Bible, in their Christian family life, and in the worship of a community gathered together to praise God. Moreover, their form of worship not seldom displays notable features of the liturgy which they shared with us of old.

Their faith in Christ bears fruit in praise and thanksgiving for the good things received from the hands of God. Among them, too, is a

[1] Cf. Rom 6: 4.

strong sense of justice and a true charity towards others. This active faith has been responsible for many organizations for the relief of spiritual and material distress, the furtherance of the education of youth, the improvement of the social conditions of life, and the promotion of peace throughout the world.

While it is true that many Christians understand the moral teaching of the Gospel differently from Catholics, and do not accept the same solutions to the more difficult problems of modern society, nevertheless they share our desire to stand by the words of Christ as the source of christian virtue, and to obey the command of the Apostle: 'and whatever you do, in word or in work, do all in the name of the Lord Jesus Christ, giving thanks to God the Father through him' (Col 3: 17). For that reason an ecumenical dialogue might start with discussion of the application of the Gospel to moral conduct.

24. Now that we have briefly set out the conditions for ecumenical action and the principles by which it is to be directed, we look with confidence to the future. This sacred Council exhorts the faithful to avoid not only all weakness but also any importunate zeal, either of which would only hinder real progress towards unity. Their ecumenical action must be fully and sincerely Catholic, that is to say, faithful to the truth which we have received from the Apostles and Fathers of the Church, in harmony with the faith which the Catholic Church has always professed, and at the same time directed towards that fulness to which our Lord wills his Body to grow in the course of time.

It is the urgent wish of this sacred Council that the measures undertaken by the sons of the Catholic Church should in practice develop in step with those of our separated brethren. No obstacle must be placed to the ways of divine Providence or any limit set to the future inspirations of the Holy Spirit. The Council moreover professes its awareness that human powers and capacities cannot achieve this holy objective—the reconciling of all Christians in the unity of the one and only Church of Christ. It is because of this that the Council rests all its hope on the prayer of Christ for the Church, on our Father's love for us, and on the power of the Holy Spirit. 'And hope does not disappoint, because God's love has been poured into our hearts through the Holy Spirit, who has been given to us' (Rom 5: 5).

COMMENTARY

The History of the Decree on Ecumenism

To write the full history of all the events which led up to the Decree would demand a treatment of origins of all christian divisions, and of all the efforts made to overcome them. The Decree itself makes no attempt at this; but begins simply with the existing situation in which Christians are in fact divided.[1]

Pope John XXIII, on 30th January 1959, spoke about the coming Council to the clergy of Rome and used the following language: 'We do not intend to set up a tribunal to judge the past. We do not want to prove who was right and who was wrong. Responsibility was divided. All we want to say is: "Let us come together. Let us make an end of our divisions." '[2]

In his address to the delegated observers on 17th October 1963, Pope Paul VI said much the same as John XXIII:

'In what direction does our thought instinctively turn when there is question of giving a precise significance to the encounter—which is taking place, as you can see, in the highest quarters and at the level of highest responsibility—of the Catholic Church with the other Christian confessions? Thoughts might be tempted to turn to the past. That would mean getting lost in the labyrinths of history, and, undoubtedly, would re-open wounds which are not completely healed.

'In our address of 29th September, we ventured to give the first place to Christian forgiveness, mutual if possible. *Veniam damus petimusque vicissim* (We grant pardon and we ask it in turn: Horace). Our spirits need this tranquility if they are to enter into friendly relations, serene conversations. First of all, because

---

[1] On the comparatively recent history of Catholics and ecumenism, cf. George H. Tavard, *Two Centuries of Ecumenism*, London, 1960, and Gregory Baum, *That They May Be One: A Study of Papal Doctrine, Leo XIII—Pius XII*, London 1958 & E. C. Messenger, *Rome and Reunion: A Collection of Papal Documents*, London 1934. It must be said, however, that in recent years the situation has changed so much that much previous writing becomes almost of purely historical interest. There has unquestionably been a development in Catholic doctrine regarding the relation of dissident Christians to the Church.

[2] Cited in *Herder–Korrespondenz*, Mar., 1959, p. 274.

it is Christian: 'So if, says the Lord, you are offering your gift at the altar, and remember that your brother has something against you, leave your gift there before the altar and go, first be reconciled to your brother and then come and offer your gift' (Mt 5: 23–4). And then, it is the better method for us: to look not towards the past but to the present and, above all, the future. Others can and ought to pursue their studies of history; we now prefer to focus our attention, not on what has been, but on what ought to be. New things must come into existence, a dream must be made real. May we be permitted to borrow the words of St Paul: "Forgetting what lies behind and straining forward to what lies ahead, I press on toward the goal for the prize which God calls us to receive, in Christ Jesus" (Phil 3: 13–14). Hope is our guide, prayer our strength, charity our method, all at the service of the divine truth which is our faith and our salvation.'[1]

The Decree follows these directions given both by Popes John and Paul. It says nothing of the historical causes of christian divisions, but begins with the existing facts and seeks remedies. Not, indeed, that historical studies have no bearing on the relationships of divided Christians. The contrary is the case, and the Decree itself recommends study of the relations which existed between the Eastern Orthodox Churches and the Roman See before the separation.[2] Moreover, through recent historical research judgements are being revised regarding the causes, circumstances and motives through which divisions among christians came about.[3]

---

[1] A.A.S. 55 (1963), pp. 879–80.   [2] No 14.

[3] It is impossible here to give an adequate bibliography—but I mention, as indicative of the changed historical outlook towards the Byzantine Empire, Professor J. M. Hussey's article 'Gibbon Re-written: recent trends in Byzantine Studies' in E. J. B. Fry and A. H. Armstrong (eds), *Rediscovering Eastern Christendom*, London, 1963, pp. 90–105, and Professor Francis Dvornik, 'Byzantium, Muscovite Autocracy and the Church', *ibid.*, pp. 166–78, in both of which valuable references will be found. Professor Dvornik's reappraisal of Photius in the *Photian, Schism, History and Legend*, Cambridge, 1948, and his *The Idea of Apostolicity in Byzantium and the Legend of St Andrew*, Harvard, 1958, are of fundamental importance, as also, are the works of Fr Joseph Gill on the Council of Florence, cf. his *The Council of Florence*, Cambridge, 1959; and his series of articles entitled 'Personalities of the Council of Florence', in *Unitas* during the years 1957–60. As regards Catholic reappraisal of the Reformation, cf. Erik Persson, 'The Reformation in the recent Roman Catholic Theology', an article which first appeared in English in *Dialog* (315 Fifth Ave, S, Minneapolis, Minnesota), and was reprinted in *New Theology I*, ed. Martin E. Marty and Dean G. Peerman, New York, 1964, pp. 94–108. It gives brief indications about the work of the Catholic scholars Joseph Lortz, Johannes Hessen, Adolf Herte, Albert Brandenburg, Y. M. Congar, L. Bouyer and J. Jedin. Cf. also

But the Decree neither makes nor presupposes any judgement about the sad history of the origins of the divisions. It says simply that after apostolic times, extensive and quite large communities made their appearance and came to be separated from full communion with the Catholic Church—for which, often enough, men of both sides were to blame. But the text continues: 'the children who are born into these communities and who grow up believing in Jesus Christ cannot be accused of the sin involved in the separation, and the Catholic Church looks upon them as brothers, with respect and affection.' (No. 3, par. 1.)

The First Session

In the first session of the Council, three distinct documents were produced relative to relations between separated Christians. The first was composed by the Theological Commission, the second by the Congregation for the Eastern Churches and the third by the Secretariat for Unity. The *Schema* regarding the Eastern Orthodox was discussed from the 25th to the 31st November, and some eighteen Catholic Orientals spoke, voicing convictions which were afterwards incorporated into the Decree on Ecumenism. On the 31st the Fathers voted by 2,088 to 36 that the three drafts should form a single document, to be drawn up by the Secretariat for Unity.[1] In the *Constitution on the Church*, Chapter I, n. 15, a brief paragraph deals with general relations between the Catholic Church and separated christian brethren;[2] and the Decree on the Eastern Catholic Churches, promulgated 21st November 1964, deals more specifically with *communicatio in sacris* (perhaps in English best translated as 'intercommunion') between these Churches and the separated Eastern Churches.[3]

In preparation for the second session, a *Schema*, or draft, was distributed to the Fathers of the Council in June 1963 which contained three chapters on Ecumenism together with one on

Walther von Loewenich, *Modern Catholicism*, translated by Reginald H. Fuller, London, 1959, chapter 9, pp. 265–92; M. Piette, *John Wesley and the Development of Protestantism*, London 1937; J. M. Todd, *John Wesley and the Catholic Church*, London 1958.

[1] Fuller details are given in *Irénikon*, 35 (1962), pp. 519–36.
[2] Cf. Appendix II, p. 255.   [3] Cf. Appendix III, p. 256.

the relation of Christians and Jews and one on religious liberty. After some discussion it was agreed that the last two subjects might be somewhat out of place in a document dealing with the relationships of Christians; and, since they raised distinct and separate issues, would better be treated elsewhere.

The Second Session

At the second session, the welcome given to the *Schema* on ecumenism surprised even the most sanguine hopes. The document was accepted as a basis for discussion by 1996 votes to 56, which meant that not five per cent of the Fathers were unsympathetic to the ecumenical idea. The vast majority of the Fathers clearly re-echoed Pope Paul VI's words: 'the Council aims at complete and universal ecumenicity. . . . It is a Council of invitation, of expectation, of confidence, looking forward toward a more widespread, more fraternal participation in authentic ecumenicity.'[1] Perhaps Bishop Arthur Elchinger, Coadjutor Archbishop of Strasburg, summed it up with the words: 'the Decree on ecumenism is a gracious gift of God to these our times.'

Moreover, the comments made during the sessions from 18th November to 2nd December showed that the *Schema* was regarded rather as too cautious than as too bold. A comparison between the *Schema* of 1963 and the final Decree is sufficient evidence of this.[2]

Terminology

Terminology was a first difficulty. Two titles of chapters were changed. The 1963 *Schema* began Chapter I with the heading: 'Principles of Catholic Ecumenism'. This was changed to

[1] Address at the opening of the second session of Vatican Council II.

[2] Complete evidence must await the publication of the *Acta* of the Council. The book edited by Küng, Congar and O'Hanlon, *Council Speeches of Vatican II*, New Jersey and London, 1964, gives the speeches of nineteen Fathers on ecumenism, and these are very useful. But a complete history should include some 110 other speeches made and all the modifications suggested to the texts of both 1963 and of 1964, together with the reasons why the Secretariat rejected or accepted them. The most scrupulous attention was paid by the Secretariat to every single suggestion made, so that the final Decree represents as faithfully as is possible the mind of the whole Council. I regret to say that some accounts of the Council, due doubtless to need for compression, are not absolutely accurate.

'Catholic Principles of Ecumenism'. The difference might seem to be merely verbal, but, if analysed, is indicative of outlooks and attitudes which are deeply different, though perhaps unconsciously so.

During the second session, the matter was thus explained by the Greek Melchite Patriarchal Vicar for the Eparchy of Damascus, Joseph Tawil: 'Instead of speaking of principles of Catholic ecumenism, it would be better to speak of Catholic principles of ecumenism. If ecumenism really is a movement of all Christians towards a greater unity, it cannot strictly be called Catholic, Orthodox or Anglican, or by any other such name.

'But it is possible to speak of Catholic or Orthodox or Anglican or other principles of the same ecumenism.'[1]

The movement towards Christian unity cannot be the possession of any one church; and so 'the ecumenical movement', or 'ecumenism', cannot belong to any one church, even though that church believes itself to be the sole true Church of Christ. Cardinal Bea has written: 'I should like to say that we Catholics must recognize with sincere gratitude that it is our separated brethren, Orthodox, Anglican and Protestant, who gave the first impulse to the modern unitive movement, and that we have learned much from them, and can learn still more.'[2]

Bishop Elchinger of Strasburg put it even more strongly: 'It is a certain historical fact that in our times, the most enthusiastic and certainly most numerous experts and promotors of the ecumenical movement came from churches separated from our church, while on the contrary, in our church, the pioneers of the movement often, even more often than not, met with exasperating obstruction.'[3]

This change of title, then, indicates, as indeed does the whole Decree, the intention of the Catholic Church to take part in the ecumenical movement, and in so doing be fully loyal to its own principles; but indicates, also, that there is not the slightest intention or desire to assume any leadership in the movement, but rather to co-operate, humbly and fraternally, with others.

[1] *Council Speeches of Vatican II*, ed. Küng, Congar and O'Hanlon, p. 193.
[2] *Unity in Freedom*, London and New York, 1964, p. 205.
[3] *Council Speeches of Vatican II*, p. 217.

The Word 'Church'

The second change occurred in Chapter III, where, after special consideration of the Eastern Orthodox Churches, the title was: 'Concerning communities arising in the sixteenth century and thereafter', which was changed to: 'Concerning churches and ecclesiastical (or ecclesial) communities separated from the Apostolic-Roman See.'

The first objection to the earlier title lies in the words 'arising in the sixteenth century and thereafter'.[1]

The bodies which separated from the Roman See from the sixteenth century onwards claim that they maintained 'continuity in faith, doctrine and worship with the One Holy Catholic and Apostolic Church of all past ages';[2] consequently the very title opened the way to theological controversy. This was doubtless not the intention of the Secretariat, and the term 'arise' or 'arose' can be used without theological implication. The Lutheran Professor Einar Molland, in his *Christendom, the Christian Churches, their Doctrines, Constitutional Forms and Ways of Worship*,[3] uses the term 'arose' or 'emerged' or 'sprang up', or 'began', or 'came into being', merely to indicate the origins of the distinctive features of religious bodies, without implications about their ultimate origins. He says, for instance, 'the Methodist Church arose as the result of the great revival in England initiated by the work of John Wesley (1703–91) and his collaborators',[4] and clearly does not mean to make any implications about Methodist continuity with the past. However, since the words were open to misconstruction, they were changed.

The use of the word 'communities' instead of the word 'churches' was criticised by a number of the Fathers.

Archbishop Paul Gouyon, of Rennes, said: 'The word 'community' suggests a meaning which belongs almost exclusively to sociology or the non-religious world.'[5] As a result, the Secretariat chose the expression 'Churches and ecclesiastical com-

---

[1] *Inde a saeculo XVI exortis*, which bears the more exact meaning, 'which *arose* in the sixteenth century and thereafter'.
[2] R. Newton Flew and Rupert Davies, *The Catholicity of Protestantism*, London 1950, p. 16.
[3] London 1959.
[4] p. 267, and cf. pp. 175, 241, 261, 280, 289, 313.
[5] Küng, Congar & O'Hanlon, *Council Speeches*, p. 176.

munities' (the word 'ecclesial' is often used, but is not strictly an English word). But it should be carefully noted that the Decree abstains from specifying which bodies are to be called 'churches' and which 'ecclesiastical communities'. My friend Canon Bernard Pawley misses, I think, this deliberate abstention from specification when he says: 'The Orthodox Patriarchates (and some others) are given full recognition as churches, and as possessing acknowledged sacraments and ministries. Other bodies are recognized as "ecclesial communities" because they possess some, though not all, of the "signs" or "marks" of the true church. This slightly patronizing attitude is none the less a great improvement on the status of "heretics and schismatics" which was their lot only a few years ago.'[1]

It is true that the word 'churches' has been for centuries used of the Eastern Orthodox; but it is also true that the Old Catholics of Holland are regarded by Catholic theologians as having as good a claim to the word 'church' as have the Orthodox, and as 'possessing acknowledged sacraments and ministries'. On the other hand, some christian bodies do not call themselves 'churches', for instance, some of the Moravian Brethren (Herrnhuter Brüdergemeine, of Würtenburg). The title 'churches and ecclesiastical communities' was deliberately chosen in order to express the complex and sad reality of the existing situation, and it was not the business of the Council, nor its intention, to make a judgement which of the 'ecclesiastical communities' ought to be called 'churches' in the theological sense. Among the Christians of today there are many kinds of groupings or forms of association which fit only with difficulty into traditional theological categories and terminology.

Among our separated brethren, also, the use of the word 'church' causes difficulty. The World Council of Churches provides that membership in it 'does not imply that one church must regard all other members as churches in the full sense'.[2]

Bishop Tomkins, Secretary of the Conference on Faith and

---

[1] *Anglican-Roman Relations*, London 1964, p. 36.
[2] *The Third World Conference on Faith and Order, Lund, 1952*, ed. Oliver Tomkins, London 1953, p. 164. The Toronto Declaration of the Central Committee of the World Council of Churches, made in July 1950, puts it that 'membership does not imply recognition of other member churches as churches in the true and full sense of the word'.

Order at Lund in 1952, put the distressing position caused by our present state of divisions as follows:

'I suspect that there will be many members of this conference who have not yet grasped the implications of being in a fellowship in which not all the churches are prepared to say of other bodies in it that they consider them to be *churches* in the full and true sense of the word. It is equally embarrassing to have one's own church treated as though it were not really a church, and to have to treat bodies which one does not believe to be churches practically as if they were.'[1]

Thus hesitation about indiscriminate application of the word 'church' is not confined to Catholics. It should be noted, however, that sometimes the term 'communion' is used to designate both the Catholic Church and separated bodies of Christians (as in no. 4, par. 2).

More Humble, Generous and Dynamic

Apart from these matters of terminology, many of the Fathers wanted the *Schema* of 1963 to be revised so as to be more humble, more generous and more dynamic. The final Decree shows that account was taken of these desires. The faults and sins of Catholics against unity were acknowledged (n. 2, n. 7, par. 2); reform must take place not merely in the members but also in the institutions of the Church (n. 3, par. 5; n. 4, par. 5; n. 6, par. 1; n. 7, par. 2); unity not only permits but demands variety (n. 2 and n. 4, par. 7); the question of sharing sacraments with others is more fully discussed (nn. 5 and 15); 'the riches of Christ' and true endowments of the Holy Spirit exist among separated brethren (n. 4, par. 8); two clear and approving references are made to the World Council of Churches and its work for unity (nn. 1 and 20); a sharp distinction is drawn between work for individual conversions and ecumenical activity (n. 4, par. 4); a certain autonomy of the Eastern Orthodox Churches is solemnly acknowledged as a fundamental principle, and special mention made of their Patriarchal Sees (n. 14, par. 1); study is commended of the relations existing between the

[1] *Lund Report*, p. 33. I may refer here to Appendix I, 'The Meaning and Use of the word "Church" ' in my *The Churches and the Church*, 2nd ed, London 1963, pp. 291–4.

Eastern Orthodox Churches and the Roman See before the separation (n. 14); with the Eastern Orthodox *communicatio in sacris*—or a sharing in sacraments and worship—is, under due conditions, to be encouraged (n. 14, par. 2); regarding the endowments of separated brethren it is made clear that these exist among them not merely as individuals but also as churches or communities (n. 3, par. 4), and that the sacred actions they perform can beget the life of grace and the means of salvation (n. 3, par. 3); 'dialogue', or conversations with separated brethren, is between equals (n. 9), and need not be confined to exposition of differing beliefs but can also be a common effort to penetrate more deeply into the unsearchable mysteries of Christ, in which there is a hierarchy of truths (n. 11, p. 3); the objection from certain countries about the proselytism of certain groups, mainly sects, was met by expressing the hope that the ecumenical spirit would spread more widely (n. 14, par. 3); and, at the end, it is clearly stated that the ecumenical effort tends to the fulness of the faith and that divine providence and the inspiration of the Holy Spirit may still have much to teach us (n. 24). Special mention was made of the Anglican Communion (n. 14, par. 3).

The position of the Eastern Churches united to the Roman See and their ecumenical importance presented a certain awkwardness, since in some countries their relationship with separated Eastern Orthodox are most friendly, in others they are disliked and even their suppression is desired. The awkwardness in the concrete situation is met by an expression of gratefulness to God that many Eastern Churches maintain both full communion with their Western brothers and complete faithfulness to their Eastern inheritance (n. 17, par. 2).

Objections

Objections were made by some Fathers during the 1963 session to various substantial matters in the Decree, but as they did not result in any change in the text they will be discussed later in this Commentary. Some Fathers, however, felt that in n. 3, there was insufficient assertion of the necessity, faithfulness and unicity of the Church, and so the last seven lines were added.

A few days before the Decree was due to be proclaimed, some forty emendations were submitted to the Secretariate, at the desire of Pope Paul VI; of which nineteen were accepted. They were, in fact, of a minor character, but as there has been some misunderstanding about them, I deal with them all in Appendix I (p. 251), giving the Latin text where it seems helpful.

The Fathers accepted the Decree as thus amended.

The Authority of the Decree

The Decree, as is explicitly said in the Introduction, is directed only to Catholics, and is to be taken in conjunction with the other Decrees and Constitutions of the Council, particularly with that on the Church. It is clear that the Decree is not an infallible pronouncement, but a pastoral directive—a directive, however, which comes from the highest form of the Church's teaching office (the *magisterium*). Catholics may well recall the words in the Constitution on the Church: 'And hence the sacred Council teaches that the bishops by divine institution have succeeded to the place of the Apostles, as shepherds of the Church, and who listens to them, listens to Christ, but who spurns them, spurns Christ and him who sent Christ.'[1]

Previous to this directive, it may have been understandable that some in the Church felt certain hesitations, doubts or reluctance regarding the general 'ecumenical' approach, and may have been far more impressed by the dangers of indifferentism than by the benefits of seeking unity. These dangers, however, were most fully discussed at the Council. The theological principles relative to Catholic relationships with dissident Christians were exhaustively examined. Consequently, doubts, hesitations and reluctances ought to yield to this clear directive from the Church's teaching authority, and a loyal effort made to understand the Decree and the outlook, attitude and charity which it commends to us all.

When St Pius X in 1902 commended frequent Communion, there were many who, being used to older customs, found it

---

[1] Cf. Lk 10: 16; Const. on the Church, Ch: III, n 20. For a discussion of the authority of the ordinary teaching of the Church, cf. J. Hamer, O. P., *The Church is a Communion*, London 1964; 'What Authority has the Encyclical *Mystici Corporis* and the pronouncements of the *Magisterium* in general?' Pp. 25–30.

very hard to attune their minds to the saintly Pope's directives. Nevertheless, in loyalty they set aside their reluctance and in sincere docility accepted what to them was a new outlook, which they found difficulty in understanding. With due reservations, the same should apply to the Decree on Ecumenism, if there are any who feel difficulty or reluctance.

Loyalty, however, to the Decree and its general spirit does not necessarily demand acceptance of every statement made in it. The Decree closes no doors hitherto open to theological disputation. Moreover, the Decree leaves open the possibility of difference of emphasis on different statements made in it. The aim of the Secretariat in the various revisions of the text was to obtain a moral unanimity in acceptance of the Decree by the Fathers of the Council; and this, some may think, means that the document may be thought to be, to some extent, a 'compromise' document. But about approval of the general 'ecumenical' spirit, there is no compromise whatever, as is clear from the last paragraph of the Introduction, and from the general conclusion expressed in no. 25; and what might be regarded as 'compromise' between different attitudes ought really to be considered as well balanced judgement. It would be difficult for a Catholic to hold that the main mind and intent of the Council, as expressed in this document, does not involve the obedience of faith, in the sense that to affirm that the Decree may be entirely neglected or disregarded would imply that private judgement can be followed even against the judgement of the highest authority, short of an infallible definition in the Church.

Nevertheless the Decree leaves the door open to differing theological opinions about particular points, and to differing stress on various of its statements. The ordinary rules, however, of interpreting a document according to its main purpose and intent, and of judging particular passages by the full context, are obviously to be observed. Above all, the charity that pervades the Decree must never be overlooked. Finally, the Decree very definitely envisages future development both in theology and in concrete relationships between Christians who differ.[1]

Thus the teaching authority of the Church commends the

[1] Cf. no 24.

Decree to all loyal Catholics. This, however, apart, a merely human authority attaches to the document because of the knowledge, theological competence and wide experience of those who drew it up and of those who approved and commended it.

Cardinal Bea has said that the Decree marks 'a peaceful and constructive revolution in the Church'.[1] The Catholic Church is irrevocably committed to the ecumenical movement. The period of the 'Counter-Reformation', with its 'war-psychology' and its juridical outlook, is ended. The new era will doubtless be full of difficulties, upsets, bewilderments and trials, and the Decree neither disguises this nor can a Decree merely by itself produce effects. These depend upon the understanding of its spirit and its directives by those to whom it is directed, and by their intelligent and energetic implementation.

[1] *Civiltá Cattolica*; 1965, 1, p. 11.

THE INTRODUCTION

The Purpose of the Council

On 25th January 1959, Pope John XXIII announced that he
would call an Ecumenical Council for the Universal Church,
and hoped that it would contribute to the 'enlightenment, edification and happiness of the whole Christian world, and would
be a renewed invitation to the faithful of the separated communities to follow us in a friendly spirit in the search for unity
and grace, yearned for by so many souls all over the earth.'[1]

It is no secret that there were those in the Catholic Church
who saw no need for a Council, felt that Pope John could not
define its purposes and regarded the attainment of Christian
unity as practically impossible. Pope John's faith overcame all
the objections. He set the general purpose as an *aggiornamento*, a
modernization of the Church, an effort to meet the spiritual
needs of the new 'atomic age'; and, if not to attain the unity of
all Christians, at least to take some steps towards it. The Secretariat for the Promotion of Christian Unity (suggested by a
prominent ecclesiastic in Germany) and the invitation to
separated brethren to send 'observers' were concrete actions
whose effects were, and will continue to be, far-reaching. Confidence was shown in the 'observers'; they had all the documents which the Fathers had. They were as fully aware of the
proceedings as were most of the Fathers. They made known their
views to the Secretariat, and found them not seldom voiced in
the Council itself. Their very presence in a prominent place in
St Peter's, before the eyes of the Fathers, gave reality to the
question of the division in Christendom and brought home the
fact that unity must be a reconciliation not merely of doctrines
but of living men. Pope John had hoped that the Council might
give proof to separated brethren of sincerity, agreement and
charity; the observers gave, in turn, proof to Catholic bishops

[1] *A.A.S.* 51 (1959), p. 69.

of their sincerity, learning and good will. Some bishops may have never met 'a Protestant' in the whole of their lives.

Not everything went smoothly at the Council. There were difficulties in procedure—how could there not be in an assembly of over two thousand, all with an equal right to be heard?—and there were differences of opinion, sometimes sharply expressed. But at least our separated brethren came to know us as we are. And, knowing us as we are, I think from conversations with several of them, that on the whole they like us better and understand our problems better, and this, though it is by no means agreement, is yet a definite step in lessening the suspicions and hostilities on both sides, which have accumulated over the centuries.

Pope Paul VI, in his address at the second session, apostrophized Pope John.

'Oh dear and venerated Pope John! May gratitude and praise be rendered to you. Surely under a divine inspiration, you convoked this Council to open new horizons for the Church and channel over the earth the new and yet untapped spring waters of Christ our Lord's doctrine and grace.'[1]

Pope Paul VI assigned four main purposes of the Council: to examine the intimate nature of the Church, and from the examination to draw 'an illuminatory, uplifting and sanctifying self-knowledge'; secondly, the renewal of the Church; thirdly, the reunion of all Christians; and lastly, the 'building of a bridge towards the contemporary world'.[2] These four purposes are intimately connected. What Pope Paul said about the third, the reunion of all Christians, will be found in Appendix V (p. 271).

The restoration of the unity of Christians is indeed one of the purposes of the Council.

The rest of the Introduction makes four statements, simple yet well worth pondering:

(a) Christ founded only one Church.

(b) In fact many different communions claim to follow Christ's plan for his Church.

---

[1] *A.A.S.* 55 (1963), p. 844; as I write this I see a book has been published by Herder & Herder of New York, entitled *Pope John XXIII, Pope Paul on his Predecessor*, with a documentation by the editors of *Herder Correspondence*; I regret not having been able to make use of this book.

[2] *A.A.S.* 55 (1963), p. 847.

(c) The divisions among Christians cause many evils.

(d) The Holy Spirit arouses desires and efforts to overcome divisions.

A. CHRIST FOUNDED ONE CHURCH AND ONE ONLY

Scripture

The evidence of the New Testament is unmistakable. The Church is indeed a mystery and is depicted in the New Testament in many metaphors. It is a manifestation, not yet complete, of the Kingdom of God; it is a sheepfold, a vine, the building of God, the family of God, the temple of God, the Spouse of the Lamb, the body of Christ, our mother, the people of God, all of which imply unity, although variety within the unity.[1] Christ said: 'Upon this rock I will build my church, and the powers of death shall not prevail against it' (Mt 16: 18); and about a brother sinning against another . . . 'if he will not listen to them, tell it to the church, and if he refuses to listen even to the church, let him be to you as a Gentile and a tax collector' (Mt 18: 17). The existence of 'the Church' is taken for granted, nor is there the slightest possibility envisaged that what one 'church' might judge another 'church' might revise. There is no appeal from 'the Church'; refusal to accept the Church's judgement means to be dismissed from the Church.

St Paul likewise assumes that there is only one Church, and suggests the reason why there can be only one Church: 'husbands love your wives as Christ loved the church and gave himself up for her' (Eph 5: 25). As there is only one redemption by Christ, so there is only one Church: Christ died for the Church, 'to sanctify' her and lead her to complete holiness.[2]

Christian Agreement

About the foundation by Christ of one Church and only one,

---

[1] Cf. *The Constitution of the Church* of Vatican II, chs I and II; and cf. Paul E. Minear, *Images of the Church in the New Testament*, London 1961.

[2] Cf. the whole passage. In no 4, par 6, the Decree indicates that the purification and renewal of the Church is progressive; only the triumphal Church in heaven will be absolutely without spot or wrinkle.

there is no dispute among Christians. The first World Conference on Faith and Order, held at Lausanne in 1927, declared in a Report accepted by all:

'As there is but one Christ, and one life in Him, and one Holy Spirit who guides into all truth, so there is and can be but one Church, holy, catholic and apostolic.'[1]

A multitude of statements could be adduced to the same effect, but only one more may be added. In the famous Declaration by the Central Committee of the World Council of Churches made at Toronto in July 1950, the following is read in Part II:

'THE MEMBER CHURCHES OF THE WORLD COUNCIL BELIEVE ON THE BASIS OF THE NEW TESTAMENT THAT THE CHURCH OF CHRIST IS ONE.

'The ecumenical movement owes its existence to the fact that this article of the faith has again come home to men and women in many Churches with an irresistible force. As they face the discrepancy between the truth that there is and can be only one Church of Christ and the fact that there exist so many Churches which claim to be Churches of Christ but are not in living unity with each other, they feel a holy dissatisfaction with the present situation. The Churches realize that it is a matter of simple Christian duty for each Church to do its utmost for the manifestation of the Church in its oneness, and to work and pray that Christ's purpose for His Church be fulfilled.'

B. MANY COMMUNIONS CLAIM TO FOLLOW CHRIST'S PLAN FOR HIS CHURCH

The Decree assumes the good faith of those who desire to follow Christ and yet are divided (cf. no. 3, par. 1, and indeed, the whole tenor of the Decree). Probably the word 'Communion' was here chosen to indicate that there is a complex unity as well as disunity among the followers of Christ. In the following pages I amplify what the Introduction to the Decree says very briefly, and do so deliberately in order to indicate something of the complexity of the concrete situation and to

[1] *Proceedings of the World Conference of Faith and Order at Lausanne*, ed. H. N. Bate, London 1928, p. 464.

bring home the difficulties involved in the task of uniting all Christians. It is not merely doctrines which have to be reconciled, but living human beings who exist in complicated associations with one another. The Decree does not envisage merely individuals who are separated from us, but the corporate entities called churches and ecclesiastical communities.[1] A 'church' itself is a complex entity, as the Constitution on the Church of the Vatican Council makes plain, and this complexity ramifies greatly among our Anglican and Protestant brethren; and there are, as will appear, other organizations of different kinds which affect relations between Christians.

Outlooks and attitudes are rapidly changing. One instance of this is to be found in Professor George A. Lindbeck's article in *The Journal of Ecumenical Studies*[2] in which he holds that 'a catholic Protestant' can reasonably hold that the Roman Catholic Church has an ecclesiological character which makes it in important respects a fuller manifestation of the Church than are the Protestant churches, and yet a Protestant is justified in remaining outside it. I only mention this article of Professor Lindbeck's to indicate that in the last twenty years, and, indeed, in the last five years, great changes have come about which inevitably make older views outdated.

In these somewhat lengthy comments on the Introduction to the Decree I do not discuss the theories held about the nature of the Church, but try to show the actually existing complex of associations among our separated brethren.

General Lines of Division

Among Christians there are Catholics, Orthodox, Anglicans, Protestants and a variety of bodies often called 'sects'. Within the World Council of Churches there are over two hundred 'churches', and one may well ask: 'in what sense are these bodies 'churches' and how do they differ from a parish, a diocese, or from a religious Order of the Catholic Church?' The criteria applied by the World Council of Churches is helpful as an answer.

---

[1] Cf. no. 3, pars 4 and 5; no. 4, par 4; and the whole of chapter III.
[2] Vol. 1, no. 2, Spring, 1964, 'The Ecclesiology of the Roman Catholic Church', pp. 243–70, Duquesne University Press, Pittsburg, U.S.A.

'The following criteria, among others, shall be applied, in addition to the primary requirement of the Constitution that churches eligible for consideration for membership shall be those "which express their agreement with the basis upon which the Council is formed".

(a) *Autonomy.* A church which is to be admitted must give evidence of autonomy. An autonomous church is one which, while recognizing the essential interdependence of the churches, particularly those of the same confession, is responsible to no other church for the conduct of its own life, including the training, ordination and maintenance of its ministry, the enlisting, development and activity of the lay forces, the propagation of the Christian message, the determination of relationships with other churches and the use of funds at its disposal from whatever source.

(b) *Stability.* A church should not be admitted unless it has given sufficient evidence of stability in life and organization to become recognized as a church by its sister churches, and should have an established programme of Christian nurture and evangelism.

(c) *Size.* The question of size must also be taken into consideration.

(d) *Relationship with other churches.* Regard must also be given to the relationship of the church to other churches.'[1]

Merely to state that there are over two hundred and fifty such 'autonomous churches' may give a greater impression of disunity than the actual facts warrant. The Eastern Orthodox Churches, for instance, although they are 'autocephalous' or autonomous, all hold strongly to the 'Tradition' which gives them an admirable cohesiveness and faithfulness in belief, sacraments and episcopal rule. The Anglican Communion, in 1958, consisted of some fourteen legally and canonically independent churches in England, Ireland, Wales, Scotland, Canada, Australia, New Zealand, South Africa, West Indies, Japan, China, West Africa, Central Africa and the U.S.A. All these have representation in the Lambeth Conference, a consul-

[1] *The First Assembly of the World Council of Churches held at Amsterdam, August 22nd to September 4th, 1948*, ed. W. A. Visser 't Hooft, London, 1949, pp. 202–3.

tative body which meets every ten years. The Anglican Communion, likewise, has very considerable unity, due partly to historical associations, community of language (save in China, Africa and Japan), derivation of their liturgies—again speaking in the main—from the Book of Common Prayer and to their common acceptance of what is called 'the Lambeth Quadrilateral'—which includes the Scriptures, the Apostles and the Nicene creeds, the two sacraments of baptism and the Eucharist and 'the historic episcopate'.[1]

Seven main groups

The others who are generally called 'Protestant' belong to what may be called 'families' and include Baptists, Congregationalists, Lutherans, Methodists, and 'Reformed' or Presbyterians. In addition to these, there are various comparatively smaller groups such as the Disciples of Christ and the Brethren, together with a diverse number of other groups usually called 'sects'. But of Anglicans and Protestants, probably 94 or 95 per cent belong to the six major 'families', namely, Anglicans, Baptists, Congregationalists, Methodists, Lutherans and Presbyterians; the others, though often stridently vocal and obtrusive, forming a comparatively small proportion of the bodies separated from the Roman See in the West. These main 'families' have formed World Federations, or Alliances, or Conferences or Fellowships, for consultative purposes. There are, too, various organizations which cut across denominational boundaries, such as Bible Societies, national or regional Councils of Churches, Conferences of Missionary Societies, Evangelical Alliances or Fellowships, and diverse similar organizations.

Yet, granting all mitigating factors, it remains sadly true that the followers of Christ have differing convictions and 'go their

[1] The 'Quadrilateral' was first formulated by the General Assembly of the Episcopal Church (in the United States of America) in 1886. It was taken over by the Lambeth Conference in 1888. It may be noted that the General Convention of the American Protestant Episcopalian Church in 1949 approved a statement about the Quadrilateral in which it is said that 'in addition to the sacraments of Baptism and the Supper of the Lord, the church recognizes sacramental rites or mysteries, namely, Confirmation, Absolution, the Marriage Blessing, Holy Orders and the Unction of the Sick'. Cf. 'Documents on Church Unity of the Protestant Episcopal Church' in *The Challenge to Reunion*, ed. Robert McAfee Brown and David H. Scott, New York and London 1963, p. 287. Among them, the Church of England is the only 'established' church.

own ways'. Disunity is real and shows itself in doctrine, in worship, in methods of administration and, perhaps most important, in psychological attitudes and general outlook. This is evident at the local level. If there are two 'churches' in one town—and in a large city there might be even a hundred or more—the physical buildings are different, with different titles, such as Baptist, Congregational, Methodist, Presbyterian, etc.; and each has its distinct 'secondary standards about doctrine', its own form of worship, often with celebration of the Eucharist at differing intervals and different prayers and hymns, its minister or priest educated at a denominational college, with distinct relation to the central organization, its own youth clubs, men's and women's societies, its own way of educating children in religion, its own missionary bodies to support, its own moral standards and outlook, and its own distinctive 'tradition' with its own religious heroes, its own distinctive 'witness', and, finally, its own outlook and attitude towards other Christian 'churches', and the way in which Christian disunity can be overcome. The separation at the local level corresponds—with variations—to the separation of the more central organizing or directive or authoritative bodies. To some extent these central bodies reflect the three main beliefs about the proper ordering of the Church, the 'episcopal', 'presbyterian' or synodical, and the 'congregational'.

Three different 'polities'

The three polities of church administration reflect in some degree answers to the question: 'what is the church?'

1. Episcopal Polity

Generally speaking, the episcopal form of Church order, even though there are different concepts of episcopacy, tends to lay more stress upon succession in the episcopal ministry as at least a sign of the continuity of the church; and very generally doctrinal and liturgical decisions are either made ultimate by the decision of the bishops, or at least cannot be accepted against the will of the bishops.[1]

[1] In the Church of England, the Convocation of Canterbury and York, with bishops sitting in the Upper house and representatives of the clergy in the Lower,

In all episcopal churches, the bishops, with representative members of the clergy and the laity (except in the Orthodox and the Catholic Churches), form a permanent Synod or Council, to decide matters affecting the whole body, the decision of the bishops in matters of doctrine and liturgy, usually being at least negatively determinative, that is, the bishops cannot be overruled.

2. *Presbyterian Polity*

The Presbyterian system, as it has hitherto been, is characterized by its systematic gradation of ruling bodies, the session of the local church, the presbytery, drawn from a group of local churches, the synod, drawn from the presbyteries (at least in some countries) and the General Assembly, which has the highest authority. Thus the governing councils form a graded hierarchy. The 'Elders', who are, in some Presbyterian churches, usually ordained for life, though they need not be in active service for life, 'in association with the pastors or ministers, exercise government and discipline, and take the oversight of the spiritual interests of a particular church, and of the Church generally, when called thereunto.'[1]

Many Presbyterians, likewise, have held the essential equality of all the 'pastors' or ministers; but others judge that this is not a fundamental Presbyterian principle. The most conspicuous leader of the early Church of Scotland, John Knox, appointed superintendents in the Church of Scotland and there are

decide matters of doctrine, liturgy and Canon Law, neither house being able to override the other; the Church Assembly, which is made up of the members of the Convocations sitting with representatives of the laity, elected by the lay members of diocesan conferences, deals with finance and with legislation needing the assent of Parliament. Cf. Archdeacon Guy Mayfield, *The Church of England*, London 1958, pp. 121–34; and E. W. Kemp, *Counsel and Consent, Aspects of Church Government*, London, 1961, in the chapter 'Parliament, Laity and Provinces', pp. 187–231, gives some account of the formation of the Church Assembly and puts the case for a modification of the terms of the establishment, that is, the fixed laws concerning the relation of Church and State. These laws are in fact gradually being modified; for instance, the *Alternative and Other Services Measure* approved by the House of Lords, 19th February 1965, gives the Convocations and the House of Laity a certain autonomy as regards changes in the Book of Common Prayer. Many Anglicans desire the same freedom from Parliamentary control as is enjoyed by the established Church of Scotland.

[1] Cf. Eugene Carson Blake (ed.) *Presbyterian Law for the Local Church* (revised 1960), Philadelphia, U.S.A., p. 28. The best account of the theory of eldership that I have seen is given by J. M. Ross, *What Is An Elder?*, London, revised ed., 1955.

bishops in the Reformed Church of Hungary; and there are Presbyterians today who hold that 'certain ministers might be appointed to be permanent moderators of presbyteries, for the purpose of acting as pastors to the ministers and congregations, and to help in expressing the Church's unity and continuity.'[1] But there remains, among many Presbyterians, a deep conviction, based partly on historical memories, against episcopacy.

3. Congregationalist Polity

The 'congregationalist' polity which is followed by Baptists, Congregationalists and Disciples of Christ, rests upon the primacy and the sufficiency of the local church or congregation. The 'Church' manifests itself in all the different local congregations, and each of these is strictly autonomous, having power to formulate its own affirmations of faith, to order its worship, to receive, teach and discipline members, to 'call' its own ministers, and, generally, to witness to the Lordship of Christ in every sphere. In practice, however, Baptists, Congregationalists and Disciples of Christ have formed 'Unions' and 'Conventions', which have their own constitutions, make affirmations of faith, have charge of missionary activities, guide the expansion of the local churches, provide for training for the ministry and pensions for ministers, undertake and manage various publications, are the organ for inter-church relations and, in general, while respecting the autonomy of the local congregations, give a cohesion and continuity to their co-operation.[2]

[1] Cf. J. M. Ross 'The Presbyterian Church', in *The Churches and Christian Unity* R. J. W. Bevan (ed.), London, 1963, p. 197, and John M. Mackay, *The Presbyterian Way of Life*, New York, 1960. The Joint Report on *Relations Between Anglican and Presbyterian Churches*, Edinburgh, 1957, admitted the proposal of 'bishops-in-presbytery' and was signed by nineteen prominent Scots and English Presbyterians, but was rejected in 1958 by the General Assembly of the Church of Scotland. More recently, in 1960 and 1963, Dr Eugene Carson Blake has proposed union between the Protestant Episcopal Church, the Methodist Church, the United Presbyterian Church and the United Church of Christ, and on the basis of episcopacy, though he wants the bishops to be constitutional and, in their manners, democratic. Cf. *The Challenge to Reunion*, edited by R. M. Brown and D. H. Scott, New York and London, 1963, p. 278.

[2] Considerable development is still going on in churches of 'congregationalist' polity. Cf. E. A. Payne, *A Short History of the Baptist Union*, London, 1959; J. W. Grant, *Free Churchmanship in England, 1870–1940, with Special Reference to Congregationalism*, London, 1951; Paul M. Harrison, *Authority and Power in the Free Church Tradition. A Social Case Study of the American Baptist Convention*, Princeton, N.J., 1959; and P. M. Harrison, 'Sociological Analysis of the Participating Communions', in

It has been maintained, notably by Professor Paul Harrison, that these three general 'polities', however different in theory, amount in practice to much the same, namely, a comparatively small group in fact making most of the decisions. However this may be, the local congregations of all churches have to refer many matters to higher decision-making bodies, and the difficult organizational 'set-up' causes delay at best, and a sense of frustration at worst. At the Nottingham Conference of the Faith and Order Department of the British Council of Churches, in September 1964, 'it was felt that administrative organization at the intermediate levels of diocese and district or similar divisions, was not geared to present-day needs and to a changing population. Lack of co-ordinated administration led to dissipation of effort and overlapping. To some extent the churches are imprisoned or hampered by traditional methods of decision-making, and even by their physical buildings.

'A definitely "centralizing" tendency was evident, and the central agency was generally named as the British Council of Churches. The B.C.C. was asked to prepare material about actual liturgical practices in the churches; "to convene forthwith consultation between member churches regarding the varied doctrine and practice of Christian initiation"; to strive "to co-ordinate all agencies of member churches", "education of children up to the age of fifteen"; to consider the ecumenical education of ministers and the possibility of setting up an ecumenical college, and to act as a clearing-house for information about suitable ministers to be appointed "in areas of ecumenical experiment". On the last day, two resolutions were unanimously accepted: that the member churches should make a "concentrated, comprehensive and united effort" at understandable communication of the Gospel; and that there should be "the necessary interdenominational machinery" at diocesan and similar levels "to promote united planning and action". Incidentally, it was suggested that to support local councils and

Digest of the Proceedings of the Consultation on Church Union for 1962 and 1963, ed. George L. Hunt, Fanwood, New Jersey, no date. The 'Proceedings' referred to the proposal to unite the Protestant Episcopal Church, the Methodist Church, the United Church of Christ, and the United Presbyterian Church in the U.S.A. Cf. also the *Revised Draft Constitution* of the Congregational Union of England and Wales, printed May 1964.

committees ten pounds from each congregation rather than ten shillings would be suitable; and that larger cities and regions should consider the appointment of full-time officers and the establishment of ecumenical centres.'

The power of 'Institutionalism'

In short, the 'denominational' organizations have been and are a difficulty in attaining the unity which so many desire. In a real sense denominational "institutionalism" is a potent factor which causes the followers of Christ to 'go their different ways'. Attitudes, convictions, historical 'traditions' (often of comparatively recent origin) become embodied in fixed organizational patterns which it is difficult to change. Not infrequently the property and investments are held on conditions which require denominational teaching at least in adherence to certain doctrinal formulations. Mr Stringfellow, a New York lawyer of the Protestant Episcopal Church, holds that the law in the States of the United States presumes that polity and theology are severable, which presumption itself involves a theological judgement. In practice, if disputes arise about the merger of two or more churches, the civil law tends to favour the minority, and thus encourages a theology of separatism.[1]

Granted that the Courts must decide that property must be used in accord with the expressed will of the donor, Mr Stringfellow suggests that the Courts, in doubtful cases, are influenced by the idea that religious pluralism is a support for freedom of religion, which in effect makes religion a matter of human choice.

The union of the Free Church of Scotland with the United Presbyterian Church of Scotland caused some sixty three congregations of the Free Church to apply to the civil courts for possession of the whole of the property of the Free Church, on grounds that they alone maintained purity of doctrine. The civil courts accepted their claim and only an Act of Parliament secured an equitable division of the property. The union of Methodist Bodies in 1932 required an act of Parliament regarding property. In the *Plan of Church Union in North India and Paki-*

[1] Cf. William Stringfellow, *Law, Polity and the Reunion of the Church*, Faith and Order Commission, paper no. 32, 1960, pp. 29–30.

stan, Third Revised Edition 1957, the Westminster Confession of Faith, and the Confessions and Canons of the Synod of Dort, the Heidelberg Catechism, Luther's Catechism and the Augsburg Confession are commended 'as worthy exponents of the Word of God, and as systems of doctrine to be taught in our churches and seminaries'.[1] The Committee Report on Church Unity of the 1958 Lambeth Conference 'understood that the primary reason for including' this provision 'is to secure the legal continuity' of the United Church with the Churches from which its membership will be derived, and for the safeguarding of property'.[2] I cite these instances only to indicate the difficulties involved in reunion efforts.

Our separated brothers of today have inherited, not made, such difficulties.

Multiplicity of churches exists to a depressing extent, due to a complicated intertwining of causes, historical, linguistic, nationalistic, political, cultural, doctrinal, devotional and emotional. In the sixteenth century, too often the principle *cuius regio eius religio* was accepted, that is 'the choice of religion belongs to the Government of each State'.[3]

Later, the European divisions were transferred to America, where greater liberty led also to the growth of new denominations and sects.[4] But whatever the causes, the fact of over two hundred and fifty autonomous 'churches' is undeniable. A glance through the lists of churches in *The World Christian Handbook*[5], or at the *Yearbooks of American Churches*,[6] will impress anyone with a sense of depression and bewilderment. The *Handbook's* list of Christian organizations working in Japan numbers one hundred and twenty, and in India two hundred and six. It is true that many of these organizations are missionary agencies connected with churches; and many of them have exceedingly few workers and belong to what the larger

---

[1] p. 39.   [2] pp. 2, 31.
[3] Cf. H. G. G. Herklots, *These Denominations*, London, 1946; even today many Lutheran churches are national, territorial churches, to which the inhabitants nominally belong. The so-called 'wars of religion' of the sixteenth and seventeenth centuries were, in fact, wars for control of the State. In the Thirty Years' War in Germany and Austria, Catholics quite often fought on the 'Protestant' side, and Protestants on the 'Catholic' side.
[4] Cf. W. L. Sperry, *Religion in America*, Cambridge, 1945.
[5] Eds.: H. Wakelin Coxell and Sir Kenneth Grubb, London, 1962.
[6] Ed. Benson Y. Landes, issued yearly, New York.

denominations would regard as 'sects'. To some extent, these organizations might be compared to religious orders or congregations in the Catholic Church.

All this granted, and even granted that there are varieties of Buddhism and Hinduism, one can still understand Japanese and Indian feeling that something must be wrong with Christianity.

Membership in the World Council of Churches and its very effort to attain unity, gives concrete evidence of Christian disunity. Merely to instance this, I enumerate some of the categories of churches which are listed in its membership:

General Category	Number
Anglican	18
Baptist	10
Catholic—not Roman	2
Congregationalist	7
Disciples of Christ	7
Lutheran	44
Methodist	15
Mennonite	2
Moravians	5
Presbyterian (or Reformed)	26
Old Catholics	4
Orthodox	15
'United' Churches[1]	8

This appearance of separateness and disunity is, especially in members of the World Council of Churches, to be modified by a very large degree of mutual charity and co-operation, by general acceptance of certain fundamental Christian truths and

[1] 'Churches' (namely those which fulfil the requirements for membership in the W.C.C. as stated on p. 36). In this list, ten Lutheran churches of Germany, though members of the Evangelical Church in Germany, are directly members of the World Council of Churches, the Evangelical Church of Germany being 'a federation (*Bund*) of confessionally determined churches'. The Danish Evangelical Lutheran Church is now part of the American Lutheran Church. The Baptists, Congregationalists, and the Disciples of Christ are represented through their 'Unions' or 'Conventions'. Of the Orthodox in the U.S.A., the Rumanian Orthodox Episcopate of America, and the Syrian Antiochene Orthodox Archdiocese, the Church of the East (Assyrian)—the Russian Orthodox, Greek Catholic Church of North America, and in India, the Mar Thoma Syrian Church of Malabar and the Orthodox Syrian Church of the East are represented as members of the World Council of Churches.

by efforts to overcome the divisions. To some extent the differences between 'churches', especially between those of the same 'family', may be compared to the differences between dioceses in episcopal churches, and, as the Decree says (in no. 4, par. 7), unity is compatible with a very considerable amount of diversity. All this granted, the disunion, even between churches within the World Council, is distressingly deep and intractable. Each church maintains its right to decide about its doctrine or its doctrinal emphasis (always indeed, accepting Scripture as its guide), and to order its own life and action. Within these churches, moreover, there is considerable diversity of conviction, so that it is sometimes said that division within churches is greater than between the churches. This division within churches is generally between those of an 'evangelical' or even 'fundamentalist' outlook, and those of a 'modernist' or 'liberal' or even 'catholic' outlook (not necessarily Roman Catholic, but approaching in many matters the Anglo-Catholic, Orthodox or Roman Catholic outlooks on tradition, episcopacy, the Eucharist, grace and even the Church). The distinction is not so sharp as it is with Catholics between 'dogma' and legitimate theological difference of opinion. Differences, however, between the churches themselves are important: episcopacy, as regards non-episcopal churches and the concept of the ministry and of the Church's continuity; Lutheran-Reformed convictions differ about the Lord's Supper, Christology, election and predestination, polity and discipline. The relation of the faith of the individual to the faith of the religious community is another area of disagreement, involving wide-ranging issues about the authority of creeds and doctrinal formulations.

Three other factors must be taken into account: the bodies which do not belong to the World Council, 'World Confessionalism', and the 'missionary' activities of our Anglican and Protestant brethren.

The 'Third Force'

As regards this Dr Van Dusen speaks of the growth in the United States of church allegiance, and says:

'Within this general growth in church allegiance, by far the largest proportionate gains have been made not among the traditional Protestant bodies affiliated with the ecumenical movement, but among groups of more recent origin—Adventist, Holiness, Pentecostal—which, for the most part, hold aloof from ecumenical participation. To be sure, none of these as yet rivals in size the larger traditional denominations. Adherents to the six largest 'sect' groups—Adventists, Assemblies of God, Christian and Missionary Alliance, Churches of God, Churches of God in Christ, Church of the Nazarene, Churches of Christ, and Pentecostals—number 4,500,000 in the United States, but at least 20 million in the world. These facts have led to the growing recognition that there is rapidly emerging a third major type of Christianity (the 'Third Force'), alongside traditional Catholicism, whether Roman or Eastern, and traditional Protestantism.'[1]

Two Pentecostal Churches in Chile were admitted to the World Council in 1961, but the majority stand apart, as do likewise the Southern Baptist Convention, the largest single non-Catholic church in the United States, the Missouri Synod Lutherans and some others. These churches keep aloof, generally from fear of dilution of doctrine, and possibly partly from fear of too close an approach to the Orthodox and Roman Catholics. Their outlook is generally very conservatively 'evangelical' and is represented by the periodical *Christianity Today*. Moreover, some members of churches which are in the World Council are suspicious of the whole ecumenical movement, likewise holding conservative 'evangelical' positions. They are represented in England by the *Church of England Newspaper*, a weekly, and by *The Churchman*, a quarterly.[2]

---

[1] 'The Church in the U.S.A. . . . 1961', in *The World Christian Handbook*, op. cit., p. 52.

[2] On the 'evangelicals', cf. Dr Norman Goodall, *The Ecumenical Movement*, Oxford, 1961, pp. 153-4, where the Basis of Belief of the Evangelical Alliance, and the Statement of Faith of the Evangelical Fellowship, are reproduced. In the issue of *The Churchman* for March 1962 is printed the Basis of Faith for the Evangelical Fellowship of the Anglican Communion. Cf. also Dr Eugene Smith, 'The Conservative Evangelicals and the World Council of Churches', *Ecumenical Review*, January 1963, pp. 182–92; and Dr Norman Goodall, 'Evangelicalism and the Ecumenical Movement', *Ecumenical Review*, July 1963, pp. 399–406. Dr Erik Routley, writing about more general issues in his book *Congregationalism and Unity*, London, 1962, declares: 'It happens to be a fact at present that the dispute concerning the conservative-evangelical position has opened a rift in the church deeper than that caused by any denominational difference, except that between

World Confessionalism

World Confessional organizations are associations of 'families' of churches and include the Lutheran World Federation, the Anglican Communion, the Presbyterian World Alliance, the World Methodist Conference and the World Baptist Alliance, the International Congregational Council, the World Convention of Churches of Christ (Disciples), the World Conference of Pentecostal Churches and the Friends' World Committee for Consultation (Quakers). Each of these bodies has its own specific conception of the link that binds it together and of its role in the total ecumenical life of the churches; yet these bodies have this in common:

(*a*) 'that their member churches share together not only the general traditions which are common to all Christian churches, but also specific traditions which have grown out of spiritual crises in the history of the Church.

(*b*) 'that they desire to witness to specific convictions of doctrinal or ecclesiological character which they consider to be essential for the life of the whole Church of Christ.'[1]

The New Delhi Report on Unity spoke as follows about the effect of these organizations in fostering either unity or disunity:

'*How may world confessional bodies contribute to the ecumenical movement and the unity of the churches?*

'Most of these organizations existed many years before the founding of the World Council. Their purpose is not only to clarify and strengthen confessional understanding and loyalty but to serve responsibly in the wider ecumenical movement. Their contributions to the whole movement are well known and much appreciated. Their leaders are, for the most part, leaders in the World Council of Churches also. But opinion today is divided over the effects of their existence and work upon the participation of their churches in the movement for unity and upon the course which they ought to take in the future.

'Some hold that a deepening understanding of the doctrines and traditions of the various confessions will in the long run en-

Protestants and Roman Catholics in Liverpool and Glasgow. Everybody knows this, and there is no need to labour it here,' p. 86.
    [1] This 'working definition' was formulated at a meeting of representatives of the 'world confessional organizations' at Geneva in April 1962.

hance the possibilities of unity in the truth, even though for the present it may seem to restrain the churches from joining into full fellowship with one another. It is possible that unity could be further advanced by more frequent conversation between leaders of the confessions at the level of world organization. Already there are theological conversations in process between the Presbyterians and, respectively, the Lutherans and Congregationalists.

'A contrary view is held by those who see the world confessional bodies as a threat to wider unity in particular areas, a view which some Asian and African Christians have often expressed with vigour.

'Probably the critical question is whether or not the leaders of confessional bodies agree with the emphasis we have already made upon the centrality of unity of all Christians *in each place*, which must, of course, always seek to be a "unity in the truth". If they agree, they will not consider the union of one of their churches as a loss, but as a gain for the whole Church. And a service can be rendered to such churches if the confessional bodies assist them in the responsible study of all issues which are involved in a proposed union.'

In the *Lutheran World* for January 1963, four leading ecumenists discussed the question whether these 'world confessional organizations' impede or help unity.[1] On the whole, their opinion seems to be that these organizations help rather than hinder unity, since they tend to keep before Asians and Africans the need for one worldwide Church and to hinder local unions which could unite with churches of other lands only on a 'federal' and not an 'organic' basis.

These discussions, however, bring home the concrete facts of disunity. In Tanzania, for instance, the seven Lutheran Churches are in process of uniting to form one Lutheran Church in Tanzania, and they envisage, also, union with Anglicans and Moravians in Tanzania and with Presbyterians, Methodists and Anglicans in Kenya, in the hope of one East African Church emerging. The problem arises about the rela-

---

[1] Dr Kurt Schmidt-Clausen, Dr Lewis S. Mudge, Dr Norman Goodall and the Rt Rev Stephen Bayne Jr., connected, respectively, with the Lutheran, Presbyterian, Congregational and Anglican 'world confessional organizations'.

tion of the new united bodies of the 'world confessional organizations'. For Anglicans, the question is whether the new church would be in communion with the rest of Anglicans throughout the world and whether its bishops would attend the Lambeth Conference.[1] As yet no clear answer has emerged to these problems, but the Report on 'Institutionalism' presented at the Faith and Order Conference at Montreal in 1963 had contained the recommendation that 'new churches' should maintain 'full fellowship with the sister churches and the world denominational associations of the uniting bodies'.[2] Yet I am unable to find any explicit endorsement of this specific recommendation in the Montreal Report. There is clearly danger lest certain unitive movements and unions might result only in the multiplication, on too pragmatic a basis, of independent national or regional 'churches', which would, in effect, be divisive and not unitive on a wider scale. But there is the danger, likewise, of carrying to Asia and Africa principles of division quite irrelevant to their situation.

Missionary expansion and Disunity

The effort to carry the Christian message to countries predominantly non-christian gives sad evidence of disunity. In Great Britain and Ireland, there are some fifty-nine societies interested in various forms of 'missionary' activity. To some extent they may be compared to the multitude of religious orders and congregations, and of societies to help the 'missions', which exist in the Catholic Church; there are, however, distinct differences. Some of the non-Roman societies are 'interdenominational', and their connection with their churches is hard to define. Even in societies of the same church or denomination, there are differing 'emphases' or outlooks, manifest for instance, between two Anglican missionary societies, the Society for the Propagation of the Gospel, which tends to an 'Anglo-Catholic' outlook, and the Bible Churchman's Missionary Society, which tends to be 'evangelical'.

Missionary societies have formed themselves into associations

[1] Cf. Donald E. Johnson, 'After Union—What?' *Lutheran World*, January 1963, pp. 68–70.
[2] Faith and Order Paper, no. 37, p. 28.

with one another in very complex patterns. The International Missionary Council, integrated into the World Council of Churches in 1961, as both a Commission and a Division of World Mission and Evangelism, was a 'Council of some 38 Councils', that is, its constituent members were neither churches nor missionary societies, but regional and national councils; and these councils were sometimes councils of churches, with the 'missionary' agencies forming a branch of the Council of the Churches. Sometimes the missionary agencies were 'interdenominational' (at least in theory) and were members of the regional or national council in their own right. In practice, co-operation with the churches, especially as regards collection of funds, was and still is, fairly close. The International Missionary Council from its foundation in 1910[1] has always tried to help on unity in the work of evangelism, and has followed the most enlightened and 'comitive' policies, as is shown by the periodical *The International Review of Missions*. It was, however, only a consultative and not an administrative body. It is in no way answerable for the plans or deeds of its member councils, much less of the various missionary societies. A great deal of its work has been in the field of study, research and publications. While the proposal to integrate the I.M.C. with the W.C.C. was being discussed, some Orthodox and some Roman Catholics expressed misgivings, largely through fear lest the World Council of Churches might be distracted from its search for unity or might indirectly become involved in 'proselytism'. By the time of integration in 1961, however, these misigvings were largely dissipated.

There are, however, groups, mainly in America, which either stand aloof from or are even hostile to, the I.M.C. as it was and as it is in its integration with the World Council of Churches. These groups have been listed as follows:

(a) The Interdenominational Foreign Missions Association of North America.

(b) The Evangelical Foreign Missions Association of the National Association of Evangelicals.

[1] Technically it may perhaps be said to date only from 1921 when the name was adopted and some changes introduced into its structure. Cf. *International Missionary Council Report* to the Assemblies of the I.M.C. and the W.C.C., New Delhi, 1961, pp. 249–57.

(c) The International Council of Christian Churches.

(d) The Southern Baptist Convention.

(e) The New Tribes Mission.

These groups include a considerable part of Protestant missionary effort. It is difficult to ascertain the exact numbers of Protestant missionaries at work in lands foreign to their own, but it is safe to say that more than half do not co-operate in any way with the World Council of Churches or its Division of World Mission and Evangelism. The percentage of these bodies is increasing, due to the growth, already mentioned[1] of 'holiness', 'faith', 'pentecostal' and similar movements, whose zeal is sometimes greater than their discretion. It may be doubted if all of them would follow the spirit of the W.C.C. document entitled *Christian Witness, Proselytism and Religious Liberty*.[2] Generalizations, however, are dangerous, for some of these missionaries are most simple, humble and charitable men and women; I say 'some' because of the comparative few whom I have actually met.[3]

Lack of co-operation

At the Nottingham Conference of the Faith and Order Department of the British Council of Churches, at which some five hundred and fifty persons were present, including five Catholic 'observers', Dr Visser 't Hooft stressed the concrete evidence of disunity:

'There is still a great lack of common strategy with regard to mission and evangelism and a corresponding waste. To take the example of theological education: in Latin America 94 per cent, in Africa 80 per cent, of the theological education of the non-

[1] Cf. pp. 45–46.

[2] This document is represented as an appendix to Cardinal Bea's *Unity in Freedom*, London, 1964.

[3] In Columbia the *Confederación Evangelica de Colombia* numbers among its members the following bodies:

Assemblies of God, Calvary Holiness Church, Christian and Missionary Alliance, Conference of Mennonite Brethren, Cumberland Presbyterian Mission, Evangelical Union of South America, Foursquare Gospel Mission, Gospel Missionary Union, Independent Evangelical Church of Vallarrica, Independent Gospel Tabernacle of Casanare, Inter-American Mission, Mennonite Mission in Columbia, South American Indian Mission, Evangelical Tabernacle of Columbia, World-Wide Evangelical Crusade, Wesleyan Methodist Church. I take this list from Eduardo Ospina, *The Protestant Denominations in Colombia, A Historical Sketch with a Particular Study of the So-called Religious Persecution*, Bogotá, 1954.

Roman churches is carried on on a denominational basis, and this means generally in very small, inadequate schools and seminaries. In many weighty matters which affect other churches, our churches take decisions without consultation with their sister churches. And perhaps more important: the ecumenical movement has not affected in any radical way the local situation. It has not succeeded in manifesting "in each place" that the time for disunity is over and the time for unity has come. So we hear from many sides that the ecumenical movement has not lived up to its promise, that its best days are over.'[1]

The General Secretary of the World Council of Churches spoke thus at the beginning of the Conference partly no doubt to stimulate those present to more effective action, but what he said is only too true.

'Everyone who has concerned himself,' says Dr Lesslie Newbigin, 'in the practical issues of Christian reunion knows the fearful strength of the corporate pride of a denominational group, the terrifying power of group-egotism when it has taken into its service memories of great and godly men, scholars, saints and martyrs of the faith. Only one thing can subdue it, and that is the word of the Cross, before which no flesh can glory.'[2]

And Catholics?

Here, inevitably, arise questions about the Catholic Church: is the Catholic Church as united as it ought to be? Are we free from parochialism, nationalism and absorption in comparatively local interests, to the detriment of the wider needs of the Church? Have we tended to make a certain administrative unity the sole criterion of unity, to the loss of the sense of a real unity of spirit and spontaneous unity in action? And, as regards the unity of all Christians, have we had enough sincere concern, or have we assumed that *they* were wrong and we were right and the only solution to the problem of Christian disunity is that

[1] *Unity Begins at Home. A Report from the First British Conference on Faith and Order, Nottingham, 1964*, London, 1964, p. 34.
[2] *The Reunion of the Church*, revised ed., London, 1960, p. 102. Dr Newbigin was bishop of South India, then Secretary of the Division for World Mission and Evangelism of the W.C.C., and has recently returned to India to be Bishop of Madras.

they should return to us? Have we given ground for the very widespread feeling that 'Rome wants to dominate'? Have we, as Fr Gregory Baum says, frankly and fairly bluntly, and as Bishop John Wright says more gently and delicately, a 'sectarian spirit'?[1]

More must be said about this in commenting on no. 7 of the Decree; but even in this general picture of the divisions among Christians, it is well to remember that the Decree declares that 'the words of St John hold good about sins against unity: "If we say we have not sinned, we make him a liar, and his word is not in us" (1 Jn 1: 10). So we humbly beg pardon of God and of our separated brethren, just as we forgive them that trespass against us.' (No. 7.) To describe the divided state of Christians ought immediately to move us to examine our own consciences, and to ask ourselves not if others have sinned, but if we have sinned. It is not for us to judge others, but for us to submit ourselves to the judgement of God.

C. DIVISIONS AMONG CHRISTIANS CAUSE MANY EVILS

The Decree briefly says that divisions among Christians are contrary to the will of Christ, are a scandal to the world and a hindrance to the preaching of the Gospel.

Contrary to the will of Christ

Dr Samuel McCrea Cavert, who was Executive Secretary of the World Council of Churches, 1954–7, expresses the matter thus:

'The basic consideration is whether union has any inherent connection with the mission of the church in the world. That mission is most plainly indicated in our Lord's word, 'and I, when I am lifted up from the earth, will draw all men to myself' (Jn 12: 92). The Church exists to draw men to Christ—not to some dynamic leader, not to a doctrinal system, not to a form of

---

[1] Cf. Gregory Baum, O.S.A., *Progress and Perspective, The Catholic Quest for Christian Unity*, New York, 1962, pp. 176–7; Bishop John Wright, 'Reflections on Ecumenism' in *Christian Unity Lectures at the Maynooth Union Summer School, 1961*, Maynooth, 1962, pp. 7, 8 and 9; 'The Impact of the Ecumenical Movement', in *Dialogue for Reunion. The Catholic Premises*, ed. Leonard Swindler, New York, 1962, pp. 27–8.

government, not to a special interpretation of Scripture or sacraments. Whenever a church points to any of these things in a way that obscures its sole mission of drawing men to Christ, it stands in need of correction.

'The great weakness of a denomination is that it does exactly this. It does not mean to do so. It may not realize that it is doing so. Yet it is for such secondary reasons that the denomination, as such, comes into being. That is why a great Presbyterian missionary leader, Robert E. Speer, once said that he was glad the adjective "Presbyterian" could not be effectively translated into Chinese. Each denomination, in its separate existence as a denomination, testifies to the insight of some vigorous founder, to a form of polity, to a mode of worship, to a certain view of baptism or the Eucharist, to the effect of cultural differences, or to some special historical circumstance. Each of these testimonies may have its own value, but not as the ground of existence of a Christian Church.

'The only ground for existence as a church is to draw men to Christ. Anything which makes that less luminous is open to challenge. That is why St Paul so sharply criticized what he saw happening among Christians in Corinth. They were drawing attention to figures like Paul and Peter and Apollos (1 Cor 1: 10–17) and thereby dimming the truth that there is "no other foundation" than Jesus Christ.

'All denominations are, of course, in their various ways, testifying to Christ. But their separate traditions make this witness less concentrated and distinct, and their insistence on a continuing separateness beclouds the sole reason for His Church. Each denomination is unconsciously saying to the world that it regards something else than Christ as justifying it in remaining apart from others who have the same loyalty to Him.'[1]

Disunity and charity

It may be added that the actual divisions among Christians

[1] *On the Road to Christian Unity. An Appraisal of the Ecumenical Movement*, New York. Dr Cavert's book was published in 1961, but probably written some little time before that; this is probably why he makes no mention of the Vatican Council II, or even of Pope John XXIII. His chapter on 'Roman Catholics and the Ecumenical Movement' is friendly in tone, but, since things have moved so fast in these last years, just a little out of date.

have led in the past to a distressing lack of the charity which Christ commended so strongly to all his followers. 'By this shall all men know that you are my disciples, if you have love one for another.'[1] Of recent times, due largely to the ecumenical movement, there has been a great lessening of antagonisms, bitterness and controversies; differences are expressed in courteous language and with considerable respect for other convictions. Nevertheless, where there is basic disagreement about the faith and ordering of the Church, charity demands conscious effort and is less spontaneous, and hostility dies too slowly. It is undeniable that there is on the side of 'non-Romans' a deep-seated suspicion that Rome really wants to dominate and to deny true freedom; and on our side a deep-seated suspicion that separated Anglican and Protestant brethren 'can believe what they like' and thus favour 'indifferentism'. Both these suspicions have some foundation and deserve sympathetic consideration, though I think neither is fully justified.

I am sorry to say that I have known Catholic bishops who will not allow even the appearance of their priests 'fraternizing' with 'non-Catholic' ministers, lest they seem to compromise the purity of the faith. One priest of my acquaintance (and a most devoted and personally humble priest) will not meet a 'non-Catholic minister' because he judges he would be insincere in extending friendliness to one whom he believes to be 'spreading heresy'. On the other hand, the Rev. Erik Routley, a Congregationalist from Scotland, writes as follows:

'Informal meetings between ministers of the Church of Scotland and Roman Catholic priests have been held, and publicly reported, during the past year or two, with spiritual consequences that all parties to the meetings agree in valuing most highly. It might well be that it is a pleasant obligation for a Congregational minister to observe the Week of Christian Unity by calling on the neighbouring Catholic priest. If it seemed good to him so to do, it is the duty of his congregation not to vilify him or spread foolish rumours; indeed, it might well be the duty of his congregation openly to state that such a visit should be paid at that season in their name, as a gesture of goodwill—for probably there are a few ministers who find themselves able to risk the

[1] Jn 13: 35; and cf. Jn 15: 12–13; 17: 20–5.

consequences of such an action without the assurance that these will not be disastrous in their own churches. [I may perhaps say that I am so fortunately placed, and that this course of action is my habit during that January week.] The irrational hatred of Rome in which all Protestants shared a century ago is at present beginning to evaporate; anything that can be done to dissipate it, and to place controversy on rational lines, and to promote charity, must be regarded as a first-class priority. The way, I suspect, is somewhat harder in Scotland than it is in England; that is why the conversation between Scottish ministers and Roman Catholic priests is so significant a development just now.'[1]

Things have, thank God, greatly changed in recent years, largely through the influence of good Pope John and of many other leaders in the ecumenical cause. Nevertheless, there is still a latent suspicion of desire to dominate on the one hand, and of religious 'indifferentism' on the other. The divisions among Christians unquestionably make more difficult the charity which should characterize all Christians.

'A scandal to the world'

Christ prayed that his followers might be one 'in order that the world may believe that Thou hast sent me' (Jn 17: 20). It is clear, then, that any disunity among Christians reduces the effective impact of their witness to an unbelieving world. This is a constant theme among ecumenists.[2] Who can say how great has been the influence of Christian disunity in the growth of scepticism, materialism, communism and 'scientific humanism'?

'It is arguable', says a very knowledgeable journalist, Christopher Driver, 'that there exists in Britain today a climate of

[1] Erik Routley, *Congregationalists and Unity*, 'Star Books on Reunion', General Editor the Bishop of Bristol (Dr Oliver Tomkins) London, 1962, p. 67. In the last five years, however, a great change has come about in Scotland and friendly feelings have increased.

[2] Cf. Donald M. Baillie and Henry Smith Lieper, in the *Lund Report*, London, 1953, pp. 144 and 207; Dr W. A. Visser 't Hooft, *The Pressure of our Common Calling*, London, 1959, pp. 82–3; Dr James E. Wagner, 'The Compulsions of a Church Unionist' in Brown and Scott, *The Challenge to Reunion*, London, 1963, pp. 24–7; an attempt to list all who wholeheartedly agree that Christian disunity is a scandal would be foredoomed to failure; on this Anglicans, Catholics, Orthodox and Protestants are in complete agreement.

opinion which is conditionally pro-Christian, wanting to believe but judging the churches—and it is a very fair criterion—at least partially on their willingness to resolve their disunity. (Curious that where the Church itself cannot see that unity and mission are different aspects of the same scriptural obligation, the unevangelized masses themselves are pointing it out.) But it is improbable that even this limited receptiveness to sincere and realistic mission will still be found thirty or fifty years on, if no progress towards reunion is made in the intervening period.'[1]

Christian disunity is made manifest to people generally in varying ways: by the very notice boards outside church buildings; by what appears in newspapers, radio and television, which report doings and 'events' in different 'churches', generally with fairness and equity, sometimes with 'slants' or emphases, which are unwelcome to diverse groups of Christians. The image of divided Christendom is projected into the public mind, which is inevitable so long as Christians are in fact divided. Journalistic and television comment is usually well informed and shrewd, though perhaps unduly conscious of 'news value' and less aware of the solid but less startling good work that goes on.

Disunity affects the Education of Children

In the United States religious teaching is excluded from schools supported by the government, a solution to the difficult question of 'denominational' teaching in a pluralistic society; and it may be wondered whether this system does not at least indirectly favour the idea that religion is something separate which need only play a small part in ordinary life.[2] In England a report from a Committee of the Free Church Federal Council in 1960 said that 'in day schools, Sunday Schools, Girl Guides, youth clubs and children's addresses, different material was being presented by people with patently different attitudes to the Bible and the young people were being given their Christian education not only by different instructors, but by different instructors working to diverse programmes, with diverse

[1] Christopher Driver, a Congregationalist, in *A Future for the Free Churches?*, London, 1962, pp. 128–9.

[2] Cf. Dr Daniel Jenkins, *Congregationalism. A Restatement*, London, 1948, p. 127, who raised the question whether education should be 'religiously neutral'.

standards, from diverse points of view and with different aims. . . .'

Mr Driver comments: 'It would certainly not be surprising if children exposed to this degree of pedagogic confusion fled into fundamentalist funk-holes at the earliest opportunity. The committee lays the blame fairly and squarely on the disunity of the churches.'[1]

In Theological Colleges there is likewise evidence of the practical evil effects of Christian divisions. Dr J. Robert Nelson a Methodist, points out that there is a tension in the minds of some students for the ministry between ecumenical interest and denominational allegiance:

'Because of their strong convictions about the need for manifesting the unity of the Church, many theologians of the ecumenical movement have taught and written in such a way as to persuade young Christians of the reality and the urgency of this unity. Since the sixteenth Century Reformation it is unlikely that so large a proportion of theological students have set their affections on the universal Church, rather than on their own communion, as do the students of the present generation. And yet it is precisely this fact which has been counterbalanced by the renewed confessional and denominational interest, which is also stimulated by the challenge of the ecumenical movement. Many a student's dissatisfaction and perplexity spring from the paradoxical situation which is brought about by the concurrent claims of ecumenism and denominationalism. The student may feel frustrated in anticipation of having to minister in the confining sphere of his denomination. But this frustration cannot be overcome so long as there exists no fully united Church in which he can serve. This unhappy feeling is naturally most

---

[1] Christopher Driver, *A Future for the Free Churches?*, London, 1962, p. 93. In English State schools religion is taught usually from 'an agreed syllabus'. Mr Driver rejects the idea that 'the Bible' and 'non-sectarian' religion in a school curriculum amounts to a Christian education (p. 88) as, indeed, do many other educationalists. On the other hand, the mere existence of 'denominational', Catholic or Anglican schools, is not of itself a guarantee of good religious teaching. Our Catholic schools have recently met criticisms in English-speaking lands on grounds of inadequate methods of teaching religion, though determined efforts are being made to introduce new methods and outlooks. The centre called *Lumen Vitae* in Brussels, which reflects the renewed interest in Scripture, is spreading its influence ever more widely; and the level of religious training in Teachers' Training Colleges is steadily rising.

acute in lands where denominational pluralism is most pro-
nounced. It is less of a problem, though not entirely dissolved, in
lands where there are comprehensive united churches or where
one confession is overwhelmingly dominant.'[1]

Thus the problem of divided Christians ramifies into concrete
situations and is no mere theoretical question.

A hindrance to the task of preaching the Gospel to all men

The World Council of Churches took its original inspiration
from the Missionary Conference at Edinburgh in 1910, at which
it was made conspicuously clear that in non-Christian countries
the divided witness of Christians brought Christianity itself into
disrepute. Since then the evidence has grown: a divided Christianity cannot convert the world. At Willington, Germany, in
1952, at the Conference of the International Missionary Council, the younger church delegates presented a statement which
included the following: 'We believe that the unity of the
churches is an essential condition of effective witness and advance. In the lands of the younger churches divided witness is a
crippling handicap. We of the younger churches feel this very
keenly. While unity may be desirable in the lands of the older
churches it is imperative in those of the younger churches. . . .
Division in the Church distorts its witness, frustrates its mission,
and contradicts its own nature. If the Church is to demonstrate
the Gospel in its life as well as in its preaching, it must manifest
to the world the power of God to break down all barriers and to
establish the Church's unity in Christ.'[2]

Ten years later Bishop Lesslie Newbigin put it like this: 'As a
missionary in India I have often been asked, "Are you really so
narrow-minded as to think that you are going to enrol the whole
human race in your little group? Are you like the frog that
thinks its little pond is the whole ocean?" With all my heart I
can answer that I long for every human being to be a Christian.
But—in all loyalty to the Church of my fathers—I have to con-

---

[1] 'The Theological Education of *Homo Ecumenicus*', *Ecumenical Review*, January
1963, p. 166. Dr Nelson also lists hopeful signs and indicates where there is room
for improvement. The Decree in no. 10 refers to the need for a more ecumenical
outlook in our Catholic seminaries, faculties and universities.
[2] Cited by Norman Goodall, *The Ecumenical Movement*, London, 1961, p. 38.

fess that I cannot wish for every human being to be a Presbyterian.

'This is one way of stating the burden which our destiny places on the heart of the evangelist. None of our Churches is a big enough fellowship to be a home for the human race. Only a universal fellowship can be the adequate bearer of a universal Gospel. The missionary cannot evade the question: 'What is the body which you are asking me to join?'' For St Paul the answer is that it is a body—one body—in which men of every sort and kind are at home. We cannot give that answer, because we represent broken fragments of that body, none of them entitled to make that claim, all of them representing some segment of Christian experience stemming from some limited part of the religious history of the western world. If you stay inside the confines of our western world you can forget that. But if you stand in the streets of a great Asian city to preach the Gospel, you cannot escape facing the question.'[1]

Catholic failings

The Orthodox and the Catholics would, of course, deny that 'we represent broken fragments' of the body of Christ, and both claim that they represent the one body of which St Paul speaks, in which men of every sort and kind are at home. Nevertheless, it must be frankly admitted that our Catholic missionary effort has carried the stamp of the western world, and we may well ask ourselves if our 'adaptation' of accidental matters to the customs of those whom we wished to make Christians has always been what it should. Have we not tended to identify the law, the liturgy, the manner of conduct and manner of dress with the essential message of Christianity? Have we always been free from a spirit of nationalist, or of excessive devotion to a particular Religious Order or Congregation?[2] Have we been sufficiently aware of the missionary obligation inherent in the very fact of being a Christian?

[1] Bishop Lesslie Newbigin, *Is Christ Divided?*, Grand Rapids, Michigan, 1961, pp. 12–13.
[2] Cf. for instance, *Réforme des Missions au xxe Siècle*, Cardinal Celso Constantini (tr. from Italian by Jean Bruls), Paris, 1960; Cardinal Constantini did not approve of Catholic Missions being under the protection, and to some extent, the tutelage of diplomatic representatives.

Has our missionary effort been really commensurate with our total numbers? Have we done enough to stimulate and foster missionary vocations? It is possible that some of the smaller Protestant bodies could put us to shame by their zeal and enterprise and spirit of sacrifice. There are about 392,400 priests in the world and of these only 33,000 work in predominately non-Christian countries; that is, there are 359,000 priests for about 510 million Catholics and about 33,000 for 1,900 million non-Christians.[1] There are many reasons for this disproportion, but perhaps all of them together do not justify the existing deployment of our forces, and this may well be one reason why Vatican Council II proposes to set up a Central Mission Board or Mission Senate to be composed of bishops, experts and representatives of missionary organizations, to work within the Congregation for the Propagation of the Faith.

The *Schema* on the Missions recommends that Catholic missionaries should collaborate with Christians of other churches, in the spirit of the Decree on Ecumenism. In the past, mutual prejudice has often led to open antagonism and competition.

Missionary organizations

There is unquestionably too great a multiplicity of Christian groups who hold differing versions of the Christian message. *The Directory of North American Protestant Foreign Missionary Agencies*[2] lists one hundred and sixty-seven 'Denominational Sending Boards' and one hundred and sixteen 'Interdenominational and Non-Denominational Missionary Sending Societies'. As Bishop Neill says, difficulty is found in the unwillingness of mission boards and other authorities to make any surrender of their own autonomy and sovereignty.[3] In spite of this, many of their achievements have been most noteworthy. All over the world they build hospitals, clinics, primary, secondary, agricultural schools and colleges; establish boys' and girls' clubs and youth organizations and have a healthy interest in sport. They do admirable work in linguistics and in translation of the Bible.

[1] Cf. the summaries of Adrien Buffard's book *Perspectives sur le Monde*, Quebec, 1959, which appeared in *Christ to the World*, Rome, vol. vi, 1961, pp. 17–31, with the subsequent comment and amplifications.

[2] Missionary Research Library, New York, 1960.

[3] *The Unfinished Task*, London, 1958, p. 211.

They make use of radio networks and introduce modern drainage systems and sanitation. Generally they create a warm friendly atmosphere and have the welfare of less developed peoples at heart. They inculcate sobriety and industry. Through the Bible they make Christ known and loved. Yet the devotion of some of these bodies to their own particular interpretation of Christianity causes the image of Christianity to be one of dividedness and even competition, even granted the personal charity of so many missionaries.

An Opposition Group

The Associated Missions of the International Council of Christian Churches, which in 1960 had some eight hundred and seventy-seven missionaries and 'overseas appropriations' of $3,111,631,[1] seems to have small charity towards the World Council of Churches and is even accused of running 'a smear campaign against it'. Dr Norman Goodall says that he is, he believes, a tolerant creature with no love of controversy: 'I even cherish a sneaking affection for the tender-hearted schoolgirl who wrote that "even the Devil in another walk of life would have been a good man." Bickerings within the Household of Faith "hurt my understanding" and I would be charitable to others even as I need the charity of men and the mercy of God.' But even Dr Goodall shows a restrained indignation against the activities of many in the International Council of Christian Churches and their virulent opposition to unitive movement.[2]

Many other missionaries of an 'evangelical' outlook raise in their converts an admirable spirit of self-reliance and a sense of personal dignity. Yet one may wonder whether the sense of order and of christian obedience has received equal attention. In South Africa over nine hundred and seventy-three independent African 'churches' have arisen, and thus the 'pluralism' in America and Europe spreads, to the loss of the sense of Christian unity.[3]

It has been a regrettable fact that some 'evangelical' and

[1] Cf. the *Directory of the Missionary Research Library*, 1960, p. 61.
[2] *The Ecumenical Movement*, London, 1961, p. 151–2.
[3] Cf. B. G. M. Sundkler, *Bantu Prophets in South Africa*, London, 2nd ed., 1961; F. B. Welbourn, *East African Rebels*, London, 1961; C. G. Baëta, *Prophetism in Ghana*, London, 1962.

other groups which try to expand Christianity (or perhaps one may say their own version of Christianity) show an aggressive hostility to the Catholic Church and magnify what failings exist among us, through lack of understanding of the complex historical, economic and psychological causes which to a considerable extent explain our failings, sometimes all too evident.[1] The remedy is surely not a correspondingly aggressive hostility, but a following of St Paul's exhortation—'Do not be overcome by evil but overcome evil with good' (Rom 12: 21). Much can be done by sincere respect for their good qualities both personal and corporate, through friendly understanding and, as far as possible, helping them.[2]

D. THE ECUMENICAL MOVEMENT

This is a movement towards universal unity among Christians. First it is a 'movement'; a time and temper of mind and heart, an 'outlook', a general aim and feeling; 'it is not a fixed and stable profession of faith or programme of action, but a moving tide of inquiry and search, with cross-currents in it, backwaters, ebbing waters, and sometimes whirlpools'.[3] Secondly, the movement finds concrete embodiment in the World Council of Churches, in the reunions and proposals for reunions of various churches, and, among Catholics, in the Secretariat for the Promotion of Christian Unity, though obviously it is not confined to these. There are various organizations, such as The Friends of Reunion, an interdenominational group in England, the International League for Apostolic Faith

[1] The complexity, for instance, of the situation in Latin America is not easy to grasp and generalizations are hazardous. This can be gathered from one of the most interesting books on the subject, Fr. John J. Considine's *New Horizons in Latin America*, New York, 1958; Bishop Stephen Neill's *The Unfinished Task*, op. cit., has most penetrating reflections about missionary work, mainly with reference to Asia.

[2] *The Lutheran World* for January 1963, carries an excellent summary entitled 'Principles, Strategy and Theology of Roman Catholic Missions', pp. 78–87, by Oberkirchenrat Hugo Schnell. For an indication of the attitude of some Catholics towards non-Christian religions, cf. Raymond Panikkar, *The Unknown Christ of Hinduism*, London, 1965, with the useful bibliographies there given; Fr Panikkar holds strongly that Hinduism, at least at its best, is a preparation for acknowledgement of Christ. *The International Review of Missions*, published in London, is invaluable on the whole question of the expansion of Christianity.

[3] *The Churches and the Church*, op. cit., p. viii.

and Order, the Anglican Fellowship of Sts Alban and Sergius, 'national and local "councils of churches"', various 'inter-church relations committees' of different churches. Among Catholics, a number of organizations like the Una Sancta movement and the Adam Moehler Institute in Paderborn, the Benedictines at Trier in Germany, the Unitas Association in Rome, with branches or tentacles throughout much of the Catholic world, and a number of institutes or monasteries, such as the Augustinians in Paris, the Benedictines at Chevetogne in Belgium, the Dominicans at Boulogne-sur-Seine in France, the Centre at Montreal and the Bombay Ecumenical Group. To attempt to enumerate them all would be a very difficult task, since associations take many different forms. I apologize for omissions, but mention in England particularly the St John Chrysostom Society for fostering good relations with the Ortho-dox, and the Dominican Spode House in Staffordshire, which is rapidly developing into an ecumenical centre.

The World Council of Churches

Founded in 1948, the World Council of Churches was a com-ing together of three movements, called respectively, Life and Work, Faith and Order and the International Missionary Council.[1] Of this last, I have already spoken.[2]

The Life and Work movement originated in efforts for peace, mainly during the 1914–18 War, and developed into efforts to apply christian principles to international relations, to econo-mics and to social matters. In the World Council it survives, though divided, in the Commission for International Affairs, the Division of Inter-church Aid and Service to Refugees, and lastly also, in the Division for study of Church and Society and in activities for youth, laity and for collaboration of men and women. It studies the sociological aspects of the churches, and practices charity as a means of unity.[3]

[1] Though this latter was not formally 'integrated' into the World Council until 1961, there had always been an 'association' between the two so that the headings on note-paper read 'The World Council of Churches, in Association with the International Missionary Council', and vice versa.

[2] Cf. pp. 49–51.

[3] Cf. E. Duff, *The Social Thought of the World Council of Churches*, London, 1956; on the development of the various departments of the W.C.C., cf. *Evanston—New*

The Faith and Order Movement began in an attempt to find unity in doctrine and the 'order' of the Church in liturgy, ministry and administration. It became part of the Division of Studies in the W.C.C., though before 1948 it had held world conferences at Lausanne in 1927, at Edinburgh in 1937, and after its integration into the W.C.C., has held conferences at Lund in 1952 and at Montreal in 1963. At the first World Conference in 1927, when men of so many different traditions, convictions and languages met one another for the first time in great goodwill, it was natural to seek agreements, even though merely verbal, and to fail exactly to define the purpose of the Conference.[1] Did all the participating churches presuppose that we do not know what is the unity which Christ wills for his Church and have to confer together to find out? After the Conference at Edinburgh in 1937, and the formation of the World Council in 1948, this question was definitely answered in an official statement made at Toronto in 1950, which made clear that no church by membership in the W.C.C. compromises its doctrine about the Church and that the World Council itself makes no presuppositions about the nature of the Church, but simply seeks to overcome the existing disunity. It has often been said that the World Council exists to bring about its own dissolution by all 'churches' uniting in the one holy catholic Church of the Creed.

Growth of Catholic understanding

The period between the Lausanne Conference in 1927 and the Lund Conference in 1952 shows a growing resolution to base unity upon truth, and an increasing awareness of the firmness with which doctrinal convictions are held. Catholics gradually came to understand this and the strictures of Pius XI in 1928 against dilution of doctrine gave place in 1949 to an Instruction of the Holy Office in which the growing desire for

---

Delhi, 1954–1961, Geneva, 1961, a volume prepared for the Assembly of December 1961, which contains all the major documents published by the W.C.C. and which is essential for any real appreciation of its aims, methods and convictions.

[1] Cf. the account given by the late Canon Tissington Tatlow in Rouse and Neill, *History of the Ecumenical Movement*, London, 1954, p. 423ff.

the reunion of all who believe in Christ, and the change in out-looks, were attributed to the inspiration of the Holy Ghost. Bishops were exhorted 'to make a special object of their care and attention this work of "reunion" which is a particular charge and duty of the Church'.[1] All over the Catholic world under-standing and sympathy grew, and books, articles in periodicals, and conferences multiplied. Catholic 'observers' were present at the meeting of the Faith and Order Department of the W.C.C. at Edinburgh in 1937, at Oberlin in 1954 and at St Andrews, Scotland, in 1960, at New Delhi in 1961, at Montreal in 1963 and since 1960 at the yearly meetings of the Central Committee of the W.C.C.[2]

The Basis of the World Council of Churches

From the time of the first proposals in 1910 by the American Protestant Episcopal Church for conferences in faith and order, belief in a confession of 'Our Lord Jesus Christ as God and Saviour' was regarded as the essential basis for the attempt to unite the Communions; this 'basis' was accepted by the World Council at its formation in 1948 and was enlarged in 1961, to read:

> 'The World Council of Churches is a fellowship of churches which confess the Lord Jesus Christ as God and Saviour according to the Scriptures and therefore seek to fulfil to-gether their common calling to the glory of the one God, Father, Son and Holy Spirit.'[3]

[1] *A.A.S.*, 42 (1950), pp. 142–51. The document was printed as an appendix to my book *The Churches and the Church* in 1960.

[2] On the development of Catholic appreciation of the unity movement among separated brethren, cf. the excellent chapter 'The Evolution of Ecumenism in Papal Documents' in Gregory Baum's *Progress and Perspectives*, London, 1962, pp. 25–45; George H. Tavard's *Two Centuries of Ecumenism*, London, 1960, and the account by Bishop Oliver Tomkins 'The Roman Catholic Church and the Ecumenical Movement, 1910–1948', Rouse and Neill, *A History of the Ecumenical Movement 1512–1948*, London, 1954, pp. 677–97. 'As the Movement has changed and developed, the emphasis of Roman Catholic pronouncement upon it has also varied,' wrote Bishop Tomkins.

[3] Cf. Tissington Tatlow, 'The World Conference on Faith and Order', Rouse and Neill, *History of the Ecumenical Movement*, op. cit., pp. 4 and 7; *The New Delhi Report*, London, 1961, pp. 152–9; for a statement on the function and purpose of the Basis, cf. *Evanston to New Delhi, Report of the Central Committee to the Third Assembly*, Geneva, 1964, pp. 215–16; and the report on Tradition presented at the Montreal Conference in 1963, *Report*, London, 1964, p. 58.

The Goal

At New Delhi in 1961 the following definition of the goal of the movement was drawn up:

'We believe that the unity which is both God's will and his gift to his Church is being made visible as all in each place who are baptized into Jesus Christ and confess him as Lord and Saviour are brought by the Holy Spirit into one fully committed fellowship, holding the one apostolic faith, preaching the one Gospel, breaking the one bread, joining in common prayer, and having a corporate life reaching out in witness and service to all and who at the same time are united with the whole Christian fellowship in all places and all ages in such wise that ministry and members are accepted by all, and that all can act and speak together as occasion requires for the task to which God calls his people. It is for such unity that we believe we must pray and work.

'This brief description of our objective leaves many questions unanswered. We are not yet of a common mind on the interpretation and the means of achieving the goal we have described. We are clear that unity does not imply simple uniformity of organization, rite or expression. We all confess that sinful self-will operates to keep us separated and that in our human ignorance we cannot discern clearly the lines of God's design for the future. But it is our firm hope that through the Holy Spirit God's will as it is witnessed to in Holy Scripture will be more and more disclosed to us and in us. The achievement of unity will involve nothing less than a death and rebirth of many forms of church life as we have known them. We believe that nothing less costly can finally suffice.'[1]

Fr Jérome Hamer remarks that this statement is not content with a purely spiritual unity or invisible unity, nor yet with a purely federal unity, that is, an external association of autonomous groups. This visible unity requires one ministry, one body of doctrine, one sacramental life.[2]

[1] *The New Delhi Report, op. cit.*, p. 116.
[2] 'The World Council of Churches' in *Christian Unity, a Catholic View, being an*

To some extent, the character of the World Council of Churches is changing, or at least developing. It has no authority over its member churches, disclaims the idea of being a church, ordains no ministers and administers no sacraments. And yet to some extent it may be said to be exercising the prophetic office of the church, by its proclamations about unity, and by the help it gives in discussions about plans for union and about missionary activity. But in this it does no more than voice the common aspirations or convictions of its member churches and stream-line certain activities. The ecclesiological significance of the W.C.C. was discussed at Toronto in 1963.[1]

In 1963 two former officials of the W.C.C., Drs Keith R. Bridston and Walter D. Wagner, gave space to some criticisms of the administration of the W.C.C. in a volume of essays by different writers, *Unity in Mid-Career*, New York, 1963. Professor Alexander Schmemann in an essay entitled 'The Moment of Truth for Orthodoxy' expressed some misgivings about Ortho-dox-Protestant relations. For myself, I confess my deep sym-pathy with the W.C.C., even though as a young organization it may suffer some 'growing pains' and I think the Eastern Ortho-dox have had a great beneficial effect, through their firmness to Orthodoxy.

Unions of Churches

Unions of churches made and proposed, are difficult to classify. First, however, there are 'intra-confessional' unions, that is between churches of the same family. Thus in 1900, the Free Church of Scotland and the United Presbyterians became the United Free Church of Scotland, and this in turn united in 1929 with the Church of Scotland; their separate General Assemblies fused to form only one Assembly of the Church of Scotland. Various Methodist, Lutheran, Presbyterian and Congrega-tionalist bodies have formed 'organic unions', this term meaning a fusion of sacramental, ministerial and administrative func-

account of the first official conference organised by the Bishops' Committee for Christian Unity, Heythrop, August 1962, edited by John C. Heenan, Archbishop of Liverpool, London, 1962, p. 151.
[1] Cf. *The Fourth World Conference on Faith and Order,* Report, London, 1963, pp. 23 and 48-9.

tions, the general 'confession' or profession of faith and often historic loyalties remaining unchanged.[1]

'Trans-confessional' corporate unions (to use the terminology of Bishop Stephen Neill), are unions of churches of different historical traditions, of different 'polities' and sometimes of different traditional professions of faith. In 1925 Canadian Congregationalists, Methodists and Presbyterians united to form the United Church of Canada. In 1961, the Congregational Christian Churches and the Evangelical (of Lutheran origin) and Reformed (Calvinist) Church united to form the United Church of Christ.[2] In 1947, Anglicans, Congregationalists, Methodists and Presbyterians united to form the Church of South India, the only instance thus far of a union of episcopal and non-episcopal churches. Those elected to be bishops at the inauguration of the union were 'ordained and consecrated' but the Anglican bishops received no new consecration. All ordinations in the Church of South India are by bishops; but the ministers, called 'presbyters', who were not episcopally or-

[1] Cf. the excellent article by Bishop Stephen Neill, 'Plans of Union and Reunion 1910–1948' in Rouse and Neill, *History of the Ecumenical Movement*, op. cit., pp.445–505. This, however, must now be completed by the *Survey* in the *Ecumenical Review*, April 1954, p. 300; October 1955, p. 76; April 1957, p. 284; January 1960, p. 231, and the last *Survey* by Dr Lukas Vischer, April 1962. In 1960 Dr Stephen J. Bayne Jnr. edited the texts of the proposed unions in Ceylon, and in North India and Pakistan; together with the counsel given by the Lambeth Conference of 1958 to the Anglicans affected by the proposals, and a comment by the Archdeacon of Allahabad, the Venerable T. D. Sully. Dr Bayne's book was published in London, 1960. Cf. also, M. G. Capon, *Towards Unity in Kenya*, Nairobi, 1962; *The Church its Nature and Functioning*, the text of the proposed union of Congregationalists, Methodists and Presbyterians in Australia, Melbourne, 1963; *Proposed Basis of Union* in Ghana (affecting an Anglican diocese and a province, Presbyterians and Methodists), published by the Ghana Church Union Committee, Accra, 1963; and *Scheme of Church Union in Nigeria* (seven Anglican dioceses, Methodists and Presbyterians), Lagos, 1960.

[2] Cf. Dr Douglas Horton's *The United Church of Christ*, New York, 1963. The Union was of special interest since the Congregationalists were of English origin, the Evangelicals of Continental European origin. Dr Horton says that the United Church considers itself 'a Protestant Catholic Church'. Administratively, the union brought greater centralization, for the United Church recognizes responsibilities at home and abroad for missions, fraternal and service, ecumenical relations, inter-church relations, and Christian unity, education, publication, the ministry, ministerial pensions and relief, evangelism, stewardship, social action, health and welfare and any other appropriate area of need or concern. (Article VIII of Constitution.) These areas are cared for by 'boards, Commissions, Councils, offices or other instrumentalities which act in accordance with the Constitution, By-laws and instructions given them by the General Synod'. There are, however, provisions in the Constitution to safeguard the congregationalist principle of the autonomy of the local congregation.

dained at the time of the union maintain their standing and can minister in any of the congregations of the Church of South India, with the proviso that 'no forms of worship nor ritual, nor a ministry, to which they have not been accustomed or to which they conscientiously object will be imposed on any congregation'. At the end of thirty years the position is to be reviewed, the hope being that by that time all the ministers will be episcopally ordained.

The Anglican Communion (with the exception of the Church of the Province of the West Indies) has established a limited measure of 'intercommunion' with the Church of South India during the thirty-year interim period. This permits the bishops and episcopally ordained presbyters of the C.S.I. to celebrate the Holy Communion in Anglican churches conditionally upon their willingness to confine their celebrations to Anglican churches, and permits their own bishops and priests to accept the hospitality of the C.S.I. for celebrating Holy Communion within it. But non-episcopally ordained presbyters of the C.S.I. may not normally celebrate in Anglican churches. Thus the Anglican Communion maintains the need for episcopal ordination.[1]

Willingness to accept episcopacy

In several other proposals for reunion of episcopal and non-episcopal churches—Anglican-Presbyterian, Anglican-Methodist, Anglican-Methodist-Presbyterian, United Church of Christ in the U.S.A., Anglicans and others in Ceylon, North India and Pakistan and in different parts of Africa[2]—a fair number of non-Anglicans have expressed willingness to accept episcopacy in practice, as a concentration of the general episcopé or oversight in the Church as a normal means or ordination, and is at least a symbol of the continuity of the Church, and perhaps also a guarantee of continuity.

These plans usually contain a provision that no specific theory about the nature of episcopacy is to be required. This

---

[1] Cf. *The Lambeth Conference, 1958*, Report of the Committee on Church Unity and the Church Universal, pp. 225–8. Cf. also Bishop Lesslie Newbigin, *The Reunion of the Church*, ed. 2, 1960, pp. xvii–xxvii, and his concluding chapter 'South India and the Ecumenical Movement', pp. 181–190.

[2] Cf. note on page 69 above.

might, indeed, leave open the possibility of holding that episcopacy is merely a suitable manner of administration, having no theological significance; but a feeling is very general that what is called the 'Anglo-Catholic' view makes the mere succession by laying on of hands the sole criterion of the continuity of the Church, as if the Church were constituted by an 'apostolic-succession' irrespective of the continuity of the whole believing community.

This most certainly is not the teaching of the Orthodox or of Catholics. Nor do I think it is the Anglo-Catholic view. It is certainly not the conception of episcopacy explained by the Church of England in both *Anglican-Methodist* Reports and, presumably accepted in principle by the Methodists.[1] But liberty in the interpretation of episcopacy, which many reunion proposals demand, must be viewed in relation to the views attributed to 'Anglo-Catholics' or Catholics in general.

Even when churches are willing to accept episcopacy (and sometimes as an effective sign of unity and continuity), there is an aversion to any action which would reflect adversely on non-episcopal ministries. In the Interim Statement about possible Anglican-Methodist union in 1958, the Methodists declared 'Methodists could never accept either the contention that without episcopacy there is no Church or any theory of the transmission of grace and authority which would deny her place in the Catholic Church or reduce her ministry and sacraments to spurious imitations'.[2] It may be noted in passing that the Decree on Ecumenism, no. 3, para. 3 and no. 22, para. 3, by no means reduces ministries and the Eucharist of separated churches to 'spurious imitations', in spite of lack of what we consider to be authentic orders. The South India method of union permitted presbyters not episcopally ordained to function alongside those episcopally ordained, save where congregations choose only the latter.

Reconciliation of Ministries

To avoid the 'anomaly' of a dual kind of ministry in the same church, in several proposals for reunion a ceremony of 'recon-

[1] Cf. *Report*, 1958, pp. 16–27, pp. 35–7; *Report*, 1963, pp. 24–7.
[2] p. 36.

ciliation of ministries' has been devised with the aim of securing a ministry acceptable to all members of the uniting churches. In the Anglican-Methodist proposals there is after a prayer a mutual, though successive, laying on of hands by Anglican bishops and ministers of the Methodists. In the prayer before the laying on of hands, the Anglican bishop says:

'Renew thy blessings already given and upon these thy servants do thou pour out thy Holy Spirit, to endue each according to his need with grace for the office of a priest in the Church of God.'

At the laying on of hands by the bishop, he says:

'Take authority to exercise the office of priest, to preach the Word of God and to minister the holy Sacraments among us, as need shall arise and you shall be licensed to do.'

Then the Methodist ministers lay hands on the bishops and priests of the Church of England, in silence, and says:

'Take authority to exercise the office of a minister to preach the Word of God and to minister the holy sacraments among us, etc.'[1]

The *Reports* of 1958 and 1963 contain summaries of doctrine about Scripture and Tradition, the Gospel, the Ministry, Priesthood, Episcopacy, Baptism, and the Eucharist. The Ceremony of Reconciliation of the Ministries is preceded by a Declaration of Intention:

'We of the Church of England have been accustomed, since the foundation of the Church in these Islands, to seek God's grace and authority for our bishops, priests and deacons through prayer and the laying on of the hands by

---

[1] Cf. *Conversations between the Church of England and the Methodist Church. An Interim Statement*, London, 1958; *Conversations between the Church of England and the Methodist Church. A Report*, London, 1963, pp. 43 and 47. The Church of England representatives were appointed by the Archbishops of Canterbury and York at the request of the Convocations, the Methodist representatives were appointed by the President of the Methodist Conference at the request of the conference. The representatives included well-known scholars on both sides, such as Canon S. L. Greenslade, Canon E. W. Kemp, Bishop G. K. A. Bell, Dr Norman Sykes, Dr C. R. Barrett, Dr E. Gordon Rupp, Dr Leslie D. Weatherhead.

bishops, and we believe this tradition, which we have received, to have come down to us from New Testament times and to be God's will for his Church. We wish to share this precious gift, which we have unworthily received, with the ministers of the Methodist Church, and at the same time to enter into the spiritual heritage which is theirs.

'We Methodists, believing that within the One Holy Catholic and Apostolic Church our communion was brought into being by the Holy Spirit to be a witness to the universal grace of God, to the gift of assurance by the Holy Spirit, and to the power of the Holy Spirit to make us perfect in love, desire to share with our brethren of the Church of England this our calling, and to enter into the spiritual heritage and continuity of commission which they treasure.'[1]

Modification of the Establishment

It must be added that the eventual complete unity of the Church of England and the Methodist Church will demand 'very extensive legal and constitutional changes for the Church of England, which are likely to be the equivalent of the granting of complete self-government'. It is to be assumed that the united church will be free to settle its own forms of doctrine, worship and discipline, to appoint its own officers and to settle disputes in its own courts with the same degree of freedom from State control as it now possessed by the Church of Scotland (p. 52). Revision of the liturgy and of the ordinals is envisaged.

Dissentient Methodists

Four Methodists refused to sign the *Report* of 1963, expressing their dissent on several grounds. Regarding episcopacy, they say that there is little help in the liberty of interpretation permitted about the nature of episcopacy. 'Actions speak louder than words and an interpretation of episcopacy as (1) the historic episcopacy and (2) absolutely indispensable to the Church of the future, is presupposed by the proposals contained in the report (p. 59).' The dissentient Methodists also object that the ceremony of reconciliation of the ministries is capable of being

---

[1] *Report*, 1963, p. 38.

and will be interpreted as an act of episcopal ordination, and thus:

'(*a*) means a mechanical and almost magical view of ordination, and (*b*) casts an intolerable (though certainly unintended) slur on Methodist ordinations and ministries in the past' (p. 60).

Doubts and Hesitations

Discussion—sometimes heated—goes on and it is unknown at present whether or not the Convocations of the Church of England and the Methodist Conference will accept the proposals. Bishop Lesslie Newbigin argued forcefully in favour of the South India method of a gradual reconciliation of ministries, partly on the ground that further unions would, on the principles admitted, require a repetition of the ceremonies of reconciliation of the ministries in each case, and this would look very like a continuing series of ordinations or 're-ordinations'. At the Nottingham Conference on Faith and Order, September 1964, a strong plea was made by members of one section that further consideration be given to the South India method.[1]

'Evangelical' Objections

It is interesting to note that some Anglicans agree with the Methodist dissentients. The Rev R. T. Beckwith, Librarian at Latimer House, Oxford, discussed the doctrines on Priesthood, the Sacraments, Baptism and Holy Communion, in connection with the *Reports*. He says in his first chapter:

'The third and most basic reason for selecting these subjects is that they, unlike some of the other matters raised by the *Report*, have not been sufficiently discussed in modern English theology. Indeed, they can hardly be said to have been *discussed* at all, since nearly all recent writing, from whatever denomination, represents the same school of thought, and maintains a high sacramental realism, often combined with a high doctrine of the eucharistic sacrifice. The progress made by such teaching since the rise of the Oxford Movement, something over a cen-

[1] *Unity Begins at Home*, a Report from the *First British Conference on Faith and Order*, 1964, p. 71.

tury ago, has been phenomenal. It pours today from Anglican presses and pulpits and commands a large majority in Convocation; it has penetrated to all parts of the Anglican Communion, bringing about in many provinces a revision of the traditional formularies; and, largely as a result of the Ecumenical Movement, which has reinforced it from Lutheran and Eastern sources, it is now spreading to many of the other denominations as well, both at home and abroad. Insofar as this trend reflects a realization of the importance of the sacraments, and a dissatisfaction with any theology which treats them as merely peripheral and thus fails to take the Biblical statements about them seriously, it is a trend that must be welcomed. But whether in other respects such teaching does justice to the statements of the Bible seems much more doubtful, especially after one has pondered the following questions: Does Scripture encourage us to account for the importance of the sacraments in this particular way? Is it possible to account for their importance in this way without derogating from the importance of faith, the word of God and the atonement? And is it not possible to account for their importance in a more satisfactory and scriptural way on the basis of the theology of our Reformers? These are questions which must be faced, and they all resolve themselves into one great question: Is the teaching which is now so prevalent really true to Scripture? But since the *Report* has also adopted the current teaching, this question must also be asked of the teaching propounded in the *Report*. For the *Report*, as we shall see, though it has not satisfied Anglo-Catholics on all matters, has on the matters of the sacraments and priesthood adopted what is unmistakably Anglo-Catholic teaching.'[1]

Anglo-Catholic Influence?

I must confess that I am doubtful whether Anglo-Catholicism has had as much influence as Mr Beckwith here supposed; I think that Anglo-Catholicism certainly has had some influence, but that new outlooks in the study of the Bible and the comparatively new interest in dogmatics, together with the ecumenical movement, have now perhaps more influence than

---

[1]*Priesthood and Sacraments, A Study in the Anglican-Methodist Report*, Abingdon, Berks, October 1964, p.p. 8–9.

Anglo-Catholicism. At any rate two other proposed unions of churches seem very similar to the Church of England-Methodist proposals. One is the proposed union of Congregationalists, Methodists and Presbyterians in Australia, in which episcopacy is to be sought from the Church of South India, not from Anglicans. Compared with the Anglican-Methodist *Report*, there are some differences of doctrinal emphasis, but the substance seems much the same. The other is the proposal made in 1961 by Dr Eugene Carson Blake, Stated Clerk of the United Presbyterian Church in the U.S.A., for a union of the Protestant Episcopal Church, the Methodist Church, the United Presbyterian Church and the United Church of Christ, accepting both episcopacy and tradition, and suggesting practically the same method for the reconciliation of the ministry.[1] I gravely doubt if Dr Blake was influenced—unless very indirectly and unconsciously—by Anglo-Catholicism. He puts 'the final question' like this:

'The final question goes: Is not the difference between the evangelical and catholic understanding of the gospel, church, and ministry so deep and essential that union of the kind proposed would water down Christian faith and make unwarranted compromise of Christian conviction? My answer to this question is that it may be so, but that neither catholic nor evangelical has a right to act on that assumption without examining it with great care.

'In general, there is much greater agreement at the heart of Christian faith than the average church member or minister normally realizes. We have for so long discussed theology polemically that it sometimes comes as a shock to find how much basic agreement on Christian truth has been exposed by the renewed Biblical study that has affected every Christian Church. I do not mean to suggest that there are no important

---

[1] Cf. Dr Blake's sermon in *The Challenge to Reunion*, ed. Brown and Scott, New York, 1963, pp. 271–83, and his 'Two Years Later', ibid., pp. 258–69. As a result of Dr Blake's sermon, a consultation on Church Union took place among representatives of the four communions, and later the Disciples of Christ and the United Brethren Church joined the Consultation. There were 'observer-consultants' from fifteen other churches. Cf. *Digest of the Proceedings of the Consultation on Church Union for 1962 and 1963*, Fanwood, New Jersey, 1963. The consultation seems rather a remote preparation for union than a discussion of immediate issues connected with an imminent union.

theological disagreements any more. But I do hold that all but one of the most important differences cut across denominational lines. When you discuss the great and central doctrines of the Church of Jesus Christ, such as Grace, Incarnation, Salvation, Atonement, Justification and Sanctification, you can find, if you are willing to look for them, statements from theologians of all the major churches of Christendom that are in basic agreement with one another. Anyone who doubts this should read such a book as *Christianity Divided* (Callahan, O'Hanlon and Oberman, eds. Sheed and Ward, N.Y., 1961). What has happened in the past is that we have tended to caricature the theologies of other Churches rather than to study them. The ecumenical movement which has brought Churches out of isolation into dialogue, has happily made that kind of polemical theology a dying phenomenon among the ablest theologians of all traditions.'[1]

Possibly Dr Blake may be just a little optimistic, but it is unquestionably true that there has been in these last few years a great increase of understanding due largely to the ecumenical movement.[2]

The willingness of so many traditionally non-episcopal churches to accept episcopacy is due to a variety of causes of which Anglican influence is certainly one, but by no means the only one. Greater study of tradition, the degree of centralization in many churches with consequent enhancement of the actual power of Secretaries of Committees, the general conviction of the urgency of the need of Christian unity, increasing friendship between leaders of many churches and general climate of theological opinion have also had their influence.

Federations

Federations of churches are of various kinds, sometimes difficult for an outsider to understand. For instance the Evangelical

---

[1] *The Challenge to Reunion*, New York and London, 1963, p. 265.

[2] In the book to which he refers, the Catholic writers are Fr J. R. Gieselmann, David Stanley, S.J., Gustave Weigel, S.J., E. A. Schillebeeckx, O.P., and Fr Hans Küng of Tubingen; the Protestants Dr Oscar Cullmann, Dr Ernst Fuchs, Professor A. A. von Ruter, Dr Karl Barth, Frère Max Thurian, Dr Helko Oberman and Professor T. F. Torrance.

Church in Germany is a federation (Bund) and a unity. It is not a church in the full sense of the term. But it is more than a mere confederation of independent churches come together for the despatch of certain business. It is a church in process of coming into existence. It includes Lutheran, Reformed and United Churches.[1] When theologians of these three churches worked out an agreed statement on Holy Communion, known as 'the Arnoldshain Theses', the Synod of the Evangelical Church could do no more than recommend further study of the 'Theses'.[2]

Lutheran Unions

In the United States, several Lutheran churches amalgamated to form the 'American Lutheran Church' and others to form the 'Lutheran Church in America'; but I must confess that I am not clear about the third Lutheran group called the 'Evangelical Lutheran Synodical Conference of North America', especially the position of the Missouri Synod Lutherans, the American Lutheran Church and the Evangelical Lutheran Synod. However, it is clear that a process of integration is continuing. Lutherans have strong convictions about the importance of clear doctrine, and although many Lutheran churches are members of the World Council of Churches, some others refuse membership lest there should be even the suspicion of tolerating 'false doctrine'.[3]

In South Africa Lutheran Churches of Swedish, American, German and Norwegian origin founded the Evangelical Lutheran Church in Southern Africa, South-Eastern Region, the confessional basis including the Augsburg Confession and the Book of Concord. It is to have a bishop, and it looks to a union with all the Lutheran churches in Southern Africa.

Intercommunion between Episcopal Churches

This is a more complex matter than at first sight appears.

[1] Cf. Bishop Stephen Neill, 'Plans of Union and Reunion 1910–1948' in Rouse and Neill, *History of the Ecumenical Movement*, op. cit., pp. 467–8.
[2] Cf. L. Vischer, 'Survey of Church Union Negotiations 1959–1961', *Ecumenical Review*, April 1962, p. 367.
[3] Cf. the article of L. Vischer, cited in previous note, pp. 373–4.

Among the Orthodox there is not 'intercommunion' but simply 'Communion' based upon the same doctrine and the same sacramental life. But the main body of the Orthodox (Patriarchates of Constantinople, Alexandria, Antioch, Jerusalem, Moscow, Serbia, Rumania, the Churches of Cyprus, Sinai, Bulgaria, Georgia, Albania, Finland and Japan, together with many under different 'jurisdictions' in America) are not in communion with the 'Nestorian' church in Irak, Syria and Malabar, nor with the 'Monophysite' Coptic Ethiopian, Syrian and Malabar (Jacobite) and American Churches. However, at the Pan-Orthodox Conference in Rhodes (September 1961), 'observers' were present from the 'Monophysite' Churches and relations seem to be improving.

The nineteen autonomous churches of the Anglican Communion are in 'full communion' with one another; the Church of England has had for the last eight years 'full intercommunion' with the Old Catholic Churches of Holland, France, Germany and Switzerland. The Church of England and some other member churches of the Anglican Communion have a limited intercommunion 'with the Church of Sweden, Denmark, Norway, Iceland and Finland'. The Church of Ireland and the Protestant Episcopalian Church of the United States have close links with the Spanish Reformed Episcopal Church and the Lusitanian Church; but no other churches of the Anglican Communion have accepted these bodies into 'intercommunion'. The Protestant Episcopal Church has a Theological Seminary in which young men of the Philippine Independent Church are trained for the ministry.

The Orthodox and Anglican Orders

As regards the Orthodox, no advance in formal relations can be recorded since the somewhat negative view expressed by the Moscow Conference of the Heads of the Autocephalous Churches in 1948. This Conference, in effect, desired union in faith, especially about the sacrament of Order, which union in faith must rest upon the official declarations of the Church of England and, that accomplished, a Council of the whole Orthodox Church could decide whether to apply the principle of

'Economy' to recognize the validity of Anglican Orders.[1] The Conference added that it understood as conditional the favourable judgement given by the Churches of Constantinople, Jerusalem, Cyprus, Rumania and some other autocephalous churches. The Conference of 1948, however, expressed views about the World Council of Churches, which later were admitted to have been based on inadequate or misleading information;[2] but by 1961 the misunderstandings were cleared up and the Orthodox Churches of Russia, Bulgaria, Rumania and Poland joined the World Council of Churches. The decision, then, about Anglican Orders is subject to revision if future developments warrant it. Friendly relations between Anglicans and Orthodox are being strengthened.

The Unitive Movement

The unitive movement, then, is taking concrete forms not only on the World Council of Churches, but also among separate bodies. Altogether, I reckon that over one hundred and sixty-five independent ecclesiastical bodies are negotiating about some form of union. These 'ecclesiastical bodies' in some cases are the former 'missions' of European and American churches and may be comparatively small in numbers; in others, old-established and large churches are negotiating. Generally, the plans necessarily involve some lessening of 'denominational' outlooks and customs, and often they deliberately envisage further unions. I confess I sometimes wonder whether nationalism plays a part in the search for union, especially in countries which have recently attained independence; but generally the plans for union provide for maintaining links of friendship, or of 'intercommunion' with the parent bodies. If in

[1] Cf. *Actes de la Conférence des Chefs et de Représentants des Eglises Orthodoxes Autocéphales*, réunies à Moscou à l'occasion de la célébration solennelle des Fêtes du 500ᵉ anniversaire de l'Autocéphalie de l'Église Orthodoxe Russe, Moscow, 2 volumes, 1950 and 1952, Russian text with French translation, Paris, 1952. Cf. Fr A. Wenger, A.A., L'Église Orthodoxe et les ordinations anglicaines; *Nouvelle Revue Théologique*, LXXVI (1954), pp. 44–55. The Resolution is also cited in Bell's *Documents on Christian Unity*, fourth series, 1948–57, pp. 35–7. The Resolution of the Rumanian Synod is given in Bell, series 3, pp. 48–9. The 'condition' was: 'It is to be understood that the above resolution will become definitive as soon as the final authority of the Anglican Church ratifies all the statements of its delegation concerning the Mystery of Holy Orders', p. 49.

[2] Cf. Bell's *Documents*, fourth series, pp. 33–8.

some cases there is ambiguity about 'reconciliation of ministries', or even about doctrine, there is nevertheless a vision of the universal Church, and the resistances, sometimes intractable, shows that religious convictions, even though mingled with 'non-doctrinal factors', are sincerely held. It is here that the World Council of Churches plays so important a role, since it stands for a universal unity, not excluding unity with the Catholic Church, however remote it may at present appear. In the World Council the Orthodox and the Anglicans uphold a 'catholic' tradition and their contribution has been and will continue to be invaluable.

The Decree on Ecumenism, at the end of the Introduction, very clearly approves this unitive movement (though not necessarily every single element in it), and lays down the principles which must guide our ecumenical activities.

GENERAL CHARACTERISTICS OF THE DOCUMENT

The general style of the document does not lend itself to easy division. It is not composed on a strictly logical plan in which each point is fully treated before proceeding to the next. The unity of the document is rather the unity of a musical composition in which the same 'theme' recurs with variations. There are repetitions of the same themes from different points of view—the effect of baptism, variety in unity, esteem of separated brethren, the need for holiness and reform, 'dialogue', co-operation—all these are recurrent. The unity of the document is not the unity of a philosophical treatise or a scholastic disputation or of a legal enactment. Indeed, legal terminology and even technical theological terminology are conspicuously absent. It is a 'pastoral' exhortation, not, in the ordinary sense, a theological treatise, though a great deal of sound theology, developed by many catholic scholars, lies behind every single statement made in the Decree.

The whole outlook is positive and constructive. It puts the Catholic position frankly and unambiguously; but it avoids the commendation of Catholic doctrine which has been so conspicuous a feature of much 'apologetic' writing. It stresses the gifts and endowments given by God to separated brethren and avoids the use of language unacceptable to them. Indeed, some of the Fathers of the Council criticized the document on the ground that it said so many good things about separated brethren and so little about the good things possessed by Catholics. To which Cardinal Bea answered that Catholics were presumed to be aware of their own teaching and of the blessings they enjoy in the Church, but might need to be instructed about the endowments and blessings possessed by separated brethren. 'The primary requirement of all ecumenical activity', he said in the Council, 'is that we have an accurate knowledge of separated brethren and their gifts, sincere admiration and genuine Christian love.'[1]

The Decree, however, does not contain a complete and final treatise on the ecumenical movement with detailed plans about Catholic participation. 'The Decree, just as it represents the slow maturation of ideas over many years and is the result of much reflection, experiment and experience, so it leaves the door open, and I might add, positively demands further reflection, experiment and experience. It represents general principles governing Catholic participation at the present time.'[2] The Decree states this explicitly in its last paragraph: 'no obstacle must be placed to the ways of divine providence or any limit set to the future inspiration of the Holy Spirit.'

The general divisions are clear; Chapter I deals with the principles and attitudes applying to relations with all separated brethren. Chapter II speaks of more detailed activities. Chapter III enters into more details about the Eastern Orthodox, Anglicans and Protestants. In the case of these last two the Decree indicates in general what is held in common between us, and something, too, of their special characteristics, but it does not attempt to deal with each group in any detail.

[1] *Council Speeches of Vatican II*, eds. Congar, Küng and O'Hanlon, p. 168.
[2] John F. Long, S.J., 'East and West in the Decree on Ecumenism', *Unitas*, XVII (Spring 1965), p. 5.

CHAPTER I

CATHOLIC PRINCIPLES OF ECUMENISM

Two preliminary observations must be made before discussing anything particular in this chapter.

First, *the principles are of universal application* to all separated Christians, to the Eastern Orthodox, Anglicans and the larger well-organized Protestant bodies, and—which must not be forgotten—the principles apply also, in modified ways,[1] to the different smaller bodies, the various 'holiness' and 'adventist' groups, the Pentecostals, the Plymouth Brethren, the Mennonites, Moravians and all whom Dr Van Dusen calls the 'Third Force'.

The Decree does indeed pay very special attention to the Eastern Orthodox, to the Anglicans[2] and to the member churches of the World Council of Churches;[3] but its general principles can be applied, in due proportion, to all separated brethren, whatever their interpretation of the Christian message, if they really accept Christ.

Two groups occupy a special position, the Friends (Quakers) and the Salvation Army. They do not use any of the normal Christian rites and yet few could doubt that they have much of the authentic christian spirit; for myself, I feel that they may be compared in many ways to the religious orders and congregations in the Catholic Church. The Pentecostals, too, are in many ways unique; they are developing and, among not a few of them, there is great ecumenical interest.

Secondly, unity *among separated brethren themselves* is something in which all of us have an interest. It is not merely unity with the Catholic Church which we must have at heart, but the whole process of the growing together of Christians. This process constitutes, if not one total problem, at least a series of

---

[1] Cf. no. 2, par. 1 and 2.   [2] Cf. no. 13, par. 3.   [3] Cf. no. 13, par. 21.

interconnected problems and the whole development of their solution affects us all.

Negotiations, or 'dialogue', between particular churches remain, of course, their own concern, and no other church or organization has a claim to participate in them or make conditions about them. The World Council of Churches has made perfectly clear that, although it is ready to help, if requested, still it has no mandate whatever as regards plans or negotiations or 'dialogue' between its member churches, or between these and non-member churches. The same applies to national councils of churches, which, like the 'World Confessional Fellowships', are meant to be servants of the churches and in no sense arbiters or official advisers.

But the Faith and Order Departments of the World Council of Churches, several national Faith and Order Departments, and some of the 'World Confessional Fellowships' have accumulated a good deal of information and experience which may be of considerable use in negotiations and 'dialogue' between churches, and there is no reason why these latter should not avail themselves of such information and experience, if they so choose.

Further, some churches, are at the same time engaged in 'conversations' about possible reunion with several different churches. The Church of England is holding conversations with Methodists and with Presbyterians, and simultaneously fostering good relations with the Eastern Orthodox and with Rome; and several member churches or provinces of the Anglican Communion are engaged in negotiations or 'conversations' with different churches. The Protestant Episcopal Church in the U.S.A. is discussing unity with Presbyterians, Methodists and the United Church of Christ, and different Anglican churches in Asia and Africa are discussing or planning unions with various different groups in those continents. In all these cases, the aim is to come to agreements or unions which will help, and not hinder, the general ecumenical cause.

Similarly, there is no reason why the Catholic Church should not simultaneously plan contacts at various levels with other churches or groups. In fact, 'dialogue' with the Eastern Orthodox and with the World Council of Churches is planned, and various Catholic groups on the continent of Europe, in the British Isles and in the Americas are meeting with various different groups. In Iowa, U.S.A., the Dominican Fathers for the last four years have been holding 'dialogue' meetings with Lutherans and the 'Reformed'. In England, several official meetings for 'dialogue' have been held between Anglicans and Catholics. 'Observers' or 'consultants' from non-negotiating churches are sometimes invited to be present at negotiations between churches planning more proximate union. At the negotiations for union of the Anglicans, Presbyterians and the United Church of Christ in the U.S.A., two other churches joined the negotiations and twelve or fourteen other churches sent 'consultant-observers'.[1] At other negotiations, e.g., the Anglican-Methodist in England, only representatives of the two churches immediately concerned are present, though they keep in mind their association with their own 'World Confessional' bodies, and their relations with other churches.

My own conviction is that Catholics will do well to encourage such mergers or 'unions' of churches, and with regard to them should apply wholeheartedly the recommendations of the Decree on Ecumenism, to make every effort to avoid expressions, judgements and actions which do not represent the condition of our separated brethren with truth and fairness and so make mutual relations with them more difficult.[2] This requires both sincerity and discretion, as well as knowledge, especially when, as sometimes happens, there is difference of view within churches, some favouring particular proposals, others opposing them. Above all, we should pray that the Holy Spirit may guide our separated brethren in these difficult and often painful matters, just as we hope they will pray for us in our efforts at reform and renewal.[3]

Hence the admonition of the Decree[4] about accurate knowledge, about 'realism' and goodwill, has particular application to 'reunion plans'. Conditions differ in different parts of the world, and what is applicable in one country or region is not necessarily applicable in another. To take an obvious example, at the Evanston Assembly of the World Council of Churches the

---

[1] Cf. p. 76 above.   [2] Cf. no. 4, par. 2.
[3] Cf. no. 6, pars. 1 and 2, and no. 7.   [4] Cf. no. 9.

theological outlook and approach of the Germans seemed unduly theoretical and abstract to the Anglo-Saxons, while to the Germans, the Anglo-Saxon approach and outlook appeared unduly practical and 'pragmatic'. This, however, is only one instance of the complications of the Christian situation, which the Decree in fact faces frankly, though possibly in such mild—and general—terms that its full implication may easily be missed.

The first chapter deals with three main subjects:

A. A description of the Catholic Church. This is significantly different from the more juridical or 'legalistic' descriptions made familiar in our post-Reformation 'apologetic' style.

B. The relation of separated brethren, individually and corporately to the Catholic Church. They are in communion, though imperfect, with us. Here arises the question of their 'endowments' or of 'our common heritage'.

C. The basic urge towards christian unity and some guiding principles of its activity. Here are discussed 'the signs of the times', the question of 'individual conversions' and 'ecumenism', and questions relative to the way in which christian truth is expressed.

A. A DESCRIPTION OF THE CHURCH

The Decree gives no 'definition' of the Church, but, relying on the Constitution on the Church promulgated at the same date as the Decree on Ecumenism, describes the outstanding features in the Catholic concept of the Church.

Brief comments may be useful on the following points:
1. Christ's redemption and the Church.
2. The Eucharist and Unity.
3. The work of the Holy Spirit in the Church.
4. The apostolic Mission and the Church's succession to it.
5. The 'pilgrim' nature of the Church.

The redemption by Christ and the Church

As the love of God is universal, so the Incarnation and redemption by Christ are universal: 'God our Saviour desires all men to be saved and come to the knowledge of the truth. For there is one God and one mediator between God and men, the man Christ Jesus, who gave himself a ransom for all' (1 Tim 2: 3–4). The Church has rejected as false and contrary to the divine goodness the idea that Christ died only for the pre-destined.[1] Christ died for all men and for each and every man and woman in the world, but how the fruits of this redemption are applied to each, is a question whose answer is not revealed to us. Indeed it may be doubtful if our limited minds could ever grasp the intricacies, the interdependences throughout human history, involved in God's plan for human salvation. St Paul suggests this in Romans 11: 33–5. Yet it is clear that Christ wills the unity and charity of those who believe in him to be a sign to the world that he was sent by God. The unity of Christians is the way in which God wills happiness and salvation to come to all mankind, the unity of the Church is intimately con-nected with the mission of the Church to bring all men to Christ.[2] The Church, then, was founded by Christ, lives in Christ, as his own body, and will find its consummation in Christ. The Church cannot be conceived without Christ; and as the Decree says, the Church 'serves all mankind through the Gospel of Peace' (no. 2, para. 5).

The Eucharist and the Church

The Eucharist is a sign of the unity of Christians, as St Paul says 'the cup of blessing which we bless, is it not a participation (or communion, *koinonia*) in the blood of Christ? The bread which we break is it not a participation in the body of Christ? Because there is one loaf, we who are many are one body, for we all partake of the same loaf' (1 Cor 10: 16–17). The Eucha-rist then is 'a sign of unity', 'a bond of charity', 'a symbol of

---

[1] Cf. the famous five proposition of Cornelius Jansen, in Denzinger, *Enchiridion Symbolorum Definitionum et Declarationum*, ed. Rahner, Herder, Freiburg, ed. 30, 1955, no. 1096. The Church likewise condemned statements of the Jansenists that Christ died only for faithful Christians, and that 'pagans, Jews, heretics and such-like people receive no influence from Christ', ibid. nn. 1294 and 1295.

[2] Cf. Cardinal Bea, *Unity in Freedom*, chapter 6, 'The Dynamic Unity of the Church', pp. 90–9 and pp. 214–32, where he discusses the unity of the whole of mankind and of the Church; 'unity and mission' is a constant theme among all ecumenists.

concord'.[1] Indeed, the early Fathers of the Church often understood the 'real body' in the Eucharist as the Church, and the 'mystical body' as the physical body of Christ, made 'mystical' in the Eucharist in as much as it signifies the union of God and man in the Incarnation, the death and resurrection of Christ, and causes the union of the Church with Christ and with God.[2] To take away the Eucharist would be to take away unity itself from the Church. Leo XIII said:

'This sacrament is, as it were, the soul of the Church, and to it the grace of the priesthood is ordered and directed in all its fullness and in each of the successive grades. From the same source the Church draws and has all her strength, all her glory, her every supernatural endowment and adornment, every good thing that is hers.'[3]

As St Thomas Aquinas puts it: 'In this sacrament the whole mystery of our salvation is summed up (comprehenditur).'[4]

This, surely, is what is meant by Chapter 6 of St John's Gospel: 'He who eats my flesh and drinks my blood, abides in me and I in him. As the living Father sent me, and I live because of the Father, so he who eats me will live because of me' (Jn 6: 56–7). Here Christ, as most exegetes agree, referred to the Eucharist: and to live in Christ is surely to 'abide' with all others who 'abide' in Christ. And the strange words—which so many of Christ's hearers did not understand—about flesh and blood, refer to Christ's words at the Last Supper: 'This is my body which is for you . . . this cup is the new covenant in my blood' (1 Cor 11: 24–5). The 'abiding in' Christ is the reality

[1] Cf. the Council of Trent, Session 13, Denzinger, op. cit., 875 and 882. The *Constitution on the Church* of Vatican Council II declares that the Church always lives and grows by the Eucharist and that the Church of Christ is present wherever the Eucharist is celebrated, and hence, local congregations are truly called the Church, for just as the whole Christ is present in every Eucharist, so too the whole Church is present in every local congregation, however small and poor; cf. chapter III, no. 26.

[2] Cf. *my Principles of Sacramental Theology*, London, 1960, pp. 255–6 and 371–6; and H. de Lubac *Corpus Mysticum*, Paris, 1944, who traces a change in terminology. In earlier times the Church was called the 'real' body of Christ and what we now name the 'real' body of Christ was called the 'mystical body'; whereas in later times the 'mystical body' was named the Church and the eucharistic body was called the 'real body'.

[3] Encyclical *Mirae Caritatis*, 28th May 1902, English translation in *The Great Encyclicals of Leo XIII*, New York, 1903, p. 531.

[4] *Summa* III, q. 83, a 4.

produced by these mysterious symbols of Christ's sacrifice; it is 'communion'—'holy communion'—with Christ in his self-giving for, and even with, all his followers.

Recently Father Jérome Hamer has published a book which in many ways breaks new ground and throws new light upon the Eucharist and the Church. The book is entitled *The Church is a Communion*.[1] Dr Hamer is particularly illuminating about the origin of the Encyclical of Pius XII *Mystici Corporis*, and about the relations of the institutional elements of the Church to the invisible elements, and has enlightening considerations about the interrelations between eucharistic 'communion' and ecclesiastical 'communion'; in earlier times each was understood as a sign of the other, though communion with Christ through the Eucharist was the ground of the communion of the faithful with one another; the faithful could not have complete unity with Christ and could not 'abide in' Christ, without likewise having complete religious unity with one another.[2]

The Holy Spirit and the Church

The references to the Holy Spirit are significant. Four main assertions are made: that at Pentecost Christ, through the Holy Spirit, calls and gathers the people of the New Covenant; that the Holy Spirit dwells in each believer and likewise rules the whole Church, bringing about the 'communion' (*koinonia*) of the faithful; that the Holy Spirit distributes different functions and a variety of gifts; and lastly that it is by the action of the Holy Spirit that the Church increases and the faithful are given fellowship in unity. All these are Scriptural statements and it would not be difficult to show that patristic exegesis lies behind the references; but obviously the Decree cannot be a treatise on the Holy Spirit.[3] St Basil says that the Holy Spirit is the 'com-

[1] Published first in French in 1962, under the title *L'Église est une communion*, trans. Ronald Matthews, London, 1964.

[2] On the question of *communicatio in sacris*, sharing in the worship of others, cf. below pp. 130–36.

[3] The treatises on the Holy Spirit by Sts Athanasius, Basil and Gregory of Nazianzus retain their appositeness today, even though they were written in reference to particular historical conditions; and most doctrinal or historical works on the Trinity have special chapters on the Holy Ghost. Leo XIII's Encyclical on the Holy Spirit, *Divinum Illud*, 9th May 1897, is likewise classical. But anything like a complete bibliography would extend this Commentary to undue lengths. Cf. the *Dogmatic Constitution on the Church*, chapter I, no. 7, n. 8.

munion' (*koinonia*) between Father and Son[1] and hence the Holy Spirit's work of uniting Christ's followers is a reflection on earth of the eternal relation of Father, Son and Holy Spirit (cf. 2 Cor 13: 13).

Two observations, however, may be mentioned. The 'Re-baptism' and the 'Donatist' controversies raised the question of the activity of the Holy Spirit among dissident Christian bodies; St Cyprian (died A.D. 258) held that a heretic could not 'give' the Holy Ghost, because being outside the Church he is not with the Holy Ghost . . . for there is one Baptism, and one Holy Ghost, and one Church.[2] St Augustine denied that the Holy Spirit works exclusively in the one true Church[3] though he, and indeed the vast majority of Christians have held that the Holy Spirit does not work indifferently in heretical sects, like the Donatists, and in the true Church. Moreover, Augustine denied the operation of the Holy Spirit in a man outside the Church, but qualified this by adding 'is so far as he consents to the per-versity of the heretics'. Augustine said in a letter to some Donatist Bishops:

'These are not to be accounted heretics who do not defend their opinion with pertinacious animosity, even though it be a false and perverse opinion, especially if they did not bring forth their opinion from their own audacious presumption, but received it from parents who had been seduced and fallen into error and if they are prepared to investigate the truth and follow it when they find it', and added that he believed his correspondents to be such.[4]

Thus, the statements, in the description of the Church, re-garding the work of the Holy Spirit in maintaining the 'com-munion' of the faithful, by no means deny his action, likewise, among separated brethren. Indeed, the ecumenical movement is attributed to the Holy Spirit (n. par. 2, no. 4, para. 1); the Holy Spirit works in the hearts of our separated brethren (n. 4, par. 9); and gives 'interior gifts' as well as faith, hope and charity (n. 3, par. 2); the separated churches and communities,

---

[1] *De Spiritu Sancto*, chapter 18, no. 46.
[2] *Ep* 70, Hartel's ed. *Corpus Scriptorum Ecclesiasticorum Latinorum*, III, 2, p. 767.
[3] Cf. *De Baptismo Contra Donatistas*, 5, 24, 34, and often.
[4] *De Baptismo Contra Donatistas*, 3, 10, 13.

as such, are used by the Holy Spirit as a means of grace (n. 3, par. 4).[1]

A second observation is this: an exaggeration of the work of the Holy Spirit brings serious dangers. Dr J. E. Fison, at present Anglican Bishop of Salisbury, speaks of the 'self-effacing Paraclete who points always and only to Jesus Christ' and adds, 'Here is the tragedy of almost all movements in church history that have claimed in any special way to honour, worship or follow the Holy Spirit. The temptation has always been the same: to claim the guidance of the Holy Spirit for the whims of individual intuition or for the corporate decisions of a mass, hypnotized by the direction of its leader or group of leaders. And where this happens the result is always the same: fanaticism and an almost pathetic robot-like mechanical movement replace the free co-operation of a living organism. The church gives way to the clique and the development of free and integrated personality is lost in the forced hot-house product of a highly pressurized technique.'[2]

Dr Fison wrote so in 1950, and the 'Pentecostal' movement has developed since then; nevertheless Dr Fison's warning is still needed.[3] And yet with regard to them, and to all similar movements, the truly 'catholic' attitude is one of glad recognition of the truths they hold and a charity which tries to lead them on to a deeper understanding of the wholeness of Christ's truth. It would be a sad mistake to image that only the larger and well-organized groups should interest us. A good deal of impression of 'divided witness' to the non-christian world arises from the sometimes strident and exclusivist claims of these 'sect-type' bodies. Only through personal interest and contacts can this impression be lessened.[4] Dr Bloch-Hoel ends his account of the Pentecostal movement as follows: 'Not even the Roman Catholic Church can claim the unconditional attribute

---

[1] The issue of *Lumière et Vie*, XIV, n. 67 (Mar-Apr 1964), is devoted to 'The Spirit and the Churches'. The reflections of Fr René Beaupère, OP, on an article by Dr Lukas Vischer, are particularly well informed and perceptive.

[2] J. E. Fison, *The Blessing of the Holy Spirit*, London, 1950, p. 174; new Libra Book ed. 1965.

[3] Cf. Nils Bloch-Hoel, *The Pentecostal Movement, Its Origin, Development and Distinctive Character*, London, 1954.

[4] Cf. the judicious reflections of Fr Prudencio Damboriena, quoted in *The Churches and the Church*, op. cit., pp. 234-6.

semper eadem. How much more then can the law of change be applied to the dynamic Pentecostal Movement? With regard to liturgy, the Movement has been subject to a marked evolution during the years from 1900 to 1960, as the extreme charismatic spontaneity is gradually replaced by a more static institutionalism. The ethics of the Movement are still puritan, but the puritan rigor is decreasing, at least within the greater Pentecostal denominations. The Movement has long ago forsaken the principle of non-organization, and is everywhere organized into local churches and denominations. The first sixty years of the Pentecostal movement have also involved changes of doctrine consisting partly in the subduing of the original doctrines, such as that of entire sanctification, and partly in a general doctrinization of the Pentecostal message. The Pentecostal Movement is, in fact, an outstanding example in Church history of a movement of reaction gradually developing in the direction of the very type of religious body or denomination against which it originally arose as a movement of reform.'[1]

The Apostolic Mission of the Church

In this section (n. 2, paras. 2 and 3) the Decree is dependent upon the Constitution on the Church (nn. 18–30 and chapter 4 on the Laity); and the short statements of the Decree are illumined by the lengthier exposition of the Constitution. It is in this section, too, that the faith of the Church is briefly but unequivocally stated, as sincerity demands, about the position of the bishops with the successor of Peter at their head. It is the bishops with Peter's successor who are to be leaders in carrying on the reconciling work of Christ and to ensure the confession of the one faith, right worship and 'the fraternal harmony of the family of God' (n. 2, para. 4).

Many of our separated brethren agree that the 'episcopé' or oversight exercised by the Apostles must be continued in the Church; and, as I have already indicated[2] many besides the Orthodox, Anglicans and the Old Catholics are beginning to accept episcopacy. Yet our separated brethren are not in full communion with us, mainly, though not solely, because they

---

[1] *The Pentecostal Movement*, pp. 176-7. [2] Cf. pp. 70-71.

cannot conscientiously accept either St Peter's position with
regard to the other Apostles or that of his successors with regard
to the bishops and the Church, though some, like Dr Cullmann,
accept St Peter's primacy over the Church and the other
Apostles, but deny its transmission.

Separation of particular doctrines from their whole context
and historical setting is dangerous. This has been remarked on
by Cardinal Bea, who points out that, 'historical difficulties of
the time led the Council of Trent and the First Vatican Council
to lay special stress upon the juridical and organizational
aspects of the Church. These Councils did not explain the whole
reality of the Church and left somewhat in the background the
living supernatural functions and relationships implicated in
the "Body of Christ" concept. In studying the history of dogma,
therefore, it is always necessary to bear in mind on the one hand
the limitations placed on dogmatic formulations by historical
circumstances and on the other the inexhaustible treasure
hidden in every truth of faith.'[1]

The Constitution on the Church endeavours to avoid this
juridical outlook and to complete the First Vatican Council,
particularly regarding the role of bishops. The Constitution
contains eight chapters: (1) The Mystery of the Church, (2) The
People of God, (3) The hierarchical structure of the Church
and in particular the Bishops, (4) The Laity, (5) The universal
call to holiness in the Church, (6) Specially consecrated people,
i.e., Religious, (7) The eschatological character of the pilgrim

---

[1] *The Unity of Christians*, p. 98. The limitations of the definition of the Church
given by St Robert Bellarmine, and very generally accepted by post-Reformation
writers, both 'Roman' and 'non-Roman', are well brought out by Fr Jérome
Hamer in his *The Church is a Communion*, op. cit., pp. 82–94. Here again I despair of
giving anything in the nature of an adequate bibliography, which should include
articles in periodicals as well as books. I mention, however, H. de Lubac, *The
Splendour of the Church*, London, 1955, and, even though he wrote before the Council's Constitution on the Church, Hans Küng, the *Living Church*, is stimulating still,
especially in parts 4 and 5. But many books are now simply out of date, which I
greatly regret to have to say of Wilhelm Niesel's *Reformed Symbolics, a Comparison of
Catholicism, Orthodoxy, and Protestantism* (tr. David Lewis from 2nd German ed. of
1960), a book of solid merit which, however—inevitably, perhaps—takes no account of the reform and renewal which has been going on in the Catholic Church,
even before 1960, nor of the changes in outlook among the Orthodox, Anglicans,
Baptists, Congregationalists, Methodists and Presbyterians. I say this only to warn
my own Catholic brethren of the difficulty of knowing our separated brethren as
they actually are, and I add that I myself feel more and more conscious of my
ignorance of separated brethren in their concrete situations.

Church and its union with the heavenly Church, (8) The Blessed Virgin Mary, Mother of God in the Mystery of Christ and the Church. All these chapters are closely interrelated and none stands independent of the others.

Collegiality

Collegiality of the bishops is an important element in the Constitution and has a significant ecumenical bearing. The emphasis on the Constitution is upon the ministry of the Church as a service (*diakonia*, Constitution, n. 24) and a service in humility—'the leader should be as one who serves' (Itrd. no. 27, citing Lk 22: 26–7). The 'collegial' character of the hierarchy is based upon the commission given to St Peter (Mt 16: 19) and given also to the Apostles (Mt 18: 18; 28: 16–20), with Peter at the head (Jn 21: 15–17); and since the gospel was to be preached to the whole world, the pattern of the Apostolic ministry was likewise to remain for all time (ibid., n. 20). Hence the concept of 'collegiality' means the solidarity in the episcopal office of the whole Catholic episcopate united with the pope as head and focus of communion.[1]

The concept of 'collegiality' cannot be understood in legal terms, as if the pope were president of a state and the bishops members of a Congress or Parliament. This is explicitly said in a note of explanation.[2] The concept is one of 'communion', meaning an organic reality, as is the union between the head and the body, neither being able to act—or even be conceived —save in connection with the other. It is the Holy Spirit who 'always supports this organic structure and its concord' (n. 22); and the assent of the whole Church can never be lacking to the

[1] Cf. Robert Murray, 'Collegiality, Infallibility and Sobornost', in *One in Christ* (a Catholic ecumenical review continuing *The Eastern Churches Quarterly*), vol. I, no. 1, 1965, pp. 19–42. Fr Murray in this article tries to restate the Catholic doctrine with due respect to all that a Catholic must respect, so as to present it as a more acceptable basis of discussion than has, perhaps, often been thought possible either by Anglicans or by Orthodox. With the latter, especially, it is hoped to show a considerable basis for agreement, particularly with the positions of Professors Nicholas Afanassiev and George Florovsky. Cf. Afanassiev 'The Church which presides in Love', in *The Primacy of Peter in the Orthodox Church*, by J. Meyendorff and others (tr. Katherine Farrer), London, 1963; Florovsky, 'Sobornost: the Catholicity of the Church' in *The Church of God*, E. L. Mascall, London, 1934, and J. Meyendorff, *The Orthodox Church*, London, 1965.

[2] At the end of the official version, pp. 72–3.

authentic witness of the Pope and the Bishops 'because of the action of the Holy Spirit by which the whole flock of Christ is preserved and advances in unity' (Const., n. 25, para. 3).

This reference to the Constitution on the Church is given here, not as though it were adequate, but merely to indicate that the brief statement in the Decree on Ecumenism about the Apostles and St Peter, with the succession to them of the bishops and the Pope, must be understood in conjunction with the Constitution on the Church, and, indeed, in the full context of Catholic teaching about the whole Church's share, including that of the laity, in the prophetic, priestly and kingly offices of Christ.

About 'papal claims' the Decree is conspicuously silent. Commendations of what we believe to be the divinely given centre of unity will be found not so much in explanations or 'apologetics' or 'defence' as in the continual reformation and renewal of which the Decree speaks (n. 4, para. 2 and 5; n. 6, paras. 1 and 2) in more responsible collaboration between the Holy See and the bishops[1], the reorganization of the Curia[2], in the intrinsic worth of statements made by the Popes, in a spontaneous loyalty on the part of Catholics, in a developing trust in the laity,[3] in evidence of concern for the problems of the modern world, in evidence of freedom in unity (n. 4, para. 7), and in solid charity towards separated brethren. The liturgical changes in the Church will not be without their ecumenical effect.

Separated brethren, in turn, are engaged in a deeper study of all the scriptural and patristic data about the whole nature of the Church; they are meeting the difficulties in maintaining unity amid the complex problems of organization experienced by almost all organized Christian bodies; some, though still only a few, are beginning to look upon Rome in a new light.[4] Anything like the 'importunate zeal' against which the Decree warns us (n. 24, para. 1) would hinder rather than help; we can

[1] Cf. Pope Paul VI's opening address to the Second Session of the Council, in Küng, Congar and O'Hanlon, *Speeches of Vatican II*, p. 28.

[2] *A.A.S.* 55 (1963), pp. 793–800.

[3] It is of interest that in the chapter on the Laity the Constitution on the Church has a section on the prophetic office of the laity, chapter IV, no. 35.

[4] Cf. my essay 'The Papacy', in *Christian Unity*, Lectures of Maynooth Union Summer School, 1961, pp. 116–39.

trust the Holy Spirit's action in our separated brethren, and trust their sincerity and perspicacity.

The 'pilgrim' Church

The Decree makes two passing, but significant, references to the 'pilgrimage' of the Church on earth (n. 3, para. 5; n. 6, para. 2). These refer back to chapter 7 of the Constitution on the Church,[1] and means that neither any man nor the Church itself finds its perfection and consummation in this present age. The Church looks forward to the final judgement of God and to the age to come (Mt 25: 31-46; 2 Peter 2: 12), and hence nothing within the Church is absolutely final but all looks forward to the second coming of Christ and the union of all in the new heaven and the new earth (Rev 21: 24 etc.). This does not mean, of course, that the revelation given by Christ is not final, but it does mean that this life is transitory and that 'while we are in the body we are exiled from the Lord, for we walk by faith and not by sight' (2 Cor 5: 6). It is a reminder that our true home is in heaven, in the communion of all the saints who have gone before us and who will come after us, and that meantime we must judge by eternal and not earthly standards, by God's judgement, not by human judgement.

B. THE POSITION OF SEPARATED BRETHREN, INDIVIDUALLY AND CORPORATELY, AS REGARDS THE CATHOLIC CHURCH

A Thorny Question

I confess I could have wished that it had been possible to omit all this discussion from the Decree. I feel the utmost sympathy with Pope Paul VI when at Grottaferrata on 18th August 1963, he cried out:

'I also venture to make my own the sudden and spontaneous call of my predecessors, especially of John XXIII: Let our voice turn into a shout of angels saying—Come! Let the barriers which separate us fall, let us discuss the points of

[1] The title is 'The Eschatological Character of the pilgrim Church and its union with the heavenly Church'. The word 'eschatological' simply means 'having reference to the end of all things on this present earth'.

doctrine which divide us and which are still the subject of controversy! Let us seek to make our creed a common one, render articulate and join together our sacred union.'[1]

By this I mean that I regret that it is necessary to enter into discussions of 'churchly status' since it inevitably seems somehow condescending. It is, however, necessary in order to found solid respect and to show the common basis in the search for unity. But it should be noted that the Decree does not attempt to give a full account of the 'ecclesiological status' of separated Christians; it confines itself to the positive elements possessed in common with the Catholic Church. It does not, for instance, give any account of the Orthodox, Anglican or Protestant views of the Roman Communion; nor does it give any account of their concept of the Church.[2]

The Decree in this chapter speaks of all our separated brethren, Orthodox, Anglican, the major Protestant denominations and does not exclude the 'sect-type' groups.[3]

A Misunderstanding corrected: 'only a desire for membership'

In a book published in 1961, entitled *The Papal Council and the Gospel, Protestant Theologians Evaluate the Coming Vatican Council*,[4] Professor Peter Brunner of Heidelberg University, writing of the 'Mystery of the Division and the Unity of the Church' concludes from a consideration of Pius XII's Encyclical on the Mystical Body that outside the Roman Catholic Church 'one cannot even find traces of the reality of the Church, but at best only a hardly comprehensible, indistinct longing for member-

---

[1] Quoted in the first English edition of *Herder Correspondence*, October 1963, p. 28. It is unfortunate that the English translation, probably due to lack of a written Italian text, is defective.

[2] For a recent account, cf. Heinrich Fries, 'The Ecclesiological Status of the Protestant Churches from a Catholic Viewpoint', *Journal of Ecumenical Studies*, 1, no. 2 (Spring, 1964), pp. 195–212; cf. also Gunter Biener, 'Theology of Encounter', Heinrich Fries's 'Theological Contribution Towards Ecumenical Understanding', ibid., pp. 213–42. But these two authors have mainly in mind the larger and more organized Protestant bodies; cf. also, the admirable article by Emilien Lamirande, O.M.I., 'La Signification ecclésiastique des Communautes dissidentés et la doctrine des *vestigia ecclesiae*. Panorama théologique des vingt-cinq dernières années', *Istina*, Jan–Mar 1964, pp. 26–58.

[3] This term is derived from Ernst Troeltsh, *The Social Teaching of the Christian Churches*, New York, 1931. Cf. also, Franklin H. Littell, 'Church and Sect', *Ecumenical Review*, VI (1954), n. 3, pp. 262–75, with the references there given.

[4] Ed. Prof. Skydsgaard, Minneapolis, Minn.

ship in the Church, of which the person himself is often uncon-
scious' (p. 201–2). This, he adds, may be found in 'unbaptized
Jews or heathens'.

Whether that is a judicious interpretation of the Encyclical
on the Mystical Body is here beside the point.[1] But Professor
Brunner enumerated the following bonds which link non-
Roman Catholics to the body of Christ: a true baptism, acceptance of revelation in Scripture and of the Apostles' Creed,
repentance of sin, missionary zeal, works of charity and compassion, suffering for the gospel 'under the anti-christian persecution in our own country, various spiritual gifts, hymns which
even Catholics use, devotion to the Holy Spirit'. It may, also, be
of interest to list what at that time I enumerated as common:
baptism, true faith in God's revelation in Scripture, in the
Trinity and the Incarnation, in the foundation of the Church by
Jesus Christ, in at least two sacraments of the Gospel, and in the
general Christian ethic and ethos, together with various devotional traditions and religious and moral qualities. This faith
and all it means is not merely individual but is in a true sense
corporate, and comes to the individual through the corporate
body.[2]

Imperfect Communion

The Decree is far more cordial and more profound. Responsibility for the original break was shared; subsequent genera-
tions are not answerable for it, and if they believe in Christ, they
are looked upon 'as brothers with respect and affection' (n. 3,
para. 1). If baptized, they are in real, though imperfect communion with the Catholic Church, even though there are
differences which prevent full ecclesiastical communion.

The ecumenical movement strives to overcome these differences and in spite of them 'those who have been justified by
faith in baptism are members of Christ's body'.[3]

[1] Cf. my article in *The Heythrop Journal*, III, n. 4 (October 1962), p. 361, where I
discuss this.

[2] *Art. cit.*, p. 367–8.

[3] Cf. Bea, *The Unity of Christians*, pp. 26–7, 30–2, who draws a sharp distinction
between what the theologians call 'formal heresy' and 'material heresy', the former
culpable, the latter not. Yet who but God can judge of culpability? Cardinal Bea
appealed to 1 Cor 12: 13 and Gal 3: 26, where baptism clearly incorporates into
Christ. Canon Law likewise declares that by baptism one is made 'a person in the

Endowments, Individual and Corporate

The concrete meaning of this 'imperfect communion' 'membership in Christ's body' and brotherhood are enumerated: 'the Bible; the life of grace; faith, hope and charity, with other interior gifts of the Holy Spirit, and visible elements too'. These are, indeed, possessed by individuals, as 'our common heritage' which 'properly belong to the Church of Christ'; but the Decree explicitly speaks of the separated Churches and Communities as such. Their liturgical celebrations can truly engender the life of grace, though in ways varying according to the conditions of each, and they 'can give access to the community in which is salvation'.[1] The Holy Spirit uses them as means of salvation, 'their efficacy springing from the grace and truth which in all its fulness has been entrusted to the Catholic Church'. (no. 3, par. 4.) Here is their significance and importance in the mystery of salvation.[2]

To a very large extent our separated brethren use this same concept of 'elements of the Church of Christ', and, indeed were the first to use it; the Toronto statement on the nature of the

Church with all the rights and obligations of membership, save that the exercise of the rights may be impeded. *Codex Iuris Canonici*, canon 87, with the references given in the Gasparri edition of 1917 to the sources of this canon. The Encyclical on the Mystical Body implies that separated brethren are not *reapse* members of the Church, which probably means that they are not in full ecclesiastical communion. Abbot Butler of Downside used the phrase 'members in exile', cf. 'Schism and Unity', *Downside Review*, LXXI, no. 226 (October 1953), p. 368. Professor Lindbech develops this comparison, and says that young people who have quarrels at home and go abroad still remain members of the family, cf. 'The Ecclesiology of the Roman Catholic Church', *Journal of Ecumenical Studies*, 1, n. 2 (Spring, 1964), pp. 246, 252, 253.

[1] Cf. no. 22, par. 3, about the absence of the sacrament of Orders.

[2] On the true supernatural faith possessed by our separated brethren, of the enlightening articles of Fr Charles Davis 'Faith and Dissident Christians', in *The Study of Theology*, London, 1962, pp. 71–92; and 'Unity and Christian Truth', *Eastern Churches Quarterly*, XVI, n. 2 (1964), pp. 101–16. 'Paradoxically, the sincere believer who is in error about the content of faith (and Catholics may be in such error) implicitly believes what he expressly denies. That this is not a contradiction is because of the nature of faith. Faith is not an assent to a truth that is personally known in its intrinsic truth by the believer; he accepts it on the authority of God. His assent to this authority embraces in intention all that is covered by it. He submits to the Word of God because it is God's, and implicitly therefore to every word that is likewise God's. Even when a statement is mistakenly repudiated because it is not recognized as God's word, the acknowledgement of it remains implicit in that general acceptance of God's Word as God's which constitutes the submission of faith and in that general surrender to Christ as the Word of God which constitutes Christian faith' (p. 103).

World Council of Churches reads: 'the member churches recognize in other churches elements of the true Church', and 'the member Churches consider the relationship of other Churches to the Holy Catholic Church which the creeds propose as a subject for mutual consideration' (nn. 4 and 5). But to give here an account of the ecclesiologies of our separated brethren is plainly impossible. The Orthodox hold the same concept of the unbroken unity of Christ's Church as do Catholics, but hold that it exists only in Orthodoxy;[1] many Anglicans and Protestants tend to hold that the Church's unity has been broken, that diversions exist within the Church, and that 'the coming Great Church alone will manifest the unity which God wills'.[2] Discussion about this seems to me sterile; the important matter is to overcome our divisions, and the Decree lays down the basic principle on which we can begin, namely, the heritage we share in common, the endowments from God which exist among our separated brethren and must not be lost.

An equally important conclusion follows from the Decree: in the 're-integration' of Christian unity, which is the first sentence of the Decree, there need be no 'surrender', 'capitulation', 'submission', or 'absorption';[3] there will be integration, reconciliation, restoration of perfect communion, instead of a merely 'imperfect' communion, and all their endowments will be retained.[4]

---

[1] Cf. for example, *Orthodoxy, a Faith and Order Dialogue*, Geneva, 1960, in which Professor Parragiotis Bratsiotis, Fr George Florovsky and Professor Chrysostomos Konstantiniadis explain the Orthodox doctrine; cf. also, the last-named's article 'The Orthodox Church and Christian Unity', in *The Eastern Churches Quarterly*, XVI, no. 1 (1964), pp. 19–27; and Professor Alexander Schmemann 'The Moment of Truth for Orthodoxy' in *Unity in Mid-Career. An Ecumenical Critique*, ed. Keith R. Bridston and Walter G. Wagner, New York, 1963, pp. 47–56, who expresses some unease lest the Orthodox position be misunderstood through membership in the World Council; Orthodoxy does not 'accept the denominational principle' and 'is the Church herself'.

[2] About the divisions being *within* the Church, cf. Oliver Tomkins, *A Time for Unity*, op. cit., pp. 62–8.

[3] But when a smaller body merges with a larger, it is easy to think it is 'absorbed' by the larger. This certainly was the case with some Methodist bodies in the union of 1932; only patience and charity can overcome the feeling of being 'absorbed'.

[4] The editor of the *Civiltà Cattolica* in the issue of 16th Jnanuary 1965, stresses the difference between the idea of a 'return' and the idea of 'restoration of unity' and 'perfect ecclesiastical communion'. The former indicates an immobilism on the part of the Catholic Church, the latter that not only should separated brethren move towards the Catholic Church, but that the Catholic Church must move toward separated brethren, and in a real way, pp. 106–7. On the use of the word 'return', Professor George Lindbeck is illuminating, 'There is a taboo in the case of

C. THE GENERAL APPROACH BY CATHOLICS

'Signs of the Times'

In the beginning of n. 4, the Decree exhorts all the Catholic faithful to 'recognize the signs of the times and to take an active and intelligent part in the work of ecumenism'.

The expression 'signs of the times' was first used in an official document by Pope John XXIII in the Bull for the convocation of the Council, 25th December 1961. He quotes Christ's words to the Pharisees and Sadducees, whom he accused of being able to foretell good or bad weather by the appearance of the sky; 'but you cannot interpret the "signs of the times" ' (Mt 16:14). The Council was, therefore, to make the Church better adapted to the modern situation, and better able to answer the questions put by men of our time.[1] Pope Paul VI in his first Encyclical, against those who would place perfection in an immutability of the forms of the Church throughout the centuries, analyses 'the signs of the times', and declared that it is necessary 'to stimulate in the Church a constant and lively attention to the 'signs of the times'. He also told the Spanish National Eucharist Congress at Sion that the movement towards Christian unity is 'a sign of the times'.[2]

What then are these 'signs of the times'? Pope John at the end of each of the main sections of his Encyclical Peace on Earth, enumerated factors in the contemporary situation of mankind

the word 'return' and every Vatican statement is judged by whether it has avoided this term or its equivalent. The catholic Protestant is as likely to be just as offended as anyone by the traditional Roman use of the notion of 'return' but yet his own position requires him to admit that there is a sense in which it is applicable. For him the full restoration of visible unity can occur only by the reincorporation of Protestantism into the re-united catholicisms of East and West.' 'The Ecclesiology of the Roman Catholic Church', *Journal of Ecumenical Studies*, I, n. 2 (1964), p. 251. Nevertheless, all recent official documents avoid the use of the word 'return', since it conveys an unfortunate impression. Archbishop Casinier Morcello of Saragossa, Spain, said in the Council: 'We know that our separated brethren completely regret the invitation to "return". They do not see themselves as responsible for the division, they believe that they belong to the Church of Christ and have preserved the cultural core of Christianity with complete fidelity. The idea of "return" is intolerable to them and dries up at the roots any possibility of working together', *Council Speeches*, op. cit., p. 156-7.

[1] *Humanae Salutis*, A.A.S., 54 (1962), p. 6 and p. 8.
[2] Quoted in *Unitas*, XVI, n. 3 (Autumn, 1964), p. 225.

of which account should be taken.[1] Dr Oliver Tomkins in his work *A Time for Unity*,[2] enumerates six 'signs'; and in a study of the ministry of the Church in modern times a 'Working Party' composed of members of different church allegiance, enumerated no less than eighteen sociological and theological factors of which account should be taken in planning training and development of the ministry.[3] I summarize briefly these three enumerations of 'signs of the times'.

(a) *World phenomena*

The rapid rise in the population of the world is at present at the rate of about 1·6 per cent a year, at which rate the present population of 3,000 million will double itself in forty-five years. Asia increase by 22,000,000 a year. In Latin America it is calculated that the present population of 200,000,000 will, by the year 2,000, have increased to 600,000,000.[4] Other phenomena are worldwide: urbanization of people; the increased sense of human dignity in workers and among women; the rise in education, or at least the demand for it; automation in productive processes; rapidity of travel and of communications; the increasing development of a 'multi-racial' society in the world.[5] The world has effectively grown smaller and scientific, economic and cultural changes quickly affect all mankind.

(b) *The desire for Peace*

International phenomena revolve largely round the desire for peace, the United Nations, the dreadful threat of nuclear weapons and the immense amount of money, time and energy spent on development of this dreadful destructive power. Space exploration is likewise comparatively new and its effects are as

---

[1] Cf. nn. 39–45; 75–9; 126–9; 142–5.

[2] Op. cit., pp. 11–33.

[3] *The Shape of the Ministry, The Report of a Working Party*, published in multigraph form by the Consultative Committee on Training for the Ministry of the British Council of Churches, no date, but available by the end of March 1965. The *Report* has particular reference to sociological conditions in England, Scotland and Wales, but has much that is relevant to the world generally.

[4] Cf. John L. Russell, *The Population Problem*, London, 2nd ed., 1958, where other authorities are quoted.

[5] By this is meant the living together of people of different racial origins which presents problems all over the world, in Europe as well as in Africa and America.

yet incalculable. The interest in it, however, is shown by the popularity of 'science fiction' among the young.

The ideological differences between East and West affect almost all international relations and even the internal affairs of individual nations.

(c) *These world phenomena affect all Christians*

The relative number of Christians in the world steadily decreases; at present Christians (including nominal Christians) may make up one-third of the human race; but the proportion steadily decreases, since the rate of rise of the population in predominantly non-Christian lands is greater than in predominately Christian. In Europe the population is about 417 million and the rate of increase 0·7 per cent; in Asia the population is about 1,592 million and its rate of increase 1·8 per cent. The prestige of Christianity in the eyes of Asians and Africans has declined, partly because of two world wars. The need of independence of many nations affects the standing of Christians in them, by contrast to the old 'colonial' patterns. There is a resurgence and a new vitality in non-Christian religions, Mohammedanism, Hinduism, Buddhism; there is the rise of a new 'secular humanism'. The State has taken over by 'social services' much that used to be done by the churches. Everywhere 'a pluralistic society' develops. Family life is changing through earlier marriage, the 'working wife' and frequent changes of residence. 'Teenage' unrest, and increase of juvenile delinquency causes universal concern. There seems much evidence that vocations to the priesthood and to religious life are not increasing as quickly as the population. Educational patterns are changing, perhaps specialization is increasing; at any rate, the old familiar 'parish school' is less in evidence. Questions are being raised whether the older form of organization by parishes is adequate to meet the rapid social changes which are in process. The older idea of 'missions' is giving place to the 'indigenous church'. Increasingly the need to entrust more to the laity is being realized.

In this general world picture a divided Christendom appears not only sad, but disastrous. Bishop Oliver Tomkins puts it that 'it would be silly to try to catch a shoal of herring with fifty shrimping nets'.[1] It is in such a context that the Decree exhorts *all* the catholic faithful to recognize the signs of the times and to take an active and intelligent part in the ecumenical movement.[2]

Ecumenical work and 'individual conversions'

The word 'convert' sounds ill in many ears. I do not know how to avoid it—even though the Decree avoids it. Perhaps 'individual restoration to full communion' would be preferable, but even this is lengthy. Language changes slowly, and I use the term as it is so commonly used among Catholics. Here I venture to reproduce part of what I wrote in the January 1964 issue of *The Catholic World*,[3] before the Decree on Ecumenism declared in n. 4, para. 5 that the preparation and reconciliation of individuals, though distinct from ecumenical activity, are in no wise opposed to it. 'Whereas the older outlooks about 're-union' centred mainly on the Orthodox and the Anglicans, the 'ecumenical approach' includes *all* Christians. It is clear that there is greater agreement in doctrine with the Orthodox; nevertheless, in the modern setting, no group of Christians is excluded from ecumenical concern. There has been a great development in thought and outlook. In the 1930's who would have imagined that a Presbyterian would have proposed a union which included episcopacy and tradition, as had Dr Eugene Carson Blake? Who would have imagined that we could speak of 'high-church Baptists'? We live in a new situation and things have moved fast and continue to move fast.

It is plainly too early to attempt to give exact specifications of the outcome of this 'ecumenical approach'. Needless to say, Catholic ecumenists hold as strongly as anyone—and perhaps more strongly than some—to the totality of Catholic dogma,

[1] *A Time for Unity*, op. cit., p. 14.
[2] On the theological import of 'the signs of the times', cf. M. D. Chenu, 'Les Signes du Temps', *Nouvelle Revue Théologique*, t. 87 (January 1965), pp. 29–39, to whom I am much indebted. God shows his will not merely by his revelation, but also by events, currents of thought, development of social institutions, that is, by the concrete circumstances in which the Church must carry on Christ's saving mission. More light is to be expected from the Council's expected document on the Church in the modern world.
[3] Reprinted in *The Catholic Mind*, vol. LXII, no. 1181, March 1964.

especially the Church and the papacy, the Mass and the Eucharist, and the doctrine concerning our Lady. Yet the 'image' of these dogmas in the minds of many non-Roman Catholics is not as we wish. Part of the ecumenical task is to change these images and bring about spontaneous Christian love instead of suspicions, dislike and resistance. In this, as Cardinal Bea has said, a first requisite is an approach in sincere humility, in honest esteem for others, and in reliance on the work of the Holy Spirit.

The 'ecumenical approach' certainly envisages our separated brethren not only as individuals but as united in churches having a corporate existence. It takes account of the true Christian values and the true Christian virtues which are to be found in these corporate entities or 'churches'. It does not leave out of account their cathedrals, churches, theological colleges, schools, monasteries, convents, retreat houses, or the missionary associations and charitable organizations which show such vitality and evoke such generosity. The world of dissident churches is not a mere conglomeration of individuals. It is a world of complex and often interlocking associations and societies organized for the support of various educational enterprises, of a multitude of 'missionary' commitments such as hospitals, orphanages, asylums for lepers, for the blind and other diversely afflicted. It is a world in which much true Christian education is going on, including translations of the Bible into various foreign languages —languages into which we Catholics have not been able to translate it. The 'ecumenical approach' tries to be realistic in assessing all the facts.

It is plain that there is not the slightest opposition between the work of Information Centres and the 'ecumenical approach'. Both can, and must, continue simultaneously; both to some extent interlock, for Information Centres must take account of the 'ecumenical fact' and the changed climate of opinion, and on the other hand, ecumenical work can only benefit by the accession to the Church of new members, who are usually fervent. Nor does there seem any great problem in assignment of personnel to be trained and formed for one or other of these works. To some extent this may be dictated by local conditions, aptitudes of individuals and estimate of long term results. The ecumenical approach is definitely a long term not a short term enterprise.

Concern has been expressed lest the ecumenical approach result in a decrease in the number of individual reconciliations or of baptisms in the Church. To some extent this concern may be an aftermath of the older and outdated opposition between 'corporate reunion' and 'a policy of individual conversions'. But it would be unrealistic to assign this as the sole cause for the concern.

I can say from personal experience that there are some good, holy and intelligent clerics and lay people who feel that the ecumenical approach tends to lessen emphasis on the distinctive elements of the Catholic faith, to soften forthright and vigorous assertions of the unique character of the Catholic Church, to stress the good in dissident bodies, to admit the need of 're-newal' or even 'reform' in the Church, and by such outlooks to weaken the urgency of personal decision and action by indivi-duals. Those who feel so are inclined to cite less wise statements made by some Catholic ecumenist; and I have heard reference made to the decreasing number of converts in the United States during the past three years.[1]

The number of converts is nowhere large enough either seriously to weaken non-Catholic bodies or to give any out-standing increase to the Catholic Church. Most converts are from the ranks of the unchurched or the uncommitted. Two or three years ago, a writer in the *Catholic Gazette*[2] estimated that at the rate converts are coming to us (perhaps 12,000–14,000 a year), it would be over a thousand years before England became Catholic. Statistics, naturally, are not the sole consideration, since many converts are of a high calibre, intellectually and spiritually. Even so, the prospects for the future through indivi-dual accessions are not very encouraging. In some regions the vast majority of converts come through marriage.

Nor are the prospects very much brighter in the United States; 140,000 in one year looks large absolutely, but looks small by comparison with a total population of 183 million, and

---

[1] *The Official Catholic Directory* gives the following statistics: 1960: 146, 212; 1961: 136, 141; 1962: 128, 430; 1963: 125,670. Note that the citations of the 1960 and 1963 *Directories* show a decrease amounting to some 20,542.

[2] Published at the Catholic Enquiry Centre, Hampstead, London.

a Catholic population of 43 million. Taking the non-Catholic population as 140 million, only about one per thousand becomes Catholic in a year; and taking the Catholic population as 43 million, the increase is a little less than three hundredths of 1 per cent a year (·0028), which means that scarcely three out of a thousand Catholics are converts each year. Even granted a steady increase at the rate roughly maintained between 1944 and 1959, the prospects of a significant increase by individual accessions are not encouraging.

As regards the fall in the number of converts during the last three years, to say anything worthwhile would require an analysis of the diocesan, and even city, returns, of which I am certainly not capable. It would require also some analysis of the religious state of the country.[1]

The proportion of the number of priests and nuns to the general Catholic population is said to show a steady decrease, sharper in the last five years or so; if this is true, it obviously would affect the amount of work done to attract individuals. Possibly, also, some of the most able and zealous priests may have diverted their time and interest to the ecumenical approach, and Vatican II undoubtedly has occupied much time and attention, and perhaps has not impeded a 'wait and see' attitude, with consequent slowing down of zealous efforts. I have heard, also, that there has been in some circles a certain 'hardening' against the Church, due perhaps to dislike of our stand on marriage and to fear of our increasing numbers and influence.

Even if fewer individuals came to the Church, the ecumenical approach should still be no less enthusiastically fostered and followed.[2]

To this I have only two remarks to add. The first is that Catholics accept the statement made by the World Council of

---

[1] The latest returns in the *Year Book of American Churches* indicates a general recession in the 'religious boom' which had marked the post-war period; in 1955 Protestants were 35·5% of the total population; in 1960, 35·4%; and in 1961, 35·2%—a steady decrease. Some denominations reported decreased membership, or at least not such an increase as corresponded with the increase of the total population. Religious statistics, however, as is well known, are often unreliable at their source, and any conclusions drawn from them must be comparative to a variety of other factors.

[2] Cf. *The Catholic World*, January 1964, pp. 226–9.

Churches in 1956 and revised in August 1960 on Christian Witness, Proselytism and Religious Liberty. Cardinal Bea reprinted the document as an appendix to his book *Unity in Freedom*.[1] It can be said that there is no issue between our separated brethren and ourselves about this, although the matter of 'mixed marriages' still causes concern and even indignation among some of our best friends among ecumenists.[2] But even on mixed marriages Cardinal Bea is hopeful that a solution may be found.[3] Secondly, I think that many who are reconciled to the Catholic Church enable Catholics to understand better and esteem more highly, the Communions in which these 'converts' were brought up. Very many of those who join the Catholic Communion retain a lasting affection for their old allegiance and are able to speak with intimate knowledge of the religious faith and inspiration they received in it. Their change to the new Communion they regard not so much as a denial as a fulfilment and retain their old friends, and, often, many of their old outlooks and manners. There are, of course, exceptions to this; but, striking a balance, I should say that Anglo-Saxon Catholics owe an immense debt to the Anglican Communion which nurtured so many who played—and still play—a most important part in universalizing and spiritualizing the English-speaking Catholic world. I think particularly of Newman (whose influence is perhaps greater on the Continent than in his own country); and of Gerard Manley Hopkins, Robert Hugh Benson, G. K. Chesterton, and Ronald Knox, to mention only a few. To a larger extent than it may realize, Anglicanism has influenced the development of English-speaking 'Roman Catholicism'; and I think Anglicanism has gained thereby and not lost.

What do separated brethren lack?

To this question, raised in the minds of a number of Catholics

[1] New York and London, 1964, pp. 240–51.

[2] Cf. Gregory Baum, in chapter 8, 'Ecumenism and Conversion Work', in *Progress and Perspectives*, New York, 1962, pp. 181–205.

[3] Cf. 'Contributo del Concilio alla causa dell' unione dei cristiani', *Civiltà Cattolica*, 2753, January 1965, p. 427. The Decree regarding Eastern Catholic Churches admits the validity, though not the lawfulness of marriages between Catholics and Orthodox, provided a sacred minister is present, cf. no. 18, p. 9 of the Latin text.

(as I have indicated on p. 107), the Decree, as Cardinal Bea says, gives a delicate but frank answer; they lack 'the blessing of the unity which Christ wished to bestow on all who through him were born again into one body and with him quickened to newness of life; only through Christ's Catholic Church can they benefit fully from the means of salvation' (no. 3, par. 5).[1]

It should be noted that this affirmation of lack of unity does not deny or minimize the gifts and endowments possessed by separated brethren, such as 'the life of grace; faith, hope and charity, with interior gifts of the Holy Spirit, and visible elements of the Church (no. 3, par. 2). About the degree in which these are possessed by separated brethren, the Decree makes no judgement. It asserts no spiritual superiority. But it does affirm the lack of the unity which Christ wills; and, in this, there are few separated brethren who would disagree, since the evil which springs from disunity is a constant theme among them, even among the Orthodox.[2]

This frank statement about Catholic belief shows, as Cardinal Bea also says, that the Council intended no retraction of any dogma already defined. It has, indeed, put Catholic doctrines into a new light and setting, more suited to modern mentality, but certainly has not changed or attenuated anything in the deposit of the faith. Just as in all previous Councils, dogmatic definitions were regarded as untouchable. But no Council regards such definitions as closing the way to further attainment of truth, but rather as indispensable signposts amid the uncertainties of our earthly pilgrimage. The same holds as regards previous condemnations of errors which are still looked upon as 'dead ends' or as 'no through roads'. To act otherwise would be to lack a sense of responsibility for the eternal salvation of men.[3]

This statement, however, about lack of unity, must be read in

[1] Cf. Cardinal Bea's article in *Civiltà Cattolica*, op. cit., p. 425; and cf. also, 'Il decreto conciliare', *Civiltà Cattolica*, no. 2748 (December 1964), p. 12.

[2] Cf. Professor Alexander Schmemann, 'Problems of Orthodoxy in America, The Canonical Problem', *St Vladimir's Seminary Quarterly*, vol. II (1964), pp. 67–85; and Michael Lacko, S.J., 'The Churches of Eastern Rite in North America', *Unitas*, xvi, no. 2, (Summer, 1964), pp. 82–115, with statistics and a bibliography. The difficulties, however, were almost bound to happen. In the United States there are Orthodox of eleven 'rites', and in Canada, of thirteen. Moreover the Catholic Eastern Churches in America have not been without their troubles.

[3] Ibid, p. 426.

conjunction with the equally frank admission of the faults and sins of Catholics (n. 4, para. 5 and 6), of the need of reform in the Church (n. 6), about which more will be said in comments on Chapter II. The Decree (n. 4) indicates that by restoration of unity there will come an enrichment, an authentic growth, a contribution to the manifestation of the catholicity of the church. As the editor of the *Civiltà Cattolica* rightly says, to prepare itself for contact with separated brethren, the Church must strive to recover its true image, its true appearance, by freeing itself from superstructures and incrustations of the past, perhaps venerable, but also, suffocating, and must strive to deepen, develop and rethink the heritage she has received, so as to be more faithful to Christ and so never to try to impose on separated brethren more than is necessary for authentic unity.[1]

In this first chapter the Decree also commends 'dialogue' and co-operation in good works, about which, also, this commentary will deal in Chapter II. But Chapter I ends with a further exhortation to realize and appreciate the 'truly christian endowments to be found among our separated brethren' and to recognize that 'whatever is truly christian is never contrary to the faith'. The observation made by the Decree about bearing witness to Christ even to the shedding of their blood has particular application to Lutherans in Germany and to the Orthodox.

Very many Lutherans refused to accept Hitler's perversion of Christianity and endured imprisonment and death in consequence.[2] The 'Confessional Church' resisted Hitler's attempt to form a 'German Christianity', and in 1937 virtually the whole leadership of the Confessional Church was put behind bars as common criminals. Dietrich Bonhoeffer, being in safety and in honour in America, in 1939 chose to return to Germany in order to bear witness to the real Christianity, and after some years in prison was executed. Many others like him suffered for their faith.

The full history of the sufferings and martyrdoms in Russia

---

[1] 'Immobilismo cattolico nel dialogo ecumenico?' *Civilta Cattolicà*, 2750, n. 2.
[2] Cf. Karl Barth, *The German Church Conflict*, London, 1965. A very full account of this is to be found in K. D. Schmidt, ed., *Arberiten Zur Geschichte des Kirchenkampfen*, Göttingen, two vols., 1958 and 1963.

and behind the Iron Curtain has not been written and perhaps never can be written.[1] In 1929 thousands of priests were executed or exiled; in 1939, several prominent bishops were shot, over fifty bishops were sent to prison or to concentration camps, and about 9,000 priests were in prison. The tragedy was that the Orthodox bishops, priests and people were, and still are, most loyal to their own country; but it is a miracle of faith and fortitude that the Orthodox Church has survived at all, and this is to be attributed, under God, to the spirit of martyrdom which has existed in Orthodoxy for centuries, and to the 'home church', that is, the faith maintained in family prayers and devotions, often before an icon. Perhaps one of the most agonizing aspects of some persecutions is that the mere telling of them may increase them.

In January 1956 five young American Protestant missionaries were massacred by the Auca Indians in Ecuador. Each of them was a man of ability and generosity who risked all they had in sincere faith.[2] Our Protestant brothers do not lack heroism in the cause of Christ.

Unity in Variety

In n. 4, para. 6, the Decree speaks of maintaining both unity in essentials and freedom 'in various forms of spiritual life and discipline, in liturgical rites and in theological elaboration of revealed truth'. The reference here, I think is mainly to the Catholics of Eastern Rites, who in the Second Vatican Council played an important part in affirming the principle of diversity in the unity of the faith. Their complaints against 'Latinization' can be read in the interesting book *The Eastern Churches and Catholic Unity*, edited by Maximos IV Saigh, head of the Catholic Melchites and Patriarch of Antioch and all the East, of Alexandria and of Jerusalem; and that their complaints were largely met by the Council is clear from the Decree on the Eastern Catholic churches. Examples are the milder norms about sharing in worship (*communicatio in sacris*) with the Eastern

[1] An account up to 1945 is given by Professor M. Searle Bates in his *Religious Liberty. An Inquiry*, New York, 1945.

[2] An account of them is given in John J. Considine's, *New Horizons in Latin America*, New York, 1958; a book on them was written by the wife of one, Elizabeth Elliott, *Through Gates of Splendor*, New York, 1957.

Orthodox,[1] and this admission of the validity of a Catholic Easterner's marriage before an Orthodox priest.[2] Several Eastern Catholics have accepted the Cardinalate.

Apart, however, from the case of the Eastern Catholics, the principle asserted here is of great moment, namely, that catholic unity is fully compatible with different customs and ecclesiastical rules, with different forms of liturgy and with different ways of developing theology. In this respect, the Eastern Orthodox Churches have an importance far beyond their numbers, in that they stand for a conception of unity that is of a different order than administrative unity, and yet of a different order, also, than that of the invisible or purely spiritual unity which some of our Western Protestant and Anglican brethren are inclined to regard as sufficient.

Speaking merely for myself, I have the impression that in the West several plans for reunion turn too largely upon the question of a single administrative unity. In some plans, for instance, it is desired that diocesan boundaries, and even parish boundaries, should co-incide. This is, no doubt, desirable from a practical point of view, but it may be doubted whether it is essential for real Christian unity. Similarly, a liturgy more or less uniform, especially for instance in the Calendar of the Ecclesiastical year, may be a great focus of unity. But is it essential?[3]

This paragraph of the Decree does not, I think, refer to the general question of religious liberty, which had a special *Schema* of its own. Many of the Fathers at the Council regretted that this draft on religious liberty was not approved, at least in principle, at the third session of the Council. There were, however, even among those who wish for a declaration about religious liberty, certain differences of opinion as to the manner of expressing the ultimate ground on which to base religious

---

[1] Cf., pp. 256–7.   [2] Cf., *Const. on the Eastern Churches*, n. 18.

[3] Cf. *Prayer Book Revision in the Church of England* and *A Memorandum of the Church of England Liturgical Commission*, London, 1958, p. 36, where liturgy is regarded as at least one way of 'safeguarding the unity of the Anglican Communion'. Cf. also, *Principles of Prayer Book Revision*. The Report of a Select Committee of the Church of India, Pakistan, Burma and Ceylon appointed by the Metropolitan to review the principles of Prayer Book revision in the Anglican Communion, London, 1957. The discussion of anamnesis and sacrifice is particularly interesting (pp. 47–50). Most Western Churches, however, are engaged in liturgical studies with a view to change in practice.

liberty, and there seems no reason to doubt that the next session will see a satisfactory declaration. In any case, the Encyclical of Pope John XXIII, *Peace on Earth*, speaks most adequately about the right to follow even an erroneous conscience.[1] Cardinal Bea devoted a book to 'Unity in Freedom',[2] which deals with the subject at length, and prints as an appendix the Universal Declaration of Human Rights made by the United Nations, which Pope John XXIII approved in *Peace on Earth* (nn. 143–4). The World Council of Churches at New Delhi in 1961 issued a Statement on Religious Liberty, which which I have no doubt the expected document from Vatican Council II will in substance agree. There are, however, some respected persons who associate 'religious liberty' with the old 'liberal' or 'rationalist' contention that 'liberty' means in practice the emancipation of the individual conscience even from divinely revealed standards and make a cult of freedom based on religious indifferentism. Since the aim of the Council is to secure moral unanimity, and not to go by mere counting of heads, perhaps it is well that more time has been available for general opinion to focus itself.

'*Dialogue*'

Apart from care to avoid 'expressions, judgements and actions which do not represent the situation of our separated brethren with truth and fairness', the Decree speaks in general of two means towards unity, 'dialogue' and co-operation in duties for the common good of humanity. In this section I refer only to 'dialogue'.[3]

What is called 'dialogue' can take many forms. It can be in books written by individuals in which accounts are given of different religious communions, comparing and contrasting them and making them better known and understood. There are, also, symposia in which various authors either describe their own Communion or some aspect of the relations between Christians. Then, there are books in which authors discuss differing views on selected topics. A large number of periodicals carry articles about the doctrine, sociology or ethos of various

---

[1] Cf. v.g. nn. 14 and 158.
[2] Op. cit.
[3] Cf. no. 4, para. 2; n. 9 and n. 18.

Christian bodies. This 'written dialogue' goes on steadily and is of inestimable value in increasing understanding.[1]

Spoken 'dialogue' can also take many forms. Sometimes, of several speakers addressing an audience, and perhaps answering questions at the end; or, which is more fruitful, if a comparatively small group, not more than six to ten on each side, discussing some doctrinal or ecclesiastical theme together. Usually one or more speakers read papers and a general discussion follows.

The advantages of such 'dialogue' are many.[2] It can help to clear away 'non-doctrinal' factors which affect the relations of Christians; it can discuss pastoral methods; it can correct misconceptions about the doctrine or practices of others. But it need not consist merely in presenting differences and discussing them; it can be an attempt by members of different Communions to penetrate more deeply into truths about which there is already agreement in the hope that deeper understanding may cause differences to fade away of themselves, as it were. In presenting the christian message to an unbelieving world, collaboration of Christians is becoming more and more important.

Experience has shown that the method of 'comparative ecclesiology', that is, of direct confrontation of differing doctrines, though it may be a necessary beginning, leads to an impasse. After the Lund Conference on Faith and Order in 1952, this was recognized and four general topics were taken for study by groups of theologians over a ten-year period: the Union of Christ and the Church; Tradition and Traditions; Ways of Worship (liturgy); and Institutionalism, i.e. something of a sociological study of ecclesiastical institutions. At Montreal in 1963 the following subjects had been studied and 'sections' of the Faith and Order Conference conferred and reported:

1. The Church in the Purpose of God.
2. Scripture, Tradition and Traditions.

[1] An excellent list of books and periodicals in English will be found in *The Ecumenist*, 2, n. 3 (March-April 1964), pp. 46-9. Cf. also *The Churches and the Church*, op. cit., bibliography, pp. 333-48. Ecumensim, however, is a subject with so many ramifications that a complete bibliography is impossible.
[2] Cf. Bea, *Unity in Freedom*, op. cit., pp. 187-93.

3. The Redemptive Purpose of Christ and the Ministry of his Church.
4. Worship and the Oneness of Christ's Church.
5. The Process of Growing Together, beginning with the local Church and the Church Universal.[1]

These are only examples of the kind of themes which our separated brethren discuss in their sincere and earnest search for unity. But, as Pope Paul VI said in his first encyclical, 'dialogue' must go on with the world, with fellow Christians and with fellow Catholics.[2] The Faith and Order Commission of the W.C.C., in its meeting at Aarhus, Denmark, in August 1964, proposed the following four themes for study:

1. Creation, New Creation, and the Unity of the Church.
2. Christ, the Holy Spirit and the Ministry.
3. The Eucharist, Sacrament of Unity.
4. Spirit, Order and Organization.

Mgr J. Vodopivec, one of the Catholic observers at this meeting, adds: 'Then there are several other study projects: the examination of what Church councils were in the life of the Church and what they mean to us today; the study of the hermeneutic presuppositions with which various Christians approach the Scriptures and the confrontation of these different presuppositions; a similar examination dealing with the interpretation of patristic writing; the study of old and new Covenant in their reciprocal relation and the bond between Israel and the Church; the revision of catechetical methods and religious education in general; and finally a study of two concrete problems related to the special ministry, namely the role of deacons and the position of women in the ministry.'[3]

Such themes can well be discussed among Catholics, and a method of 'group study' can prove most fruitful.

[1] Cf. *The Fourth World Conference on Faith and Order, The Report from Montreal 1963*, eds. P. C. Rodger and L. Vischer, London, 1964, p. 6. At this Conference there were five official Catholic 'observers', and some fifteen 'guests'. Altogether there were 489 persons present, and, as Bishop Tomkins said, the traditional method of such conferences proved inadequate to cope with so many and such varying convictions and outlooks. In the meeting of Faith and Order in Denmark in August 1964, a permanent committee of ten theologians was set up to co-ordinate the work going on in various parts of the world.
[2] Cf. Appendix V, p. 280 ff.
[3] Cf. his account in *The Ecumenist*, 3, n. 1, Nov-Dec 1964, pp. 4–6.

'Dialogue' does not mean—and this cannot be stressed too much—an attempt to persuade others of the truth of one's own faith. Firmness in our faith is to be taken for granted, and that being so, 'dialogue' can teach us much. Bishop J. Blomjous, of Mwanza (Tanzania) puts this well, towards the end of a striking article entitled 'Ecumenism in Africa—Reflections of a Bishop':

'Ecumenism means that we listen to God speaking to us through other Christians. The existence of separated Christians accuses the one true Church of the Lord of infidelity, for if she had been more faithful to the Gospel, God would not have permitted the division of his people. Our division is a constant call to conversion of heart. But we must also listen to others as partners in a dialogue. They have left the unity of the church because of an emphasis, excessive in our eyes, on a particular Christian truth and hence this very truth may be alive among them in a specially developed form. We must learn in whatever way possible, knowing that whatever is wise and holy comes from God.'[1]

Official 'dialogue', however, in the concrete circumstances in which churches exist, sometimes presents a variety of preliminary difficulties, and, unhappily is not free from political implications at least in some minds. Thus at the Pan-Orthodox Conference at Rhodes in November 1964 it was decided that the time was not yet ripe for Orthodoxy as a whole to engage in conversations with Rome, but that each Church could take its own course in the matter.[2] It is sad but true that tensions caused by Communism and by Arab-Jewish hostility have repercussions in the religious sphere. To enter here into these difficulties would not be to the present purpose and, in any case, the full facts are not always easy to ascertain.

It is clear, however, that the more 'dialogue' is on a wide and official scale, the more need there is that those taking part in it should be at once representative of their Communions and competent in theology. Consequently for international meetings representatives are chosen by the Secretariat for Unity;

[1] *The Ecumenist*, 2, n. 2, (Jan-Feb 1964), p. 20.
[2] Cf. *Unitas*, XVI (Winter, 1964), p. 311; *Chrysostom*, no. 20 (Winter, 1964-5), p. 7.

while in more local meetings the bishop's approval is sufficient.

In 'dialogue', however, no one begins with the least inclination to call in doubt the convictions of his own communion. Thus the Orthodox do not question their faith about tradition, nor Anglicans about episcopacy, nor Lutherans about confessions of faith, nor Baptists about 'believer's' baptism, nor Catholics about the papacy. If antecedent conditions about religious convictions were to be laid down in advance, no dialogue would be possible between those firm in their belief. But maintaining firmness in faith, the hope is that in the total vision things may appear different, and, at the very least, the way may be prepared for co-operation in good works. Antecedent difficulties have, indeed arisen; but, as they seem either solved or on the way to solution, there is no need to discuss them.[1] Recently six Catholic representatives have met eight representatives of the World Council of Churches, though so far no results of these conversations have appeared.

Competency?

Cardinal Bea speaks wisely about this in chapter 11 of *Unity in Freedom*.

'A difficulty about such dialogue with learned men among separated brethren may be felt on grounds of sufficient theological competency and sufficient time; for many of the clergy are already almost over-burdened with urgent pastoral or teaching tasks and are unable to find time for study and reading. The difficulty, however, is not insoluble. Dialogue need not be restricted to theology proper, for most useful conversations can take place about methods and problems in pastoral duties, about devotional matters and about methods of preaching and of instructing young people and the faithful generally. Nor need dialogue be carried on only between theologians of the highest grade or only between Professors; it is not a trial or test of intellectual or theological attainments, but a meeting of brothers who are glad to know one another and to be known to one another as they actually are. If ignorance is revealed, it is re-

---

[1] Cf. the admirable article of Fr M. J. LeGuillou, O.P., 'Interrogations sur l'avenir de l'œcumenisme', *Istina*, 1964, n. 1, Jan-Mar, pp. 7–24; and Charles Boyer, S.J., in *Unitas*, XVI, no. 2, (Summer, 1964), pp. 127–30.

vealed among friends, and its revelation can be a stimulus to find time for inquiry or reading. What is most needed is sincere humility and charity, and patient trust in the power of God, especially when hopes sink low.

'I add that such dialogue can be a very definite stimulus to the deeper theological knowledge which a more educated laity is seeking, and a stimulus, also, to better teaching of religion in our secondary schools and colleges.'[1]

[1] Op. cit., p. 191.

CHAPTER II

THE PRACTICAL SIDE OF ECUMENISM

This chapter deals with five main topics about which some comment may be useful. 1. The concern all in the Church should have for ecumenism (no. 5). 2. Reform and renewal, both in the whole Church and in individuals (nos. 6 and 7); 3. Prayer in common and general principles about sharing in worship with others (*communicatio in sacris*, no. 8); 4. The manner of expressing the truth (nos. 10 and 11); and 5. Co-operation in works for the common good of society and mankind (no. 12).

A. ECUMENISM MUST BE THE CONCERN OF ALL CATHOLICS

The concern of everyone in the Church must be engaged. Ecumenism is not, as it were, a special 'subject' or department to be left to a comparatively few specialists. It is a work, as the Decree plainly says (no. 4 end, and no. 5) of the whole Church, faithful and clergy alike. Ecumenism is now as much a part of the Church's work as is the spread of the faith to non-Christians; indeed it is more and more clear that both the maintenance of our own faith and the spread of the faith to non-christians are intimately bound up with the unity and charity which Christians have for one another.

When asked after a lecture, 'But what can we do, Father?' I have sometimes answered smilingly, 'That is your problem. Don't ask me to solve it.' That answer is deliberately provocative, for it is impossible to lay down an exact blue-print which is applicable to all times, people and circumstances. An apostolic spirit is ingenious in finding ways and means.

There are, however, certain general matters which may be mentioned. First, to inform oneself, reasonably, about ecu-

menism. There are various ways of doing this, it is possible to
ask neighbours about their church life and their organizations
—even granted that today there are, alas, only too few people
interested in the Church. All Catholic societies (and these are
many), parish, inter-parish and national, can put ecumenism
into their interests. Sermons can be preached about it, special
services arranged and special prayers said, even at other
times of the year besides the Unity Octave in January. Periodicals can be circulated. Small meetings at home for reading of
the Bible and prayer can be arranged with separated brethren
in the neighbourhood. Discreet requests to newspapers, to the
radio and television managers can be made by brief notes—for
they are sensitive to public opinion. Poems, plays, mimes can be
composed and recited or enacted, especially by school children.
Friendly relations can be cultivated with the clergy of other
Communions.

Perhaps most important of all, ecumenism should become
part of religious instruction and education, beginning in the
seminaries and the training colleges. It should have a place,
too, in any new catechisms or books on religious instruction.
Unions of Catholic students can arrange lectures, and bible
vigils; groups could study liturgy together.

It often happens that the clergy are so overburdened with
urgent work that they feel ecumenical concern is too much to
expect of them. Nevertheless the Council expects it; and if the
instructions of the Council in the Constitution on the Church
are taken seriously, concern for ecumenism need not go by de-
fault. In the Constitution on the Church (chapter 4, about the
Laity, no. 37), priests and bishops are exhorted to acknowledge
and foster dignity and responsibility in the laity, and not only
to take their advice and trust them, but to welcome initiative
from them and to make the work of the Church a co-operative
effort. The presence of lay auditors at the Council is a sign of
the times.

B. REFORM AND RENEWAL

This has been the object of the Second Vatican Council, as
was clearly said by Pope Paul VI in his opening speech at the

second session of the Council.[1] The Decree affirms very plainly: 'Christ summons the Church to continue reformation in her pilgrimage on earth' (no. 6, par. 2), and this emphasis in the Decree on reform and renewal was inserted at the requests of a large number of the Fathers in the second session; and a comparison of the Decree with the original *Schema* shows that their requests were accepted.

The Decree does not enter into detail about the particular reforms needed in the Church. It may, however, be recalled that Pope Paul VI has referred to two matters. In his opening address at the second session, he expressed the hope that the Council might indicate ways in which he himself might 're-ceive more help and support, in ways to be determined, from a more effective and responsible collaboration with our brothers in the episcopate'.[2]

The Roman Curia

In his address on 21st September 1963 to the Curia, he made mention of this association of diocesan bishops with the head of the Church 'on the study and responsibility of ecclesiastical government'.[3] In this address, Pope Paul also spoke to the Curia, with the utmost trust, kindness and gentleness, of the peace with which possible reform should be adopted in its regard. 'That some reforms should be introduced in the Roman Curia is not only easy to realize but good to desire. As everybody knows this old and complex organization traces back in its present form to Pope Sixtus V's celebrated constitution of 1588, *Immensa Aeterni Dei*. St Pius X gave it new life with the constitution *Sapienti Consilio* of 1909, and the Code of Canon Law in 1917 made this substantially its own form.

'Many years have passed. It is understandable, therefore, how such an establishment would have grown ponderous with its own venerable age, how it feels the disparity of its organs and of its practices with respect to the needs and customs of new times, how at the same time it feels the need of being broadened and made fit for new functions.

---

[1] Cf. *A.A.S.* 55, p. 850.   [2] Cf. ibid., p. 847.
[3] *A.A.S.* 55 (1963), pp. 793–800. A translation of this address is printed as Appendix I, in Xavier Rynne, *The Second Session*, London, 1964, pp. 338–46.

'Therefore various reforms will be needed . . . they will be formulated and promulgated by the Curia itself.'[1]

Eastern Patriarchs made Cardinals

Another reform was the offer and the acceptance of the cardinalate by three eastern patriarchs and an eastern bishop: Maximos IV Saigh, Melchite Patriarch of Antioch; Paul Peter Meouchi, Maronite Patriarch of Antioch; Stephen I, Coptic Patriarch of Alexandria; and Josyf Slipyi, Archbishop of Lvov (Lwow).

This action seems to presage that all the Eastern Catholic Patriarchs will be made cardinals, who, like the first three, will keep their titles and not be assigned any titular churches in Rome, and thus the gesture has the significance, as the Holy Father said, of showing that the Roman Church is not 'a closer fold, immobile, self-centred and exclusive, but rather should be the indispensable centre of a flock, one that is open and has a variety of forms within it, the flock of Christ, wonderfully characterized by the complementary nature of its constituent parts, unity and catholicity, authority and fraternity, the identity of the faith in the boundless and vast breadth of charity'.[2]

This gesture of the Holy Father and of the Eastern Catholic Patriarchs is significant of a development in the conception of one of the traditions which had grown up, namely that all those who elect the Pope are, by title at least, in some way part of the clergy of the diocese of Rome. This tradition is now broken and it becomes explicit that it is not the clergy of Rome who elect the Pope. Hitherto, Cardinals from all over the world were given a title to a Roman church, as a survival of the time when difficulties of travel—to say nothing of the Pope being bishop of Rome—made election by the Roman clergy a necessity. The Pope is also Patriarch of the West, and now we have Eastern Patriarchs taking part in the election of a Patriarch of the West.[3]

---

[1] *A.A.S.* 55 (1963), p. 797.
[2] Quoted in *Chrysostom*, no. 21 (Spring, 1965), p. 5.
[3] Cf. below, p. 166.

Renewal in process

The Decree (n. 6, para. 3) mentions the movements of re-newal which are proceeding: the biblical and liturgical move-ments, the apostolate of the laity, new forms of religious life, the spiritualizing of married life and the Church's social teaching and activity—all have ecumenical import.

A Common Bible

To treat in any way adequately of these topics would require several whole books. I mention, however, the matter of a com-mon Bible. In Ceylon, Tanzania, the Congo and Samoa, translations into the vernacular are either accepted by Catho-lics and separated brethren, or seem likely to be so. In Scotland, Archbishop Gordon Gray of Edinburgh in 1964 gave an im-primatur to the Revised Standard Version of the New Testa-ment and the edition of the Old Testament is being prepared. A few changes were introduced, such as, for instance, 'Hail full of grace' for the Revised Standard's 'O favoured one' and the 'apocrypha' will appear in the traditional places in the new version; but the spelling of biblical names is the same, and the text is made from the original languages and not, as are the Douay and the Knox, based upon the Vulgate. The American owners of the copyright, the American Council of Churches of Christ in the U.S.A., as Dom Bernard Orchard said, 'made us a present of their most cherished possession'. The 'Confra-ternity' version in the United States is a Catholic enterprise and proceeds steadily.[1]

Liturgical Renewal

Much common study of the liturgy is in progress, the Calen-dar being one of the most troublesome matters on which to secure agreement. A fixed Easter would greatly help, and a common 'lectionary', i.e. the reading of the same passages from Scripture on Sundays in all churches. But reforms here are in progress,[2] as is made very manifest by the use of English in

[1] Cf. Walter M. Abbott, *The Ecumenist*, II, 5, (July-Aug 1964), pp. 77–9. Cf. also *Herder Correspondence*, I, 2 (Feb 1964), 'Common Bible Projects', pp. 35–7.

[2] Cf. J. D. Benoit, *Liturgical Renewal*, London, 1958; J. H. Srawley, *The Liturgical Movement*, London, 1954.

much of the Mass and by the revised Holy Week services, with concelebration on Holy Thursday where suitable. Concelebration is now a common daily practice in some colleges.

Secular Institutes

I have already briefly referred to the apostolate of the laity,[1] 'New forms of religious life' refers, I think, to what are called 'secular institutes'. These are organizations of a new kind, which rose up spontaneously in the Church, of people who dedicate themselves to a life of special apostolic work in the world. They have grown from small beginnings. Some have two or three thousand members; some have only a handful of members, some two or three hundred. Some admit only priests, some both lay men and women; some only men or only women. Their special form of dedication and of work and methods varies greatly; but usually poverty, as far as it can be observed consistently with an occupation in the world, and some form of obedience, is required. Some help the missions, some devote themselves to various forms of teaching religion, some to the spread of Christian principles in the whole of 'secular' life. Some are highly organized and have official papal approval; others await this and still others wish to maintain spontaneity and not to become too 'institutionalized'. Some like to work in obscurity and do not make their membership public.

Like any other 'movement', they have met some suspicion and some opposition. Their zeal has not always been discreet— or so it is alleged. But they are a sign of vitality, of spontaneity, of the realization of new needs, and of a sense of corporateness in striving for holiness.[2] It is claimed that they do not hinder, but rather help, the ordinary religious orders and congregations.

The 'Spiritualizing of marriage' (matrimonii spiritualitas)

This does not mean any lessening of esteem for all that marriage implies, but means that the vocation to married life is a

[1] Cf. p. 96.
[2] Cf. *Secular Institutes*, A Symposium on the modern lay community, Blackfriars Publications, London, 1952; T. M. Perrin, *Secular Institutes, Consecration to God in the World* (tr. Roger Capel), London, 1961.

means of holiness to both husband and wife, and, if God gives them, to children. On this subject I think that canonists and lawyers have given an emphasis to the 'making of the contract' of marriage, which has tended to lessen the necessary Christian emphasis on the vocation and the state of marriage. Pius XI, in his encyclical on Christian marriage, tried to revitalize the opinion of St Robert Bellarmine and of other eminent theologians that marriage is a *permanent* sacrament, and hence is a permanent influence of God's grace for husband, wife and children.[1]

Of the social teaching of the Church it must be enough here to refer to Pope John's two Encyclicals, *Peace on Earth* (1963) and *New Light on Social Problems* (*Mater et Magistra*, 1961).

The Agonies of Reform

There is no doubt that this reform and renewal in the Church brings difficulties and even agonies. Some think that the renewal is going too fast, that what they regarded as fixed and settled is now being called into question and in consequence they feel uneasy and almost rootless. On the other hand, others think the renewal is too slow and do not hesitate to voice their criticisms sometimes in shrill or harsh terms. To some extent this divergence corresponds to the divergence between the 'progressives' and the 'conservatives' in the Vatican Council. It is, I think, a transitory phase; not, indeed, that the reform and renewal will be transitory, but that the upsetting elements will gradually fall into place. The exhortation in the Decree (n. 7) should help, especially the quotation of the words of St Paul, 'I beg you to lead a life worthy of the calling to which you have been called, with all humility and meekness, with patience, forbearing one another in love, eager to maintain the unity of the spirit in the bonds of peace' (Eph 4: 1–3). The Decree adds that this exhortation is directed especially to those in sacred orders.

As the Decree says, ecumenism is a summons to holiness: un-

[1] Cf. my *Principles of Sacramental Theology*, chap. III, on the nature of Sacramental Grace, where Pius XI is quoted. The sacred significance of marriage is not solely or even principally, in the marriage ceremony, but in the permanent lifting up of the love of husband and wife to have a new meaning in Christ and the Church.

less we give an example of unity and of unity combined with freedom, among ourselves, it is idle to hope for unity with others.

Repentance

The Decree, in speaking of 'a change of heart' uses the Latin word *conversio* (in Greek, *metanoia*), meaning a change of mind, outlook, desires and conduct; and the Decree also adds that St John's words about us saying we have not sinned, and thereby contradicting God, apply also to sins against unity. It may be asked whether the 'we' in the phrase about 'us' sinning against unity, and asking forgiveness, applies only to each individual and means at least sins of neglect, or whether it applies to the Church in general?

Pope Paul VI spoke of this in his address at the opening of the second Session:

'Yes, the Council aims at renewal. Note well, however, that in saying and desiring that, we do not imply that the Catholic Church of today can be accused of substantial infidelity to the mind of her divine Founder. Rather, it is the deeper realization of her substantial faithfulness that fills her with gratitude and humility and inspires her with courage to correct the imperfections of human weakness.

'The reform at which the Council aims is not, therefore, a turning upside down of the Church's present way of life or a breaking with what is essential and worthy of veneration in her tradition. It is, rather, an honouring of tradition by stripping it of what is unworthy or defective so that it may be rendered firm and fruitful.'[1]

Can the Church repent?

The Church, then, cannot repent as if Christ through his Holy Spirit had not protected her from error in dogmatic teaching, or had not given her the means of holiness or had not raised up in the Church many saintly men and women, some known, many unknown. And yet the Church in absolute sincerity can repent of the faults of her members which react upon

[1] Cf. *A.A.S.* 55, pp. 850–2.

the whole body and tend in practice to obscure the Church's substantial faithfulness and to lessen the corporate charity of the Church. St Augustine says:

'The whole Church says: Forgive us our trespasses. . . . This is because she is spotted and wrinkled. But by confession the wrinkles are smoothed out, the spots are washed away. The Church is constant in prayer so as to be purified by confession. And as long as she lives on earth it will be the same.'[1]

What, then, calls for sincere repentance and forgiveness? Firstly our lack of religious fervour and devotion, which clearly makes the church less vigorous in its total impact on men. Then, possibly excessive interest in our own affairs, personal, parochial, national, and not enough interest in the world-wide mission of the Church. Next, in some cases, at least, too controversial an attitude and lack of positive appreciation of the 'heritage' we share in common with separated brethren. Possibly, also, in English-speaking countries, there has been a lack of appreciation of methods of approach to separated brethren used by continental Catholics. Here let me endorse the unanimous expression of gratefulness at the Heythrop Conference in the summer of 1962 that 'we ought to pay tribute to the work of the French, Belgian and German theologians. They have made a great advance in Christian unity without sacrificing the principles of Catholic Theology.' This was unanimously accepted by all the sixty-five priests present. I should myself now go further than this and judge that over the last hundred and twenty years or so, our continental brethren have had a wider, deeper and more far-seeing general outlook than have Catholics in English-speaking lands. This does not mean that I think every action and every word of our continental Catholic brothers was correct; on the contrary I think that sometimes they misread the actual position in English-speaking countries, and left out of account the 'evangelicals' in the Church of England and the wide range of the Free Churches. This granted, I am convinced that their

[1] Serms. 181, 16, Migne, *Patres Latini*, 38,983. I owe this reference to Georges Dejaifve, S.J., who quotes it in his article 'Is ecumenical repentance possible for the Catholic Church?' *Eastern Churches Quarterly*, XV, nn. 1–2 (1963), pp. 25–41. Fr Dejaifve notes that the Evanston Assembly in 1954 declared: 'We cannot in sincerity repent of our various understandings of God's will for his Church, unless the Spirit himself reveals that our understandings have been in error.' Report of Section I, *The Evanston Report*, London, 1953, p. 89.

general approach was right and that time has proved that they were right. For my part, I can only say: *peccavi*, and I say it in honesty and without abjectness.[1] The clear implications of the Decree are that the restoration of unity with Anglicans and the major Protestant churches does not *in principle* differ from the restoration of unity with the Orthodox churches, granted, of course, the differences between the latter and the former.

Triumphalism; clericalism; legalism

In the Council, and out of it, criticisms of us Catholics have been made on the ground that we have been 'triumphalist', that is inclined to boast of our unity, our doctrine and of our achievements generally; 'clericalist', that is, inclined to present the Church as consisting only of the Pope, the bishops and the priests, and consequently to exaggerate their importance and authority; 'legalist', that is, inclined to make Christianity to consist in the observance of ecclesiastical laws, and to regulate our theological thinking by legal-like theological formulations, to the neglect of the true spirit of the Gospel of Christ.

To appraise these criticisms would be difficult and, indeed, not here apposite. It would be easy to cite non-Catholics who express sincere appreciation of Catholic loyalty to the Pope and to their clergy, of the definiteness of Catholic doctrinal teaching and of the clearness of Catholic moral principles and of religious education for which Catholics have sacrificed so generously. Neither non-Christians nor Secularists will be attracted to a body which does not know what it believes and what it does not. Christ taught with authority and the Church teaches by Christ's authority. I must say that I think that Christians all over the world owe a debt to the Catholic Church which none of our failings can obscure: if Catholicism (or 'Roman' Catholicism) had disappeared from this world, say in 1800, or 1850, I do not think the Christian cause would have been advanced, just as I think the same about so many of the dissident churches. But appraisal of all this is irrelevant to the new situation which all Christians must face in the world; and, with all their goodness and generosity, Catholics must be honest in admitting our

[1] Cf. my note 'The Abbé Portal Then and Now', *Heythrop Journal*, II, no. 4 (1961), pp. 345-55.

deficiencies. It is possible for right confidence in the one true Church of Christ to exceed into boastfulness; for right confidence in the clergy to degenerate into arrogance on the one side and subservience on the other; for due obedience to the rule of Christ in his Church to decline into passivity and lack of initiative.

The fact that these criticisms have been made is a reason for each of us to examine his conscience. The Council has done much to chasten us and possibly the temptation now is rather to depression, to a certain bewilderment and a feeling of not quite knowing where we are going. The publication, however, of the Constitutions and Decrees of the Council will have a reassuring and stimulating effect.

C. PRAYER IN COMMON

Prayer in common and sharing in worship (*communicatio in sacris*): this latter expression—*communicatio in sacris*—means sharing with others in 'holy things', such as churches, holy places, services and the sacraments, such as Penance, the Eucharist, Marriage, Orders and the Anointing of the sick.

In the long history of the Church, with the heresies and schisms which arose, there was general agreement on the part of all, orthodox and 'heretics' alike, that difference of conviction about doctrine or about the proper order to be observed in the Church demanded separation in worship and particularly separation from the Eucharist, in which unity with Christ and with fellow Christians is both signified and caused. This seems to be derived from the Gospel precept, 'if he refuses to listen even to the church, let him be to you as a Gentile and a tax collector' (Mt 18: 17). Thus 'excommunication' was regarded as normal where faith was different or due obedience refused.

Yet problems arose. What was to be done about repentant apostates? What about baptism and Orders conferred by heretics or in simony (i.e., merely for money)? What was the worth of the Eucharist celebrated by wicked priests or bishops, or by excommunicated priests or bishops? Some of these questions took centuries to solve, especially the question of 're-ordinations'; gradually, however, both the Eastern and the Western Church arrived at solutions which differ in canonical formulation, but may be thought not to differ greatly in substance.[1]

I refer to this long and complicated history merely to indicate that the problems connected with prayer in common and with 'intercommunion', that is, admission to the Eucharist, are to some extent, or in some circumstances, common to Christians divided in church 'confession' or church order, and have a long history behind them, complicated by historical circumstances and situations.

In English-speaking lands, and occasionally elsewhere, the question of attendance at the service in the 'national' church was taken to be a sign of loyalty to the religion of the country and was prescribed by law. Hence, in the sixteenth and seventeenth centuries 'conformity', i.e., Sunday attendance in the parish church, was regarded as an abandonment of any allegiance save to the national church. 'Nonconformists', among whom were Roman Catholics, were fined for non-attendance and excluded from many civil posts of trust. These laws were gradually relaxed and the distinction between religious and civil loyalty gradually admitted.[2]

What general Christian principle?

After this brief glance at a long and complicated history one may well ask: 'Has there been, and is there, any general principle on which Christians agree? Or, does this difference in practice merely reflect the changing views, or the prejudices, of varying groups at varying times without any real governing principle?'

I venture to think that the Decree does sum up the general Christian mind on the subject, and shows that there is a basic agreement behind all the variations both of the past and of the present. The principle is this:

[1] Cf. pp. 207–8 below.
[2] Cf. Maurice Bévenot's article 'Communicatio in Sacris', in *Christian Unity: A Catholic View*, London, 1962, pp. 114–39. Fr Bévenot points out that in the seventeenth and eighteenth centuries the English legislation presupposed that joining in the prayers or rites of a different church was a practical demonstration of agreement with that church, and that this supposition affected the legislation of the Catholic Church even with regard to the Orthodox, cf. pp. 117–25.

Outward manifestations of religion must correspond to the inward convictions and to the reality of the situation.

Thus, in approving prayers in common the Decree does so on the ground that such prayers express the real bonds that unite Catholics with their separated brethren—*genuina significatio vinculorum quibus Catholici cum fratribus sejunctis adhuc coniunguntur.* To refuse to pray with separated brethren would be a practical denial that they are in fact in communion with us, a real though imperfect communion (no. 3). We must not act as though we did not admit the true Christian endowments and values which they have in common with us.

And in affirming that a sharing in rites and worship is not a means to be indiscriminately used, the Decree lays down the principle that in such sharing the witness given to the unity of the Church must be considered: *significatio unitatis Ecclesiae,* that is, there should not be an outward expression which would not correspond to the real facts and to inward convictions.

The Decree does indeed say that prayer, worship and sacraments are a means of grace and that this also must be considered in conjunction with consideration of the outward expression corresponding to the reality and to convictions. Both principles must be considered together. Judgement in concrete circumstances must be left to the bishops, so that we may act in full union with the Church and have the blessing that that union brings.

Varying rules and practices find their explanation (I think among separated brethren as well as among ourselves) from these two principles. It is right to express outwardly the unity which really exists; it is wrong to try to express the fulness of unity if in fact the fulness of unity does not exist. This explains the difference of practice adopted by Catholics towards the Orthodox,[1] and also the use of the 'economy' by the Orthodox; it explains differences of practice in different circumstances, for instance during the octave of prayers for Christian Unity, and at ecumenical gatherings, and in different countries. It explains, too, I think, the different emphasis in prayers for unity given by Fr Paul Wattson in the early years of this century and by Fr

[1] Cf. the extracts from the Decree on the Eastern Catholic Churches in Appendix III, p. 256.

Paul Couturier twenty-five years later. Both saw that prayer is an essential, even the soul of the movement towards unity and both did very much to awaken Christians to that fact. But they lived in different countries and in different circumstances, which to a large extent influenced their different stress. Fr Paul lived in the United States at a time when he thought it needful to stress the need for unity with the Holy See; Fr Couturier lived in France, though he visited England, at a time when unity with the Orthodox came more into prominence and the general atmosphere was more ready to accept the prayer for the unity which Christ wills, by the means he chooses. Both have left disciples and followers behind them and surely nothing would please both more than that their followers should be whole-heartedly united.[1]

By way of a summary of what is the present position of the Church, I quote the words of Bishop Willebrands, who was asked about the matter in Bombay:

'Bishop Willebrands explained that prayer in common was permissible and recommended, subject to the ruling of legitimate authority, of course, provided that it was prayer *for* unity and did not presume that unity was already with us. Thus, common celebrations of the eucharist are ruled out. In special circumstances, e.g. the absence of sacred ministers, Roman Catholics might share in the eucharist with those who hold the same faith and maintain the same tradition regarding it. Presence at other communion services would have meaning and be justified on special occasions, such as the Unity Octave or a national event which Christians wish to celebrate together. Bishop Willebrands explained that this participation is something more than mere passive attendance yet does not amount to active participation. One is not merely present because one cannot help it, but associates oneself with the prayers of the brethren in Christ, though unable to take part in their sacred action. With regard to the faithful at large, prudence must be observed and confusion carefully avoided. Finally, there must be

---

[1] Cf. David Gannon, Friar of the Atonement, *Father Paul of Graymoor*, New York, 1952; Geoffrey Curtis, of the Community of the Resurrection, *Paul Couturier and Unity in Christ*, London, 1964. Cf. my brief remarks in *The Churches and the Church*, about the foundation of the Octave by Fr Paul Wattson and the changed stress given by Fr Couturier, pp. 54–57.

nothing that does not correspond to the real situation, that is not truthful as well as charitable.'[1]

Intercommunion

Intercommunion among our separated brethren has caused a great deal of discussion and there is as yet no agreement upon the subject. The problems revolve round exchange of pulpits, interchange of clergy and admission of members of different churches to receive the eucharist celebrated by clergy of different churches; and the problems come to a focus when there is union of two or more churches and when there are large ecumenical gatherings. If two or more churches unite, the question arises of their relation, and of their 'communion', with the other churches with which they were previously associated and with which they were 'in communion'. At ecumenical gatherings, some churches will not admit any to Holy Communion save their own members; others admit, on these special occasions, all baptized members of other churches to their Eucharist, but do not approve, or at least do not encourage, their own members to receive the sacrament at the eucharist celebrations of other churches, particularly where there is a non-episcopal ministry. The literature on the subject is immense.[2]

At the Montreal Conference of Faith and Order in 1963, a sub-section spoke of two 'poles' of diversion of opinion among the member churches of the World Council:

'Some Christians believe that the degree of ecclesial communion which we have in the Body of Christ, through Baptism and through our fundamental faith, although we are still divided on some points, urges us to celebrate Holy Communion together and to promote intercommunion between the churches. It is Christ, present in the Eucharist, who invites all Christians

[1] *The Ecumenist* 3, no. 2, Jan-Feb 1965, p. 27.
[2] Cf. J. G. Davies, *Intercommunion*, published by the British Council of Churches, London, 1961, which gives the best summary I have seen of the theological reasons which lie behind the different practices of the churches; my article, 'Intercommunion', *Heythrop Journal*, 2 (April 1962), pp. 139–51; Ruth Slade, 'Communion Services at Ecumenical Gatherings: the Montreal Recommendations', *Eastern Churches Quarterly*, XV, nn. 3–4 (1963), pp. 181–97; Oliver Tomkins, ch. 5, 'The Challenge of Intercommunion, An Anglican Position', in *A Time for Unity*, pp. 80–98; Max Thurian, in the *Ecumenical Review*, April 1961. Ample references will be found in these articles.

to his table: this direct invitation of Christ cannot be thwarted by ecclesiastical discipline. In the communion at the same holy table, divided Christians are committed in a decisive way to make manifest their total, visible and organic unity.

'Some Christians believe that Eucharistic communion, being an expression of acceptance of the whole Christ, implies full unity in the wholeness of his truth; that there cannot be any 'intercommunion' between otherwise separated Christians; that communion in the sacraments therefore implies a pattern of doctrine and ministry, which is indivisible; and that 'intercommunion' cannot presume upon the union in faith that we still seek.

'Between these two views of Holy Communion there are others, some approximating to one side, some to the other.

'But the sharp difference of conviction indicating two poles within the Council's membership must be recognized. However, as was said at the New Delhi Assembly: 'For neither view can there be any final peace so long as others who are known to be in Christ are not with us at the Holy Communion." '[1]

Both these two views accept the fact that the Eucharist is an expression of the unity of the Church; they differ, however, in their concept of what the unity of the Church involves. The first view stresses the difference between the unity that in fact exists but is not manifest, which unmanifested unity can be and should be sincerely expressed in the Eucharist, provided there is the resolve to make manifest this invisible, or unmanifested unity. The second holds that as long as churches are in part divided in doctrine and ministry, they cannot truly express the unity which the Eucharist presupposes. The two different conceptions of the nature of the Church find their concrete meaning, and their sharpest division, in the Eucharist.

This is, I think, a most hopeful development, and a recognition that the Eucharist is 'the sacrament of unity'.

It should be noted that the words of the Decree, n. 8, do not refer either to the question of Orders, or of belief about the Eucharist, or, even of doctrinal agreement, as contra-indica-

---

[1] I take this citation from Ruth Slade's article in the *Eastern Churches Quarterly*, not having access here to the reports of the sub-section of the Montreal Conference of 1963.

tions to *communicatio in sacris*, that is, to sharing in prayer, rites, holy places and sacraments with separated brethren. Not that it denies the relevance of these things, but the Decree places the whole matter upon the broader ground of the witness to the unity of Christ's Church—*unitas Ecclesiae significanda* and *genuina significatio vinculorum*. This is a general principle which admits at once of variety in practice and of development in practice as the relations between separated Christian brethren are various and may in future develop.

Spiritual ecumenism

This is a term used by the Decree to declare that the movement essentially depends upon a change of heart (a *conversio*, in Latin), upon holiness and upon prayer.

About a change of heart Pope John spoke early in his pontificate, on 25th January 1959:

'The faults of which we Catholics are not, alas, free, lie in our not having prayed enough to God to smooth the ways that converge on Christ's Church; in not having felt charity to the full; in not having always practised it towards our separated brethren, preferring the rigour of learned, logical, incontrovertible arguments, to forebearing and patient love, which has its own compelling power of persuasion; in having preferred the philosophical rigidity of the lecture room to the friendly serenity of St Francis of Sales.'[1]

At worst, our attitude used to be rather to look for arguments to confute non-Romans than to find the good and the true which they held; to some extent there was an excuse for this since we inherited the controversial tone of the 'counter-Reformation'.[2] A 'change of heart' is to a large extent intangible but is most real for all that. A controversial atmosphere can induce a certain harshness from very love of truth, from fear of compromising what Christ has entrusted to us, or of weakening the spirit of firmness of faith in others. One great blessing of the ecumenical movement has been a more general realization that

[1] Cf. Appendix IV, p. 258.
[2] My book *The Churches and the Church*, written largely in 1957 and 1958, was criticized by some of my French and Belgian friends as being too 'apologetic'; I agree with this criticism, though I still think the book contains much useful information, and I had in mind others even less 'ecumenical' than myself.

friendliness and glad recognition of all that is good in others need not lead to any spirit of compromise or of weakness in faith.

Holiness

Holiness must of course be sought for its own sake; but many motives can bring deeper realizations of the need of holiness. Among these motives, the need of Christian unity is one. Just as some great calamity, war, for instance, or in personal life some crisis, such as the death of a loved one, can force men back upon God and bring increased realization of the meaning of life in Christ and of his teaching about the cross, so too deeper realization of the evil and the sin of christian division can force us back upon the power of God and upon reliance in the whole of our lives upon Christ and his cross.

Prayer

Prayer, both private and public is universally recognized as belonging to 'the soul' of the movement. Pope John XXIII commended the Council most especially to the prayers of children and of the sick; thus showing his faith in prayer, since children and the sick are usually helpless in any other way. The whole enterprise must depend wholly upon God, and all our desires and plans must be wholly dependent upon God.

Difficulty about prayer for the unity of Christians has been felt by some on the ground that Christians have a different concept of the unity of the Church and hence will be praying for different things. All, however, can pray for the unity which Christ wills and for it to come about in the way which Christ wills; and this, like the implicit condition of all prayer, 'thy will be done', makes it possible to reconcile common prayer with the different ideas which exist regarding the specific unity which Christ wills.

Prayer of petition does not attempt, as it were, to inform God of our desires and needs, for God 'knows what we need before we ask him' (Mt 6: 8) but, as St Augustine says, prayer prepares us to receive from God what he in his goodness wants to give us. Thus prayer, even of petition, expresses and helps on our unity with God; and prayer of petition may insensibly lead on to the prayer of meditation, of contemplation and even of what is called 'mystic' prayer, or the prayer of utter simplicity. Both the example of Christ (Lk 6: 12, Mt 26: 36) and his command to us (Lk 18: 1) urge the need for prayer, which is a common Christian conviction. The Gospel overflows with clear affirmations of the power of prayer and the conditions in which it will be answered—faith, humility and perseverance.

In the world of the spirit prayer must be called 'a cosmic force', making fruitful all the powers of human intellect and will. In realization of this, Pius XI entrusted to the Benedictines a special commission of work for unity, because their life of stability is common prayer, their withdrawal from 'active' work in the world, and their 'interior' spirit place the whole enterprise of overcoming divisions into a manifestly 'spiritual' dimension; not, indeed, that they alone were to work for unity, nor that other means—knowledge, dialogue, co-operation—were to be neglected, but that the emphasis must be placed first and foremost upon prayer as union with Christ in his prayer to the Father: 'that they may all be one; even as thou, Father, art in me, and I in thee, that they also may be one is us' (Jn 17: 20). Christ's prayer is a reflection in human nature of his union with the Father, a relation of 'derived equality' in the Spirit of both; a relation of complete love and complete self-giving, of the uttermost union of understanding, will and action. Father, Son and Holy Spirit, each is truly God, yet the one is not the other: the mystery of unity with a real relation of diversity. Union with Christ—and that must come by prayer—means union, too, with the Father of Christ and the Spirit of Christ, a union which enables men to share in the divine nature (2 Pet 1: 4), and sharing in that nature to be able to understand with something of God's understanding and to love with something of God's own love. The Decree rightly says that union with Father, Son and Holy Spirit will bring union in brotherly love (no. 7, par. 3).[1] This statement of the Decree

---

[1] Fr Geoffrey Curtis, of the Anglican Community of the Resurrection, in his *Paul Couturier and Unity in Christ*, London, 1964, prints (in Appendix A, pp. 329–51), Fr Couturier's 'Prayer and Christian Unity'. Fr Couturier's large-hearted spirit in

likewise stresses that unity must be sought not merely on the 'theological' level, but also on the devotional and spiritual level, granted, of course, the right and the need of differing devotional and spiritual outlooks. It is possible that hymns and liturgy may prove a greater force for unity than any intellectualized formulations.

D. TRUTH AND ITS EXPRESSION

In Chapter II (n. 6) the Decree frankly states that the way in which church teaching has been formulated, must be carefully distinguished from the deposit of faith itself (para. 2). The faith is formulated in 'creeds', in definitions by Councils and in expressions which become usual among theologians and even among the faithful. None of these can express the full content of God's revelation, though creeds and definitions of General Councils undoubtedly affirm christian truth, usually against distortions of the christian message; formulations by theologians stand on a different footing and may in later times be accepted by the whole Church or may be changed either in substance or in emphasis.

Illustrations of this distinction between formulations of faith and the 'deposit of faith'—a distinction which some Fathers at the Council thought dangerous—may be found in the defence by the Church in the third and fourth centuries of the doctrine of the Trinity. Two heresies rose, both based upon the absolute unity of God. The one, called 'Modalism' or 'Sabellianism', held that the words Father, Son and Holy Spirit were merely names, or merely aspects of the activity of the one God who in himself is absolutely undifferentiated. They concluded that it is as true to say that the Father became man and suffered for us as to say this of the Son. On the other hand, Arians, holding likewise to the unity of God, concluded that the Son is a creature made in time by God and hence is of a different nature than the Father, being, in fact, 'son' only in the same sense in which all Christians are made sons of God. It is clear that in re-

no way dulled his sense of the need for firmness in doctrine, as is evident (see pp. 332 and 342). It is almost impossible to exaggerate the debt which the ecumenical movement owes to the simple, humble Abbé Couturier.

jecting Arianism, and affirming the absolute equality and unity of Father and Son, it was easy to appear to deny the distinction between Father and Son; and, on the other hand, in rejecting 'Modalism', to exaggerate the difference between Father and Son and to appear to favour Arianism. The Church had to keep a correct balance between the two distortions.

At the first Ecumenical Council at Nicaea in 325 it became clear that the only way in which the Arians could in practice be shown to be heretical was by using about the Son the term *homoousios*—'consubstantial' or 'co-essential' with the Father, a word chosen, although it was not scriptural, because it alone fixed the essential faith and made a touchstone by which the equality of Father and Son in very being could be at once affirmed and defended. The Arians, as St Athanasius tells us, could explain away all scriptural language, but they would not accept the formulation that the Son is 'co-essential' or 'consubstantial' with the Father; and St Athanasius said that although the word is not in Scripture, 'yet it contains the sense of the Scriptures, and expressing it, conveys the meaning of the Scriptures' to religious men.[1]

This, however, is only a necessary preliminary to discussion of the 'formulation' of catholic truth. Athanasius was the most strenuous opponent of the Arians and defender of the creed of Nicaea. There were, however, some bishops who were by no means Arians, but yet could not bring themselves to accept the formula *homoousios*—or co-essential— fearing it favoured Modalism and led to a denial of the difference between Father and Son. Athanasius says of these:

'Those who accept everything else that was defined at Nicaea, and doubt only about the Co-essential (*homoousion*), must not be treated as enemies; nor do we attack them as if they were out-and-out Arians, nor as opponents of the Fathers, but we discuss the matter with them as brothers with brothers, who mean what we mean, and dispute only about the word. For confessing that the Son is from the substance of the Father, and not from another substance, and that he is not a creature nor made, but his genuine and natural offspring, and that he is eternally with

[1] Cf. Athanasius's *Defence of the Nicene Definition*, written between 351 and 355, especially ch. 5.

the Father as being his Word and Wisdom, they are not far from accepting even the phrase "co-essential" (*homoousios*). Such is Basil who wrote from Ancyra about the faith.'[1]

Athanasius wrote no more than thirty years after the Council of Nicaea, and his large-hearted and wise understanding of the difficulties felt by sincere bishops about the formula of Nicaea is a model of the distinction to be drawn between the faith and its formulation. In fact, many of those who hesitated about the formula came to understand and accept it.

Another illustration of the difference between faith and the way of expressing it is found in Dionysius of Alexandria (d. 264–5). In arguing against Modalists who denied any real distinction between the Persons of the Trinity, Dionysius used expressions which the Arians invoked: 'the Son of God is a creature and something made, and not his own by nature, but in essence alien from the Father, just as the husbandman is from the vine, or the shipbuilder from the boat, for that, being a creature, he was not before he came to be'.[2] St Athanasius in his defence of Dionysius lays down principles of universal application: judgement must be made not of isolated expressions, but of the whole of a man's writings, taking each in its full context, and of the complete mind of the writer; and Athanasius adduced a whole series of quotations from Dionysius showing that he held the complete equality of Father and Son, and was ready even to accept the term 'homousios' or 'consubstantial'. The suspect expressions he explained by the need to confute the Modalists, or Unitarians.

Words change in meaning

This was very obvious, in the Church of the third and the fourth centuries, regarding the word 'hypostasis', used by many earlier writers to mean the same as 'essence' or 'substance'. Thus in their understanding there was only one *hypostasis* in God and at the Council of Nicaea in 325 the word was taken as

---

[1] *De Synodis*, n. 41, *P.G.* 26, 765. Cf. the introductions and notes in Robertson's edition of Newman's translation of St Athanasius, in Wace and Schaff, *Select Library of Nicene and Post Nicene Fathers of the Christian Church*, vol. IV, *St Athanasius: Select Works and Letters*, pp. 448–9, and LVII (3).

[2] Cf. Athanasius, 'On the Opinion of Dionysius', Robertson's ed., op. cit., p. 177; *P.G.* 25, 485.

the equivalent of 'essence' or 'substance'.[1] Later, however, the word took on the meaning of what we now call 'person', and orthodoxy confessed three *hypostases* in the one nature, essence, or substance, of God. Indeed, writing in 362 Athanasius says that he found that some bishops spoke of three *hypostases* in God, while others of only one *hypostasis*. On further inquiry, however, Athanasius understood that both usages of the word meant the same, and each maintained the unity of the Godhead and the distinction between Father, Son and Holy Spirit.[2] Athanasius in his readiness to go behind mere words to the real meaning is a model of an 'ecumenical' mind.

The inadequacy of all language about the inner nature of the Godhead is well put by Augustine:

'We do not dare to say one essence, three substances; but one essence or substance and three persons; as many Latin writers of authority on the subject spoke, since they cound find no better way to put into words what they understood without words. In truth, since the Father is not the Son, and the Son is not the Father and the Holy Spirit is neither Father nor Son, there are three. . . . Nevertheless, when one inquires three *of what*, then speech reveals its inadequacy. The expression used, however, is three persons, not that thereby the truth is positively expressed, but only it is not left in complete silence.'[3]

Nevertheless progress in understanding is made partly through doctrinal formulations. The Councils of Nicaea (325) and of Ephesus (431) made clear that the Son of God is truly God and truly is a divine person incarnate; but the Councils of Chalcedon, A.D. 451, of Constantinople II and III, 553 and 681 A.D., made it equally clear that the Son of God was really and fully man, with a human mind and will, his manhood not lessened or absorbed by the divinity which was equally his.[4]

---

[1] Cf. Denzinger, *Enchiridion*, n. 54.

[2] Cf. Athanasius's 'Letter to the Church of Antioch', nn. 5 and 6. Cf. also the interesting discussion by the late Dr G. L. Prestige in chapters VIII and IX of his *God in Patristic Thought*, London, 1963, pp. 157–90.

[3] *De Trinitate*, bk. 5, n. 10 and cf. bk. 7, nn. 8–9.

[4] An instance of a misused formulation is found in the refusal of some adherents to the Council of Ephesus to accept the formulation that Christ has two natures, out of loyalty to the formulation of Cyril of Alexandria that 'one nature of God the Word was incarnate'. Cf. Constantinople II, Canon 8, Denzinger *Enchiridion*, 290. These men were called 'Monophysites', but in some cases, at least, the doctrine

The way, then, of formulating truths of faith may differ from the faith itself, and this principle, asserted by the Decree (n. 6) and presupposed in nn. 10 and 11, is fully justified from the history of the Church. Cardinal Bea well remarks: 'The first task of the dogmatic theologian is to grasp accurately, deeply and in its different bearings the content of the truths of faith, as they are contained in scripture and tradition and authoritatively taught by the Church. Next he must distinguish the timeless and eternal content amid the historically conditioned interpretations and formulations of past centuries; and in doing this he must avoid any dilution of the truth and any over-emphasizing of the non-essential.'[1] This is a delicate and important task requiring attention not only to the texts of Councils but to the *Acta* and to the whole historical situation.[2]

A symbolic character, however, in creeds and definitions of faith should be recognized. In Greek and Latin a creed is still called a *symbolum*. Creeds, definitions and even theological formulations are not merely statements of fact, or a catalogue of propositions saying what we believe; they are also symbols pointing beyond themselves, conveying a meaning which is transcendent and is evocative not merely of the assent of the mind, but of the response of the heart. In the Liturgy, the Nicene creed is not merely a declaration of faith, but is also a hymn of praise expressing human awe before the majesty and the mystery of God, recalling, asserting and anticipating the whole of the divine ecstasy in which God's goodness descended to us, dwells among us and lifts us up to the life of the world to come.

Progress, however, in understanding the Christian revelation may arise from many causes: meditation, reflection and con-

held about the Incarnation was correct, though its formulation at Chalcedon in 451 was rejected.

[1] *The Unity of Christians*, op. cit., in chapter 7, 'How University Research and Teaching can further Christian Unity', p. 99.

[2] This is particularly true of the Council of Trent (1545–63). It is not enough to quote an 'anathema' from Trent and conclude that the contrary is part of the faith; cf. H. Lennerz, 'Notulae Tridentinae', *Gregorianum*, 27 (1940), pp. 136–42; P. Fransen, 'Die Formel "si quis dixerit . . ." ', *Scholastik*, 25 (1950), pp. 492–517, and 'Réflexions sur l'anathème au Concile de Trente', *Ephemerides Theologiae Lovanienses*, 29 (1953), pp. 657–72; J. Cahill, *The Development of Theological Censures after the Council of Trent (1563–1709)*, Fribourg, 1955; M. Bévenot, 'Faith and Morals in the Councils of Trent and Vatican I', *Heythrop Journal*, III, 1, January 1962, pp. 15–36; '*Traditiones* in the Council of Trent', ibid., IV, October 1963, pp. 333–47.

templation of revealed truth and its implications, particularly in 'schools' of theology, the attacks or distortions of heretics; the effort to relate philosophical views to revealed truth, manifest, for instance, in the thirteenth century and in Thomas Aquinas's synthesis of Aristotelianism and the faith; the on-going life of the Church, its prayers, liturgies, its spiritual movements like monasticism and the rise of the 'Friars' with a great sense of poverty; various facts of history, such as the barbarian invasions, the decline of the Roman Empire, the break-up of 'Christendom'; the rise of 'liberalism' and the political changes it brought; wars and revolutions. All these had repercussions upon theology, sometimes helping progress, sometimes hindering it.[1]

Method in Theology

The Decree gives a warning against a controversial attitude in the study of theology, against an unintelligible style in expressing theological truths, and against a 'false irenicism' which either omits some catholic doctrines or 'tones them down' merely to secure agreement.

The warning against a controversial outlook is still, unhappily, needed. The age-long 'war psychology' dies hard and there are still many mutual prejudices between Catholics and Protestants, which reveal themselves in efforts to show the worst side of the other in books and writings. I refrain from giving examples.

Fortunately controversial literature plays small part in modern theology, even though older manuals still in use to some extent perpetuate the battles of the past and those who use them are sometimes unaware of the new outlooks.

Theological concern has changed. There is a new biblical movement, with enormous developments in archaeology and discoveries about the languages, laws, customs, literature and religions of the ancient peoples of the Middle East; and in scriptural studies there are no denominational boundaries. The

[1] Cf. Y. M. J. Congar, *La Foi et la Théologie*, Tournai (Belgium), 1962, part I, ch. IV, 'le progrès de l'Eglise dans l'intelligence de la foi', pp. 93–120. Newman's, *Development of Doctrine* is, of course, a classic; but cf. O. Chadwick, *From Bossuet to Newman. The Idea of Development of Doctrine*, Cambridge, 1957. A brief summary of catholic views up to 1952 is in M. Flick, 'Il problema dello sviluppo del dogma nella teologia contemporanea', *Gregorianum*, XXXIII (1952), pp. 5–23.

'neo-orthodoxy' associated with Karl Barth has put 'liberalism' in the shade. The new philosophies of 'analysis' and of 'existentialism'[1] give theological language a new dimension; sociology throws light on church communities and institutions.[2] The question of making the Christian message intelligible to modern man, in an age of technology and social change is common to theologians of all Communions; the 'meaning of history' raises in new forms the old question of the relation of nature and grace; liturgical study has placed the Eucharist both as sacrament and sacrifice into new perspective.[3] The old opposition between Scripture and Tradition is fast disappearing. In 1960 Dr Eugene Carson Blake said:

'The reformation churches have traditionally found their authority for faith and life in the Scripture alone. So long as the wording *sola scriptura* is required, no bridge can be made between catholic and evangelical. But it is now clear in ecumenical conversations that Protestants generally have come to recognize the right place of tradition, just as catholics have generally become aware of the rightness of judging all tradition by the Scriptures as interpreted to the Church by the Holy Spirit.'[4]

This is only an instance of the changed climate in theological writing. As Dean Roger Hazleton puts it in his *New Accents in Contemporary Theology*, 'real theological progress is already being made, as the old defensive rigidities are given up for more generous and spacious modes of christian thought'.[5]

The task of the theologian was never more important or more difficult. It is increasingly important because those not of our faith, and sometimes of no faith, are beginning to be interested in Catholicism, and any superficiality, any lack of strictly verifiable methods, any mere flat assertions or take-it-or-leave-it propositions, are quickly detected and cast a shadow upon our theology as a whole. It is, moreover, a mistake to imagine that

[1] Cf. David Roberts, *Existentialism and Religious Belief*, Oxford, 1957.
[2] Cf., for instance, Ehrenström, Nils, and Walter G. Muelder, eds., *Institutionalism and Church Unity*; *A Symposium Prepared by the Study Commission on Institutionalism*, Commission on Faith and Order, New York, 1963.
[3] Cf. Report of the *Theological Commission on Worship*, Faith and Order paper no. 39, Geneva, 1963; but the literature on this subject is enormous.
[4] *The Challenge to Reunion*, op. cit., p. 277, cf. also Paul S. Minear (ed.), *Faith and Order Findings; the Final Reports of the Theological Commissions to the Fourth World Conference on Faith and Order, Montreal, 1963*, Minneapolis, 1963.
[5] New York, 1960, p. 107.

only such theologizing is 'ecumenical' which aims at direct en-encounter with separated brethren. In fact, some of the theologians who have had the most influence in ecumenism have not been interested in ecumenism but only in some aspect of theological truth; this is true of de la Taille, Lepin, and to a large extent of Vonier, Masure, Journet (now a Cardinal), to mention only a few, in their writings on the Eucharist. Although its day, so to speak, has not yet come, I think that much of the study of patristic and mediaeval literature will prove most valuable to the ecumenical cause. The Decree speaks of 'due regard for the ecumenical point of view', but this by no means signifies that all theological study must be directly related to the present 'ecumenical encounter'.

Systematic theology can be of immense help. To have undertaken a course of theology divided into 'treatises' so that the whole range of Christian doctrine is covered, even though somewhat sketchily, gives a wholeness to the mind, prevents a too early specialization which leads to onesidedness and lack of balance, and may be compared to the study of anatomy by medical students. The ordinary course of four years pursued in our seminaries and faculties of theology, although it has many defects, and tends sometimes to give the impression of reducing living faith and contact with God to a series of abstract propositions about God, nevertheless when rightly used, can give a sense of the articulation of the various 'parts', into which inevitably the human mind divides theology, into a coherent whole, with some perception of the interdependence of each part with the others and with the whole. It is a fascinating question whether the various 'treatises', v.g. on God as one, on the Trinity, on creation and the fall, on the Incarnation, on sin and on the sacraments, could be better arranged, so as to give a greater sense of unity, without omission or repetition. There certainly are individual Professors who could make their own divisions and unify the whole; but the problem is to secure a teaching of theology which will not be too dependent upon individual brilliance and will secure a reasonable continuity.

Deficiencies there certainly have been and still are in our theological training, but open-minded and thoughtful attention to them is steadily proceeding, the need for more integration of all the branches of theology is being fully realized, and the need to attend to the questions being asked of Christians in the world today.[1]

Difficulties

The difficulties of a theologian are many. 'The most serious student', wrote Fr John J. Sweeney of Woodstock College, Maryland, 'is in danger of engulfment in the torrent of theological works that threatens to flood us all.'[2] A writer on theology must face new lexicons, dictionaries, encyclopaedias, new editions, new discoveries of documents, new translations, specialized books, monographs, dissertations and articles. There are whole books on single texts of Scripture, whole books on particular aspects of almost every ancient writer, batteries of works on mediaeval theology, exhaustive disquisitions on the Councils of the Church, and practically whole libraries on modern theology.[3] 'Dogmatic Theology' is not independent of philosophy, history, canon law, liturgy, ascetics, and, in recent times, of sociology and psychology.

To some extent this difficulty is being met by surveys and summaries in theological journals; in the long run useful contributions make their impact and eccentricities are dropped by the wayside. Yet the difficulty remains, and can be oppressive to the spirit of a conscientious scholar. I am convinced that in theological research and, indeed, in theology generally, there could and should be far more co-operation and combined work both among Catholic scholars themselves, and among both Catholics and separated brethren. Moreover, I am convinced that too much attention—note that I say 'too much'—to immediate problems and needs can defeat its own purpose. Truth must be sought for its own sake, according to the Gospel precept, 'seek first God's kingdom and his glory, and all these

[1] Cf. on the whole subject, Cardinal Bea, 'How University Research and Teaching can further Christian Unity', in the *Unity of Christians*, chapter 7, pp. 94–111; and *Apostolic Renewal in the Seminary in the light of Vatican Council II*, ed. James Keller and Richard Armstrong, New York, 1965.

[2] *Theological Studies*, 17 (1956), p. 368.

[3] This year Professor Paul A. Crow Jr. has published *The Ecumenical Movement in Bibliographical Outline*, New York. It runs to seventy-nine pages merely listing books published for the most part since 1945. Professor Crow speaks of 'the avalanche of literature' in these last years.

things shall be yours as well' (Mt 6: 33). Theology is an end in itself, not a means to something else, not even the salvation of souls.

Unintelligible terminology

This is a snare not only in theology but also in other sciences, such as psychology and sociology; but it is most particularly obnoxious in theology, which deals with communication of the living God to living men. It is undoubted that Catholic theology, though justified in using a reasonable amount of technical language, has tended to develop a terminology which is not understandable by ordinary people, much less by Anglicans, Orthodox or Protestants. We have tended to speak of abstractions, for example the 'humanity of Christ', as if they existed as concrete realities. We have introduced the 'causes', formal, material, efficient, final, with the addition of 'dispositive' and 'meritorious', into our account of God's encounter with men; rightly understood, this type of language is defensible, and even necessary, but to explain it, even to our own students becomes almost intolerably burdensome. In a treatise on grace published fifty years ago by a Catholic theologian whose manuals enjoyed considerable authority, one reads about grace as uncreated and created, as arousing and assisting, as operating and co-operating, as prevenient and subsequent, or antecedent and concomitant, as sufficient or efficacious, and one cannot help feeling that such distinctions—introduced partly because of the Jansenist controversy and the controversy between Molina and Bannez, in the seventeenth century—are of small relevance today even though a sympathetic consideration by Anglicans, Orthodox and Protestants of the issues raised by the Jansenists could be of solid use in ecumenical understanding. The problems connected with the interpretation of God's absolute sovereignty and human freedom have tended to be dismissed too readily, and even though the human mind cannot hope for an adequate solution, certain ways of speaking can be recognized as apt to be misleading and so to be avoided.[1]

Similarly our use of the word 'valid' about sacraments is not

[1] Cf. Peter Fransen, 'How should we teach the treatise on grace?' in *Apostolic Renewal in the Seminary*, ed. Keller and Armstrong, New York, 1965, pp. 139–73.

understood by separated brethren;[1] nor indeed is our concept of 'merit', of the 'sacramental character', of 'infused virtues', of 'created grace' and of many other matters which our theology has expressed in language neither biblical nor suited to modern ways of speaking. All the truths contained in such terminologies—and important truths are contained in them—can and should be put into different language, so that the real meaning may appear; but, above all, the historical conditions in which these terminologies developed must be made clear.

A *Schema* on the training of priests has been prepared for the Council and there is good reason to believe that its provisions will favour and foster renewal in methods of teaching and learning theology.

A hierarchy of truths

It was Archbishop Andrea Pangrazio of Gorizia, Italy, who introduced this distinction between truths which are on the level of our final goal, and those which are on the level of means to salvation; the full text of his speech can be found in Appendix VII, p. 298. The distinction does not fall upon the firmness of our belief, but upon the importance of the object of our belief: the mystery of the Blessed Trinity, the Incarnation and Redemption, God's love and mercy towards sinful humanity, eternal life in the perfect kingdom of God—such truths will not pass away, as will faith and hope, but will remain for ever, as charity remains for ever (1 Cor 13: 13). Sacraments, the hierarchical structure of the Church, the apostolic succession—the whole present organization of the Church, all these are only means to an end given by Christ to the Church on her pilgrim journey here on earth, and will pass away.

If I understand him rightly, Archbishop Pangrazio feels that the common faith and belief in the truths concerning our final goal not only already makes a unity among Christians, but also has a dynamism within it which can lead Christ's Church 'along paths which none of us can foresee or predict', to the fulness of unity which Christ wills.

There is, here, a vision which all ecumenists should take to

[1] Cf. my *Principles of Sacramental Theology*, 2nd ed., London, 1960, pp. 265–73 and 650–3.

heart: do we tend to think too much of the means to the end, and not enough about the end itself? Have many 'ecumenical' writings concentrated on the nature of the Church, the ministry, the sacraments, the nature of the faith, the differing ways of worship, to the neglect of study of the Trinity, the Incarnation and Redemption and of God's love for sinful humanity? Have we all attended too much to the temporal, neglecting the eternal?

These are searching questions, touching very fundamental outlooks. The inward vision of God, one in three, essentially self-giving, essentially love; contemplation of Christ's revelation of the nature of God by his sacrifice on the cross, remembrance that Christ 'loved me and gave himself for me' (Gal 2: 20), a deep and honest conviction of the transitory nature of this world and of the solid reality of the 'life in the future age'—such a vision has a dynamism within it which can of itself dissolve apparently insuperable obstacles. And it is this vision that is the deepest 'ecumenical' vision, because it sees the whole universe as Christ's and as Christ's must be one.

False irenicism

I take it on faith that there must be such a thing, because people speak of it so often. I have never met it in any Catholic ecumenist; if it did exist, separated brethren would quickly expose it, for they are very acutely aware of the Catholic position, and some know our authorities as well, or even better, than we do ourselves. Indeed some Protestant brethren have accused Catholic theologians of unorthodoxy or of undue subtlety when they interpret papal and conciliar pronouncements by reference to the historical setting in which they were made. Professor Lindbeck has defended Catholic theologians against this charge, on the ground that pronouncements of a legal nature might rightly be interpreted legally. The *Syllabus*, for instance, of Pius IX can only be understood by reference to the views against which the *Syllabus* was directed.[1] But such inter-

[1] Cf. Lindbeck's articles 'The Evangelical Possibilities of Roman Catholic Theology', *Lutheran World*, VI (1960), pp. 142–52; 'Reform and Infallibility. A Protestant view of the place of unalterable dogma in contemporary Catholic Theology', *Crosscurrents*, XI, no. 4 (Fall, 1961), pp. 345–56.

pretation of documents is far, indeed, from a 'false irenicism' by which the purity of Catholic doctrine suffers loss and its assured genuine meaning is clouded (n. 11, para. 1).

There were and are, of course, differences of opinion, even in the Council about the 'purity of Catholic doctrine'. Some thought that the assertion of the collegiality of the bishops would weaken the position of the Pope, that Marian doctrine should not be treated in the Constitution on the Church, but should have a special document to itself. In both cases the Council decided against those who so thought. As regards revelation, some judge that Tradition should be regarded as a source distinct from Scripture; and, as regards religious liberty and the relation of Christian and Jews some would prefer the Council to make no statement. In these matters, as in many matters of theology, there is legitimate difference of opinion. But neither opinion can justly be accused of 'clouding the assured genuine meaning of Catholic doctrine'.

Many separated brethren are well aware of these differences of opinion among us, especially those of them who were 'observers' at the Council, and those who, like Professor Skydsgaard, Jaroslav Pelikan, Robert Macafee Brown, George Lindbeck, George Williams (to name but a few), have made serious studies of Catholicism. Such men—and they are increasing in numbers—would despise any attempt to 'water down' Catholic doctrine.

A Protestant estimate of Catholicism

In 1961, a group of Lutheran scholars wrote about the coming Council, and Professor George Lindbeck's account of 'Roman Catholicism on the eve of the Council' remains still of value in estimating the futility of any 'false irenicism'. He recounts, as evidence of renewal in the Church since the time of the First Vatican Council; disengagement from political ties, renewal of learning and return to the sources, especially the Bible, a forward-looking social policy begun by Leo XIII's *Rerum Novarum*, codification and revision of canon law, the increasing role of the laity especially in intellectual circles, reassessments of the Reformation, adaptability to changing conditions, an immense missionary enterprise, a more flexible and adventurous attitude in theology, the liturgical movement and, finally, the calling of the Vatican Council. On the other hand, he deprecates the definition of the Assumption, the growth of interest in Mariology and the tendencies among some Catholics to be excessively legalistic, conservative, passively obedient and perhaps repressive.[1]

On this last matter, Pope John's Encyclical *Peace on Earth* asserted plainly, strongly and repeatedly the freedom of the individual conscience, even though erroneous, and the right to religious liberty. There is no doubt that the fourth session of Vatican Council II will endorse this teaching and make clear that the whole Catholic Church not only accepts but vindicates the right to religious liberty and repudiates any theory or practice contrary to freedom in religion.[2]

After this short digression, it must be evident that any false picture of the Catholic Church made to separated brethren would be unwise as well as dishonest. Thus to 'play down', or 'soft pedal', the uniqueness of the Church, or the authority of the Pope and of the Bishops, or the deep Catholic devotion to the Mother of God, or the Sacrifice of the Mass, or even normal Catholic devotions and practices, would be disloyal in itself and would only incur the disapproval or even disgust of Anglican, Orthodox and Protestant brethren. Reasonable and charitable criticism of the use of authority, or of exaggerations in devotion may be justified and are by no means 'a false irenicism', nor need there be any hesitation in acknowledging our defects, as the Decree itself does, and in urging reform and renewals (nn. 3, n. 4, paras. 5 and 6; n. 6, para. 2; n. 7, paras. 1 and 2, n. 10, para. 2, n. 11). Criticism, however, should be judicious and designed rather to bring reform and renewal than irritation or discouragement.

But I must confess that of the 'weakness' and 'importunate zeal' against which the Council warns us (n. 24), the latter— 'importunate zeal'—seems among some, at least, the greater danger at present. Dr E. L. Mascall has remarked that the

---

[1] *The Papal Council and the Gospel, Protestant Theologians Evaluate the Coming Vatican Council,* Minneapolis, Minnesota, 1961, pp. 61–93. Cf. my summary of this book in *The Heythrop Journal III*, no. 4 (1962), pp. 358–70.

[2] Cf. above, p. xii.

documents on the Church, ecumenism and the Eastern Catholic Churches 'mark nothing less than a complete transformation and reorientation of the Roman Communion as regards its official teaching about the church and its attitude to other christian bodies and the repercussions through Christendom are bound to be far reaching'.[1] The word 'transformation' is perhaps too strong, for the Decree only makes explicit what was already implicit in Catholic teaching; nevertheless, the 'reorientation' is true—and it has unhappily upset some devoted and saintly Catholics, who even feel that the Decree itself favours a false spirit of peace and even of weakness. This is, of course, simply not true and the Decree should be carefully read and quietly pondered. Catholics who have not been aware of the developments in the Church during the last thirty years have certainly been sometimes bewildered, sometimes irritated at what they consider weakness and failure in firmness and definiteness. This is partly due to delay in producing good translations of the documents, and it is to be hoped that reading and discussion of the documents will allay all fears.

In my experience the clergy and the laity generally in English-speaking countries, have welcomed the ecumenical outlook and are disposed whole-heartedly to welcome the Decree on Ecumenism and to work to implement it.

E. CO-OPERATION WITH SEPARATED BRETHREN

The chapter ends with two general suggestions, the first, that Christians should, on occasion, make public their faith in the Trinity and the Incarnation and the hope that inspires all Christians. This can be done in various ways, for instance, by discreet efforts to make Christmas a Christian and not merely a secular feast, by doing all that is possible to ensure that greeting cards are Christian and not merely secular or even pagan, by common tableaux, carol singing and even Christmas cribs. Similarly, Good Friday can be marked by a common procession, with the cross conspicuous. Sunday observance can be

---

[1] 'The Church and Ecumenism at Vatican II', *Graham Street Quarterly* (Spring, 1965), p. 12, and cf. Dr Mascall's 'Vatican II on the Church and Ecumenism: an Anglican Comment', *Blackfriars*, April 1965, pp. 386–95.

prudently advocated and the christian calendar as far as possible followed. On special occasions, whether of distress or of thanksgiving, Christians can unite in expressing their common faith. The recommendation of the Decree is general, leaving it to the ingenuity and prudence of Christians in different parts of the world to find ways and means of carrying it out.

The second general suggestion refers to combined christian efforts to maintain 'a just evaluation of the human person, to the establishment of peace, the application of Gospel principles to social life and advancement of the arts and sciences in a truly christian spirit'. Pope John's *Peace on Earth* deals with all this at more length.

Cardinal Gracias of Bombay quoted in the Council some figures which must disturb the conscience of all Christians:

'In the underdeveloped countries 150,000,000 families are living in subhuman conditions; two-thirds of the population of the world are not receiving 2,500 calories daily, considered to be a vital minimum; infant mortality still stands at 185 per 1,000 in India and the expectation of life in the new-born is only 32 years in India. The nineteen richest countries representing together only 16% of the world's population control 75% of the world's income. In the underdeveloped countries 150,000,000 families are living under subhuman conditions and 30,000,000 in countries called prosperous. India has an illiteracy percentage of 83·4%.'[1]

No individual can solve this heartrending problem. Nor can it be solved merely by provision of food and goods. The problem is massive and demands a whole variety of measures for its solution, among them the provision of technical instruction. Much assistance has been given, and is being given, by the wealthier and more developed countries, not only in goods but in personal service. The question, however, remains whether enough is being done and whether Christians generally show sufficient concern. Many agencies, national and international, are working on the problem and patterns of co-operation are complex. And yet one may still ask whether Christians are sufficiently concerned. Would it be possible, for instance, for Christians in particular cities, towns and regions in the weal-

[1] *Council Speeches*, op. cit., pp. 203–4.

thier countries to 'adopt' similar cities, towns and regions in less developed countries, and, if unable to solve all the complicated problems, at least to send tokens of concern and brotherly charity? To carry out any such suggestion would cost time, trouble and money—and doubtless many would judge that the work might better be left to the agencies which have experience and an already existing organization. Nevertheless, Christians should feel themselves personally involved in the distress of their fellow human beings.

On a smaller scale Christians are collaborating in such works as the Samaritan telephone service, which offers help to anyone in distress of mind; schools are co-operating in visiting the aged and the sick; sometimes parish visiting is co-ordinated, with exchange of information between the clergy. Catholics are becoming 'observers' at the different sub-committees of the British Council of Churches, and 'observers' likewise, at local councils of Churches. Publishers of different Communions have met to discuss common interests, various professional groups have also sometimes met, marriage advisory councils generally maintain contact with one another. In Canada, a Christian Association has been formed to provide houses at cheap rates to young married couples. Mixed groups have met to read and discuss the teaching of Pope John in *Peace on Earth*. Gradually 'isolationism' is breaking down, without surrender of principle, and this is according to the recommendations of the Decree.

CHAPTER III

CHURCHES AND ECCLESIASTICAL COMMUNITIES SEPARATED FROM THE ROMAN APOSTOLIC SEE

The Decree mentions three main classes separated from the Roman Apostolic See: (1) the Nestorians who refused to accept the Council of Ephesus in 431 and the use of the title Mother of God (*theotokos*), and the Monophysites, who did not accept the Council of Chalcedon in 451, holding to Cyril of Alexandria's formula: 'one nature of God the Word incarnate'.[1] (2) the Orthodox Church, whose separation from Rome may perhaps be said to date from 1054; and (3) the Anglicans and Protestants separated from the Roman allegiance in the sixteenth century and thereafter.[2]

The Decree does not attempt to give any full account of these separated 'Churches and Ecclesiastical Communities', but it indicates a number of considerations which may act as guiding principles for present ecumenical action.

[1] The Decree says nothing more of these Churches, sometimes called 'Non-Chalcedonian'. They retain many of the characteristics of the main Orthodox Church and perhaps their doctrinal differences are more verbal than real, cf. Donald Attwater, *The Christian Churches of the East*, vol. II, as regards the Nestorians of Iraq, Iran and Syria, p. 178; as regards the Copts, p. 190, the Ethiopians, p. 200, the Syrian Jacobites, p. 208, the Malabar Jacobites, p. 217 and the Armenians, p. 228. The Nestorians from the sixth to the fifteenth centuries showed great missionary activity and evangelized Tibet, Mongolia, Manchuria, China and the Malabar coast of India; they now number only about 60,000 and are sometimes known as 'Assyrians'. Together with the Monophysites they may number eight million. In January 1965 they held a conference in Addis-Ababa and showed themselves aware of the problems facing the modern Church, cf. *Vers l'Unité Chrétienne*, published by the ecumenical centre 'Istina', outside Paris, Jan-Feb 1965, pp. 9–12.

[2] The Decree in n. 13, par. 3, makes special mention of the Anglican Communion; but I postpone consideration of the Anglicans until later, since in many ways they act as a 'bridge' between Catholics, Orthodox and Protestants.

Special Consideration of the Eastern Orthodox Churches

Here the following general divisions seem pertinent:

A. Catholicity, apostolicity and the Orthodox.

B. Some general characteristics of Orthodoxy.

C. The debt owed by the West to the East.

D. Differences in theological expression between East and West.

E. The solemn declaration by the Council of the right of the Orthodox to maintain their own rites, laws and customs.

A. CATHOLICITY, APOSTOLICITY AND THE ORTHODOX

Cardinal Bea has made a most pertinent comment upon the special consideration given in the Decree to the Orthodox. He quotes the following passage and then comments:

' "Nor should we forget that anything wrought by the grace of the Holy Spirit in the hearts of our separated brethren can be a help to our own spiritual growth. Whatever is truly christian is never contrary to the genuine good of the faith; indeed, it can always bring a deeper realization of the mystery of Christ and the Church" (n. 4, par. 9).

As a significant example of this willingness to learn from separated brethren, the Decree gives an incisive exhortation relative to the spiritual riches of the christian East:

' "Catholics are earnestly recommended to avail themselves still more of the spiritual riches of the Eastern Fathers which lift up the whole man to the contemplation of the divine.

' "The rich liturgical and spiritual heritage of the Eastern Churches should be known, venerated, preserved and cherished by all. They must recognize that this is of supreme importance for the faithful preservation of the fulness of Christian tradition, and for bringing about reconciliation between Eastern and Western Christians" (n. 15, par. 5).

'Careful note should be taken of the fact that knowledge and preservation of the Eastern spiritual heritage is commended not merely as springing from love and hope of unity, but also as demanded by very loyalty to the Christian tradition itself, since only so can that tradition be preserved in all its fulness. And in fact, a little later, the Decree declares very explicitly and decisively that "all this heritage of spirituality and liturgy, of discipline and theology, in its various traditions, the sacred Council declares to belong to the full catholic and apostolic character of the Church" (n. 17, par. 2).

'The principle here laid down is general, and in consequence there can be no doubt that it applies to the endowments possessed by separated brethren both of the East and of the West. These latter are acknowledged and exemplified further on in the Decree. But it will surprise no one in touch with the situation to see that this conciliar document contains a special, explicit and most significant exhortation to diligent study of the spiritual treasures of the East, in order to enrich our own christian life.'[1]

I think that this last sentence means that Catholics can and should enlarge their general outlook by better knowledge of the history, theology, liturgy and customs of the Eastern Churches. We have been, I venture to think, inclined to conceive 'the Church' exclusively in terms of the Western Church of the Latin rite, overlooking both the Eastern Churches in union with us and the Orthodox who are not in full communion with us. Fr Georges Florovsky, speaking of the problems of ecumenical encounter, stresses the tendency to overlook, especially in historical writing, the common history of East and West:

'It is hard even in our own time to recover a common idiom. It is even harder to recover the vision of common Christian history. One can in the West, even in our own days, write a history of the Church universal without mentioning the Eastern Churches except casually and sporadically.[2] This attitude, however, can be formally justified by the assumption that, strictly speaking, since the Schism with Rome, there was

[1] 'Il decreto conciliare sull ecumenismo: l'azione da svolgere', *La Civiltà Cattolica*, 2nd January 1965, p. 13.
[2] Fr Florovsky gives one instance which I omit for reasons of reverence and charity; but I could easily add other instances.

actually no "Church" in the East but only scattered Christians. Of course, this contention may be dismissed as a polemic exaggeration, and many Catholic theologians and historians would wish to tone it down, or, at least, to qualify it carefully. Yet the prejudice is widely spread and does actually control the ecumenical vision in many quarters. Christian universality is readily interpreted as universality of the West. Again, there are notable exceptions.'[1]

I should like to think that the 'exceptions' were not so very rare; nevertheless the insistence of the Decree upon the need for greater and wider knowledge and esteem for our Orthodox brethren indicates a conviction that not enough has yet been done, in spite of most admirable work done by those whom Fr Florovsky calls 'exceptions'.[2] It is largely due to the interest aroused by the action of these popes, together with the presence at the Council of the Eastern Catholic hierarchy, that the Decree is so insistent upon the importance of the Orthodox.[3] The concept of the Church's catholicity and apostolicity must include the Eastern Churches, which are so closely united to us in doctrine, outlook and spirituality; and for the fulness of catholicity and of apostolicity union with the Orthodox, and indeed with all separated Christian brethren, is a clear postulate. I repeat: the assumption must not be made that the Catholic Church is the Church of the West. To make that assumption and to act upon it by exclusive attention only to the Western tradition is to impoverish, or even deny, the very idea of the Church's catholicity.

---

[1] 'The Problem of Ecumenical Encounter', *Rediscovering Eastern Christendom*, op. cit., p. 66.

[2] Pope Pius IX issued five documents dealing with the Eastern Churches, Orthodox and Catholic; Leo XIII, seven; Pius X, five; Benedict XV, two; Pius XI, eight; and Pius XII, eight. Benedict XV set up the Pontifical Oriental Institute; Pius XI united the Oriental Institute with the Biblical Institute, prescribed courses in Oriental Theology in all seminaries and gave the Benedictines a special charge with regard to the Eastern Orthodox.

[3] The literature is large. Bibliographies will be found in Donald Attwater's *Eastern Churches English Book-list*, Newport, Rhode Island, 1960; Henry Brandreth's *An Outline Guide to the study of Eastern Christendom*, London, 1951; and Dean Timothy Andrews, *The Eastern Orthodox Church*, New York, 1957. Mr Attwater's, *The Christian Churches of the East*, 2 vols., London, 1961, contains a good deal of bibliographical matter, and, at the end of the second volume, a list of periodicals. Dr Nicolas Zernov has a brief but select bibliography at the end of his *Orthodox Encounter*, London, 1961, as has, likewise, Timothy Ware, *The Orthodox Church*, London, 1964; cf. p. 169.

The Eastern Catholic Churches

The Eastern Catholic Churches, who belong to the Alexandrine, the Antiochene, Chaldean, Armenian and Byzantine Rites,[1] and number between seven and eight million, have an importance far beyond their numbers, since they bear witness both to loyalty to Eastern traditions and customs and to the centre of unity in the successor of St Peter. There have been many indications that these Eastern patriarchs and bishops had very considerable influence in the deliberations of the Council.

These Eastern Catholics, small in numbers and often poor, have nevertheless a most important role to play: to maintain a twofold and equal loyalty towards Catholicism and the East.[2] This role, or rather vocation, is a difficult one. In the past, says the Patriarch Maximos, many Westerners have either disliked the Eastern Catholics, or tolerated them, or found them, with their own clergy, discipline and rites, an abnormal and uncomfortable thing, at least a source of problems. There has, however, been a change:

'In the Western Church, ignorance, incomprehension, and occasional hostility have been superseded, especially in recent years, by an immense desire for a more intimate acquaintance with the East, by a sincere will to understand it and by a beginning of frank and loyal collaboration.

'The last few years have witnessed in the West an admirable growth of scientific institutions devoted to oriental research.

---

[1] They live in Egypt, Syria, Iraq, the Lebanon, Bulgaria, Turkey, Palestine, Rumania, Russia, Poland, Jugoslavia, Galacia and India: and many of them have emigrated to North America. Cf. Donald Attwater's first volume, *passim*. Michael Lacko, S.J., gives a history of Eastern Christians in the United States and Canada in 'The Churches of Eastern Rite in North America', *Unitas*, XVI (Summer, 1964), pp. 89–115; the tables giving nationalities and numbers are particularly useful, pp. 110–13. Since 1950 the Ukranians in Canada have had one Metropolitan and four 'eparchies'; the Ukranians in the United States have had one Metropolitan and three eparchies; and since 1963 the Ruthenians in the U.S.A. have had two eparchies. Eastern Catholics in North America number about one million. Fr Lacko gives an up-to-date bibliography relative to Orthodox and Catholic Easterners in North America.

[2] Cf. *The Eastern Churches and Catholic Unity*, ed. by Maximos IV Saigh, Patriarch of Antioch and of all the East, of Alexandria and of Jerusalem, London, 1963, trans. by John Dingle. Cf. also the judicious review of this book by Père Robert Clément in *The Heythrop Journal*, IV, no. 4 (October 1963, pp. 392–8). Père Clément himself wrote a most illuminating account of the Eastern Orthodox, *Chrétiens d'Orient, Initation à l'Orient chrétien et perspectives oecumeniques*, Paris, 1961.

There exist today many scientific or high-quality popular publications investigating the various aspects of the spiritual heritage of the East, and uncovering these riches for the benefit of their readers. Travel, meetings, conventions, and business lead to numerous personal contacts between Eastern and Western Catholics. As an Arab proverb says, 'Man hates only that of which he is ignorant.' A better mutual knowledge will, no doubt, soon result in mutual respect and love between Easterners and Westerners. The younger generation of apostolic workers imbued with this spirit, identify themselves more and more thoroughly with the Church they come to serve. Many of the older missionaries sent to be helpers in the East were a terrible burden for the East through their attempts at dominating or absorbing it under the pretext of more efficient assistance. The younger generation, on the other hand, comes truly in a spirit of service, adopts the East, and identifies itself with it, without human ambition or mental reservation.'[1]

To the Orthodox, however, the very existence of Eastern Catholics is unwelcome. 'Very often they consider us', says the Patriarch Maximos, 'spies and agents of the political and religious imperialism of the Vatican. . . . The Orthodox authorities are inclined to consider us as ravening wolves in sheep's clothing, and, consequently, persecute us as the chief agents of Roman proselytism. Those among our Orthodox brethren who, knowing us, refuse to believe that we are capable of such sinister designs, pity us as unwitting victims, who without realizing it, tend to strengthen the ambition for supremacy and universal domination which, in their opinion, constantly inspires the Roman Church. At any rate, it is undeniable that our Orthodox brethren feel deeply hurt by what they call our premature, unconditional union, comparable in their minds to a separate peace treaty signed by political powers without the knowledge or approval of their allies.'[2]

Possibly the Patriarch forgot some instances of good feeling between Orthodox and Catholic Christians. In 1948, for instance, when the Byzantine Catholics in Transylvania were

---

[1] 'The Eastern Role in Christian Reunion', *The Eastern Churches and Unity*, pp. 51–2.
[2] Ibid., p. 53.

'disrupted' by the government, seventy-six Orthodox priests were imprisoned for refusing to take over Catholic churches, and there were mutual expressions of esteem.[1] During the Nazi occupation of Jugoslavia many Catholic priests risked their lives to protect the Orthodox.[2] Other instances of friendly feeling could be given, though Père Dumont gives instances of Catholic failure in courtesy towards the Orthodox.[3] In an article in *Herder Correspondence* we read: 'It looks as if the problem of the Eastern Catholic Churches has lately lost much of its acuteness, due presumably to the attitude of the Uniate Melchite Patriarch Maximos at the Council and to the good personal relationship between Maximos and Athenagoras (the Patriarch of Constantinople). Surprisingly enough, Archbishop Jakovos (the Greek Exarch in America) declared in an interview that the Catholic Eastern Rite Churches might even further a reconciliation between East and West. As long as there was no proselytizing activity, all could live together as good neighbours.'[4] Nevertheless, such statements are recent and seem exceptional. The general attitude of the Orthodox towards the Eastern Churches united with the Roman See is generally unfavourable, as the Patriarch Maximos says.

These Eastern Catholics manifest first of all a passionate conviction that it is right and necessary to retain their Eastern heritage:

'We must be convinced that Christianity can never accomplish its mission in the world unless it is Catholic, that is, universal, not only in law but also in actual fact. If someone cannot be Catholic unless he gives up his own liturgy, hierarchy, patristic traditions, history, hymnography, art, language, culture, and spiritual heritage, and adopts the rites, philosophical and theological thought, religious poetry, liturgical language, culture and spirituality, of a particular group, even though it be the best, then the Church is not a great gift of God to the whole world but a faction, however numerous, and a human institu-

---

[1] Attwater, *Christian Churches of the East*, vol. II, p. 93.
[2] R. Clément, *Chrétiens d'Orient*, p. 11.
[3] Cf. his comments of Archibishop Medawar's 'Reflections on the Union of the Churches', *Eastern Churches and Catholic Unity*, London, 1963, pp. 106 and 109.
[4] *Herder Correspondence*, I, no. 8 (August 1964), p. 247. The interview is quoted from *Orthodoxoi Paratiritis*, February 1964.

tion subservient to the interests of one group. Such a church is no longer the true Church of Christ. In resisting, then, the latinizations of our institutions, we are not defending any petty parochial interests or an out-dated traditionalism; rather, we are aware of defending the vital interests of the apostolic Church, of remaining faithful to our mission, our vocation which we could not betray without betraying ourselves and disfiguring the message of Christ before our brothers.'[1]

The Patriarch Maximos and other Eastern Catholic bishops both within the Council and during its deliberations pressed for more definite acknowledgement of the rights of patriarchs, of the apostolic traditions of the East, of a normal use of the vernacular, and, in general, an eastern understanding of man and of his obligations, independent of western moralism and avoiding the excesses of casuistry through its own traditional norms without falling into laxity.[2] The general trend of the ideas advocated by the Patriarch had been repeatedly approved by the successive popes.[3] They joined, too, with many Western bishops in urging the importance of the 'collegial' concept of the Church.[4]

The Latinization of the Church

Of this Eastern Orthodox and Eastern Catholics have often complained; it is perhaps a general mental outlook which is not easy to define. It is found in the assumption, often the more

[1] 'The Eastern Role in Christian Reunion', op. cit., pp. 60–1.
[2] Cf. Clément, The Heythrop Journal, IV, no. 4 (October 1963), p. 396.
[3] Cf., for instance, the quotations given by Archbishop Neophytos Edelby from Benedict XIV's Constitution of 26th July 1755, Allatae Sunt, and from Leo XIII's encyclical, Orientalium Dignitas of 30th November 1894, 'Our Vocation as Eastern Christians', The Eastern Churches and Catholic Unity, pp. 41 and 42–3.
[4] Council Speeches of Vatican II, op. cit., gives a number of the speeches of Eastern Catholic patriarchs and bishops: Elias Zoghby, Greek-Melchite Patriarchal Vicar in Egypt, 'Eastern and Western Tradition in the One Church', pp. 49–54; Michael Doumith, Maronite Bishop of Sarba, 'The Significance of Episcopal Consecration', pp. 64–8; the Patriarch Maximos of Antioch, 'Servant of the Servants of God', pp. 72–8, and 'The Supreme Senate of the Catholic Church', pp. 133–7; Ignatius Ziade, Maronite Archbishop of Beirut, Lebanon, 'Pastoral Need of Permanent Deacons', pp. 98–103, and 'The Rights of Bishops', pp. 111–20; Joseph Tawil, Greek-Melchite Patriarchal Vicar for the Eparchy of Damascus, 'A Voice from the East', pp. 193–6. These are merely random examples; any final estimate of the contribution to the Council of various groups of Bishops must await the publication of the complete Acta. Meantime, estimates must be tentative and subject to revision.

irritating because unconsciously made, that the Church is the Latin Church; that the customs, laws and rites of the Eastern Catholics are 'permitted', 'conceded' or 'allowed' and hence are not as much a right as the customs, laws and rites of the West.[1] It is found in the identification of the pope's role as Patriarch of the West and his role as centre and guardian of the unity of the people of God.[2] It is found, too, in the tendency of the Western canonists to regard the Eastern Patriarchs as practically the same as Western metropolitans or archbishops.[3] The origins of the patriarchate would appear to lie in a concentration in one man of certain powers of the collegial episcopate in a region, and not as a grant of powers by Rome, as tended to be held after the appointment of Latin Patriarchs in the East at the time of the Crusade.

Other 'latinizations' of which the Eastern Catholic bishops complained were found in restrictions placed on the powers of the bishops (though Latin bishops complained of this, also), and restrictions in such matters as the vernacular liturgy, sharing in rites with the Orthodox (*communicatio in sacris*), the invalidity of mixed marriages except before a Catholic priest, and the choice given to those being reconciled to the Church to enter an Eastern or a Latin rite.

A kind of 'osmosis', however, takes place between the East and the West as regards customs. Thus the determination that the sacrament of Orders is conferred by an imposition of hands rested largely on Eastern authorities;[4] the Easter Vigil and concelebration derive from the East. On the other hand, the synod of Charafé in 1888 for the Catholic Syrians, and of Alexandria in 1898 for the Catholic Copts, adopted a law of clerical celibacy;[5] the month of May instead of the Eastern month of

[1] Cf. Clément, *Chrétiens d'Orient*, op. cit., pp. 19, 20; Archbishop Neophytos Edelby, 'The Byzantine Liturgy in the Vernacular', *The Eastern Churches and Catholic Unity*, ed. by Maximos IV, p. 212. Archbishop Edelby speaks in particular of the use of the vernacular, but the principle he urges is general.

[2] Cf. John F. Long, S.J., 'East and West in the Decree on Ecumenism', *Unitas*, XVII (Spring, 1965), p. 7.

[3] Cf. Archbishop Peter K. Medawar, 'The Cairo Synod of the Greek Catholic Church, February 1958', *Eastern Churches and Catholic Unity*, op. cit., p. 148–52. On the origins and theology of the Patriarchate, cf. W. de Vries, *Rom und die Patriarchate des Ostens*, Freiburg, 1963.

[4] Pius XII's *Apostolic Constitution*, A.A.S., XL (28th January 1948), pp. 5–8.

[5] E. Herman, art. 'Célibat', *Dictionnaire de Droit Canonique*, vol. III, Paris, 1942, col. 155.

December is chosen for particular devotion to the Mother of God; a shortened form of the Liturgy is used on Sundays for the convenience of workers and students, and to meet the desire of some clergy to celebrate daily. Statues and diverse church decorations are sometimes imported from France and Italy; and literature from the West tends to be appreciated more and more.[1]

The principles for which the Eastern Catholic patriarchs and bishops, together with many others, had stood were fully accepted by the Decrees on the Eastern Catholic Churches and on Ecumenism and by the Constitution on the Church. Both in the Decree on the Eastern Catholic Churches and on Ecumenism the general rights of the Eastern Churches were solemnly asserted.[2] In the Decree on the Eastern Catholic Churches the rights and the position of the patriarchs were asserted, nn. 7–11, including the right of the Patriarch and his Synod to nominate bishops and erect Eparchies; the principle is set down in virtue of which a separated Christian who is received into the Catholic Church is to be incorporated, as a regular thing, into that Eastern Church that corresponds to the rite to which he previously belonged (n. 4);[3] mixed marriages before an Orthodox minister are valid (n. 19); the obligation of Sunday Mass is modified by Eastern customs (n. 15); priests

---

[1] Cf. R. Clément, *Chrétiens d'Orient*, op. cit., pp. 14–18. On the difficulties of emigrant Eastern Catholics in North America, cf. Michael Lacko, 'The Churches of Eastern Rite in North America', *Unitas*, XVI (Summer, 1964), pp. 104–9.

[2] Cf. below no. 5, pp. 209.

[3] Fr Clément Pujol, S.J. remarks that there was a spirited debate among the Council Fathers on this matter, 'The Conciliar Decree on the Eastern Catholic Churches', *Unitas*, XVII (Spring, 1965), p. 32. Archbishop Peter K. Medawar, Auxiliary Bishop to the Patriarch Maximos, objected strongly to the provision in the newly published Code of Canon Law for the Eastern Catholic Churches that those coming into full unity could choose the rite they preferred, *The Eastern Churches and Christian Unity*, pp. 152–5. In his English translation and commentary on the new Code, Victor J. Pospishil, of the Archeparchy of Philadelphia, maintains that Protestants could be received into any Catholic Rite of their choice, cf. *Code of Oriental Canon Law: The Law on Persons*, Ford City, Pa., U.S.A., pp. 38–9. The Eastern Catholics are sensitive about anything which appears to suggest any inferiority of Eastern Rites to the Latin Rite. In North America, Fr Lacko recounts that some 300,000 Slovaks and some 300,000 Ukranians went over to the Latin Rite, and 800,000 went to different Orthodox jurisdictions, mainly because of lack of priests. The exact date, however of these changes is not easy to gather from the information given by Fr Lacko, cf. 'The Churches of Eastern Rite in North America', *Unitas*, XVI (Summer, 1964), pp. 106–7. The situation is greatly changed today, and Latin bishops help the Easterners in the erection of parishes and schools.

may regularly confirm (n. 13); a permanent diaconate is approved (n. 17); the date of Easter, in some regions, may be fixed by agreement with Orthodox authorities (n. 17); regulations about liturgical language is left to the Patriarchal Synods (n. 23); rules about sharing in sacred rites (*communicatio in sacris*) with the Orthodox are made broader (nn. 28–32). The obvious purpose of the Decree is to give added strength and prestige to Eastern Catholic Rites.[1]

The Patriarch Maximos was indeed critical of the section about patriarchs in the Decree, mainly because the patriarchs were not given a place in the universal government of the Church;[2] but in January 1965, together with the Maronite Patriarch of Antioch and the Coptic Patriarch of Alexandria, he accepted the cardinalate, and declared: 'by the entrance of the Patriarchs of the East into the college of cardinals, the institution of the cardinalate witnesses a new stage in the history of its long evolution, which is perhaps not yet complete. . . . In their role as cardinals, the patriarchs of the East will participate equally in the election of the Pope. They will be called to be his counsellors and to aid him at closer hand in the general affairs of the Church and in the central organisms and administration.'[3]

Ultimate Destiny of the Catholic Eastern Churches

When union with the Orthodox comes, the express anticipation of some Eastern Catholics is that their own heirarchical organization will disappear. The Patriarch Maximos has declared:

'In suggesting this union (with the Orthodox) we seek no personal advantage. On the contrary, we further our own disappearance as a hierarchical community. To be exact we are hoping that once the union is achieved, there will no longer be a united or uniat Eastern Church but simply an Eastern Church,

[1] Cf. C. Pujol, 'The Conciliar Decree on the Eastern Catholic Churches', *Unitas*, XVII (Spring, 1965), pp. 28–32. Cf., also, Julian Walter, A.A., 'The Voice of the East in the Church', *Chrysostom*, no. 21 (Spring, 1965), pp. 3–4.

[2] 'Maximos IV on the Institution of the Patriarchate', *One in Christ* (a continuation of *The Eastern Churches Quarterly*), vol. I, no. 1 (1965), pp. 74–7.

[3] The full text of Patriarch Maximos's letter is given in *Chrysostom*, no. 21 (Spring, 1965), pp. 5–6. Maximos understood that the Patriarchs of the Armenians and of the Chaldeans would also be made cardinals.

among whose ranks we ourselves shall re-enter as if we had never departed.'[1]

'This radical declaration', comments Père Clément, 'comes from the Patriarch himself. It met, by anticipation, the demand of a theologian from Constantinople for the disappearance of the 'Uniates' as a condition of Union. . . . It indicates the temporary role of the Greek Catholic Church as a Church distinct from the rest of Eastern Orthodoxy.'[2] This seems to be confirmed by the Decree on the Eastern Catholic Churches, which says at the end: 'The sacred council feels great joy in the fruitful zealous collaboration of the Eastern and Western Catholic Churches and at the same time declares: All these directives are laid down in view of the present situation till such time as the Catholic Church and the separated Eastern Churches come together into complete unity.'[3]

Meanwhile the effect of the Eastern Catholic Churches in the predominately Western Church can hardly be overestimated. Contacts with the Orthodox are apt to be rare, and although there are in the Western Church many who have a deep and even intimate knowledge of Orthodoxy and an even deeper sympathy and affection towards it, nevertheless they remain somewhat 'specialists', and their publications which absolutely speaking are many, reach comparatively few. At the Council this was to a considerable extent changed, especially by the liturgical celebrations each morning in St Peter's. Bishop Thomas Holland of Salford explains how the liturgy became a symbol of a deeper principle:

'It was a providential feature of the First Session that, morning after morning, the Fathers attended the Sacred Mysteries celebrated in the different rites now flourishing in the Church. There, before their eyes, in three dimensions, the unchangeable mystery of the Mass was clothed in a rich variety of forms. This

---

[1] 'The Eastern Role in Christian Reunion', *The Eastern Churches and Catholic Unity*, p. 58.

[2] 'The Voice of the East', *Heythrop Journal*, IV, no. 4 (October 1962), p. 395.

[3] No. 30. Père Georges Dejaifve, in his account of the Third Pan-Orthodox Conference in Rhodes, remarks that 'the decree on the Oriental Churches is far from pleasing Orthodoxy, which is inclined to see in it the canonization by the Roman Church of an institution which they regard as unbearable', *One in Christ*, vol. I, no. 2 (1965), p. 153. The Decree explicitly declares that it refers only to the present situation and hence it does not in any way prejudice the future.

was deliberate: the Holy Father himself, delivering a homily at the Ambrosian Mass on St Charles' Day, quoted Psalm 44 and spoke of the Church as the Queen in her vesture of gold "circumdata varietate". The vesture of gold may be interpreted as the divinely-given mystery she celebrates; the 'surrounding of variety" as the differing forms of speech, music, ceremony in which the mystery is enacted.

'The effect upon the Fathers was profound. One heard them say: "How can we be so narrow in liturgical concessions to the needs of the times when already this rich variety is not only tolerated, but encouraged?" The high point of the experience perhaps was the morning when we heard the drums of Abyssinia throb within the baroque splendours of St Peter's, to the accompaniment of hand-clapped rhythms unknown in the church music of the West.

'I would venture to say that it is in these terms that gradually the first duty of the Fathers has dawned collectively upon them: in the recognition that their task is to render all the ecclesiastical forms in which the unchangeable realities are transmitted, more flexible, more adaptable to the needs and the genius of different peoples. The Council has meant a face-to-face encounter with the principle of variety-in-unity; it has forced upon the Fathers the realization that this is the ideal and the decisions of the Council must vigorously display and extend it.'[1]

B. SOME GENERAL CHARACTERISTICS OF ORTHODOXY

The Orthodox Archbishop Michael, in the United States, described Orthodoxy as follows:

'When we speak of the Orthodox Church, by this term we mean, first, those churches founded by the Apostles themselves or the disciples of the Apostles, and which have remained in full communion with one another. Secondly, those churches which have derived their origin from the missionary activity of the former, or which were founded by separation without loss of communion. To the first class belong the four Patriarchates of Constantinople, of Alexandria, of Antioch, of Jerusalem, and

[1] 'Ecumenism at the Council', *Eastern Churches Quarterly*, XV, 1–2 (1963), pp. 12–13.

the Church of Cyprus. To the second class belong: (1) the Church of Sinai; (2) the Church of Russia; (3) the Church of Greece; (4) the Church of Jugoslavia; (5) the Church of Rumania; (6) the Church of Georgia; and (7) the Church of Poland. All the enumerated Churches are independent in their own administration and, at the same time, in full communion with one another. All these Churches, although independent of each other, have the same faith, the same dogmas, the same Apostolic Traditions, the same sacraments, the same services and the same liturgies. There is no significance for the Orthodox people of all these Churches in the ecclesiastical authority to which they give allegiance. The only essential for them is the Orthodox Church, to which they attach great importance.'[1]

It is significant that Archbishop Michael refers first to the apostolic origins, Jerusalem by St James—or by the apostles collegially(?)—Antioch by St Peter, Alexandria, according to an ancient tradition, by St Mark; to the missionary expansion of Orthodoxy into Russia and into the other countries mentioned; and to unity of faith without administrative unity.[2]

[1] I owe this reference to an article by Thaddaeus F. Horgan, 'A General View of Orthodoxy', in *At-one-ment*, Washington, D.C., 1961, p. 26. Bishop Michael omits to mention the Churches of Albania, Cyprus, Finland and Japan. The Orthodox was found mainly in the 'Near East', Egypt, Palestine, Syria, Lebanon, Jordan, Turkey; the Balkans, Jugoslavia, Rumania, Bulgaria, Greece, Albania, Crete, Cyprus; and in Russia, Georgia, Poland, Hungary, Czechoslovakia and Finland. Emigrant members of these Churches now live in many countries of Europe and North and South America. The number of the Orthodox is impossible to ascertain exactly; in Russia, the figure is put at between 20 and 30 million, though before the revolution in 1917 the Orthodox Church was nominally 90 million. All told, the Orthodox today are estimated as numbering between 170 and 200 million. In the United States there were in 1958 some 3 million, and the others in different parts of Europe, Canada, South America, Australia may amount to half a million. I refrain from giving references here.

[2] On p. 159 are listed books in which bibliographies of the Orthodox Church may be found; to these may be added: M. J. Le Guillou, *The Spirit of Eastern Orthodoxy*, London, 1962, and *Mission et Unité, les exigences de la communion*, Paris, 1960; J. Meyendorff, *The Orthodox Church*, London, 1965; A. Schmemann, *The Historical Road of Orthodoxy*, New York, 1963; on recent developments in Greece, P. Hammond, *The Waters of Marah*, London, 1956, and Père G. Dejaifve, 'The Revival in the Greek Orthodox Church', *Eastern Churches Quarterly*, XXX (1957), pp. 458–67. On Russian missions, cf. S. Bolshakoff, *The Foreign Missions of the Russian Orthodox Church*, London, 1943, and, as regards North America, M. Lacko, 'The Churches of Eastern Rite in North America', *Unitas*, XVI (Summer, 1964), pp. 90–102. A brief but most valuable sketch is the booklet of Joseph Gill, S.J. and Edmund Flood, O.S.B., *The Orthodox. Their Relations with Rome*, London, 1964. For a Catholic student this booklet is perhaps the best introduction.

Indivisible Unity

An indivisible unity is a concept specially characteristic of the Orthodox Church, that is, unity in doctrine, liturgy and spirituality. This is manifest from the Declaration of the Orthodox Delegation to the Second Assembly of the World Council of Churches concerning Faith and Order, at Evanston, Ohio, August 1954:

'The Orthodox conception of church unity implies a twofold agreement:

'(*a*) The whole of the Christian Faith should be regarded as one indivisible unity. It is not enough to accept just certain particular doctrines, basic as they may be in themselves, e.g. that Christ is God and Saviour. It is compelling that all doctrines as formulated by the Ecumenical Councils, as well as the totality of the teaching of the early, undivided Church, should be accepted. One cannot be satisfied with formulas which are isolated from the life and experience of the Church. They must be assessed and understood within the context of the Church's life. From the Orthodox viewpoint, reunion of Christendom with which the World Council of Churches is concerned can be achieved solely on the basis of the total, dogmatic Faith of the early, undivided Church without either subtraction or alteration. We cannot accept a rigid distinction between essential and non-essential doctrines, and there is no room for comprehensiveness in the Faith. On the other hand, the Orthodox Church cannot accept that the Holy Spirit speaks only through the Bible. The Holy Spirit abides and witnesses through the totality of the Church's life and experience. The Bible is given to us within the context of Apostolic Tradition in which in turn is the authentic interpretation and explication of the Word of God. Loyalty to the Apostolic Tradition safeguards the reality and continuity of church unity.

'(*b*) It is through the Apostolic Ministry that the mystery of Pentecost is perpetuated in the Church. The Episcopal Succession from the Apostles constitutes an historical reality in the life and structure of the Church and one of the pre-suppositions of her unity through the ages. The unity of the Church is preserved through the unity of the Episcopate. The Church is one

Body whose historical continuity and unity is also safeguarded by the common faith arising spontaneously out of the fullness (*pleroma*) of the Church.'[1]

Similar statements have often been made by the Orthodox.[2]

The Holy Tradition, in Orthodox belief, is the living continuity of the Church's life, guided by the Holy Spirit. In the Section on Scripture, Tradition and Traditions of the Faith and Order Conference at Montreal in 1963, the Orthodox view was that 'Tradition includes an understanding of the events recorded in the New Testament, of the writings of the Fathers, of the ecumenical creeds and Councils, and of the life of the Church throughout the centuries'.[3] A more detailed list of the principal forms of Tradition was given by Professor Chrysostomos Konstantinidis, of the Theological School of Halki, Istanbul: (1) the valid and authentic interpretation of Scripture; (2) the official formulations and confessions of faith; (3) the formulations, definitions and creeds of the Ecumenical Councils; (4) the larger accords of the teaching of the Fathers and ecclesiastical authors, in other words, the *Consensus Patrum*; the forms, acts and institutions of worship and liturgies of the early Church, which form the living expression of the apostolic spirit in the ways of worship in the Church. Everything which remains outside these forms of the *depositum* of the faith of the Church, can be a tradition in the Church, but it cannot be Tradition of dogma and saving faith; it is not the Holy Tradition.'[4]

[1] Bell, *Documents on Christian Unity*, 4, London, 1958, pp. 42–3.

[2] On the statement made at New Delhi in 1961, but, through some misunderstanding not printed in the Report, cf. M. J. Le Guillou, 'The Orthodox Church and the World Council', *Eastern Churches Quarterly*, XV, nos. 1–3 (1963), pp. 136–51. At the Faith and Order Conference at Montreal in 1963, the Orthodox made no separate statement, but their position on Tradition was briefly put, cf. p. 58 of the Montreal *Report*, 1964.

[3] *Report*, p. 58. Earlier in the Report it was said: 'For the first time in the Faith and Order dialogue, the Eastern Orthodox and other Eastern Churches have been strongly represented in our meetings. A new dimension of Faith and Order has been opened up, and we only begin to see its future possibilities. It is clear that many of our problems of communication have arisen from an imperfect understanding of the Eastern Churches to be found even among scholars of the West, and vice versa, p. 56.

[4] 'The Significance of the Eastern and Western Traditions within Christendom', *Orthodoxy. A Faith and Order Dialogue*, Geneva, 1960, p. 66. Cf., also, Fr G. Florovsky, 'The Function of Tradition in the Ancient Church', an offprint from *The Greek Theological Review*, IX, no. 2 (Winter, 1963–4), pp. 181–200. Cf., also, the essays of Fr Florovsky and of the late Fr S. Bulgakov in *The Church of God: An Anglo-Russian*

The Orthodox accept seven Ecumenical Councils: Nicaea I, in 325; Constantinople I, in 381; Ephesus, in 431; Chalcedon, in 451; Constantinople II, in 553; Constantinople III, in 681 and Nicaea II, in 787. Local Councils have an authority which needs careful appraisal. Such, for instance, are the Council of Jassy in Rumania, which in 1643 approved the Confession of Peter Moghilia, and the Council of Jerusalem (also known as the Council of Bethlehem), which in 1672 ratified the Confession of Dositheus, Patriarch of Jerusalem; both are regarded as at least inadequate by some Orthodox because of their dependence on Latin sources.[1]

Different liturgical forms and languages

These are considered by the Orthodox as perfectly consistent with the wholeness of unity and with the Holy Tradition. Sometimes the same forms are used with different languages, sometimes the language is the same but the form different. St Cyril (d. 869) and St Methodius (d. 885) translated the Scriptures and the Liturgy into the Slavonic language, and in spite of the objection of the Germanic bishops, Pope Hadrian II gave full approval.[2]

The twelve principal feasts of the Church are: (1) The Nativity of the Virgin Mary, Mother of God (*Theotokos*), 8th September; (2) The Presentation in the Temple, 21st November; (3) The Annunciation, 25th March; (4) The Nativity of

Symposium by Members of the Society of the Fellowship of St Alban and St Sergius, ed. by E. L. Mascall, London, 1934.

[1] *The Acts and Decrees of the Synod of Jerusalem* were translated into English by J. N. W. B. Robertson and published in London, 1899.

[2] The term 'rite' does not refer merely to liturgy. In Catholic canon law it is defined: 'A Rite is a group of faithful who are governed by laws and customs of their own, based on ancient traditions not only in regard to liturgical matters, but also in respect to canonical order, which group is acknowledged by the Holy See as autonomous and distinct from others.' E. Herman, *De ritu in Jure Canonico*, Orientalia Periodica, XXXII (1933), p. 339, and cf. V. J. Pospishil, *Code of Oriental Canon Law. The Law of Persons*, Ford City, Pa., U.S.A., 1960, p. 9. Omitting the reference to the Holy See, this definition applies also, in general, to the Orthodox. Among the Orthodox, an autocephalous Church is one subject to no jurisdiction outside itself; an autonomous Church is self-governing but acknowledges the jurisdiction of a patriarch or other hierarch outside itself. The Liturgy used by the Orthodox Churches is the Byzantine, sometimes with minor variations. The liturgies used by the 'Non-Chalcedonian' Churches not in communion with the main Orthodox Church, are the Chaldean, the Armenian, the Coptic (and Ethiopian), and the Syrian. On the derivation of these liturgies, cf. I. H. Dalmais, O.P., *Introduction to the Liturgy*, London, 1961, pp. 79–194.

our Lord, 25th December; (5) His Presentation in the Temple, 2nd February; (6) The Epiphany, 6th January; The Transfiguration, 6th August; (8) Palm Sunday; (9) The Ascension; (10) Pentecost; (11) The Assumption, or the Falling asleep of the Mother of God, 15th August; (12) Easter is the main feast, standing above all others.

Devotion to the Mother of God

Eastern liturgies are marked by a strong sense of the unity of the whole Church, living and dead, and, as can be seen from the list of feasts, by great devotion to the Mother of God. The Decree makes mention of this:

'In their liturgical worship, the Christians of the East pay high tribute, in beautiful hymns of praise, to Mary ever Virgin, whom the ecumenical Synod of Ephesus solemnly proclaimed to be the holy Mother of God, so that Christ might be acknowledged as being truly Son of God and Son of Man, according to the Scriptures.'

Indeed long before the Council of Ephesus (431), the Theologian among the Greek Fathers, St Gregory of Nazianzus, writing about the year 382, made the dogma of Mary's motherhood the pivot of the Church's teaching about the Incarnation:

'If anyone does not believe that Saint Mary is the Mother of God (*theotokos*), he is severed from the Godhead. If anyone should assert that he passed through the Virgin as through a channel, and was not at once divinely and humanly formed in her (divinely, because without the intervention of a man; humanly, because in accordance with the laws of gestation), he is in like manner godless. If any assert that the manhood was formed and afterwards was clothed with the Godhead, he too is to be condemned. For this would not be a generation of God, but a shirking of generation. If any introduce the notion of two Sons, one of God the Father, the other of the mother, and discredits the unity and identity, may he lose his part in the adoption promised to those who believe aright. . . . If anyone assert that his flesh came down from heaven, that is, not from hence, nor of us but above us, let him be anathema. . . . If anyone put his trust in him as a man without a human mind, he is really bereft of mind himself, and quite unworthy of salvation. For that which he has not assumed he has not healed; but what which is united to his Godhead is also saved.'[1]

This letter was a guide to the Fathers of the Councils of Ephesus, A.D. 481, and of Chalcedon, A.D. 481, and give the basic conviction that recognition of the place of the Virgin Mary in the dispensation of salvation is the greatest protection against doubts about Christ's true Godhead and against any etherializing of Christ's true manhood.

There are in all the Eastern Liturgies many invocations to the Mother of God, the general titles used being 'our all-holy, immaculate, most blessed and glorified Lady, Mother of God and ever-Virgin Mary'. In the Liturgy of St John Chrysostom, used in the Byzantine Rite on certain feasts, she is reverenced as 'the most exalted among God's creatures, more honourable than the Cherubim, incomparably more glorious than the Seraphim.'[2]

Steadfastness

The steadfastness of the Eastern Churches to the faith, and the sufferings they have endured and are still enduring because of that steadfastness, are mentioned briefly in the Decree (no. 14, par. 2). To give any adequate account of this is here impossible; but I cite Archbishop Peter K. Medawar: 'The misfortunes of the centuries imposed harsh trials on the apostolic churches of the East. There were the Persian, Arab, Seljuk, crusader, Mongol and Turkish invasions, with civil wars, feudal clashes and many other disturbances.' To describe all these would need a lengthy history. The Archbishop adds a note about the crusaders:

[1] Letter 101, cited by Johannes Quasten in vol. III of his *Patrology*, Utrecht/ Antwerp, and Westminster, Maryland, 1960, p. 253. The translation is from *A Select Library of Nicene and Post-Nicene Fathers of the Christian Church*, ed. by Philip Shaff and H. Wace, Oxford, 1893.

[2] Cf. M. Gordillo, *Mariologia Orientalis*, no. 141 of *Orientalia Christiana Analecta*, Rome, 1954, on the Byzantine Liturgy, pp. 44–6. On the famous hymn, used in the East somewhat as we use the *Te Deum*, cf. the translation by Donald Attwater, *The Akathistos Hymn*, London, 1934; and on the Latin translations, dating from the ninth century, cf. G. G. Meerssemann, *Der Hymnus Akathistos in Abendland*, Freiburg (Switzerland), vol. I, 1958, vol. 2, 1960. Hilda Graef, in her *Mary: A History of Doctrine and Devotion*, vol. I, London, 1963, gives a brief summary, explaining that poetic exuberance is not meant to be taken as exact theology, pp. 127–9. On Eastern devotion to the Mother of God, cf. Timothy Ware, *The Orthodox Church*, op. cit., pp. 258–65.

'The reader must not be surprised that we name the crusades at the same time as the wars provoked in our countries by non-Christian nations, which ended by weakening Christians and their patriarchates. Whatever were the intentions of the crusaders, and exception must be made for the spiritual, moral and material benefit which would have accrued here and there, the practical result of the crusades in the East was on the one hand to confirm the hatred between the Moslems and the Christians, and on the other hand to increase the ill-feeling between the Byzantines of the Orient and the Latins of the West, because of numerous injustices committed by the crusaders against the Byzantines, which contributed to weaken the Christians of the East in the face of Islam. In that, the expeditions of the crusaders resemble other invasions.'[1]

Much has been written about the sufferings of Eastern Christians behind the 'iron curtain' in the struggle against an atheistic onslaught. The history is complicated, for conditions and actions differed much at different times and in different regions.[2] Exact statistics and accurate accounts are difficult to secure. It is clear, however, that up to recent times our Orthodox brethren have suffered, in the U.S.S.R. and in allied countries, arrests, imprisonments, deportations and executions. In 1918 and 1919 about twenty-eight bishops were killed; between 1919 and 1926 some fifty more were murdered, and it is said that some 2,700 priests, 2,000 monks and 3,400 nuns were killed. Some writers have estimated that since 1917, among priests alone, at least 12,000 were executed or died through ill-treatment.[3] Churches, monasteries and church plate were confiscated. In Moscow before the revolution there were 600

---

[1] 'The Rights of the Eastern Church', *The Eastern Churches and Catholic Unity*, edited by Maximos IV Saigh, Patriarch of Antioch, London, 1963, p. 134. It is almost impossible to exaggerate the effect upon the Eastern mind of the sack of Constantinople by the crusaders in 1204, especially of the sacrileges committed in the church of the Holy Wisdom; this is a constant theme among all who discuss the schism between East and West.

[2] I rely upon Kenneth Scott Latourette, *Christianity in a Revolutionary Age*, vol. I, 'The Twentieth Century in Europe', London, 1962, chapters XIX and XX; Walter Kolarz, *Religion in the Soviet Union*, London, 1961; Donald Attwater, *The Christian Churches of the East*, vol. II, 'Churches not in communion with Rome', London, 1961; and Timothy Ware, *The Orthodox Church*, 1964. Inevitably these accounts refer to past history and judgements based upon them should be applied only with caution to present conditions.

[3] Ware, op. cit., p. 156; Latourette, pp. 495, 497.

Orthodox churches; in 1958 there were, including the suburbs, only fifty-five. In Georgia, of the pre-revolutionary 2,455 churches, only a hundred remain, including eleven in Tiflis.[1] Many seminaries were closed. There were campaigns of calumny against the clergy, attempts to spread disunion in the Church by support of dissident groups, the 'Living Church' being an example. There was systematic intellectual and cultural starvation by denial of Christian literature; attempts to bribe the clergy in subtle ways, infiltration of spies into ecclesiastical circles; and, by no means to be underrated, the general materialistic atmosphere, such as affected many Western Christians. This is the barest outline.

In spite of all this, the Orthodox Church in Russia has survived and 30 million is a conservative estimate of its practising members. Whatever may be said of the relations of the Church with the State, the doctrinal faithfulness of the Russian Orthodox has never been questioned.

Kolarz, speaking of the 1922 attack on the Orthodox Church, makes an observation which seems of general application:

'Seen in retrospect, it seems almost a miracle that the Russian Orthodox Church did not disintegrate and that after à time of bitter trial it was able to reassemble the scattered sheep and rebuild the framework of its organization. All prerequisites for its annihilation seemed in being. The assets which the Soviet régime held when fighting the Church were not only superior material power but also superior tactical skill, in which many ecclesiastical leaders were lacking. The Soviet régime succeeded in falsifying the issues and manœuvred the Church into a position where it did not appear to be fighting for the defence of the faith against unbelief but for the retention of church property with the help of which the Government wanted to feed the the starving population.'[2] The survival of the Orthodox Churches, with the full integrity of their doctrinal tradition, is, indeed, little less than a miracle, and must be attributed to special graces from God.

The charge is sometimes made that the Orthodox hierarchy has appeared to not a few as merely a tool of the Soviet govern-

---

[1] Kolarz, pp. 80, 105.   [2] Op. cit., p. 38.

ment.[1] Care should be taken before accepting this charge. Donald Attwater speaks of criticisms of the Patriarch Sergius (d. 1944), and of the present Patriarch, Alexis, elected in February 1945, and goes on:

'He (Alexis) has been widely accused of allowing himself to be used by an atheistic government for its own ends, of making extravagant professions of civil allegiance, denouncing the Pope and fellow Christians of the West, and all the rest of it, in return for concessions to his church. It is too simple a way of looking at a highly complex and delicate situation, one about which "outsiders" are emphatically not qualified to make a final judgement. Alexis has to serve his flock as seems best to him, whatever mistakes he may make, or appear to make in the process. Nor, indeed, has his attitude towards the régime been wholly passive and "conformist": witness his public speech in February 1960, when he expounded to an astonished audience in the Kremlin how much the Russian people owed to the Orthodox Church in the past, and this just after he had announced the excommunication of the apostate priest Ossipov, a man who had been enthusiastically taken up by the propagandists of atheism!'[2]

On 30th December, 1959, the Holy Synod of the Russian Orthodox Church issued a courageous decree which amounted to a wholesale excommunication of all apostates who had supplied anti-religious and anti-clerical material to the communists and who thus committed 'public acts of blasphemy.'[3]

It should not be forgotten that Catholic bishops and administrators, particularly the younger ones, have used all the clichés of the régime about 'Anglo-American warmongers', 'the Anglo-American imperialists and their henchmen', and have praised 'the achievements of the democratic states, led by the Soviet Union'. 'A particularly obnoxious statement by a leading Catholic Church dignitary was published soon after the Hungarian revolution. It condemned the Anglo-French Israeli aggression in Egypt whilst at the same time denouncing Western "slander" about Hungary.'[4]

[1] Cf. J. Meyendorff, *The Orthodox Church*, London, 1965, pp. 135 ff.
[2] Op. cit., p. 63.
[3] Kolarz, op. cit., p. 71.
    Kolarz, op. cit., p. 209.

Such statements, both by Orthodox and Catholics, need not be attributed solely to desire to protect the Church; churchmen, as others, are affected mentally by nationalistic feelings and by the presentation of news which is available to them.[1]

The emigration from Russia

The emigration from Russia after the revolution had one incidental good effect, that of making far better known the Orthodox doctrine and outlook. The Theological Institute of St Sergius, Paris, became famous for its theologians; a list of books and articles published by teachers at the Institute between 1925 and 1947 runs to ninety-two pages, and includes seventy full-scale books.[2] St Vladimir's Seminary in New York is the centre of an active intellectual life, the review *St Vladimir's Seminary Quarterly* enjoying well-merited esteem.[3]

Other emigration, mainly though not exclusively, to America, which may have reached the number of five million or thereabouts, presented and still presents problems of various kinds. The emigrants were of different nationalities, Albanian, Bulgarian, Greeks, Byelorussians, Russians, Rumanians, Carpo-Russians, Serbians, Ukranians, and, from the non-Chalcedonian Churches, Armenians and Syrians. Usually, at the beginning especially, these groups depended jurisdictionally upon the authorities of the countries from which they came; and in some cases this has been retained, so that there are at least eight groups dependent upon the Old Patriarchates or Archbishoprics, while others have become independent. In 1960 was formed the Standing Conference of the Canonical Orthodox Bishops. The President changes each year, being elected in turn from the different jurisdictions. There is a permanent secretary, and eleven commissions to deal with such matters as relations

---

[1] I omit more than a reference to the sad and complicated history of the Greek Catholic Church of the Ukraine and its incorporation into the Orthodox Church; cf. Kolarz, op. cit., pp. 227–44. Kolarz's book is certainly ecumenical in that he considers the position of all religions in the Soviet Union, and is particularly sympathetic to the Lutherans, Baptists and Jews.

[2] Cf. Ware, op. cit., p. 186.

[3] Much bibliographical matter will be found in *Re-Discovering Eastern Christendom*, op. cit. The essay by Irene Posnoff, 'Roman Catholics and Ecumenism in the Twentieth Century', throws light on little-known aspects of the relations between Catholicism and Orthodoxy.

with other churches, education, College work, youth movements, scouting, liturgical texts, missionary enterprises and
fund-raising. In 1963 the Russian Church announced that it
was prepared to concede autocephaly to an American Church;
and it looks as if an American Orthodox Church would be the
ultimate outcome, although ties with the countries of origin are
still strong.[1] Archbishop Jakovos, who acts—at least often—as
spokesman for the Patriarch of Constantinople (the Ecumenical
Patriarch), and who has some 1,200,000 faithful and 386
parishes under him, carries considerable weight, perhaps
especially with non-Orthodox.[2]

In 1960 Fr Alexander Schmemann wrote as follows:

'The fateful "jurisdictional divisions" in the Russian Church
outside Russia are ultimately rooted in the question of ecclesiastical *submission* to the various "supreme authorities", i.e. to
the question of primacy. . . . The development of Church life in
America is deeply handicapped by the absence of any connection between the ten national jurisdictions, which for lack of *a
centre of communion* are practically isolated from one another.
Here also the question of primacy, and consequently, of an
initiative of "rapprochement" is quite central.'[3]

The Pan-Orthodox Conferences at Rhodes

The first of these took place in October 1961, for the purpose
of planning a Pro-Synod of the whole Orthodox Church. Official observers from the 'non-Chalcedonian' churches were present; and Père C. Dumont, O.P. (who is an honorary Archimandrite), Fr A. Wenger, A.A. editor of *La Croix*, as also the
editors of the periodicals *Irenikon, Proche Orient Chrétien*, and *Una
Sancta*, were guests of the Patriarch Athenagoras[4]. The Con-

---

[1] The book by Alexander A. Bogolepov, *Towards an American Orthodox Church*,
New York, 1963, was favourably reviewed by Professor Nicholas Arseniev in *St
Vladamir's Seminary Quarterly*, vol. 8, no. 1 (1964), p. 50.
[2] Cf. Michael Lacko, 'The Churches of Eastern Rite in North America', *Unitas*,
XVI (Summer, 1964), pp. 79–102, and the tables annexed; Timothy Ware, op.
cit., pp. 181–93; D. Attwater, op. cit., II, pp. 131–42. Fr Lacko takes account of
the special number devoted to the problems in *St Vladimir's Seminary Quarterly* in
1961.
[3] *St Vladimir's Seminary Quarterly*, IV, nn. 2–3 (1960), pp. 71–2. Cf., also, Professor
Schmemann's, 'Problems of Orthodoxy in America', ibid., VIII, no. 2 (1964),
pp. 67–84.
[4] John F. Long S.J. was present as a correspondent and wrote an account of the

ference placed relations with the Roman Church on the *agenda*
of the future Pro-Synod and approved study of these relations in
the meantime.

The second Conference was brief, for three days in September
1963, and left the question of observers at the Vatican Council
to the decision of the individual Churches, but approved in
principle future 'dialogue' with the Roman Church.

The third took place 1st–15th of November 1964, and after a
considerable discussion, decided that dialogue between the
Orthodox Church as a whole and the Church of Rome should
take place only after due preparation had been made and
appropriate conditions created. Each of the local Orthodox
Churches was left free to cultivate fraternal relations with the
Church of Rome, and, indeed, 'the Third Pan-Orthodox Conference asks our local Churches to study the details of the dialogue from the Orthodox point of view and to exchange between themselves the results of their studies as well as any other
relevant information'.[1] But as regards dialogue with the Anglican Church and the Old Catholic Church, the Conference decided on the immediate formation of Inter-Orthodox Commissions to prepare the subjects for discussion on the basis of previous discussions, and to arrange dates of meetings.

Various conjectures have been made at this caution in
arranging dialogue with Rome.[2] Père Dumont, however, takes
the decision at its face value and indicates that the Orthodox
regard conversations with Rome at an official level as a grave
matter.[3] At the time of the third Rhodes Conference the Vatican
Council had not published the Constitution on the Church nor

Conference in *Unitas* (Winter, 1961). The proposed subjects for the Pro-Synod
were, almost as numerous as those for the Vatican Council, and the general headings were: 1. Faith, Dogma and Liturgy; 2. Administration and government; 3.
Relations of Orthodox Churches with one another; 4. Social problems; 5. Relations of the Orthodox with separated Churches both in the East and in the West.
Cf. Père Dumont, *Vers l'Unité Chrétienne*, Nov-Dec 1961, pp. 97–100, and Jan-Feb
1962, pp. 1–9. The sub-divisions of the main themes present a formidable list and
considerable preparation was obviously needed.

[1] G. Dejaifve, S.J., who was present on behalf of the Secretariat for Unity, published an account in *One In Christ*, I, no. 2 (1965), pp. 140–56, in which the formal
decisions are listed on p. 151–2. Pères Dumont and Wenger were again present as
guests of the Ecumenical Patriarch; but no observers were invited, and a good deal
of the discussions were private.

[2] Cf. Dejaifve, art. cit., *passim*.

[3] Cf. *Vers l'Unité Chrétienne*, Jan-Feb 1965, pp. 1–4, especially pp. 3–4.

the Decrees on Ecumenism or on the Eastern Catholic Churches, much less the determinations relative to the bishops, the proposed episcopal Senate or the status of episcopal regional or national Conferences. Moreover, the distinction between 'dialogue' and 'negotiations' is fine, and may not have been understood by the Orthodox faithful, not to mention the clergy. Further, the proceedings of the Vatican Council had shown the practical difficulties in attaining general agreement, even in a Church so homogeneous as the Catholic Church. Finally, although the Orthodox have among them many brilliant theologians, nevertheless the sufferings during the last world war, when so many of their countries were invaded and normal life disrupted, interfered with the theological study, and hence it seems reasonable enough that the Orthodox felt the need to concentrate their forces and prepare well before engaging in official conversations which would engage Orthodoxy as a whole. In the minds of some of the participants other reasons may have carried weight, but the need for preparation seems entirely adequate.

Signs of courtesy and charity

The most conspicuous of these and the most fruitful was the pilgrimage of Pope Paul VI to Jerusalem, with his meeting with the Patriarch Athenagoras, with the Greek Orthodox Patriarch of Jerusalem and with the Patriarch of the Armenian Apostolic Church; visits were exchanged, which was a break in the traditional papal protocol. With the exception of Greece, the Orthodox welcomed the meeting as symbolic. Archimandrite Andrei Scrima, a Rumanian, who is Rector of the Orthodox Patriarchal Church in Rome and personal representative of the Ecumenical Patriarch Athenagoras I at the Vatican Council, expressed a very general feeling when he said, a year after the event:

'The Jerusalem meeting has clearly opened a new phase in relations between the Orthodox Church and the Church of Rome, above all because this meeting was truly an act of grace in the Christian sense. The spiritual leaders of the West and East met together; they encountered, first and foremost, Christ at the heart of the Church, in the historic city of Jerusalem which even in its present humble state reminds us of the heavenly Jerusalem—of the ultimate goal of our faith and the transformation of the world by the spirit of Christ.

'Those who were present at the meeting will not forget the absolute sincerity of the two spiritual leaders, both of whom have become symbols. Neither of them sought personal honour, but rather the glory of Christ which follows from the vigour of our renewal and from the unselfish service of our Lord in the form of our neighbours.'[1]

Pope Paul VI, however, though he recognized the symbolic nature of the meeting, was under no illusions. In his address on 25th January 1964, to the diplomatic Corps who had requested an audience to render homage to him after his pilgrimage to the Holy Land, he said:

'We have already said, and are happy to repeat to you, that one of the most moving moments of our entire journey was our meeting with the Patriarch of Constantinople. When we prayed beside him, when we exchanged with him the kiss of peace on the very site where Christ effected the redemption of the world, we were conscious of renewing across the centuries the links of a chain which ought never to have been broken. We were conscious of taking the first steps along the road of a reconciliation which all Christians worthy of the name ardently desire.

'It is a road that is still a long one, and certainly also one beset with obstacles. Prejudices and misunderstandings accumulated in the course of centuries cannot be set aside in a few hours. But to have embarked upon this road, to have made personal contact again after centuries of separation, surely is an augury and a portent of developments which, with God's help, might lead one day to the union that is so desired.'[2]

In September 1964 Cardinal Bea went to Patras to restore the relic of the skull of St Andrew, taken to Rome in 1462. In February 1965 the Metropolitans Meliton of Heliopolis Thyra, and Chrostome of Myre (the latter an old student of the Oriental Institute in Rome) came to Rome to communicate officially the

[1] Interview with a correspondent of the *Herder Correspondence*, II, no. 2 (February 1965), p. 36. For the address made by Pope Paul VI at Bethlehem, cf. Appendix V, p. 273.
[2] Translation from *Herder Correspondence*, I, no. 3 (March 1964), p. 70.

decisions of the third Conference of Rhodes. They were received with the greatest courtesy, and Pope Paul VI declared that he was happy about the wisdom and the realism of the decisions taken at Rhodes, and hoped the informal contacts would gradually develop an atmosphere in which 'the dialogue of charity' could take place. In April 1965 Cardinal Bea went to thank the Patriarch of Constantinople for his message, and his reception was particularly warm, especially on the part of the people. He also addressed the students and Professors of the Theological School at Halki.

In April, shortly after Cardinal Bea had visited the United States, the Standing Committee of the Canonical Orthodox Bishops in America announced that invitations to Roman Catholic theologians to meet with their Orthodox counterparts were acceptable to Cardinal Shehan, Chairman of the Catholic Bishops Commission for Ecumenical Affairs. When the Vatican Council ends, other informal conversations may be expected.

C. THE DEBT OF THE WEST TO THE EAST

The Decree makes special mention of the Western derivations from the Eastern Churches in liturgical practice, spiritual tradition, ecclesiastical law, the definitions of the basic doctrines of the faith, and lastly, to monasticism (cf. n. 14, par. 2, n. 15, par. 4), and 'Catholics are earnestly recommended to avail themselves still more of the spiritual riches of the Eastern Fathers' (n. 15, par. 4).

The inscription on the cross of Christ was written in Hebrew, Greek and Latin, and this is indicative of the three great strands interwoven to form a single though variegated tradition. Of recent times more attention has been paid to the Jewish influence,[1] and this undoubtedly was powerful, especially through the Scriptures. Nevertheless from the second century it was in the East that the major problems inherent in Christian convictions were raised and to a large extent solved: first, the

[1] Cf. J. Daniélou, *The Theology of Jewish Christianity*, London, 1964, and *Message évangelique Culture hellénnistique aux IIe et IIIe siècles*, Tournai, 1960. E. Hatch's Hibbert Lectures for 1888, *The Influence of Greek Ideas upon the Christian Church*, reprinted as a paperback by Herder in 1937, should be compared with C. N. Cochrane's *Christianity and Classical Culture*, Oxford, 1940.

relation of spirit to matter; secondly, the nature of God as one and yet somehow mysteriously three; thirdly, the reality of the Incarnation of the Son of God; and fourthly the manner of human union with God. These solutions were not merely propounded in learned writings, but were embodied in the Christian Calendar and in the Christian liturgy, so that the minds and hearts of even simple people could enter into the Christian mystery.[1]

The Liturgy

After the edict of Milan in 313 by which Christianity became a permitted religion, the influence of the Church of Jerusalem greatly increased, and it is held that the origins of the liturgical year, with its sequence of fasts and feasts recalling the events of our Lord's life, and with different readings from Scripture, are to be sought in the fourth-century usage of the Church of Jerusalem.[2] It is certain that feasts of our Lady were introduced into the Gelasian Sacramentary from the East, the Purification, 2nd February; the Assumption, 15th August; the Annunciation, 25th March, and the Nativity of Mary, 8th September—all in the seventh century; the feast of the Assumption was probably introduced into the West by Theodore, Greek by descent and born in Jerusalem, Pope A.D. 642-9.[3]

The other very obvious derivations from the Greek in our Latin Mass (or, our Mass which used to be Latin), are the *Kyrie Eleison*, the *Gloria in excelsis Deo* and the *Credo*. The *Kyrie* is not a survival from an original Greek liturgy when Greek was the ordinary language at Rome, but was introduced into the Latin liturgy in the fifty century, perhaps by pilgrims who had

[1] On the general influence of the East, cf. G. Bardy, *La Question des Langues dans l'Église Ancienne*, Paris, 1947; P. Courcelle, *Les Lettres grecques en Occident de Macrobe à Cassiodore*, ed. 2, Paris, 1948; and J. de Ghellinck, *Patristique et Moyen Age*, 3 vols., Gemblou, 1946, 1947 and 1948.

[2] Cf. F. Cabrol, 'La Semaine sainte et les origines de l'année liturgique', in *Les Origines Liturgiques*, Paris, 1906; and *The Year's Liturgy*, vol. I, London, 1938, p. xiv. Cabrol's judgement is accepted by E. C. Ratcliff, 'Christian Worship and Liturgy', in *The Study of Theology*, ed. Kenneth E. Kirk, London, 1939, p. 432. On pilgrimages to Jerusalem, which began very early in Christian history, cf. H. Leclercq, 'Pélerinages aux Lieux saints' in *Dictionnaire d'Archaeologie et de Liturgie*, vol. 7, Paris, 1939, cols. 65–175, where all the known pilgrimages are listed in chronological order.

[3] Cf. Hilda Graef, op. cit., I, p. 142, with the references there given.

been in Jerusalem and become familiar with its use there.[1] It is noteworthy that in the East non-Greek liturgies, the Coptic, the Ethiopian and the West Syrian, use the *Kyrie Eleison* untranslated.

The *Gloria in Excelsis Deo* was certainly an Eastern hymn, practically certainly Greek, though conceivably Syrian. The Latin *Liber Pontificalis*, or chronicles of the Church of Rome, in the part written about 530–532, says that Pope Telesophorus (d. *c.* 136), ordered the 'angelic hymn' to be said at midnight Mass at Christmas, a fact which shows that the *Gloria* was in common use in the Roman liturgy in the sixth century. The *Antiphony of Bangor*, which originated about 690, has a version of the *Gloria* which corresponds to that of the Byzantine liturgy in the *Codex Alexandrinus* of the fifth century. Probably the hymn was introduced into the Roman liturgy in the late fourth or early fifty century, though its exact wording may not have been the same as that used today.

There is small doubt that hymnology was introduced into the Roman liturgy through the influence of the East. St Hilary of Poitiers, exiled to Asia Minor from 356 to 359, found there a well-developed church singing; and St Ambrose of Milan by 386 had introduced the antiphonal singing of psalms, making use of Greek tunes, as St Augustine tells us in his *Confessions* (9, 7). Writing about the year 375, the anonymous 'Ambrosiaster', tells us that people of his time used sometimes to sing in Greek, even though they did not understand the words, merely because the tune delighted them.[2]

Ignatius of Antioch, martyred about 110, shows that Greek poetic forms exercised a strong influence in Christian poetry; in his letter to the Ephesians a hymnodic style seems evident:

> 'There is one physician
> Of flesh and of spirit,
> Generate and ingenerate,
> God in man, true life in death,

[1] J. A. Jungmann, *The Mass of the Latin Rite. Its Origin and Development*, tr. Francis A. Brunner, New York, 1950, vol. I, pp. 353–46.

[2] Cf. G. Bardy, 'Formules liturgiques grecques à Rome au IV siècle', *Recherches de Science Religieuse*, XXX (1940), pp. 108–13. Even in the sixth century some Greek was sung at Arles, and the church was crowded to hear it, Bardy, *ibld.*, p. 111, n. 1.

> Son of Mary and Son of God,
> First passible, then impassible,
> Jesus Christ our Lord.'[1]

Clement of Alexandria (d. before 215), composed hymns to Christ; morning and evening hymns are found in the *Apostolic Constitutions*, probably composed in Syria about 380, and not a few old Christian prayers and hymns have come to light in Egypt of comparatively recent years. St Ephraem of Syria (d. 373) composed most of his writing in metrical forms. His poems were translated into Greek and Latin and had wide circulation.[2] It is certainly not too much to say that through the East a poetic element entered the Church and had its effect upon the liturgy.[3]

The *Credo* is the so-called Nicaeno-Constantinopolitan Creed, that is, the creed of the Council of Nicaea in 325 as enlarged by the Council of Constantinople in 381, and as approved by the Councils of Ephesus in 431 and of Chalcedon in 451.[4] By the year 536 it was customary in Constantinople to recite this creed in the Liturgy, and its use spread throughout the East after an ordinance of the Emperor Justin II issued in 568. But up to the year 589 no creed had been recited in any of the Latin liturgies. In that year, however, the third Council of Toledo, under the influence of Reccared, king of the Visigoths, ordered the creed to be chanted by the congregation 'according to the use of the Eastern churches'.[5] From Spain the usage spread to Ireland, since it is found in the famous Stowe Missal, which was written in the first decade of the ninth century and

---

[1] Translation, Lightfoot, *Apostolic Fathers*, revised text, London, 1907, p. 139.

[2] Cf. J. Kirchmeyer, art. 'Ephrem' in *Dictionaire de Spiritualité Ascétique et Mystique*, vol. iv, Paris, 1906, cols. 902–822. Ephraem was cited in Greek as early as the sixth century, and in Latin a little later, though unfortunately much was interpolated and much falsely attributed to him.

[3] Cf. Jungmann, *The Mass of the Roman Rite*, vol. I, pp. 346–59. The Council of Toledo in 633 defended the use of hymns in the liturgy, recalling that after the Last Supper Christ and his Apostles sang a hymn, Mt 26: 30, and that St Paul commends canticles in Eph 5: 1–9. The brevity of Jungmann's note 3 on p. 347 might leave the impression that the Council of Toledo disapproved hymn-singing, whereas the contrary is the case. The scholarly researches of Dr Egon Wellesz have thrown much light on the matter of church music, cf. his *The Christian Chant*, London, 1963. I regret that I have not been able to see his book *Eastern Elements in Western Chant*.

[4] Cf. J. N. D. Kelly, *Early Christian Creeds*, London, 1950, chapter X, pp. 296–331.

[5] Mansi IX, 992 ff.

indicates that the custom of reciting the creed at Mass was well established in the eighth century. From Ireland the usage spread to England, and thence to Aachen and the Carolingian Empire during the eighth century. Probably Alcuin and St Paulinus of Aquileia agreed that the use of this creed was the best means of crushing the Adoptionist heresy, which held Christ to be the adopted and not the natural Son of God; and its position after the Gospel and before the Offertory may well have been due to Alcuin's familiarity with the use in the north of England. But it was two hundred years more before the Roman Church adopted the singing of the creed. In 1014 the Emperor Henry II persuaded Pope Benedict VIII to introduce the creed into the Roman Mass.[1]

Apart from the *Kyrie*, the *Gloria* and the *Credo*, it is difficult to establish any direct derivations in the Latin Mass from the Greek, although many attempts have been made to do so.[2] It has been suggested that practically the whole of the Canon of the Roman Mass was derived from Alexandria, and certainly the agreements between the formulation of the prayers in Rome and in Egypt are striking.[3] Nevertheless, as J. H. Strawley says, the influence of the East in the third and fourth centuries was of a much more subtle character than a theory of direct borrowing suggests. 'The growth of pilgrimages to Jerusalem, and the effect of the Arian controversy, with its frequent councils and interchange of ideas and visits between Eastern and Western bishops would contribute to spread a knowledge of the more advanced teaching and practices of the Greek-speaking East among Western Christians.'[4]

Speaking, however, of a later period, between the seventh and eleventh centuries, Fr Jungmann says: 'We dare not overlook the cultural heritage of the Greek Orient which overflowed abundantly during this period into the West, into the Gallo-Frankish part of Europe in particular. It is well-known that from the fourth century the Gallican liturgy, i.e. the liturgy of the whole non-Roman West, presents numerous features which

---

[1] Cf. J. N. D. Kelly, *Early Christian Creeds*, London, 1950, pp. 351–7. On the procession of the Holy Spirit, cf. below, p. 204.
[2] Cf. Jungmann, *The Mass of the Roman Rite*, pp. 49–60.
[3] Cf. the list given by Jungmann in note 25, p. 55.
[4] J. H. Strawley, *The History of the Early Liturgy*, Cambridge, ed. 2, 1947, p. 212.

point to an Oriental origin: the pre-eminence of Epiphany, the system of weekly and yearly fast-days, the veneration of Saturday, the Trishagion (the three-fold *Sanctus*) in the Mass, the Offertory procession, the Kiss of Peace before the Consecration, the Epiclesis—to mention but a few obvious examples. Somewhat later the Oriental Marian feasts and various liturgical practices connected with Palm Sunday and Holy Week appeared in the West.'[1]

General Greek Influence

The New Testament was written wholly in Greek and St Paul wrote all his letters, with the exception of that to the Romans, to Greek-speaking communities. The Greek translation of the Old Testament, made about 250 B.C., or recensions of it, was used by the New Testament authors and by the Church both East and West, up to the time of Origen (d. 253) in the East, and of St Jerome (d. 419) in the West. Of the first thirty bishops of Rome, one-third were Greek or Syrian; and between 643 and 752 twelve of the nineteen bishops of Rome were orientals.

Up to about A.D. 240 Greek was the common language of the Christian community at Rome.[2] But after that date Latin more and more took the place of Greek, as is clear from the evidence of coins and inscriptions. Greek, however, was understood in many parts of the West; St Denis of Alexandria (d. 265) could write in Greek to Popes Stephen (254–7), Sixtus (257–8) and Denis (258–68), and be sure of being understood. Firmilian (d. *c.* 268) could write in Greek to Cyprian. But throughout the fourth century knowledge of Greek in the West became relatively rare. In 428 Nestorius, Patriarch of Constantinople, when

---

[1] *Pastoral Liturgy*, London, 1962. Fr Jungmann says that this book 'is not a complete study but rather the broad outline of a theme which can be expounded only in a greater number of specialized essays', p. 1. One may add that Greek words entered the common Latin of the Church: *baptismus, eleemosyma, episcopus, diaconus, laicus, presbyter, charisma, ecclesia, evangelism, haeresis, schisma, idolum, paralyticus, pascha, pentecostes, pharisaeus, ichthus, diabolus, amartia* (or *hamartia*), *agape, abyssus, prophetia*; all these are cited by R. F. Refoulé, O.P. in his Introduction to Tertullien Traité du Baptême, in *Sources Chrétiennes*, Paris, 1953, p. 55. To this list add *hierarchia, metropolis, synod, liturgia*, and the famous word *oikumenè*, and in recent times, *episcopé*.

[2] The first Roman theologian to use Latin was the heretic Novatian, in a metrical treatise on the Trinity, about A.D. 250. He used several Greek sources: Irenaeus (d. *c.* A.D. 202), Theophilus of Antioch (d. *c.* 200) and Hippolytus (d. 235).

accused of denying the true doctrine of the Incarnation, sent a dossier of his writings to Pope Celestine, but lack of translators caused a delay of over a year in enabling Celestine to make a judgement.[1]

Latin Esteem for the East

In the fourth century, the Latin Fathers of the Church, St Hilary (d. 367), St Ambrose (d. 397), St Jerome (d. 419) and St Augustine (d. 430) drew extensively upon the East for scriptural exegesis, theology and spirituality. St Jerome was possibly a bit caustic when he wrote in 395, about the Latin writers:

'Tertullian (d. *c.* 200) is packed with good things but is very hard to read; the blessed Cyprian (d. 258) is like a pure fountain and is steadily and completely devoted in his exhortations to virtue, but, harassed by the anxieties of persecution, he never had a real interest in Scripture; the saintly Victorinus (d. 304) understood much but could not express himself; Lactantius (d. before 320), though eloquent, is more interested in destroying error than in affirming truth; Arnobius (d. *c.* 306) is confused, uneven and verbose; Hilary (d. 367) mixes gallic artificiality with Greek flourishes, writes in complicated sentences and is unintelligible to most people.'[2]

This is possibly a harsh judgement. Nevertheless it remains true that Hilary, Ambrose and Jerome were incalculably indebted to Eastern writers and part of their greatness consists in the knowledge of the East which they brought to the West.

St Hilary of Poitiers (d. 367), spent four years of exile in Asia Minor (356–60), and his work on the Trinity depends either on St Athanasius or on sources common to them both.[3] He translated and explained the decisions of a number of Eastern Synods for the benefit of the bishops of Gaul and Britain; his treatise on Job depends greatly upon Origen.[4] He has been

[1] Cf. Fr Aloys Grillmeier, *Christ in Christian Tradition from the Apostolic Age to Chalcedon* (*A.D. 451*), trans. J. S. Bowen, London, 1965, pp. 292–3, with the references there given.

[2] *Epistle* 58, n. 10, Migne, *Patres Latini*, 22, 583.

[3] Cf. P. Smulders, *La doctrine trinitaire de S. Hilaire de Poitiers*, Romae, 1944, pp. 289–95.

[4] Cf. Bardy, *La question des langues*, pp. 211–14.

called 'the Athanasius of the West' because of his resistance to Arianism.

St Ambrose of Milan (d. 397) was a good Greek scholar and borrowed extensively from Philo and Origen, from Didymus the Blind of Alexandria, St Basil, St Gregory of Nazianzus, Sts Cyril of Jerusalem, Epiphanius and Athanasius. St Ambrose followed Origen in accepting the threefold sense of scripture, the literal, the moral and the 'allegorical-mystical'. His three booklets on the Holy Spirit were derived from Athanasius, Basil and Didymus, mostly from the last, and this work had considerable influence upon St Augustine's lengthy treatise on the Trinity. The Life of St Ambrose by Paulinus of Milan was translated into Greek and had considerable currency.[1]

Indefatigable Translators

Almost the whole life of St Jerome (347–419), and of his friend Rufinus (345–410) were devoted to the making available to the West the biblical, historical, theological and ascetical literature of the East. St Jerome spent over forty years of his life in the East (373–81 and 385–419) and it is clear he was not alone in thinking that the West needed to profit by the learning and wisdom of the East. Pope Damasus (d. 384) was aware that the old Latin versions of the Bible were discordant and corrupt and asked Jerome to revise them; Augustine begged Jerome to be informed about Greek exegesis and about heresies that arose in the East. The Life of St Antony the hermit by St Athanasius, translated by Evagrius of Antioch in 375, roused in the West the desire to know more about Eastern asceticism and monasticism.

To list all the Greek writings translated by Jerome and Rufinus would make a dull catalogue. But I give the following merely as an indication of their tireless labours:

Jerome translated the whole of the Old and the New Testaments from the original languages, with regard, however, to the Greek Septuagint and the old Latin. Of exegesis, he made Latin versions of some seventy-seven commentaries of Origen,

---

[1] G. Bardy, *La question des langues*, p. 285, n. 3. Cf. F. H. Dudden, *The Life and Times of St Ambrose*, London, 1955, vol. II, p. 556.

and Rufinus no less than one hundred and eight. Jerome's own commentaries depended largely upon the Greeks.[1]

Church History is indebted to Rufinus for a translation of the *Ecclesiastical History* of Eusebius of Caesarea, and to Jerome for a version of Eusebius's *Chronicle*. These works, in their Latin translations, became the sources from which the West learned the history of the early Church, the method of giving sources and the basis of a philosophy of history.

The first Christian treatise on systematic theology, Origen's work *On the Principal Doctrines* (*De Principiis*), written between A.D. 220 and 230, was translated by both Jerome and Rufinus.[2] Rufinus also made versions of nine homilies of St Basil, of some theological letters and nine theological discourses of St Gregory Nazianzus; and a version of the Pseudo-Clementine writings. St Jerome's account of the lives and writings of one hundred and thirty-five religious writers, *De Viris Illustribus*, produced in 392, made known to the West throughout the Middle Ages the achievements of the Eastern scholars and defenders of the faith, and laid the foundations of Patrology. His work was continued by Gennadius of Marseilles (d. *c.* 480), and by St Isidore of Seville (d. 618).

St Augustine (354–430), whose influence on the West was paramount, the greatest of the Latin Fathers, knew the Neo-Platonists,[3] and had read parts of Irenaeus, Athanasius, Didymus, Epiphanius, Gregory of Nazianzus and his namesake of Nyssa, Basil, Eusebius of Caesarea and Chrysostom.[4] Augustine studied Greek to such effect that he was able to translate Epi-

[1] Cf. Bardy, *La question des Langues dans l'Église ancienne*, pp. 271–5; and 'S. Jerôme et la pensée grecque', *Irénikon*, XXVI (1953), pp. 337–62; P. Courcelle, *Les lettres grecques en occident de Macrobe à Cassiodore*, ed. 2, Paris, 1948, pp. 78–115. On Rufinus, cf. F. X. Murphy, *Rufinus of Aquileia, his Life and Works*, Washington, 1945; M. M. Wagner, *Rufinus the Translator. A Study of his Theory and Practice as illustrated in his Version of the Apologetica of Gregory of Nazianzus*, Washington, 1945; Bardy, op. cit., pp. 273–80.

[2] Jerome's is lost and Rufinus's is only doubtfully exact, as he believed the work had been corrupted by interpolations and 'corrected' it. Jerome and Rufinus fell out over Origen.

[3] Experts do not agree how much they influenced him, Cf. *Augustinus Magister*, 'Les sources platoniciennes de l'augustinienisme', vol. II, containing the discussions, 21st–24th September 1954, Paris.

[4] Cf. Courcelle, *Les Lettres grecques en Occident*, Paris, 1948, pp. 137–209; S. Salaville, 'Saint Augustin et l'Orient', *Angelicum*, VIII (1931), pp. 3–23; J. Chevalier, 'Saint Augustin et la pensée grecque, les relations trinitaire', *Collectanea Friburgensia*, XXXIII, Freiburg (Switzerland), 1940.

phanius and to control mistranslations of Chrysostom by the Pelagians. Courcelle in 1948 judged that Augustine used the Greek Fathers only to confirm his own conviction about the faith; but subsequent studies, especially those by Bernold Altaner, suggest that this judgement needs some modification and that Augustine really learned from the Greek Fathers, especially about the Trinity.[1] But it can be said without exaggeration that through Ambrose and Augustine the allegorizing method of interpreting Scripture, especially the first chapters of Genesis, had a permanent effect upon Western writers, perhaps especially upon St Thomas Aquinas.

Monasticism

The Decree makes special mention of this, saying: 'Moreover, in the East are to be found the riches of those spiritual traditions which are given expression especially in monastic life. From the glorious times of the holy Fathers, monastic spirituality flourished in the East, then later flowed over into the Western world, and there provided the source from which Latin monastic life took its rise and has drawn fresh vigour ever since.' (N. 15, par. 4.) The main and undoubted impact of the East upon the West came through the accounts reaching the West of the hermits, monks and nuns in Egypt, Palestine, Syria and Asia Minor. St Athanasius' *Life of St Antony*, written about 357 and shortly afterwards translated into Latin by Evagrius of Antioch, roused many both in East and West to interest in the monastic ideal. Antony's character was singularly attractive: 'calm and composed, manly, intrepid, magnanimous, full of affectionate loyalty to the Church and to the Truth', as Newman puts it. 'His doctrine surely is pure and unimpeachable; his temper is high and heavenly, without cowardice, without gloom, without formality, and without self-complacency. Superstition is abject and crouching, it is full of thoughts of guilt; it distrusts God, and dreads the powers of evil. Antony has nothing of this, being full of holy confidence, divine peace, cheerfulness and valorous-

---

[1] Altaner made careful investigation into Augustine's knowledge of all the Greek Fathers who wrote before or during Augustine's life time; references to Altaner's publications are to be found in his *Patrology*, trans. Hilda Graef, London, 1959, p. 498.

ness.'[1] Antony died in 356, at the age of one hundred and six; he was a hermit, though colonies of other hermits gathered round him and he became their leader and guide.

The founder of the 'cenobitic' or strictly monastic life was St Pachomius, who between 320 and his death in 346 founded eight monasteries for men and two for women. The rule he drew up was translated into Latin by St Jerome in 404, but it was used by St Basil in composing the rule which is still that of most of the Orthodox monasteries. This rule was translated into Latin by Rufinus, and was used by the great St Benedict, the Father of Western monasticism. It was used also by St Benedict of Aniane (d. 821) in his reforms. It is interesting that many prescriptions of the rule concern work; the monks were agricultural workers, tailors, smiths, carpenters, dyers, tanners, shoemakers, copyists, camel drivers, and especially weavers who made mats and baskets from the rushes of the Nile and palm leaves. No one was admitted who could not read; the training and the life were robust, even rugged, and were designed to produce simplicity and humility. Characteristic of much of the literature about these monks is teaching by history, examples and short pithy sayings.

Knowledge of the Eastern monks reached the West through translations of the *Lausiac History* of Palladius (d. 431), which gives personal reminiscences and a series of biographies, for Palladius had known the monks of Egypt, Palestine, Syria and Asia Minor.[2] Rufinus made Latin versions of the anonymous *History of the Monks in Egypt*, given us in English by Helen Waddell as *The Desert Fathers*.[3] Rufinus also translated certain of the works of Evagrius of Pontus, who wrote numerous works which had great influence on Christian piety, and were read by many of the Byzantines, and in the West by John Cassian, founder of the famous monastery at Lerins, in France.

John Cassian, a Scythian, educated at a monastery in Jerusalem, later a favourite pupil of St John Chrysostom, came to Rome in 404 to defend Chrysostom, and remained in the West to found in 415 the monasteries in Marseilles which became

---

[1] *Historical Sketches*, vol. II, new impression, London, 1899, pp. 99 and 111.
[2] It was edited by C. Butler for the Cambridge Texts and Studies, 2 vols., 1889 and 1904.
[3] New York, 1936.

famous both for asceticism and learning. Here Cassian wrote the *Institutes of Monastic Life* and the *Conferences of the Fathers*, a work noteworthy for its concrete examples and illustrations. This last work was commended by St Benedict (d. 547), Cassiodorus (d. 583), St Gregory the Great (d. 604) and John Climacus (d. 649). Western monasticism sprang from Eastern, and its traditions persisted in spite of all the estrangements of later years.[1]

In the fifth, sixth and seventh centuries, when the West was overrun by Huns, Goths, Vandals, Lombards and Franks, peoples fierce, proud and lawless, monasticism was an effective means of inculcating self-control, industry, stability, esteem for learning, and an idealism that looked beyond this world. The early Church had expanded largely through the witness of the martyrs; the monks and nuns gave a new kind of witness, comparable to martyrdom, through their complete dedication to God. As such they fulfilled a special prophetic office in the Church.[2]

England's debt to the East

England was particularly indebted to the East. In 669 Pope Vitalian (d. *c.* 673) sent Theodore of Tarsus to be Archbishop of Canterbury. Theodore was reputed to be one of the most learned men of his time. Fr Philip Hughes, in his *History of the Church, an Introductory Study*,[3] says that Theodore 'brought with him books, equipment, a plan of organization and a live tradition of culture. With Theodore of Tarsus the English Church passes very definitely out of its pioneer stage. His school of Canterbury was to be one of the springs whence flowed the culture of the next two hundred years. . . . The school was delivered from the intellectual sterility that lay over so much of the West.' Theodore died in 690, an old man of nearly ninety. 'Of whatever unity English Catholicism possessed,

[1] St Martin of Tours (d. 397), began monastic life as early as 361, under the influence of St Hilary. The monastery near Marseilles had contacts, often literary, with the Irish monks, who were particularly interested in commentaries on Scripture.
[2] Cf. E. F. Malone, *The Monk and the Martyr*, Washington, 1950; J. E. Stewart, *The Influence of the Idea of Martyrdom in the Early Church*, St Andrews, Scotland, 1957.
[3] London, 1939, vol. 2, 139, pp. 125-7.

of its scholarship and culture, this learned Greek is the undoubted founder.' The tradition of scholarship founded in England by Theodore of Tarsus passed on to the Venerable Bede, author of the *Ecclesiastical History of England*, and through him to Egbert, who founded in 732 the Cathedral school at York, and through him to Alcuin (735–804) who had the reputation of being the greatest scholar of his age. Alcuin became Abbot of the monastic school at Tours and helped on the ecclesiastical reform and revival of learning in the Carolingian age at the end of the eighth and the beginning of the ninth century.

Latin Ignorance of the East

This was real, but should not be exaggerated. There were, indeed, after about the year 450, very few in the West who could speak Greek. At the same time the history of the Ecumenical Councils shows that Popes Celestine in 431, Leo in 481, Vigilius in 553 and Agatho in 681 were able to inform themselves accurately about differences of outlooks and convictions in the East, and that communication between Constantinople, Alexandria and Rome could be free from any misunderstanding in serious matters of faith. Yet it remains true, as the Decree states (n. 14, par. 2), that the basic definitions of the faith regarding the Trinity and the Incarnation were made in the East. Dossiers of testimonies of the Fathers, both in Greek and Latin, provided one means of understanding, and the decisions of the Councils were issued in both languages. But such intercommunications took place, so to speak, at the top level. After the sixth century Latin theologians seem to have had small interest in the East; translations of the Greek Fathers existed in the West, but how far they were read and assimilated is doubtful. The famous eleventh Council of Toledo in 675, which made a most notable profession of faith on the Trinity and the Incarnation, seems to have been derived from not a single Greek Father, though its doctrine is astonishingly like theirs, doubtless because of its reliance upon Hilary, Ambrose and Augustine.[1]

---

[1] Cf. J. Madoz, *Le symbole du XIe concile de Toldeo*, Louvain, 1938, who gives all the derivations, mentioning two from St Athanasius, though these seem indirect.

'Filioque'

The so-called 'Athanasian Creed', also called the *Quicunque Vult*, provides an instance of factual ignorance which was tragic. This 'creed' was composed between 435 and 535, probably in southern France, and the name 'Athanasius' was attached to it by the unknown author. Its doctrine is unexceptional and is an excellent summary of the universal Christian faith. But the words 'and from the Son' were added to the assertion that the Holy Ghost proceeds from the Father. The tragedy is that the whole of the West sincerely believed that this creed was really that of St Athanasius, and believed this for over a thousand years,[1] and hence that the addition 'and from the Son' was really as much a Greek formula as a Latin one. Whenever the Latins urged this authority in discussions or disputes with the Greeks, the latter answered either that the document was not by St Athanasius at all, or else that the 'and from the Son' was a bare-faced Latin interpolation.[2]

In the revival of theological learning in the twelfth century, Latin theologians had small acquaintance with the Greek Fathers. Peter the Lombard, whose *Sententiae* were used as a textbook until the sixteenth century, cites some thirty snippets from John Damascene's *Exposition of the Orthodox Faith*, and a few from St Athanasius, Didymus and St Cyril of Alexandria.[3]

Eastern Mariological influence

There were, however, two notable exceptions to this ignorance of the East in the West. The first regards doctrine and devotion to the Virgin Mother of God. Recent research has established that many preachers and poets from the sixth to the eleventh

[1] J. N. D. Kelly, *The Athanasian Creed*, London, 1964, p. 3.

[2] Cf. Dr Kelly's discussion of 'the Quicunque in the East', pp. 44–8. At the Council of Florence, as far as I can gather from Fr J. Gill's *History*, the Latins did not adduce the *Quicunque*, possibly because they were uncertain of its origin. In any case, the discussions at Florence concerned the addition of the *Filioque* to the Creed of Constantinople I, and the rest of the discussion concerned the correctness of the doctrine. Only in the nineteenth century was it generally accepted in the West that the origin of the *Quicunque* was certainly not to be found in Athanasius but in some Latin source.

[3] Cf. J. de Ghellinck, art. 'Pierre Lombard' in *Dictionaire de Théologie Catholique*, vol. 12, Paris, 1933, col. 1898. John Damascene's work had been translated into Latin about the middle of the twelfth century at the request of Pope Eugene III.

century were translated into Latin and contributed towards
acceptance by the West of the Assumption of the Mother of God
and of a deeper and wider devotion to her. Fr A. Wenger, A.A.
in comparatively recent times discovered several Latin manu-
scripts which were translations from Greek, and in other Latin
writers dependence on the Greeks is obvious. Miss Hilda Graef
has given the substance of the evidence in her *Mary: A History of
Doctrine and Devotion*.[1] To this I add by way of illustration a short
extract from Professor Constantine A. Trypanis, who holds the
chair of Byzantine and Modern Greek Language and Literature
at Oxford, and speaks as follows of the Romanos the Melodist
(*c.* 490–560) and his poem *On the Nativity*:

'The whole *kontakion* culminates in the exquisite prayer of the
Virgin, which is the counterpart of the initial prayer. It is full
of poetic vigour and tenderness. The Virgin is the voice of the
whole world and all God's creation. Here we see at its height
the Byzantine conception of the Virgin as the Mother Protector
of the world, and the mediator for all suffering mankind:

' "I am not only Thy mother, O merciful Saviour,
    nor in vain do I give suck to the Giver of milk;
    But for all men do I supplicate Thee.
    Thou hast made me the mouth and the pride of all
      my race,
    And Thy creation has me as a strong cover,
    a wall and a buttress.
    To me do they look, who are cast out
    Of the Paradise of delight,
    For I shall lead them back
    and they shall see the reason of all things
    through Me, who bore Thee
    a little child, God of all time." '[2]

Christian Mysticism

The Decree, after speaking of monasticism, adds the exhorta-

[1] Op. cit., cf. pp. 134, 165, n. 2, 180. Cf. A. Wenger, *L'Assomption de la très-sainte
Vierge dans la tradition byzantine du VIe au Xe siècle*, Paris, 1955.

[2] *The Orthodox Ethos, Studies in Orthodoxy. Essays in honour of the Centenary of the
Greek Orthodox Archdiocese of North and South America*, ed. A. J. Philippou, Oxford,
1964, p. 191. The whole essay is illuminating, as is that of Bishop Emilianos Timia-
dis entitled 'Byzantine Music', pp. 200–6.

tion: 'Catholics therefore are earnestly recommended to avail themselves still more of the spiritual riches of the Eastern Fathers which lift up the whole man to the contemplation of the divine.' (N. 15, par. 4.) The significant words here are, I think, 'lift the whole man to contemplation of the divine', for they refer to the general doctrine of the Greek Fathers of the 'divinization' of man, and perhaps more specifically to the purely contemplative Greek monks. The literature on this subject is daunting in its immensity, and I give here the most cursory and inadequate, possibly mistaken, account as far as I understand the matter. The Greek ascetics and contemplatives insisted upon the 'purification' of the mind and intellect from all images and conceptualizations, since God must be beyond all human thoughts, hidden in incomprehensibility, ineffability and inexpressibility in any human thinking: that is, the *via negativa*, the denial that God is anything we can imagine or conceptualize, plays an important part in the initiation of contemplation;[1] then through God's gift may come a certain 'nakedness' or stripping of all things created, and finally a union which can only be experienced.[2] Certain of the Greek mystics, however, joined this method of contemplation to a vocal prayer, a repetition of the 'Jesus Prayer'—'Jesus, Son of God, have mercy on me, a sinner'—in such sort that even the body becomes joined in the union with God.[3] This 'Jesus Prayer' was recommended by St John Climacus (d. 649) and entered into the spirituality of most of the monks who devoted themselves to asceticism and prayer.

As far as I can understand this 'hesychasm', or prayer of peace and quiet, the norm taken seems to have been that of the beatification of the whole man after this life, when not only the intellect and soul but also the body will in mysterious fashion be united to God, even our eyes being enlightened by the light of

---

[1] Cf. I. Hausherr, 'Ignorance infinie', *Orientalia Christiana Periodica*, II (1936), pp. 358 ff. In *Honest to God*, Dr J. A. T. Robinson laid such stress on the *via negativa* that he was understood as denying the very existence of God.

[2] Cf. art. 'Contemplation' by J. Lemaitre, R. Roques and M. Viller in *Dictionnaire de Spiritualité Ascetique et de Mystique*, by Viller, Cavallera and J. de Guibert, Paris, 1953, cols. 1875–77.

[3] Cf. I. Hausherr, 'De Doctrina spirituali christianorum Quaestiones et Scripta', *Orientalia Christiana*, XXX, 3 (1933), pp. 153–63; 'Les grands courants de la spiritualité orientale', *Orientalia Christiana Periodica*, I (1935), pp. 114–38, especially p. 129.

God, somewhat as the eyes of the Apostles were enlightened by
the vision at the Transfiguration; and hence even in this life
there may be some kind of anticipation or foretaste of the total
union with God that is to come. This, of course, was to be
attained only by a special gift of God.

The Pseudo-Denis the Areopagite, who was believed all
through the Middle Ages to be St Paul's convert at Athens
(Acts 17: 34), was in fact an unknown writer, probably belonging to Monophysitic circles, who wrote on the *Divine Names*,
Mystical Theology, the *Celestial Hierarchy* and the *Ecclesiastical
Hierarchy*, and was translated into Latin by John Scott Erigena
about 867 (though parts of his work existed in Latin as early as
the sixth century). Commentaries on his works multiplied. I
speak in considerable ignorance, but conjecture that his influence lay not only in his insistence upon the transcendence of
God and the impossibility of conceiving God as he really is (the
via negativa), but also in his conjoining this with the hierarchy
of beings both in the spiritual world and in the earthly Church in
such sort that his mysticism is related to the whole dispensation
of God in creation and in return to God through 'deification'.[1]
The books reached England and echoes of them may be found
in Richard Rolle (d. 1349), *The Cloud of Unknowing* (between
1350 and 1370), and Walter Hilton (d. 1396).

Humility, however, is particularly characteristic of Eastern
spirituality. Nicholas Arseniev in his attractive book *Mysticism
and the Eastern Church*,[2] takes 'at random a characteristic story of
the old Book of the Fathers of the Egyptian desert—a story of
the great saint, Abbot Sisoe:

'When, after a long life of spiritual struggle and endeavour,
he was nearing his end, his face was suddenly lit as by the sun,
and he cried to the Fathers gathered round him: "See, there
comes Abbot Antony!" And in spirit he gazed upon the hosts
of glorified saints, who approached him one by one, and the

[1] The *Dictionnaire de Spiritualité, Ascetique et Mystique*, vol. III, Paris, 1957, devotes
no less than 185 columns to the Pseudo-Denis and his influence both in East and
West, with articles by different authors dealing with all the great theologians and
the various 'schools' of asceticism. The adages, *bonum est diffusivum sui*—good tends
to diffuse itself—and *bonum ex integra causa, malum ex quocunque defectu*—a thing to be
good must be totally good and is spoiled by a single defect—seem derived from the
Pseudo-Denis. Thomas Aquinas remarked that he was obscure but profound.

[2] London, 1926.

radiance of his face was increased. At last one of the Fathers asked him, "With whom dost thou speak, Abbot?" and he answered them: "Angels are come to fetch me and I am begging them to grant me yet a little while that I may do penance." The Fathers said to him: "Thou hast no need of penance, Abbot." And he answered: "Verily I say unto you, I have not so much as begun my repentance." And then they all understood that he was perfect.'[1]

Orthodox Doctrine

A significant statement about Orthodox doctrine concerning the connection between the Eucharist, the Blessed Trinity and the Church occurs in the Decree, n. 15, par. 1:

'Everyone knows with what great love the Christians of the East celebrate the sacred liturgy, especially the eucharistic mystery, source of the Church's life and pledge of future glory. There the faithful, united with their bishop, have access to God the Father through the Son, the Word made flesh, suffering and glorified, and so, in the outpouring of the Holy Spirit, they enter into communion with the most Holy Trinity, being made "partakers of the divine nature" (2 Pet 1: 4). Hence, through the celebration of the Holy Eucharist in each of these churches, the Church of God is built up and grows in stature and through concelebration, their communion with one another is made manifest.'

This is clearly derived from Greek sources, and, indeed, the reference to growth through the Eucharist is explicitly taken from St John Chrysostom.[2] This account of Orthodox teaching, should be compared with chapter I, par. 2, on the action of the Holy Spirit in causing the unity of the faithful; and with the following passage in the Constitution on the Church:

'The bishop, characterized by the fulness of the sacrament of order, is "the steward of the grace of the high priesthood".[3] This holds especially in the Eucharist, which he offers or provides for being offered,[4] for the Eucharist is the perpetual

[1] Op. cit., p. 49.
[2] Cf. p. 13 n. 1, above.
[3] Prayer of episcopal consecration in the Byzantine rite, *Euchologion to mega*, Romae, 1873, p. 139.
[4] Cf. Ignatius M., Smyrn. 8, 1.

source of the Church's life and growth. This Church of Christ is truly present in all lawful local congregations of the faithful, which, in attachment to their bishop, are themselves named churches in the New Testament.[1] They are, in their own localities, the new people called by God, in the Holy Spirit and in firm conviction (cf. 1 Thess 1: 5). In these churches by the preaching of the Gospel of Christ, the faithful are gathered together, and in them the mystery of the Lord's Supper is celebrated, "so that by the food and blood of the body of the Lord the whole brotherhood may be bound together".[2] In any sharing of the altar, under the holy stewardship of the bishop, is made manifest the symbol of that charity and "unity of the mystical body without which there is no salvation".[3] In these communities, small and poor though they may often be, and widely separated from one another, Christ is present and by his power the one holy catholic and apostolic Church is held in association.[4] For "the sharing of the body and blood of Christ does nothing other than to make us to be changed into that of which we partake".'[5]

In preparing these statements about the Church's 'self-understanding', recourse was had to the Eastern tradition, not primarily for the sake of reconciliation with the Orthodox, but in order to enlarge and deepen understanding of the nature of the Church. Thus the debt of the West to the East continues down to our own days.

D. DIFFERENCES IN THEOLOGICAL EXPRESSION BETWEEN EAST AND WEST

The Decree in n. 17 makes more explicit what it had said earlier about truth and its expression in n. 11.[6]

'What has just been said about the variety that can exist in the Church must also be taken to apply to the differences in

[1] Cf. Acts 8: 1; 14: 22–3; 20: 17, et passim.
[2] Mozarabic prayer, Migne Patres Latini, 96, 759 B.
[3] Cf. Ignatius M., Smyrn. 8, 1; Thomas Aquinas, Summa Theologica, III, q. 73, a. 3.
[4] Cf. Augustine, C. Faustum, 12, 20, Migne PL 42, 265; Sermo, 57, 7. Migne PL 38, 389, etc.
[5] Leo the Great, Sermo, 63, 7, Migne PL 54, 357 C.
[6] Cf. pp. 139 above.

theological expression of doctrine. In the study of revelation East and West have followed different methods, and have developed differently their understanding and confession of God's truth. It is hardly surprising, then, if from time to time one tradition has come nearer to a full appreciation of some aspects of a mystery of revelation than the other, or has expressed it to better advantage. In such cases these various theological expressions are often to be considered as mutually complementary rather then conflicting.' (N. 17, par. 1.)

Eastern and Western ethos

Of recent years much has been written on the contrasts between the Orthodox ethos and theology and the ethos and theology of the West.[1] It is easy to give an indication of the contrasts made: the East is speculative and mystical, the West practical and juridical; the East stresses Christ as triumphant and human deification, the West Christ as a victim and human redemption; the East is 'apophatic', that is, emphasizes more God's transcendence and his inexpressibility in human language, the West is 'scholastic' and stresses the knowledge obtained by analogy; the East, in Trinitarian doctrine, goes from the distinction of Persons to the unity of the nature, the West goes from the unity of the nature to the distinction of the Persons; the East conceives sin as 'corruption' (*phthora*), the West as 'guilt' (*reatus*); the East regards the unity of the Church as based on 'communion', the West as based on authority. All these examples could be amplified and others added.

Now I am far from denying that these differences in ethos and outlook are real. At the same time, there are many exceptions. Athanasius and Gregory of Nazianzus seem to me less specula-

[1] Cf., for instance, Georges Dejaifve, 'East and West, Two Theologies, One Faith', in Armstrong and Fry, op. cit., pp. 51–62; Georges Florovsky, 'The Problem of Ecumenical Encounter', *ibid.*, pp. 63–76; Bernard Schultze, 'Catholic Theology in East and West: Uniformity or Diversity?', *Unitas*, XVI (Autumn, 1964), pp. 186–201; Nikos A. Nissiotis, 'The Importance of the Doctrine of the Trinity for Christian Life and Theology', in *The Orthodox Ethos*, ed. A. J. Philippou, London, 1964, pp. 22–70; W. E. Wiest, 'The Centenary of the Greek Orthodox Archdiocese of North and South America: An Appreciation', *ibid.*, pp. 3–20; T. Ware, op. cit., pp. 56–7; Donald Attwater, op. cit., pp. 232–43. These are merely samples, for almost every book dealing with the Eastern Churches contrasts them with the Western Churches, Catholic, Anglican or Protestant.

tive and easier to read than much in Augustine and Ambrose. Many of the Eastern Patriarchs were exceedingly able administrators and most practical men. Respect for the 'sacred canons' is something universal in the East, and, indeed, at the Council of Florence, the Greek interpretation of the prohibition to add to the creed of Constantinople I was more 'rigidly legalistic' than was the Latin attitude. Jurisdictional matters play a considerable part in Orthodox life even today. Again, the Eastern Church has always had a deep devotion to the suffering Christ.[1] Other examples could be given to indicate that the contrasts may not be as radical as they seem when announced in general terms. Above all, the full historical setting ought always to be considered: East and West had to deal with different peoples and with different distortions of the one faith: Donatism and Pelagianism made little impact on the East, and Monophysitism comparatively little on the West after the Council of Chalcedon in 451. Moreover, in both East and West there have been and are different schools of theology—the Scotist and the Thomist are examples in the West—with very different outlooks and solutions to common difficulties.[2]

There seem to be two dangers in this amassing of differences in ethos and formulations of doctrine. The one is that the oppositions are made to seem so massive that the still greater massive agreements are overlooked. The other is to take particular points of doctrine and consider them apart from the whole spirit and life with which they are closely associated. By God's grace, neither difficulty is insuperable.[3]

On some matters I think that mutual explanations could

[1] Cf. the references given in *Rediscovering Eastern Christendom*, op. cit., p. 34, n. 31.
[2] As an instance, Dr Panagiotis Trembelas, in reconciling God's immutability with human prayer, says: 'We arrive at a satisfactory answer to these questions when we remember that the foreknowledge of God did not order and predetermine the government of the world without reference to the acts of free beings eternally known to Him.' 'Prayer', in *The Orthodox Ethos*, p. 126. For most of my life I accepted this explanation of God's foreknowledge taking into account our free acts, and it is an opinion still held by many Catholic theologians. Recently, however, I have come to wonder whether it does not presuppose too anthropomorphic a view of God, and I am more ready to consider the matter an insoluble mystery.
[3] The essay of Fr Florovsky, 'The Problem of Ecumenical Encounter', in *Rediscovering Eastern Christendom*, has some penetrating observations, among them that controversy is still active—or was so when he wrote two or perhaps three years ago. I confess I have been depressed by the controversial tone of some Catholic theologians, even in comparatively recent times.

greatly help; for instance, the doctrine of original sin and the Immaculate Conception, the distinction made by some Orthodox between the essence and the 'energies' of God; and the term 'created grace'. On the Immaculate Conception, Timothy Ware says:

'So far as the Immaculate Conception is concerned, the great majority of Orthodox reject the Roman Catholic definition, although in the past there have been prominent Orthodox who believed the doctrine or at any rate something extremely close to it. Orthodox call Mary "immaculate" (*achrantos*) and they hold that she was free from *actual* sin, but most feel that the doctrine of the Immaculate Conception as formulated by the Pope in 1845 implies an understanding of original sin which they cannot accept. The whole question, however, is still a matter for discussion among Orthodox theologians, and there has never been any binding declaration on the matter.'[1] There is clearly room here for friendly explanations. Similarly, many Catholic theologians find difficulty in the distinction between the essence and the 'energies' of God, feeling that it compromises the divine simplicity; but a reconciliation may be possible if it is remembered that all hold that the beatific vision is given through what is called 'the light of glory' and that the vision of God, though immediate, does not enable the blessed to comprehend God.

Similarly, many Orthodox object to the term, often used by Catholic theologians, 'created grace'; but I confess I feel that here a reconciliation is definitely possible, especially if the question is discussed in the light of the common teaching about the indwelling of the three divine Persons in the faithful.

The procession of the Holy Spirit: here, too, a reconciliation seems possible.[2] The Orthodox felt that the addition 'and from the Son' might either destroy the distinction between Father and Son or else give ground for suspecting that the Holy Spirit was a creature of the Son; whereas the Latins seem to have added the 'and from the Son' as a means of rejecting

---

[1] 'The Communion of Saints', *The Orthodox Ethos*, ed. A. J. Philippou, Oxford, 1964, p. 147.
[2] See above, p. 196 ff.

Adoptionism, and so of protecting the equality of the Son with the Father. Both formulas are most fully orthodox in intent.[1]

The Papacy?

Here I confess I feel that the warning given in the Decree against 'importunate zeal' (n. 24, par. 1) is most relevant. Catholics can and indeed must on occasion express the religious significance and the spiritual reality which our belief in the centre of unity has for us; but anything like arguments to convince others are very dubiously wise.[2] The Decree on Ecumenism exhorts all who are interested in reconciliation to give due consideration to the concept of 'communion' in the origin and growth of the Eastern Churches and 'to the character of the relations which obtained between them and the Roman See before separation'. (N. 14, par. 4.)[3] The Vatican Council, as further study of all its documents will more and more reveal, has opened many doors; and though the way on the other side of them may still be hard and long, nevertheless doors believed closed are now definitely open.

Two instances occur where differences of theological formulation may be recognized as complementary rather than opposed. The first concerns the possible reconciliation of the 'Chalcedonian' and the 'non-Chalcedonian' Churches; the other concerns the principle of 'Economy' in the Orthodox Church.

A 'Chalcedonian' and 'non-Chalcedonian' Consultation

The main body of the Orthodox accept the first seven Ecumenical Councils; but two smaller bodies, the 'Nestorians', now often called 'Assyrians', did not accept the Council of Ephesus which in 431 condemned Nestorius, and the Monophysites (the Armenian, the Coptic, the Ethiopian, the Syrian-Jacobite and

---

[1] Cf. my essay 'Orthodox-Catholic Relations' in *Rediscovering Eastern Christendom*, op. cit., pp. 23–42.
[2] Cf. D. Attwater, op. cit., vol. II, p. 234.
[3] The *Schema* of the Decree referred to C. L. Hertling, S.J., *Communio, Chiesa e Papato nell'antichità cristiana*, Rome, 1961, and to G. Bardy, *La théologie de l'église de Saint Clément à Saint Irenée*, Paris, 1945.

the Syrian Church of Malabar) did not accept the Council of Chalcedon in 451. The Nestorians feared that the Council of Ephesus, and the expression *theotokos* (God-bearer) imperilled the true manhood of Christ; the Monophysites feared that the Council of Chalcedon, with its doctrine of the two natures of Christ, brought danger to the divinity of Christ, and cast doubt upon the formula of St Cyril of Alexandria, 'one nature of the Word incarnate'. After a period of missionary expansion, the Nestorians have become but a small number, perhaps only fifty or sixty thousand. But the Monophysites number over fifteen million.

By 1963 all the larger Orthodox Churches were members of the World Council of Churches; and so also were the 'non-Chalcedonian' Churches. The contacts made at the various meetings, especially of Faith and Order, revealed a community of faith and outlook which led, through the help of the World Council and Faith and Order, to an unofficial consultation between seven Orthodox theologians and eight 'non-Chalcedonian' theologians. The consultation was convened and helped by three permanent members of the Staff of the Faith and Order Commission of the World Council of Churches, Dr N. A. Nissiotis,[1] Fr Paul Vergese[2] and Dr Lukas Vischer.[3] The consultation took place in connection with the meeting of the Faith and Order Commission in Aarhus, Denmark, and an agreed statement was issued 14th August 1964.

Two matters are significant, the first, that 'through the different terminologies, we saw the same truth expressed', and the second, the recognition of the 'significant role of political, sociological and cultural factors in creating tension between factions in the past, which should be recognized and studied together. They should not, however, continue to divide us'.[4]

It is, I think, impossible to lay too great emphasis upon the sentence: 'Through different terminologies used by each side, we saw the same truth expressed.'

[1] Ecumenical Institute, Bossey, Orthodox.
[2] WCC Associate General Secretary, Church of Malabar.
[3] Research Secretary, Faith and Order, Reformed.
[4] Cf. John Meyendorff, 'A Consultation between "Chalcedonians" and "non-Chalcedonians" ', *St Vladimir's Seminary Quarterly*, VIII, no. 3 (1964), pp. 149–52.

'Economy'

The principle of the 'economy' in the Orthodox Church means an exception to the strict rule according to which all sacraments outside the Orthodox Church are useless and void. Thus, in certain circumstances the Orthodox have received non-Orthodox into full communion without a repetition of baptism, confirmation and orders; but on some occasions have demanded a repetition—or administration for the first time—of these sacraments. The practice up to 1775 in the Greek Church was to receive Latins and Armenians with an anointing or merely a profession of faith; but in 1775 the Patriarch Cyril V. of Constantinople, with the concurrence of the Patriarchs of Alexandria and Jerusalem, issued a decree that all Latins and Armenians who came to Orthodoxy were to be rebaptized and anointed. Lutherans and Calvinists were treated in the same way as the Latins. In Russia, also, the custom has varied.[1] Catholics on the other hand, since the fifth century have admitted the 'validity' of sacraments administered by heretics with due minister, matter, form and intention, and have not repeated sacraments received in schism or heresy.

Recently a wider conception of sacramental effectiveness has been growing among Catholic theologians, the 'matter and form' of sacraments tending to be understood not merely as a mere rite but as an expression in their totality of the meaning of the Church's real values and mind. In the case of 'wandering bishops'—*episcopi vagantes*—who are not associated with any of the larger Christian communities, and often with scarcely any community at all,[2] it is arguable that the due relation to the Church is lacking. Sacraments, in the more recent views, are conceived as 'actualizations' or effective expressions of the interlocking, interpenetrated sacramentality of Christ and his Church, and in certain circumstances the mere material rite

[1] Cf. my *Principles of Sacramental Theology*, London, 1960, pp. 543–8.
[2] Cf. R. T. Brandreth, *Episcopi Vagantes and the Anglican Communion*, ed. 2, London, 1960; Peter F. Anson, *Bishops at Large. Some Autocephalous Churches of the Past Hundred Years*, London, 1964; B. Leeming, 'Are They Really Bishops?', *Heythrop Journal*, V, no. 3 (July 1964), pp. 259–67; A. Wenger, A.A., L'Église' Orthodoxe et les Ordinations anglicaines', *Nouvelle Revue Théologique*, LXXVI (1954), pp. 44–55.

may not be sufficient to express this due relation to the Church, even though the rite be materially sufficient, since the meaning of the rite is affected by the totality of the circumstances in which it is used. On this ground I argued that ordinations performed by some, at least, of these 'wandering bishops' should be regarded as invalid.[1]

Speaking of the Orthodox theology relative to the validity of Orders, Fr A. Wenger says that in order that a rite be valid it is not enough that the externals merely be observed; it is further needful that in the Church which uses the rite, the faith or apostolic teaching relative to the rite in question should be conformed to the doctrine of the universal Church.[2] If this latter condition is not fulfilled, the application of the principle of 'economy' becomes difficult or impossible. Fr Alexander Schmemann, of St Vladimir's Theological Seminary, New York, says truly that 'the Orthodox tradition has never isolated validity into a "principle in itself", that is, disconnected from truth, authenticity and, in general from the whole faith and order of the Church.'[3]

Thus I think that there is an approach, at least, towards agreement between the Western doctrine of 'validity' and the Eastern doctrine of the 'economy'. The basic line of agreement lies in the sacrament consisting in its meaning and significance, which must include a relation to the Church.[4]

Before leaving this topic, it should be added that in the Constitution on the Church, it is stated that the 'canonical mission of bishops can take place through legitimate custom never revoked by the supreme and universal authority of the Church', which means that Orthodox bishops have a fully legitimate mission, according to the canonical law, and hence have the same jurisdiction over their priests and subjects as have the Latin bishops.[5]

---

[1] Art. cit. in previous note.
[2] Art. cit., p. 50.
[3] 'Problems of Orthodoxy in America: the Canonical Problem', *St Vladimir's Seminary Quarterly*, VIII, no. 2 (1964), pp. 73-4.
[4] I also argued that the concept of 'commissioning' held by many Anglicans and others approaches very closely to the Orthodox and the recent Catholic thinking on the question, cf. art. cit., pp. 266.
[5] Cf. *Constitutio Dogmatica de Ecclesia*, no. 24, par. 2. After this statement it is useless to refer to the somewhat varying opinions of Catholic theologians.

E. THE SOLEMN DECLARATION ABOUT THE RIGHTS OF THE EASTERN ORTHODOX

On this subject the Council made one of its most measured and weighty declarations:

'From the earliest times the Eastern Churches followed their own forms of ecclesiastical law and customs, which were sanctioned by the approval of the Fathers of the Church, of Synods, and even of Ecumenical Councils. Far from being an obstacle to the Church's unity, such diversity of customs and observances only adds to her seemliness and is of great help in carrying out her mission, as has already been stated. To remove, then, all shadow of doubt, this holy Synod solemnly declares that the Churches of the East, while mindful of the necessary unity of the whole Church, have the right to govern themselves according to the disciplines proper to them, since these are better suited to the character of their faithful and more for the good of their souls. The perfect observance of this principle which is sanctioned by long-standing tradition, but in fact has not always been observed, is one of the essential prerequisites for any restoration of unity.' (N. 16.)

The *Schema* had read: 'have the right and the duty to govern themselves, etc. (*ius et officium habere*); but very late in the day this was changed to read: 'have the power—*facultatem*, etc.' It is interesting to compare the wording in the final Decree on Ecumenism with that in the Decree for the Eastern Catholic Churches, where a similar declaration is made, reading as follows:

'Their history, traditions and many ecclesiastical institutions bear eloquent witness to the debt owed by the whole Church to the Eastern Churches. Therefore this holy Synod not only justly esteems and rightly praises this ecclesiastical and spiritual inheritance, but is firmly convinced that it is an inheritance of the whole Church. And consequently this holy Synod solemnly declares that the Eastern Churches, just as the Western, enjoy the right and are bound by the obligation of governing themselves according to their own special institutions—*iure pollere et officio teneri se secundum proprias disciplinas peculiares regendi*—since these are commended by venerable antiquity, are more adapted to the character of their people and more for the good of their souls.'[1]

In both cases the reasons assigned are the same:

(a) Old-standing practice, approved by Fathers of the Church, by Synods and by General Councils.[2]

(b) Adaptation to the character of Eastern peoples. Here, in passing it may be noted that when the Church of South India was in progress of formation, special study was made of the ancient Eastern Liturgies so that the liturgy of the new Church might be suited to the character of an Eastern people.

(c) The good in the spiritual order to be attained.

The Decree on Ecumenism observes that the principle of the Eastern Churches retaining their own institutions and customs has not always been observed, in spite of the age-long tradition. When the Venetians had possession of Crete in 1368, Pope Urban V directed that no Greek should be ordained except by a Latin or Greek Catholic bishop and added that those so ordained 'should celebrate Masses and other divine offices according to the rite that the aforesaid Roman Church observes'; any Greek monk or priest at all who declined to employ the Roman rite would no longer be allowed to hear confessions or to preach.[3]

The Council of Florence in 1439 in renewing the decisions about the precedence of the Patriarchs, namely, Rome, Constantinople, Alexandria, Antioch and Jerusalem, added *salvis privilegiis omnibus et iuribus eorum*, that is, keeping all their privileges and rights. From that time, this return to the ancient discipline has never been questioned in theory, although many complaints have been made that it was not always observed in practice, especially during the nineteenth century. The solemn declaration by Vatican Council II, both in the Decree on Ecumenism and in that on the Eastern Catholic Churches, only renews in clear form the principle repeatedly affirmed by many

---

[1] *Decretum de Ecclesiis Orientalibus Catholicis*, no. 5, p. 5.

[2] The Decree for the Eastern Catholic Churches gives a long list of authorities on which the 'venerable antiquity' relies. The list runs to a third of a page and it seems needless to reproduce it here.

[3] Cf. J. Gill, *Personalities of the Council of Florence*, Oxford, 1964, p. 290, where this and other instances are given and authorities cited.

popes (as well as by Councils), notably by Benedict XIV and by Leo XIII.[1]

It may be asked whether this question of maintenance of customs, laws and institutions could apply also to separated brethren of the West as well as to those of the East? Cardinal Bea, whom I have already cited,[2] explicitly says, 'The principle here laid down—(namely, about the heritage of spirituality, liturgy, discipline and theology possessed by the Eastern Churches)—is general, and in consequence there can be no doubt that it applies to the endowments possessed by separated brethren both of the East and of the West.' In past years, more than one suggestion has been made, by separated brethren, of an 'Anglican Rite', or some other 'Rite'. The Holy See, as far as I know, has never rejected such suggestions in principle. But the experience of the Eastern Catholic Churches shows the difficulties, and the suspicions, occasioned by such 'Rites', and in consequence such suggestions do not seem at present to be in any way practical.

Nevertheless, this declaration by the Council is a concrete denial that unity demands uniformity, and a denial that unity demands a centralized administrative body which would curb local initiative or lessen local authorities. Unity, however, in faith is essential.[3]

SECTION II

Separated Churches and Ecclesiastical Communities
in the West

Regarding this title, Dr E. L. Mascall remarks that the Decree 'tactfully refrains from specifying to which bodies each designation applies'.[4] It was perhaps more than tact which lay behind this choice of title. The Decree on Ecumenism is a pastoral document and its whole tone indicates that its purpose is

[1] For references, see the Decree on the Eastern Catholic Churches, n. 2, note 2, p. 4.
[2] Cf. above, p. 158.   [3] Cf. Decree, no. 2.
[4] 'Vatican II on the Church and Ecumenism', *New Blackfriars* (April 1965), p. 394.

not to make judgements about others, but to lay down general principles to be followed by Catholics in the search for Christian unity. To have attempted to determine where the word 'Church' is properly applied would not have been either necessary or helpful to this purpose, and it may be doubted whether it would be proper in itself.

This said, the following general divisions seem useful:

A. The general standpoint of this Section.
B. The World Council of Churches and the Catholic Church.
C. The Anglican Communion.
D. The 'endowments' possessed by these separated brethren.
E. The differences between them and the Catholic Church.

A. THE GENERAL STANDPOINT OF THE SECTION

The Secretariat for the Promotion of Christian Unity took the greatest pains to inform itself about the actual state and conditions of churches and ecclesiastical communities in the West, and received detailed accounts from competent Catholic theologians all over the world. But the Decree, save for one brief reference to the Anglican Communion, does not attempt to describe either the origins or the characteristics of the various bodies, for example, Lutherans, Presbyterians, Congregationalists, Methodists, etc. This was not a sign of failure to recognize the importance of these bodies, but was decided because of the complicated history of the Reformation, because of the difficulties in explaining the developments they have undergone, and because of the complex nature of the relationships existing between them, some of which have already been indicated in this Commentary.[1] The purpose of the Decree is to lay down in general the principles on which efforts toward Christian unity, from the Catholic point of view (and it must never be forgotten that the Decree is directed to Catholics), should be founded.

Suspicions of Roman Catholics

The Decree, however, observes that 'the ecumenical move-

[1] Cf. pp. 34-53.

ment and desire for peace with the Catholic Church has not yet prevailed everywhere, and hopes that among all ecumenical feeling and mutual esteem may gradually increase'. (No. 19, par. 3.) This means that the Secretariat and the Council is aware that Catholics are looked upon with suspicion, and, sometimes, with hostility by a number of our Protestant brethren. The fact is undoubted; the causes are often a mixture of racial, national, cultural and historical reasons as well as the purely religious. As one evidence of this, and of the attitude of some ecumenists, I venture to cite from a semi-private letter sent out by a prominent Pentecostalist, Dr David J. du Plessis, in April 1965.

'RENEWAL OF THE ROMAN CATHOLIC CHURCH. Remembering how bitter my heart used to be against R.C.'s, and how prejudiced I was against anything tainted with Catholicism, I am not surprised at the scepticism of Protestant and Pentecostal people regarding the phenomenal change that is taking place in the R.C. Church round the world. Reports in the secular and religious press are often so surprising. Let me assure you that what I find "at the grass roots" is even more than astonishing. The Holy Spirit is certainly moving upon ROMAN CATHOLIC FLESH. They are reading the Bible and they are showing a real regard for OTHERS. If you find it hard to trust them, then remember how hard it must have been for the Christians in Jerusalem to trust Saul of Tarsus, even when his name was changed to Paul. BUT nevertheless, he was God's chosen man. I suggest that we all read again the very FIRST assignment that Jesus gave to the very FIRST men that HE REGENERATED BY HIS SPIRIT on the day of His resurrection. When He had breathed upon them saying RECEIVE THE HOLY GHOST he added: "If you forgive the sins of any, they are forgiven; if you retain the sins of any, they are retained" (Jn 20: 23). Let us think of the warning of the Lord (Mt 6: 14–15): "For if you forgive men their trespasses, your heavenly Father also will forgive you BUT if you DO NOT forgive men their trespasses, NEITHER will your Father forgive your trespasses" (RSV). Remember this at Easter time and let us FORGIVE, 7 times 70. The souls and bodies of Christians will LIVE when all learn to FORGIVE.'

David du Plessis was an observer at the third session of the Vatican Council, and plans to be in Rome for the fourth session. He travels extensively and the message he gives is surely one of charity and hence is one inspired by the Holy Spirit.

Other evidence of suspicion towards the Catholic Church could easily be given.[1] This opposition is often accompanied by opposition to the ecumenical movement as a whole, but regarding it, the Rev Derek Murray made the following plea:

'May I make a plea that despite this opposition—and it is as often unexpressed as made explicit and which may not be inseparable—the British Council of Churches will not dismiss the Mission Hall and the Brethren Assembly as funny little heretical sects? For the fulness of Christ, I believe their witness, knowledge and holiness are necessary.'[2] That plea should, I think, be addressed also to ourselves. In their regard one recommendation in the Decree is particularly applicable: 'We should pray to the Holy Spirit for the grace to be genuinely self-denying, humble, gentle in the service of others, and to have an attitude of brotherly generosity towards them.' (N. 7, par. 1.)

A certain affinity among all the Western churches is remarked upon by the Decree (n. 19, par. 1), because of the long centuries in which all Christendom lived together in ecclesiastical communion. There are historical memories in common: for one thing, the Crusades, good or evil as one may judge them. There was and is a certain tradition of chivalry, and of piety: *The Imitation of Christ*, though perhaps neglected, still had its influence. The inheritance of Western theology was more pervasive than is often realized: Catholics, Protestants and Anglicans alike speak of our redemption 'by the infinite merits of Christ', a manner of speech less often found in the East, if found at all. At a Consultation between Orthodox and non-Orthodox theologians at Montreal, 8th–11th July 1963, one conclusion was: 'Critical study of different theological terminologies is essential. Our discussion suggests the possibility that joint study

---

[1] For instance, at the Nottingham Conference on Faith and Order, September 1964, the addresses of the Rev Derek Murray and of the Rev A. T. Houghton, *Unity Begins at Home*, London 1964, pp. 35–7. It should be added, however, that the address, on the last day, among the 'Courtesies', by a Catholic priest, Fr Cuthbert Rand, of Ushaw, received most warm applause.

[2] *Unity Begins at Home*, p. 36.

of the meaning of uncreated grace might prove fruitful.'[1] To some extent, all the contrasts between the Orthodox and the Westerns apply to Anglicans and Protestants as well as to Catholics. The whole of the West was influenced by St Augustine in a way in which the East was not.

B. THE WORLD COUNCIL OF CHURCHES AND THE CATHOLIC CHURCH

The Decree makes no verbal mention of the World Council of Churches, but the reference to it is clear in the beginning of n. 20: 'Our thoughts turn first to those Christians who make open confession of Jesus Christ as God and Lord and as the one mediator between God and men, to the glory of the one God, Father, Son and Holy Spirit.' This is almost the exact wording of the Basis of the World Council of Churches.[2] Catholics have certainly grown in appreciation of the World Council of Churches,[3] and this remark in the Decree is one evidence of it. It may be added that Cardinal Bea in his book *Unity in Freedom* declared: 'I would like to say that we Catholics must recognize with sincere gratitude that it was our separated brethren, Orthodox, Anglican and Protestant, who gave the first impulse to the modern unitive movement and that we have learned much from them and can learn still more.'[4]

Evidence of Goodwill

In turn, the World Council, during these years of Vatican Council II, has expressed most generous goodwill and great interest. Dr Lukas Vischer was its delegated observer at all three sessions of the Council, Dr Nikos A. Nissiotis, at the last two, and there were also at the two sessions two other observers delegated by the World Council, though not all were present throughout the whole sessions.[5] *The Ecumenical Review* and the

---

[1] *Ecumenical Review*, XVI, no. 1 (October 1963), p. 111.
[2] Cf. *The New Delhi Report*, London, 1962, pp. 37 and 152–9.
[3] Cf. p. 65 above.   [4] Op. cit., p. 205.
[5] Dr Vischer is Research Secretary in the Department of Faith and Order of the World Council of Churches. Dr Nissiotis is Associate Director of the Ecumenical Institute of the World Council of Churches, Bossey (Switzerland). At the Second

Ecumenical Press Service published frequent accounts of the sessions of the second Vatican Council, careful, generally sympathetic and free from the sensationalism which marred some other press accounts and even some Catholic writing on the Council.

The meetings of the Central Committee of the W.C.C. at Rochester, New York in January 1963, at Odessa, February 1964, and at Enuga, Nigeria, in January 1965, discussed various aspects or the relations between the World Council of Churches and the Catholic Church. In January 1965, Dr Nissiotis gave an important Conference in the Aula of the University of Geneva, and Dr Vischer has written a number of lengthy and thoughtful reports. In February 1965, Cardinal Bea went to Geneva and had an exchange of views with Pastor Mark Boegner, a veteran of the Ecumenical Movement, and ex-President of the World Council of Churches.[1] In the third week of May 1965, eight representatives of the World Council met six Catholic representatives, to discuss 'practical collaboration in the fields of philanthropy, social and international affairs; theological study programmes which have a specific bearing on ecumenical relations; problems which cause tension between the Churches (e.g. mixed marriages, religious liberty, proselytism); common concerns with regard to the life of the Church (laity, missions, etc.).'[2] The Report of this meeting has not been published; and it may be conjectured that both sides felt the need for further consultation with the bodies which they represented, a *Motu Proprio* on mixed marriages from the Holy Father being expected and the matter of religious liberty still to be further discussed at the fourth session of the second Vatican Council. Moreover collaboration in philanthropic undertakings would

Session the WCC observers included Rt Rev John Sadquid, of the Church of India, Pakistan, Burma and Ceylon, Bishop of Nagpur; and Professor Masatoshi Doi, of the United Church of Christ in Japan, Professor of Systematic Theology and Ecumenics, Soshisha University, Kyoto, Japan; and at the third, Dr Z. K. Matthews, on the Staff of Inter-Church Aid, World Service and Refugees of the World Council of Churches; and Rev Dr Jerald C. Brauer, Dean of the Divinity School, University of Chicago. At the third Session Professor Doi was present as a guest of the Secretariat for Promoting Christian Unity.

[1] Cf. *Rencontre Oecuménique à Genève*, Introduction by J. G. Bodmer, pasteur, président du Rassemblement oecuménique des Eglises de Genève, Geneva and Paris, 1965. I assume that Pastor Boegner edited the little volume.

[2] *The Tablet*, 15th May 1965, p. 560.

surely demand consultation with various more local organizations.[1]

I indicate briefly here some considerations which have, I think, more than a merely temporary bearing on relations between the World Council of Churches and the Catholic Church:

They are not comparable entities

They are not comparable entities, even though both are largely international and both are now interested in the unitive movement. The Catholic Church is a Church, with its own doctrine, sacraments and ecclesiastical unity; the World Council of Churches is strictly a council, a meeting place where churches of differing doctrinal tenets, and different conceptions of the nature of the Church's unity, may meet together without surrendering any of their convictions, recognizing in the other member churches elements, or endowments, of the one true Church. The famous Declaration made at Toronto in July 1950 made clear several fundamental matters:

'The World Council cannot and should not be based upon any one conception of the Church. It does not prejudge the ecclesiastical problem.

'Membership in the World Council of Churches does not imply that a Church treats its own conception of the Church as merely relative.

'Membership in the World Council does not imply the accep-

---

[1] The W.C.C. representatives were: Archpriest Vitaly Borovoy, Moscow Patriarchate representative at W.C.C. headquarters in Geneva and a Council observer; De Edwin Espy, general secretary of the U.S. National Council of Churches of Christ (American Baptist Convention); Dr Nikos Nissiotis, Greek Orthodox lay theologian and a Council observer; Dr Edmund Schlink, professor of dogmatic theology at Heidelberg and German Evangelical Council observer; Dr Oliver Tomkins, Bishop of Bristol, chairman of the W.C.C.'s working committee on Faith and Order; Fr Paul Vergese, of the Syrian Orthodox Church in India, an associate general secretary of the W.C.C. and director of the division of ecumenical action; Dr Lukas Vischer, a clergyman of the Swiss Reformed Church and a W.C.C. Council observer; and Dr W. A. Visser 't Hooft, formerly W.C.C. general secretary.

The Catholic representatives were: Bishop Willebrands, secretary of the Christian Unity Secretariat; Bishop Thomas Holland, of Salford, England; Mgr William Braum, secretary of the U.S. national episcopal commission for ecumenical affairs; Mgr Carlo Bayer, secretary general of Caritas International; Fr Pierre Duprey, W.F., Eastern undersecretary of the Christian Unity Secretariat; and Fr Jérôme Hamer, O.P., assistant general to the Dominican Master General and general secretary for studies in the Dominican Order.

tance of a specific doctrine concerning the nature of Church unity.

'The member Churches of the World Council consider the relationship of other Churches to the Holy Catholic Church which the Creeds profess as a subject for mutual consideration. Nevertheless membership does not imply that each Church regards the other member Churches as Churches in the true and full sense of the word.'

Friendly co-operation, discussion, a certain solidarity with each other, and avoidance of such actions as are incompatible with brotherly relations—these are also implied in membership.[1]

At the meeting of the Central Committee at Odessa, February 1964, these principles were reaffirmed, but reference was also made to the statement made at New Delhi about the nature of the unity sought.[2] The statement issued by the Central Committee ended thus: 'We warmly invite those churches outside our membership to consider how they might be able to enter into this kind of fellowship. Since all churches have a great responsibility towards each other and can learn from the renewal which is granted to them and can learn from the renewal which is granted to others we encourage them to co-operate more and more in service to the world in the name of Christ, the Lord of all.'

A slight rift in the cordiality of relations between the W.C.C. and the Catholic Church occurred in May 1964, occasioned by suggestions that the 'centre' of ecumenism was moving from Geneva to Rome, and by the meeting of Pope Paul VI with the Ecumenical Patriarch in Jerusalem, with the possible conclusion, drawn by some, that the Orthodox would move rather towards Rome than towards closer relations with Geneva.

In a radio broadcast from Germany (16th May 1964), Dr Visser 't Hooft, General Secretary of the World Council at the time, indicated that he thought relations between the Orthodox and the World Council—indeed with Protestants—were easier than either of them had with Rome: 'For both are seeking a fellowship in which all the Churches retain their independence

---

[1] The quotations are from nn. 3, 4, 5 of part I, and n. 4 of part II.
[2] Cf. p. 67 above, where the statement is quoted.

and their particular character.' Neither tells the other, 'It is a condition of unity absolutely *sine qua non* that your Church come under the leadership and jurisdiction of the head of my Church.'[1]

Cardinal Bea took occasion to say that the contacts made in the Holy Land had indeed envisaged dialogue between some Orthodox and the Catholic Church, as had been projected at Rhodes. 'But', he went on, 'these meetings in the Holy Land do not mean an intention on Rome's part to forget the Lutherans and the Reformed of the West. Every friend of Christian unity is grateful to the World Council of Churches of Geneva for all that it has done for the great cause of union; the Secretariat for Unity has sought from the beginning of its activities to collaborate with the World Council and will continue to do so. . . . The presence of the Orthodox Churches in the World Council is certainly of great usefulness for unity and it is hard to see why the Church of Rome should wish to detach them from that Council.'[2]

Dr Visser 't Hooft on the Third Session

Dr Visser 't Hooft, in his Report to the Central Committee at Enugu, Nigeria in January 1965, spoke as follows:

'When I turn next to the relations between the World Council of Churches and the Roman Catholic Church I must begin by saying that I find it this time more difficult to speak on this subject than on any previous occasion. The reason is of course that recent developments, particularly those in the last days of the third session of the Vatican Council, have created a sense of great uncertainty.

'On the one hand we cannot and must not underestimate the strength of the movement for a true spiritual renewal which is at work in the Roman Catholic Church, and which has found expression in many of the speeches and some of the actions of the Council. We know by experience that there is a great difference between the wish for renewal and its actual applica-

---

[1] Cf. M. J. Le Guillou, 'Interrogations sur l'avenir de l'oecuménisme', *Istina*, no. 1 (Jan-Mar 1964), pp. 8–10; *Herder-Correspondence*, 'World Council of Churches and Catholic Ecumenism', vol. I, nos. 9–10 (Sep-Oct 1964), pp. 283–5.
[2] Quoted by Fr Le Guillou, *art cit*.. in previous note, p. 16.

tion in daily church-life. But we must rejoice that there is so much new thinking, so much readiness to face anew the issues of the task and message of the Church in the modern world and that this new approach is to such a large extent inspired by a new listening to the biblical witness.

'On the one hand, we find that this renewal meets with powerful opposition in leading ecclesiastical circles. This has happened especially with regard to a number of matters which are of great moment for inter-church relationships. The result so far is that while in certain respects the Council has come to decisions which from an ecumenical point of view are constructive, it has postponed decision on other important matters, such as religious liberty, and in some cases has only reaffirmed the old positions.

'The question now arises: What should be our attitude at this time when there is reason for both expectation and disappointment? It seems to me that we ought to keep in mind the following considerations:

'First of all we cannot forget that in our own churches we have by no means solved the problem of the tension between the forces of renewal and the existing structures. Secondly, just as many Roman Catholics and members of other churches rejoice together when they see in each others' churches signs of genuine spiritual renewal and are thus brought into a new relation to each other, so the anxiety about developments which put obstacles in the way to renewal is an anxiety in which many Roman Catholics and many Christians of other confessions share, so that there is a sense of being involved in a common cause. Thirdly, the adoption of the Decree *de oecumenismo* creates a new situation. It means that the Roman Catholic Church is no longer standing apart. It expresses its desire to enter into fraternal relations with other churches. It does so on the basis of an ecumenism which differs in important respects from the conceptions of ecumenism held in our midst, but the fact remains that it desires to enter into conversations with other churches since it recognizes that in those churches Christ is working. Now this surely means that the Roman Catholic Church and the non-Roman Catholic Churches bear a great responsibility for each other. Through the developments of recent years they have become more than ever "their brother's keepers". Is it not already clear that we have in fact a great, as it were, subterranean influence upon each other? Has the ecumenical movement been an important factor in the new development in the Roman Catholic Church? And have we not received important spiritual stimulation from the Roman Catholic ecumenists? Or if we look at the world situation, is it not clear that we are together faced with the obligation to re-interpret the task of the Church in an increasingly secularized world and to find the prophetic word to remind men in their disorder of the order of God? There must be the acceptance of responsibility for each other and therefore intensive conversation. Is it necessary to say that such conversation does not mean that deep convictions will be silenced or minimized? In so far as this dialogue has to do with the specific issues of doctrine it will of course take place between the Roman Catholic Church and other churches. From the point of view of the World Council it is normal and necessary that such inter-church discussions shall take place, if and when the churches are ready for them. In so far as the dialogue has to do with matters in which the World Council itself is competent, the dialogue can take place between the Roman Catholic Church and the W.C.C. Our task is to work out a clear distinction between these two types of dialogue.'[1]

The Central Committee was in agreement with the substance of Dr Visser 't Hooft's practical suggestions, and the result was the meeting in May of the eight representatives from the W.C.C. and the six from the Catholic Church.

The last week of the Third Session

The events of the last days of the third session were probably what caused Dr Visser 't Hooft to speak of 'a great sense of uncertainty'. These events were, first, the postponement of the vote on the *Schema* on Religious Liberty; secondly, the modifications introduced into the *Schema* on Ecumenism; thirdly, the note of explanation about collegiality; and lastly, the proclamation by the Holy Father of the Mother of God as Mother

[1] *Ecumenical Review*, XVII, no. 2 (April 1965), pp. 169–70.

of the Church.[1] Each of these should be examined on its own account.[2]

As regards the changes introduced into the draft on Ecumenism, they were, in fact, of little significance, and some few were an improvement. There were forty changes suggested, and the Secretariat for Unity rejected all save nineteen; and when the final *Schema* was given to the Fathers of the Council, it was accompanied by a multigraphed sheet from the Secretariat approving the changes. Nevertheless, it was open to the Fathers to reject the *Schema*; but they must have felt that if the Secretariat approved the changes, there was nothing offensive or objectionable in them. All the same, it is understandable and regrettable that not a few of the observers felt hurt and offended. Cardinal Bea more than once has expressed regret that our Protestant brethren felt hurt.[3]

The explanatory note about the collegiality of the bishops, in chapter III of the Constitution of the Church added nothing to what was already in the text itself. As I understood it, 'colle-

[1] Cf. Cardinal Bea, 'Quanto il Concilio ha sinora fatto per l'unione dei cristiani', *Civiltà Cattolica*, March 1965; G. Caprile, 'Aspetti positivi della terza sessione del Concilio', *ibid.*, 20th February 1965; *Informations Catholiques*, 15th January 1965, pp. 34–42; R. Rouquette, 'Les derniers jours de la troisième session', *Etudes*, January 1965, pp. 100–20; *Faith and Order Trends*, New York, vol. 5, no. 1 (December 1964), pp. 1–5.

[2] As regards the postponement of the statement on religious liberty, the final revised text—and it was very considerably revised—was only ready in print by 17th November, and the Presidents of the Council, reasonably enough, judged that there would not be time for the Fathers to read and ponder it sufficiently, especially considering the amount of other matters to be dealt with. A number of the Bishops sent a petition, signed by some five hundred Fathers, to Pope Paul VI, asking him to overrule the procedure and have a vote taken. The Pope stood to the prescribed procedure and refused to interfere. In fact, as Canon Pawley has said (*Church Times*, 18/12/64), the delay will ensure a larger majority in favour, and a more mature approval.

Père Rouquette and Padre Caprile give more details about this postponement. The procedure of a *Schema* through various stages is complicated and designed to allow every Father's observations or objections to anything in a *Schema* to be proposed and considered by the Commission in charge of the *Schema* and then submitted to the whole Council. The procedure may leave room for obstructive tactics on the part of a small minority, but whether in this case such tactics were used can neither be proved nor disproved. The matter was also complicated by some difference of outlook among those who wished a declaration on religious liberty to be made. The World Council of Churches issued its statement on Christian Witness, Proselytism and Religious Liberty in a draft form and only after some years accepted it as final. The gravamen was, of course, that only a vote of general approval was desired but postponed in the third session. But considering the pressure of other business the Presidents certainly had a case for leaving the *Schema* to be considered during the interval before the fourth session.

[3] Cf. Appendix I, where all the changes are listed.

giality' means that the bishops and the successor of Peter form together in solidarity the main organ for the guidance and sanctification of the Church;[1] and, as Pope Paul VI put it in his closing address at the third session, it means 'a just and constitutional accord' between the episcopal body and its head, 'the Vicar of Christ, chief of the episcopal body'. This, in fact, had been the accepted doctrine and practice, as the *Acta* of the first Vatican Council make clear. But the Constitution on the Church declared authoritatively that this episcopal part in the solidarity is of divine origin, and that bishops receive their fundamental status by a sacramental consecration, though their 'canonical mission', i.e. appointment to a particular office, must be received in 'hierarchical communion'.

The explanatory note added nothing to this, but underlines four matters, that the episcopal college is not a college in the Roman legal sense, able to elect its own head (and presumably dismiss him), but is a concept derived from revelation; 'hierarchical communion' is needed for the exercise of episcopal power, though neither the Constitution nor the Note specify whether this is a requirement for lawfulness or for validity; the College of bishops necessarily includes the Pope and cannot act without him; and lastly, the episcopal college is not always in a condition to act in a strictly collegial way (though no doubt the ordinary teaching of the bishops is collegial in a wide sense), whereas the Pope can normally act as his office requires.

In practice, the bishops are taking a larger share in the administration of the Church. The 'post-conciliar Commission' on the Liturgy works alongside the Congregation of Rites, and a recent instruction is issued by the Congregation but signed first by the head of the post-conciliar Commission. This may be the pattern of other post-conciliar Commissions. Secondly, diocesan bishops have been made members of the Holy Office, perhaps as a prelude to other changes. And, lastly, Pope Paul VI in his address at the end of the third session announced his intention of inviting certain bishops on due occasion (no time was

---

[1] Distinguish this carefully from the norms they must use, v.g. Scripture, tradition, the agreement of theologians and the faith of the Christian people, the *sensus fidelium*.

specified) to meet and take counsel with him, 'so that I may have the comfort of your presence, the benefit of your experience, the aid of your counsel and the support of your authority', words carefully chosen.

However, in none of these three matters, the postponement of the vote on religious liberty, the changes in the *Schema* on ecumenism and the explanatory note on collegiality, did the Pope himself take the initiative. He acquiesced in the requests of some of the Fathers of the Council who disagreed with others. They may indeed have been a comparatively small minority, but it is clear that Pope Paul wished to secure as large a consensus as possible, and for this reason took pains to respect the consciences of honourable, if possibly scrupulous or anxious men. To suggest that the supremacy of the Pope over the Council was deliberately stressed goes beyond the facts, for the Pope acted in his character of arbiter between differing groups.

As to the proclamation of the Mother of God as the Mother of the Church, here, too, my own opinion is that the Pope was in touch with the feeling of the faithful. One man of intelligence and some standing asked me a year ago, 'Is the Council downgrading our Lady?' Devotion to the Mother of God is deeprooted among the Catholic faithful, as it is among the Orthodox. Moreover, Pope Paul took pains to safeguard the unique Lordship of Christ over the Church in the spirit of the balanced chapter on the Virgin Mary at the end of the Constitution on the Church. Cardinal Bea, whose ecumenical attitude is beyond question, remarked that four years earlier he himself had spoken of our Lady as 'the mother of all the living'.

'Only History Can Judge' is the heading of the conclusion of a Report on Vatican Council II by Dr William A. Norgren, Secretary of the Faith and Order Department of the American Council of Churches; and Dr Norgren ends like this:

'Despite the unsatisfactory events in its last days, in a broader perspective the ten weeks of the third session may have been the most important in the history of the modern church. Episcopal collegiality has been affirmed. The order of the Diaconate was restored. The Roman Church has been committed to the ecumenical movement. Religious liberty and the declaration on the

Jews were powerfully supported. The question of the relation between Scripture and tradition is left open for future dialogue. Modern biblical criticism has been discussed with a substantial measure of appreciation. The sharing of the laity in mission has been strongly supported. Only history can judge whether these last days were as crucial as has been suggested, but there can be no question that momentous things have happened.'[1]

Should the Catholic Church join the W.C.C.?

Whether the Catholic Church should join the World Council of Churches is a question which is often asked, especially in view of the Toronto statement that no church compromises its doctrine of the Church by membership.[2] Even more, a group of theologians who produced a Report, entitled *The Church*, edited under the chairmanship of Dr Newton Flew, London, 1951, listed the theological assumptions of the World Council, and number five contains this sentence: 'There is no reason why those Churches which believe that God has finally committed to them the fulness of the Catholic Church should not be in the Council as the point of contact at which the Holy Spirit will convince others of the truth which He has already revealed to them.' It seems, then, that the Catholic Church would in no way compromise her convictions about the nature of Christ's Church by membership in the World Council.

My own feeling is, nevertheless, that it would not be wise for the Catholic Church formally to have membership in the World Council, much as I esteem it and its work for unity.[3] There is a good deal of confusion about the nature of the W.C.C., especially in the popular mind. Moreover, some connected with the W.C.C. have been questioning whether or no the World Council does not in fact manifest certain elements of the Church, its universality, for instance.[4] Further, sometimes there is confusion between what is said about the Council of Churches

---

[1] *Faith and Order Trends*, vol. 5, no. 1 (December 1964), p. 5.
[2] Cf. Gustave Thils, *Histoire Doctrinale du Mouvement Oecuménique*, Paris and Louvain, new ed., 1962, pp. 220, 260–2, 259–75; Gregory Baum, 'The Catholic Church and the W.C.C., *The Ecumenist*, I, no. 6 (Sept-Oct 1963), pp. 92–5.
[3] Cf. my 'Ecumenical Conclusions', *Heythrop Journal*, I, no. 1 (January 1960); II, no. 2 (April 1961); II, no. 4 (October 1961).
[4] Cf. Dr Lukas Vischer, 'The World Council of Churches and the Vatican Council', *Ecumenical Review*, XIV, no. 3 (April 1963), p. 290.

and what is said about the Church itself.[1] It is certainly not true, as the statements from the Toronto Declaration and from the Report on *The Church* amply demonstrate, that the World Council assumes that we do not know what kind of unity God wills for his Church and have to investigate to find out; but it is true that not a few ecumenists do make that assumption. Consequently, at least in the popular mind, it might be imagined, were the Catholic Church to join the World Council of Churches, that Catholics had either given up, or were compromising about, their faith that the Catholic Church is the authentic heir of the apostolic community.[2]

As I conceive it (and my conception may be mistaken), an application from the Catholic Church to join the W.C.C. would cause very considerable difficulties to the latter. How would the Catholic Church be represented? If according to numbers, its representation would be preponderant. Again, 'conservative evangelicals', whose churches stand outside the W.C.C., and some whose churches are members of the W.C.C. have strong prepossessions against Rome, and might well be expected to object and to dislike the W.C.C., to put it mildly, were the Catholic Church a member.

At present, dialogue is proceeding between the W.C.C. and the Catholic Church. The Secretariat for Unity and the officials of the W.C.C. are in friendly relationships, even though there may be an occasional rift. And so it seems wiser to continue these friendly relations rather than to make the Catholic Church a member of the W.C.C. This is no failure to appreciate 'the ecumenical fact', or that God has been and is working in the World Council of Churches; on the contrary, there is definite belief that the Holy Spirit is drawing us all to the fulness of the unity which he wills. The Decree expresses the desire that 'the measures undertaken by the sons of the Catholic Church should in practice develop in step with those of our separated brethren'. (N. 24, par. 2.) Moreover, 'no obstacle must be placed to the ways of divine Providence or any limit set to the future inspirations of the Holy Spirit'. (*Ibid.*) But, for

---

[1] For an instance of this, cf. my *The Churches and the Church*, op. cit., p. 180, note 1.

[2] The words are those of Gregory Baum, *art. cit.*, p. 93.

the present, development of present cordial relations with the
W.C.C. seem most according to God's will.

C. THE ANGLICAN COMMUNION

The Decree makes mention of the Anglican Communion. As
a result of the Reformation, 'many Communions, national or
confessional, were separated from the Apostolic See. Among
those in which Catholic traditions and institutions in part continue to exist, the Anglican Communion holds a special place.'
(N. 13, par. 3.) The Anglican Communion includes those independent Churches which send their bishops to the Lambeth
Conference, which meets every ten years. At the last Lambeth
Conference in 1958, there were fourteen such Churches represented,[1] all of which are outgrowths of the Church of England
and have retained, largely through the King James Version of the
Bible and the Book of Common Prayer, a great deal of the ethos
and of the doctrinal outlooks of the Church of England.

In contrast with the 'Independents' and the 'Puritans', and
to some extent in contrast with the Zwinglians, the Calvinists
and even the Lutherans, Anglicanism has been marked by a
certain traditionalism. It retained episcopacy and the pre-
Reformation delimitation of dioceses and parishes, and retained
—save for ultimate appeal to the Crown instead of to the Pope
—the whole body of medieval Canon Law: Convocations,
Cathedral Chapters, the University Statutes of Oxford and
Cambridge, deaneries, and the right of patrons to nominate to
cures of souls.[2]

The Church of England retained a major portion of the
Liturgical year, including two feasts of our Lady, and retained
much of the Liturgy of the pre-Reformation Church.[3] Anglicans

---

[1] England, Wales, Ireland, Scotland, the United States, Canada, India, Pakistan, Burma and Ceylon, Australia, New Zealand, South Africa, West Indies,
Japan, West Africa, Central Africa. Since then, four more Churches have become
independent.

[2] Cf. E. W. Kemp, *Counsel and Consent, Aspects of the Government of the Church as
exemplified in the History of the English Provincial Synods*, London, 1960; and the same
author's *An Introduction to the Canon Law of the Church of England*, London, 1957. For
the present government of the Church of England, cf. Guy Mayfield, *The Church of
England; Its Members and Its Business*, London, 1958.

[3] I omit here consideration of the vexed question of the changes which Catholics

from the time of Hooker (d. 1600) generally appeal both to Scripture and to the 'ancient undivided Church' and to the first six Ecumenical Councils. Most Anglicans claim unbroken continuity with the pre-Reformation Church, and say that their ancestors only abolished abuses. Bishops and vicars display, in cathedrals and churches, lists of the names of incumbents in unbroken succession from the date of the foundation, through Reformation times, until the present day.[1]

Anglicans have always retained an admirable tradition of 'sound learning'. They are conspicuous for their interest in patristic studies, are responsible for translation into English of much patristic literature, are producing the Dictionary of Patristic Greek, and the Patristic Conferences at Oxford, inspired and directed by Dr F. L. Cross, of Christ Church, have been a stimulus to patristic scholars all over the world. There are in England today many distinguished scholars, especially about the early history of the Church.[2]

There is a division in Anglicanism between Anglo-Catholics and Evangelicals; but there are many signs that it is growing less, in spite of the strong feeling of some 'Evangelicals' and some 'Anglo-Catholics'. In the ecumenical movement Anglicans have always insisted that episcopacy is an essential condition for reunion. There are, indeed, among Anglicans different interpretations of episcopacy; 'Some Anglicans regard episcopacy as one possible form of church government, desirable it

hold to have rejected the traditional belief in the priesthood. The Church of England is in process of revising its liturgy and its Ordinal. Leo XIII's decision about Anglican Orders was based upon the older Ordinals, and a new Ordinal and Liturgy would create a new situation, especially if Old Catholic bishops took part in consecrations of Anglican bishops. For a brief comparison of the Anglican liturgies with the continental ones, cf. E. C. Ratcliff, 'Christian Worship and Liturgy', sections VI and VII, in The Study of Theology, ed. Kenneth E. Kirk, London, 1939, pp. 448–76. The standard work on the Church of England Liturgy is E. F. Brightman, The English Rite, 2 vols., London, 1915.

[1] Catholics, of course, dispute this claim, on the ground that continuity demands continuity of doctrine. In the past there have been most bitter controversies on the matter. I am convinced that such a controversy is useless and that God in his own way will lead us to perfect reconciliation, a conviction shared by many of our Anglican brethren.

[2] I name the following from memory: A. M. Ramsey, J. W. C. Wand, S. Neill, H. Chadwick, O. Chadwick, J. N. D. Kelly, F. L. Cross, E. L. Mascall, A. Farrar, T. Parker, E. C. Ratcliff, A. W. Couratin, G. D. H. Lampe, R. V. Sellers, A. R. Vidler, S. L. Greenslade, W. R. Matthews, E. W. Kemp, G. Mayfield, H. A. Hodges, O. S. Tomkins, D. Allchin—and there are others whom I have forgotten at the moment.

may be, but not essential; others regard episcopacy as an essential constituent of the Church, a necessary strand in apostolic continuity. Some Anglicans place the emphasis in the interpretation of priesthood upon its sacrificial and absolving functions, in the daily offering of the Eucharist and in regular sacramental confession; others hold views of the ministry in no way differing from those prevailing in non-episcopal communions. . . . The full extent of such liberty of interpretation is only possible within a strict invariability of episcopal ordination. For, while it is possible to hold a "low" view of episcopacy and priesthood within a strict invariability of practice, it becomes impossible to hold a "high" view where this invariability is broken.'[1]

Catholics find this liberty of interpretations not a little disconcerting. Nevertheless Anglicans, in converse with non-episcopal churches, are in practice accustomed to commend episcopacy, and as the ecumenical perspective looks more and more to the continuity of the Church through all history back to apostolic times, it becomes more difficult to give a convincing reason for the invariability of episcopal ordination in practice without tending towards a 'high' view.

D. THE ENDOWMENTS POSSESSED BY THESE SEPARATED BRETHREN

Namely, those churches and ecclesiastical communities stemming from the events which are usually referred to as 'The Reformation'. It should carefully be noticed that the endowments enumerated in this section of the Decree nn. 19–24, must be taken in conjunction with what is said earlier in n. 3, par. 2,s 3 and 4. These separated brethren are recognized as brothers, are in communion with Catholics, although the communion is imperfect; they may have the life of grace, faith, hope and charity, with the other interior gifts of the Holy Ghost; their liturgical celebrations are to be ergarded 'as giving access to the salvation we all hope for, since the Holy Spirit uses them for this purpose'. The 'ecclesiastical reality' of these communions is fully recognized.

[1] *Anglican-Methodist Report*, p. 48.

Next, it should be noticed the endowments enumerated are such as apply to all separated brethren, to 'conservative evangelicals' as well as to others more 'catholic-minded'. Thus, for instance, although many Lutherans, Presbyterians, Methodists, Baptists and others are inclining to accept Scripture in connection with tradition and the Church, nevertheless the Evangelical Alliance maintains 'the right and duty of Private Judgement in the Interpretation of the Holy Scriptures'.[1] Similarly, about the Eucharist, although many in the Protestant tradition are willing to admit a sacrificial element, yet the Constitution of the Evangelical Fellowship in the Anglican Communion makes this statement on the Ministry and the Sacraments:

'We acknowledge Jesus Christ as our only and all sufficient mediator between God and man, and His death as the only sacrifice for sin. We therefore believe that the distinctive functions of the ordained ministry are pastoral not sacerdotal; that whilst the Holy Communion service is a proper occasion for the offering of praise and thanksgiving and of ourselves and our gifts, these are responsive sacrifices offered by all the worshippers as members of the priesthood of all believers; and that the Lord's Supper itself, particularly the action with the bread and wine in which the minister alone engages, is a sacrament administered to men, not a sacrifice offered to God.'[2]

The Decree, of course, makes no judgement about the position of 'conservative evangelicals' within their own communions—and they exist in many communions—and makes no judgement whether they are truly representative of our separated brethren or not. But in listing the 'endowments' the Decree tries to speak as universally as possible and hence not so to speak as to seem to exclude any group of them, or to seem to concentrate attention merely upon those whose convictions are nearer the Orthodox and the Catholic positions.

First, then, is faith in the Incarnation and the Trinity, which faith is a gift of God.[3] Next, the desire for Christian unity is the

---

[1] The Basis of Faith of the Evangelical Alliance and the statement of Faith of the Evangelical Fellowship—the two organizations being different—are given in Dr Norman Goodall's *The Ecumenical Movement*, Oxford, 1961, pp. 153-4.

[2] The Constitution was published in *The Churchman*, March 1962.

[3] Faith is an intelligent and free self-committal to God as he reveals himself in Christ; yet, as the Council of Orange declared in 529, its first beginning, its con-

effect of the grace of the Holy Spirit (no. 1, par. 2). The 'conservative evangelicals' also share this desire: 'Although we hold that the spiritual unity of the Church already exists and has never been destroyed, since the one Spirit animates the one Body, we welcome all efforts to effect full communion between churches, provided that Biblical truth is not thereby compromised.'[1]

The Decree adds two other matters relative to ecumenism among separated brethren in the West, first that they 'look to Christ as the source and centre of church unity'; and secondly, they are inspired to 'bear witness to their faith among all nations everywhere'—a clear reference to the missionary outreach of the churches in the World Council of Churches. The Decree may have in mind the Message of the General Assembly of the W.C.C. from New Delhi in 1961, which contains the following paragraph:

'Christ is the way and therefore we have to walk together witnessing to him and serving all men. This is his commandment. There is no greater service to men than to tell them of the living Christ and no more effective witness than a life offered in service. The indifference or hostility of men may check our open speaking but God is not silenced. He speaks through worship and the sufferings of his Church. Her prayers and patience are, by his gracious acceptance of them, made part of the witness he bears to Christ.'[2]

Here it may be worth remarking that Catholic fears and misgivings about the integration of the International Missionary Council with the World Council of Churches seem to have disappeared since 1961. These misgivings were lest less attention should be paid to doctrinal issues and lest 'proselytism' might be associated with the W.C.C.; I have heard nothing further about these misgivings since the integration in 1961. Ecumenism is certainly having its influence in Africa and most encouraging reports come from Uganda and the Congo.[3]

tinuance and its increase are likewise due to the grace of God, cf. Denzinger, *Enchiridion Symbolorum*, nn. 176–200. Semi-Pelagianism is a recognized heresy.

[1] *Basis of Faith* of the Evangelical Fellowship in the Anglican Communion, n. 5.

[2] *The New Delhi Report*, London, 1962, p. 321. The reference undoubtedly is to parts of the world where freedom of religion is denied or curbed.

[3] Cf. George Every, S.S.M., 'Ecumenism in Africa', and 'Catholic-Protestant

The Bible

The Bible is the object of love and reverence among these our brethren, 'which leads them to a constant and fruitful study of the sacred text'. (N. 21, par. 1). There is no need to mention the debt which all Catholic biblical scholars most gladly acknowledge towards their Protestant confrères, since it is now a commonplace among them. Biblical scholarship seeks for light wherever it can be found and there is a kind of freemasonry among biblical scholars which largely ignores denominational lines.[1] But it is not merely this scholarly study of the Bible which is regarded as characteristic of our separated brethren of the West; the Decree goes on to say—in a passage about which there has been much dispute:[2]

'While invoking the Holy Spirit, in Scripture they seek God as speaking to them in Christ, who is the Word of God made flesh, whom the Prophets foretold. They contemplate in Scripture the life of Christ and what the divine Master taught and did for our salvation, especially the mysteries of his death and resurrection.' (N. 21, par. 2.)

The literature on the first Reformers, on Luther particularly, has grown to enormous proportions.[3] But there is universal agreement that Scripture holds a paramount and cardinal place in all Protestant outlooks and convictions. About Luther's 'new discovery' of Scripture, Fr van de Pol speaks as

Relationships at Lovanium University, Leopoldville' by Canon Alfred Vanneste, in *One In Christ*, vol. I, no. 2 (1965), pp. 157–68.

[1] Cardinal Bea is publishing shortly a new book entitled *The Study of the Gospels. The New Catholic Approach*, Ed. and trans. by Joseph A. Fitzmyer, S.J., London and New York. In the Foreword Cardinal Bea says: 'The recent Instruction of the Biblical Commission (of 24th April 1964) is obviously concerned to encourage biblical scholarship and to protect biblical scholars from the impatience sometimes manifested towards them. It gives its approval to the most modern and scientific methods of biblical research; it indicates the complexity of many problems of Gospel exegesis, and, while warning against the intrusion of dubious philosophical and theological presuppositions into exegetical matters, it approves of the methodology of a sane and balanced Form Criticism.'

[2] Cf. Appendix I, p. 253 below.

[3] Cf. v.g. the review of the literature by Gordon Rupp, *Protestant Catholicity*, London, 1960, pp. 14–28; W. H. van de Pol, *World Protestantism*, English translation, New York, 'Research on Luther', pp. 23–33. Very interesting is J. Newton Flew and Rupert Davies, *The Catholicity of Protestantism*, London, 4th impression, 1953. A useful bibliography is given in *The Ecumenist*, II, no. 3 (March-April 1964), pp. 46–9. One of the most appealing books on Protestantism is R. M. Brown's *The Spirit of Protestantism*, New York and London, 1961.

follows, his words making a certain commentary on the passage from the Decree just quoted:

'Luther discovered the gospel in an entirely new way: that of personal discovery. As a message from God addressed to him personally it contained the only means of solving his personal struggle and agony of soul. Since then one of the most important characteristics of Reformation piety and belief has been this personal, direct, living, existential relation between the individual believer and the objective character of the redeeming word of God as it speaks to man directly and immediately.

'Reformation spirituality is based on and nourished by a daily dialogue with the Bible and as a result the theology of the reformer also received its own characteristic stamp. Truth no longer has a general, abstract, speculative and theoretical meaning but rather a highly personal, concrete, existential and practical one; the science of theology is now no longer a system of premises and conclusions. Luther was perfectly convinced that human reason by itself was incapable of achieving true and genuine knowledge of God. Any such knowledge, he held, must rest on God's self-revelation, on God's own word. This word is not directed primarily at the mind but at the heart. It effects something in man and man reacts to it and draws his practical conclusions from it, but neither the operation of the word nor man's reactions are of an intellectual nature. These events cannot be expressed in a system. They can only be expressed in testimony. Luther's theology was from the very beginning marked by this testimonial character, not in the sense of a proclamation of personal opinions but in the sense of a faithful and obedient annunciation of the objective word of God, of the message of salvation which affects the lives of all men. His theology was born of a prayerful, conscientious listening to sacred Scripture.'[1]

I am not student enough of Luther to be able to guarantee the correctness of this account of Luther, but I cite it as illuminating the statement of the Decree about our separated brothers reading the Scriptures and hearing God speaking in them. It is interesting that Cardinal Bea quotes from the *Schema* on Revelation (not yet approved) the sentence: 'In the

[1] *World Protestantism*, pp. 45–6.

sacred Scriptures the heavenly Father lovingly meets his sons and converses with them.'[1]

The Decree concludes about Scripture by saying: 'But sacred Scriptures provide for the work of dialogue an instrument of the highest value in the mighty hand of God for the attainment of that unity which the Saviour holds out to all.' (N. 21, par. 4.) Here is a basic agreement, that Scripture is the revealed word of God and that nothing contrary to Scripture can possibly form part of the Christian message. Moreover, it is the living word of God, able still to help us into greater fulness of truth.

Baptism

The Decree in n. 22 makes more explicit what had already been said more briefly in n. 3, par. 1. If rightly administered and received, Baptism regenerates to a sharing of the divine life, and established a sacramental bond which links all who have been reborn by it. Cardinal Bea in his two books, *The Unity of Christians* and *Unity in Freedom* has insisted upon this doctrine as thoroughly Scriptural, and though there were doubts, the Decree makes evident that this is now the accepted doctrine.[2] But the Decree adds that Baptism of its nature should lead to the completeness of unity which eucharistic communion gives.

The Lord's Supper

The statement of the Decree in n. 22, par. 3, corresponds to the doctrine set out by the Evangelical Fellowship in the Church of England, as quoted above, p. 230. Granted, then, a denial of the real sacrifice in the Eucharist, and a denial of the real presence,[3] the significance of the Eucharist is reduced to

[1] 'What the Council has so far done for the union of Christians', *Civiltà Cattolica*, March 1965, note 18.

[2] Cf. *The Unity of Christians*, p. 32; *Unity in Freedom*, p. 204, and with more ample references, p. 202. In a most interesting article in the *Clergy Review* (December 1964), 'The Conditional Baptism of Converts', Anthony B. Boylan gives the history of the present unfavourable presumption in England against the validity of a previous baptism and urges that we ought rather to act on the contrary presumption, as is done in Egypt and in France, cf. pp. 736 and 749. Conditional baptism is not justified merely to avoid the trouble of inquiry.

[3] On this, cf. R. Newton Flew and Rupert Davies, *The Catholicity of Protestantism*, op. cit., pp. 112–14.

what the Decree says, namely, a significance of communion with Christ and an expectation of his coming in glory. Nevertheless, such a celebration of the Eucharist may still be an occasion of grace—or, as is said in n. 3, par. 4, 'can engender the life of grace in ways that vary according to the condition of each Church or Community'. We may believe that through such celebrations of the Lord's Supper, the faith of the participants is strengthened and a stimulus given, even by the action of the Holy Ghost, to have greater devotion to the life of self-giving which is expressed in the eucharistic elements. In this way such celebrations can really give access to the salvation for which we all hope.

Worship

Their form of worship, the Decree says, 'not seldom displays notable features of the liturgy they shared with us of old'. This is, I think, particularly true of many of the Lutheran Churches both in Germany and in Scandinavia; at Lund during the Faith and Order Conference of 1952 a High Mass was celebrated by the Lutheran Bishop.

The liturgical movement, however, is bringing many changes among all groups of separated brethren in the West, as is clear from observation, and is explained in greater detail by J. D. Benoit, *Liturgical Renewal*, London, 1958, and by M. J. Taylor, S.J., *The Protestant Liturgical Revival*, Westminster, Md., 1963. The Eucharist is more and more being recognized as central in all Christian worship, and even church buildings show this in the place given to the altar, which in some cases of Free Churches, which used to insist on the 'table', are of stone. The 'conservative evangelicals' are suspicious of this liturgical movement, and want all ceremonial used in worship 'to be a true expression of the biblical truths' as they see them. But perhaps nothing shows more clearly that the 'conservative evangelicals' are not representative than the progress of the liturgical movement.

The lives of these brethren show that they are nourished by their faith in Christ. It is undeniable that church membership and church attendance, over the last thirty years, has decreased in the British Isles, and, from what one hears, in Germany also. Nevertheless the members if fewer are more devoted, active and self-sacrificing. The Puritan tradition of a certain austerity still persists among the Free Churches, and the Church of England seems to be consolidating and showing an admirable adaptation to changing conditions.[1] Anglican religious communities both of men and of women continue their quiet and self-sacrificing work; the Free Churches are starting retreat houses. There is great emphasis upon 'stewardship', that is, upon the duty of supporting the Church and charitable undertakings. The community of monks—of the 'reformed' faith—at Taizé, in France is steadily increasing, and its influence is as incalculable as its monks are humble and devout.

In 1961 a Sunday paper carried two articles criticizing the Anglican and Free Church clergy. The present Cardinal Heenan, then Archbishop of Liverpool, promptly wrote to the newspaper protesting that the articles had not done justice to Protestant and Anglican clergymen—the articles 'seemed like a caricature'. He declared that Protestant clergymen as a body 'are dedicated men. It is impossible not to be impressed by their frugal living and the alacrity with which they respond to calls on their compassion. The poor, the sick, the young, the worried, and indeed, criminals turn to them as friends. The self-sacrifice and devoted charity of the wives of clergymen are also everywhere recognized and admired.'

The Decree makes special mention of their 'strong sense of justice and a true charity towards others. This active faith has been responsible for many organizations for the relief of spiritual and material distress, the furtherance of the education of youth, the improvement of the world conditions of life, and the promotion of justice throughout the world'. To give only one instance, the World Council of Churches collected and distributed in 1961 some $1,100,000 for inter-church aid and service to refugees. But this is only one of the multitudinous agencies of charity among our separated brethren.

[1] Cf. *The Anglican Synthesis*, ed. N. R. F. Browning, op. cit.; R. McAdoo, *The Spirit of Anglicanism*, London, 1965; D. Voll, *Catholic Evangelicalism*, London, 1963; Leslie Paul, *The Deployment and Payment of the Clergy*, London, 1964, suggesting very radical changes in Anglican deployment of the clergy, including abolition of the parson's freehold.

E. DIFFERENCES BETWEEN THEM AND THE
CATHOLIC CHURCH

Many prominent Protestants have praised the frankness with which the Decree on Ecumenism faced the doctrinal differences. Dr W. A. Visser 't Hooft, in his address of welcome to Cardinal Bea at Geneva said: 'We are happy to find that the decree rejects all ecumenical confusionism, and describes ecumenical action as a loyal dialogue in which the differences are taken with utter seriousness.' Pastor Boegner: 'how express to you, your Eminence, the gratefulness which we owe to you for the perfect honesty with which you have always said plainly that however much progress we have made on the way we are happy to travel together, there are still immense obstacles to be overcome?' Pastor Boegner then recalled how Cardinal Bea had said in a Conference at Paris before the Council that Protestant and other Churches separated from Rome could expect no kind of softening down of Catholic doctrine and how he had thanked him for that. 'I thank you now in the name of all who heard you, and particularly in the name of Protestants, for the straightness with which you reject all possibility of confusion, and declare yourself totally opposed to a sentimental ecumenism—as I myself have always done in my writings and my conferences, and face up to the immense difficulties which we all shall have to face and surmount together.'[1]

A series of brief comments upon the Decree was published in the April issue of *The Ecumenical Review*, all generally most favourable. Dr Oskar Cullmann said this in praise of the Decree.

'I welcome as an excellent basis for future dialogue the decree's rejection of any false ecumenical approach (para. 11); for what I consider to be the greatest danger to ecumenism today is the tendency to conceal what separates us, especially when we meet one another as "Christians open to dialogue". Now that ecumenism has come into vogue, both sides are tempted to consider as manifest actions of a highly ecumenical spirit those

[1] *Rencontre Oecuménique à Genève*, Geneva and Paris, 1965, p. 26 and 40.

discussions in which each side shifts the emphasis when presenting his point of view, in order to meet the other side halfway. However slight these shifts of emphasis may be they often distort the truth, create illusion, and thereby do harm to the ecumenical cause, because sooner or later they are bound to lead to a great disappointment.'[1]

Professor Robert McAfee Brown said: 'The clear warning against "false irenicism" is a further strength of the document. It is possible for the new atmosphere to produce varying degrees of unrealistic euphoria. We must continually be reminded that unity is not just round the corner and that extra spurts of good will are not going to resolve all the remaining differences. The advantage of the new situation is that it provides an atmosphere of charity rather than polemics in which we can proceed to discuss our hard-core differences.'[2]

The Rev Dr Douglas Horton, one of the 'delegated observers' representing the International Congregational Council, comments upon the observation made by one Father in the first session of the Council: 'Truth is the essential matter: we must not weaken it, even to meet the separated brethren': 'Remarks such as this are heard only from those who have had little to do with the ecumenical movement and really do not understand it. I am sure that the Secretariat for Unity and all those associated with it, know perfectly well that the separated brethren wish to have the Catholic truths stated as clearly as possible in simple and strong declarative sentences. The ecumenical movement calls for no recessions whatever from the truth as one sees it, but does ask for minds sufficiently open to expect that through the gracious work of the Holy Spirit a higher and more inclusive statement of the truth may be discovered. This will include and correlate convictions tenaciously held which, at the moment, may seem to exclude each other. Both ecumenical and non-ecumenical persons believe their tenets true, but the latter seems to be convinced that there is nothing more to be learned.'[3] Dr Horton reverted to this topic at a meeting of the observers and the American bishops: 'I took the opportunity to scotch

---

[1] P. 94.   [2] P. 97.
[3] *Vatican Diary 1962. A Protestant observes the first session of Vatican Council II*, Philadelphia, U.S.A., 1964, pp. 175–6.

one of the ideas which I have mentioned before in this diary and which we had recently heard several times in the council, namely, that ecumenical dialogue calls for a toning down of the truth held by the Catholic Church, to make it palatable to others. This is of course the very opposite of what is needed: Protestants want Catholics to point up the truth as they see it in as clean-cut outline as possible, for only then can we know what we are talking about. Moreover, if truth were comparable to an inanimate block of stone, even having it cleanly limned would carry no ecumenical hope for the future, but since is is a growing thing, like a flowering plant, there may be some chance for the Holy Spirit to do some grafting in the not as yet clearly discerned days ahead.'[1]

Dr Horton also expressed a general 'protestant' feeling in the same book: 'During the eight and a half weeks of this session we observers have made many Roman Catholic friends. They have appealed to us as human beings. We respect them in every way. Some of whom we have come to know well we regard with un-alloyed affection. I cannot say, however, that as yet (I speak only for myself) I understand the form of the religion which obviously means so much to them. I see the visible church as something at once human and divine. I can touch divinity in it at many points, but I cannot believe that it is divinely perfect, untrammelled by human sin and ignorance, at any point. Here my Catholic colleagues seem to part company with me. I am willing to admit the possibility of papal primacy (for must not the point of highest authority be localized in any executive system?); but it involves a further leap to hold the Pope, under certain circumstances, infallible, for infallibility is an attribute of divine perfection. The church as a whole is regarded as an inerrant teacher, the wafer on the altar as the body of Christ himself—and all through this great church there seems to be a tendency to deify what is of God but is not God. But this means, surely, not that Protestants should turn away from their Catho-lic brethren in discouragement but that they should continue to try to understand them. If they fail again and again to do so, let them remember that the rule for a comparable situation reads "seventy times seven".'[2]

[1] Ibid., p. 192. [2] Op. cit., p. 200.

Frankness

An atmosphere of charity and freedom is essential in express-ing differences. We must speak plainly, but we do not want even to seem to force our convictions upon others or even to persuade them to accept them. Faith depends upon human freedom and God's grace. If others from their own reading, thought and prayer came to share our convictions, we should be glad; but if they do not, we respect their freedom and the work of God's grace within them, and insist more strongly on the truths on which we are agreed, not letting disagreement about some things overshadow our agreements about others. The conditions for dialogue are not the same as the conditions for ultimate full communion, and they should not be confused.

Before stating the differences, two other observations are: Several commentators on the Decree have criticized certain aspects of the Roman position, and have then gone on to say that criticisms of the Roman position ought to carry with them criticisms also of certain features of the non-Roman church doctrines and practices.[1] That, however, is their affair, not ours. In listing differences, which it does here and there, the Decree does not criticize other churches, but only records ad-mitted facts which are pertinent to the ecumenical endeavour. It affirms Catholic principles, but does not enter upon any 'proofs' or justification for them. The purpose of the Decree is not to give an *apologia* for Catholic doctrine or practice, but to fix guiding principles for dialogue and co-operation with separated brethren.

Secondly, the differences mentioned must be placed in the full context of the Decree, recalling what is said about the Church as a communion, about the needs of reform, about humility, variety in unity, a hierarchy of truths, about some traditions expressing certain aspects of divine truth better than others, and about the need to study the relations which existed between the Eastern churches and the See of Rome before the separation.

[1] Cf. Dr Nikos A. Nissiotis, 'Mouvement oecuménique et Vatican II. Un point de vue orthodoxe', *Rencontre Oecuménique à Genève*, Geneva and Paris, 1965, pp. 111–14. After criticizing the Roman centralization, Dr Nissiotis turns to the lack of authority among non-Roman churches.

Specific differences: The structure of the Church

As divinely constituted, this includes the pope and the bishops; the successor of St Peter can voice unerringly the authentic teaching of the Church, and has the special charge of preserving the unity of the Church.

Although among our separated brethren there are those who would grant the pope a primacy of some kind, practically all deny his position as defined in the Constitution on the Church. There seems no need to amplify this. Courtesy and even respect has grown, but our separated brethren, Anglican, Orthodox and Protestant, do not admit that the place in the Church of the successor of St Peter has been divinely revealed.[1] Many Protestants and some Anglicans deny that episcopacy is of divine institution.

The Bible and the Church

On the relation between Scripture and the Church, the Decree says that our separated brethren differ from us—some in one way, some in another. 'For according to Catholic belief the authentic teaching of the Church has a special place in the interpretation and preaching of the written word of God.' (N. 21, par. 3.)

On this point Cardinal Bea, in his friendly discussion with Pastor Boegner in Geneva, appealed to the fact that it was the Church which fixed the canon of the New Testament: 'this fact of the fixing of the canon of the New Testament, that is the fact that the Church in the post-apostolic age defined the number of the books of the New Testament and that it declared them as the authentic norm of the doctrine and of the apostolic tradition—and we Catholics also say, as the inspired Word of God— this fact shows the Church was aware of its power and its duty to put forward doctrine in an authentic way which should

[1] In 'The Papacy', Christian Unity—*Lectures of Maynooth Summer School 1961*, Maynooth, 1963, pp. 116-39, I indicate something of the different tone and outlook towards the Vatican among Anglicans, Orthodox and Protestants. The ecumenical movement, which is largely conciliar, brings to the fore various questions of authority.

oblige the conscience, and to do so on no written foundation—
since the canon did not yet exist—but on the oral tradition
received from the Apostles. If the fixing of the canon of the New
Testament did not rest upon that foundation, then it was a
decision and an operation in the purely human order, liable
consequently to be changed in succeeding centuries—a thing
which is completely contradicted by the tradition of succeeding
centuries which regarded the canon as a thing absolutely unchangeable and untouchable.'[1]

There are differing views among Catholic theologians about
the precise relations between Scripture and Tradition; but all
agree that the Church has the duty and the power to judge the
true meaning of Scripture and to judge what 'traditions' are
sound and what unsound. Separated brethren are advancing
towards greater appreciation of Tradition. The Montreal Conference on Faith and Order in 1963 spoke as follows about the
criterion for a right interpretation of Scripture:

'In some confessional traditions the accepted hermeneutical
principle has been that any portion of Scripture is to be interpreted in the light of Scripture as a whole. In others the key has
been sought in what is considered to be the centre of Holy
Scripture, and the emphasis has been primarily on the Incarnation, or on the Atonement and Redemption, or on justification
by faith, or again on the message of the nearness of the kingdom
of God, or on the ethical teachings of Jesus. In yet others, all
emphasis is laid upon what Scripture says to the individual conscience, under the guidance of the Holy Spirit. In the Orthodox
Church the hermeneutical key is found in the mind of the
Church, especially as expressed in the Fathers of the Church
and in the Ecumenical Councils. In the Roman Catholic
Church the key is found in the deposit of faith, of which the
Church's *magisterium* is the guardian. In other traditions again
the creeds, complemented by confessional documents and the
witness of the Fathers, are considered to give the right key to
the understanding of Scripture. In none of these cases where
the principle of interpretation is found elsewhere than in
Scripture is the authority thought to be alien to the central
concept of Holy Scripture. On the contrary, it is considered

[1] *Rencontre à Genève, op. cit.*, p. 78–9.

as providing just a key to the understanding of what is said in Scripture.'[1]

This passage makes clear how truly the Decree spoke of 'some differing in one way, some in another' from the Catholic doctrine. But the Decree did not say that the Church is the guardian of the deposit of faith, but that the Church has a special place in the interpretation and preaching of the written word of God, which is just a little different, since the Church can grow in understanding of the written word of God, and can come to appreciate implications and connections which in earlier days were not realized.

The Role of Mary

The role of Mary in the plan of salvation is another divergence mentioned by the Decree (n. 20). Conservative and liberal Protestants generally are averse to devotion to the Mother of God; but the influence of several Anglo-Catholics, notably Dr E. L. Mascall, and the religious of the Church of England, and in Germany of the High Church movement, makes it impossible to generalize.[2] The definition of the Assumption was unfavourably received by many Protestants; and the proclamation of our Lady as Mother of the Church by Pope Paul VI was not welcome, though possibly many who reacted unfavourably had not read the section on the Blessed Virgin Mary Mother of God in the Mystery of Christ and the Church, which ends the Constitution on the Church. Pope Paul's proclamation remains strictly within the spirit and even the language of that section of the Constitution, and it may be hoped that the biblical and patristic basis for devotion to our Lady given in that section together with the warning against excesses, may lessen, at least, some of the objections among our separated brethren.

The Eucharist and the Sacrament of Orders

The Decree is most forthright in this paragraph 3 of n. 22:

[1] 'Section Report on Scripture, Tradition and Traditions', *Montreal Report*, London, 1964, p. 53.
[2] Cf. the article and bibliography of Kenneth F. Dougherty, S.A., 'Our Lady and the Protestants', *Unitas*, 4 (Winter, 1963), pp. 253–68.

'though we believe they have not retained the authentic and full reality of the eucharistic mystery, especially because of the absence of the sacrament of orders, etc'. The Eucharist brings to a focus the whole nature of God's intervention in the history of mankind: it sums up all the mysteries of the Christian faith and is the sign and the cause of the unity of Christ's Church. Consequently, it brings to a focus also the differing outlooks and convictions about the manner of God's intervention and the nature of the unity of the Church. Concretely, it brings to a focus the question of the continuity of the Church, shown in the need of episcopal ordination, and the manner in which Christ's redemption is made available to men.

Professor K. E. Skydsgaard, to whom Catholics owe so much for his truly ecumerical concern, speaking of the Lutheran Eucharist, says:

'In immediate connection with prayer, confession, hymns and sermon, follows the celebration of Holy Communion. At this very point the main division between the Roman Catholics and the Evangelical Lutherans has existed since the time of the Reformation. According to the Evangelical position there can be no talk of a "sacrificial mass" as Roman Catholic theology understands it. Christ died one time for all. At the Holy Communion the sacrifice of Jesus made once for all is present in the congregation. A direct line goes back from every celebration of Holy Communion to the cross of Jesus Christ, which alone gives life to the world. We approach here the innermost reality of Christianity. Time stands still in the sacrament of the Eucharist, and the congregation gathers itself about the crucified and risen Lord who is truly present to give to his people a participation in his atonement and resurrection. But in the Evangelical view there is no "sacrifice" either as a "repetition" or as a "representation". Therefore the minister is not a sacrificial priest nor is the altar table a place of sacrifice. At the table Christ himself celebrates Holy Communion with his people, by giving his body and blood to sinful men and making them partakers of his eternal sacrifice.'[1]

Professor Jaroslav Pelikan, who also is by no means unfriendly to Catholics, gives this account of the Catholic doctrine:

[1] *One in Christ*, trans. by Alex C. Kildegaard, Philadelphia, 1957, p. 175.

'The miracle of the Eucharist explains and justifies the sacrifice of the mass, which many Protestants regard as the most repulsive aspect of Roman sacramental teaching. Because the body on the altar is his true body, the same body which he offered on Calvary as the perfect sacrifice for the sins of the world, we continue to plead the merits of that sacrifice each day as we daily offer up the same body that bore our sins. Stated as carefully as that, the sacrifice of the mass may not seem as dangerous as most Protestants make it. But many Roman Catholic theologians do not state it as carefully as that, and neither do many lay people. What was originally intended as a representation ("re-presentation") of the sacrifice on Calvary has now become an extension or even a repetition of that sacrifice. No apologist for the Roman Catholic position can deny that this confusion has often appeared not only among lay people but even among theologians. The formulation of the Council of Trent itself is subject to ambiguous interpretation. To many non-Romans all of this seems to be in direct conflict with the explicit and repeated insistence of the New Testament that what Christ has done, he has done "once for all" in a single and unrepeatable sacrifice of perfect obedience. His sacrifice of Calvary cannot be extended or repeated. A sacrifice there is in the Eucharist; the very word means "sacrifice of thanksgiving". But it is a sacrifice that avails because it is "in union with his most holy sacrifice", as an ancient liturgical formula has it. Roman Catholic theology and piety have not always kept this distinction clear".[1]

Professor G. D. H. Lampe of Cambridge, writing about the English Ordinal, after having said that the Ordinal obviously intends to continue the threefold ministry of deacon, priest and bishop, proceeds:

'If this is what is meant by the ambiguous term "validity", there is no doubt that the Church of England possesses a fully valid and regular ministry. If, however, a valid ministry of priesthood is defined in terms of intention to continue, not merely the office of priesthood (that is, the pastoral ministry of

---

[1] *The Riddle of Roman Catholicism*, London, 1960, p. 110. I cite this merely to show the different outlook on the Eucharist which is held even now by many Protestants and that in general very many tend to reject the sacrifice of the Mass and to justify their rejection.

Word and sacraments as the Ordinal believes it to have existed in the Church from the beginning) but also the pre-Reformation conception of that office which defines it in terms of the power to "consecrate" and offer sacrifice, then the clear implication of the Ordinal is that Anglican orders are in this sense invalid—as Bonner, Pole, Julius III, and Paul IV evidently believed. The Anglican priest has every reason to claim that his orders place him in the historic succession of the ministry of the universal Church throughout the centuries, and that he is fully and regularly commissioned to the ministry of the Word and sacraments in the sense in which the New Testament understands that ministry. If he is loyal to the Ordinal he cannot, however, rightly claim that he has been ordained to do what the Sarum Pontifical understood to be the principal function of a priest. On the contrary he will be thankful that he has not. He will also look with gratitude and hopeful expectation to the present striking developments in the "Catholic" (both Roman and Anglican) theology of eucharistic presence and sacrifice, with increasing confidence that in the light of the revival of biblical study and fuller understanding of patristic theology the concepts which have dominated the Catholic-Protestant controversy about "sacrificing priests" from the sixteenth century to the time of Leo XIII will, before long, be drastically modified.

'It has often been maintained in the current debate about intercommunion that loyalty to the Ordinal forbids Anglicans to recognize an equality of episcopal and non-episcopal ministries. If this means that he may not ascribe to the latter the same degree of regularity and authority, this is true. If, however, it is taken to refer to the possession by the former of a *sacerdotium* which the latter necessarily lacks, the Ordinal offers no support to the contention; for it knows of no *sacerdotium* but that which is the essence of the priesthood: the ministry of Word and sacraments by which Christ's priestly mediation is made effective for all believers. In this priestly ministry others besides episcopally ordained priests obviously share, however defective their orders may be in regularity, and in the authority of the universal Church; and the Ordinal offers no ground on which Anglicans can refuse to recognize a fundamental equality between these ministries in respect of the grace of the priest-hood.'[1]

Professor Lampe in this statement disagrees with what I believe the vast majority of Anglicans now hold; and this is clear from their unwillingness that their members should receive Holy Communion from any save an episcopally ordained minister, from their insistence upon acceptance of episcopacy in all plans for reunion and from a multitude of declarations from Anglican bishops and theologians. I do not cite Professor Lampe in order to introduce controversy about Anglican Orders, for I think that such controversy will do harm to the ecumenical cause, and I am convinced that God will settle that question in his own way. The Decree makes no judgement about the official teaching of any other Church or ecclesiastical Community; but it is clear that Professor Lampe and those who share his rejection of a priesthood whose office is to 'consecrate' and offer sacrifice have not retained what Catholics hold to be the authentic and full reality of the eucharistic mystery.[2]

Yet even on this most painful subject—for must not everyone feel pain at a difference on so sacred a subject?—there are signs of a new dawn. At the Nottingham Conference of Faith and Order of the British Council of Churches in 1964, the section on the ministry, after long and painful discussion produced the following statement, which was accepted by all except thirty-seven official delegates:

'Jesus Christ is not only the one Apostle of God; he is the one Priest. As risen Lord through the Spirit he exercises his priesthood of mediating life to the world and bringing the world to the Father. Christ enables his people to identify themselves with his own love to the Father; therefore they have a corporate priesthood centred in his. This priestly action is sacramentally set forth in the Lord's Supper. Here the minister does not repeat the action of Calvary but, in union with Christ and his people, declares sacramentally, in word and action, his once-for-all

---

[1] *The Churchman, A Quarterly Journal of Anglican Theology,* vol. 76, no. 1 (March 1962), p. 30.

[2] I do not believe that the pre-Reformation Church held any other doctrine on the eucharistic sacrifice than is held today, and I think Fr Francis Clark and Mgr H. Francis Davis have done a service to the ecumenical cause in showing this cf. Francis Clark, *Eucharistic Sacrifice and the Reformation,* London, 1960, and H. Francis Davis, 'The Mass in the Middle Ages', *Clergy Review,* July 1959.

sacrifice. By Christ's action in the Eucharist he unites his people with himself in his eternal love to the Father.'[1]

The word 'priest' is not used nor the expression 'to offer sacrifice'. But the Eucharist is not described merely as a remembrance of Christ's sacrifice, for the minister 'declares sacramentally Christ's once-for-all sacrifice', an expression substituted, I believe, for the word 're-presents', which appeared in an earlier version. I think both Catholics and Orthodox would like a clearer statement, even though there is a definite approach to the doctrine held by both.

Moral Teaching

Reference is made to differences on this head in n. 23, par. 3. A good deal of this moral teaching in accord with the Gospels was contained in Pope John XXIII's Encyclical *Peace on Earth*; more will doubtless be contained in the declarations of Vatican Council II about religious liberty and the relation of the Church to the world and to non-Christian religions. The question of marriage, however, remains. Cardinal Bea in his *Unity in Freedom* pointed out that the question of mixed marriages would be eased if our separated brethren would state their belief about the whole question of marriage, especially about divorce.[2]

This list of disagreements—and more might be added—is certainly formidable, and becomes more formidable when one recollects that both Anglicanism and Protestantism have developed a certain ethos of their own. Dean Roger Hazelton, of the Graduate School of Theology at Oberlin College, in his excellent book entitled *New Accents in Contemporary Theology*[3] puts the difference thus:

'The catholic and protestant tendencies show themselves in discussion of Scripture and tradition, the sacraments, Jesus Christ, social action and responsibility, as in the doctrine of the church. The former tendency emphasizes the historic continuity and authority of Christian institutions as God-given and God-directed; the latter stresses the sovereignty and transcendence of God above all visible and historic church life. One

---

[1] *Unity Begins at Home. A Report from the First British Conference of Faith and Order, Nottingham, 1964,* 1964, p. 68.
[2] Pp. 196–200.   [3] New York, 1960.

may roughly say that the protestant tendency is prophetic; the catholic is sacramental, or that the difference is essentially between a view in which man is related savingly to Christ through the church and one in which man is related savingly to the church through personal faith in Christ. It is clear, furthermore, that within the ecumenical movement these tendencies are growing closer together and are gaining in mutual understanding and respect.'[1]

In conclusion, weighty as are the divisions and their principles, the principles which unite are weightier still. There is the change of feeling and atmosphere from antagonism and suspicion to friendliness and trust. There is the conviction of being engaged in a common cause—to bring Christ to an increasingly secularized world. There is the effort to find principles which will 'undercut' the formal differences and make the differences disappear, as it were of themselves, without the direct confrontation which may be needed at the beginning. No theological formulation exhausts the truth and in the total vision a reconciliation may be perceived almost comparable to the vision we shall have when we see God face to face after this life is over.

The Decree on Ecumenism is unquestionably revolutionary, as others have said as well as Cardinal Bea. What it says about the Eastern Orthodox Church certainly overturns much previous Catholic thinking. Sincere appreciation of Anglican and Protestant religious convictions and life gives hope of new vision. And—what must never be forgotten—God may raise up prophets among us to put things in ways we have not yet imagined.

'The Council professes its awareness that human powers and capacities cannot achieve this holy objective—the reconciling of all Christians in the unity of the one and only Church of Christ. It is because of this that the Council rests all its hope on the prayer of Christ for the Church, on our Father's love for us, and on the power of the Holy Spirit. 'And hope does not disappoint, because God's love has been poured into our hearts through the Holy Spirit who has been given to us" (Rom 5: 5).'

[1] Op. cit., p. 95. Cf. also Gregory Baum, *Prospects and Perspectives*, op. cit., p. 167, who agrees about this different ethos between the catholic and the protestant.

APPENDIX I

(1) No. 1, par. 1, the second sentence read: 'the disciples (or followers) of the Lord have different convictions etc.', which was changed to read: 'All, indeed, avow that they are disciples of the Lord, but they have different convictions, etc.'

(2) No. 1, par. 2, where it was said that 'all long for the one visible Church', the word 'almost' was inserted. In fact, there are some Christians who still believe that an invisible unity of the church is sufficient.

(3) No. 3, par. 2, last sentence . . . 'belong to the one Church of Christ', the word 'properly' (*iure*) was inserted before the word 'belong'.

(4) No. 3, par. 3, last line . . . 'has been entrusted to the Church'; the word 'Catholic' was added before the word 'Church'.

(5) No. 3, par. 5, last sentence, the phrase 'in its members' was inserted before the word 'liable to sin'.

(6) No. 4, par. 1, line 1, the phrase 'under the inspiring grace of the Holy Spirit' was put instead of 'under the inspiration of the Holy Spirit'. The Latin was '*afflante Spiritu Sancto*', which was the opening phrase of an Encyclical of Pius XII on the inspiration of Scripture.

(7) No. 4, par. 4, last line 'since both proceed from the marvellous ways of God' was put instead of 'since both proceed from the action of the Holy Spirit'.

(8) No. 4, par. 8, second sentence, the phrase 'such riches of Christ and gifts of the Holy Spirit' was emended to read: 'such riches of Christ and virtuous deeds'.

(9) No. 4, par. 9, the phrase 'by the grace of the Holy Spirit' was put instead of 'by the Holy Spirit'.

(10) No. 13, par. 2, the phrase 'in the West' was substituted for 'in the Western Church'.

(11) No. 14, par. 1, the phrase 'are proud to trace their origins to the Apostles' was put in place of 'trace their origins to the Apostles'.

(12) No. 14, par. 2, sentence two, the clause 'who took flesh from the Virgin Mary' was substituted for 'who took flesh from the Virgin Mother of God, (Deipara)'.

(13) No. 14, par. 3, in the second sentence, the word 'also' was inserted before 'from lack of mutual understanding and charity', i.e., lack of charity and mutual understanding was not necessarily the sole cause of the breach.

(14) No. 14, par. 4, first sentence, the word 'desired' or 'hoped for' was inserted before the word 'fullness', in Latin *in instaurationem plenae communionis optatae inter Ecclesias orientales et Ecclesiam.*

(15) No. 15, par. 4, in the third sentence, 'to avail themselves of the spiritual riches of the Eastern Fathers' the words 'still more' were inserted.

(16) No. 16, the sentence affirming that the Eastern Churches 'have the power (*facultatem*) to govern themselves, according to the disciplines proper to them, since they are better suited to the character of their faithful and more for the good of souls', had read: 'the right and the duty' (*ius et officium*).[1]

(17) No. 17, par. 1, in the second sentence which had said that the theological formulations of the East and West were to be regarded rather as complementary rather than as conflicting, the word 'often' was added, so as to admit at least the possibility that some formulations might be conflicting.

(18) No. 21, par. 2; as this emendation caused considerable discussion, I give the Latin both of the original and of the emended text:

Original: Spiritu Sancto movente in ipsis Sacris Scripturis Deum inveniunt sibi loquentem in Christo, etc.

(By the action of the Holy Spirit, in the Holy Scrip-

---

[1] Cf. p. 209

tures themselves, they find God speaking to them in
Christ, etc.)

*Emended Text: Spiritum Sanctum invocantes, in ipsis Sacris
Scripturis Deum inquirunt quasi sibi loquentem in Christo,
etc.*

(Calling upon the Holy Spirit, they seek God in the
Scriptures themselves, as speaking to them in Christ,
etc.)

It should be noted that the emended Latin *quasi sibi
loquentem in Christo* must not be translated as if it read
'*quasi sibi loqueretur*'—as if God were speaking to them in
Christ (but he is not), with the imputation that they seek
God, but do not find him. The old text might have implied
that all our separated brothers *always* find God speaking to
them in the Scriptures, and they themselves would
scarcely hold this, being aware of the differing interpretations of Scripture among them. On the other hand, the
new text cannot fairly be understood as if it affirmed that
they *never* find God speaking to them in Scripture: in fact,
both the old and the new texts meant to indicate, and to
indicate with approval, a general attitude towards Holy
Writ: they look upon it as God's revelation to men in and
through Christ, and in reading Scripture they are convinced that God speaks to them both as individuals and as
groups, and in Scripture they seek to find solutions both to
their personal problems and to the problems connected
with the search for unity. It was this that the old text
meant, the word 'inveniunt'—they find—being probably
intended to be taken as a 'conative present', that is to
indicate that 'they are for finding' God speaking to them
in Christ. But as the word '*inveniunt*' could be misunderstood, the word '*inquirunt*'—to search for—to examine—
was judged to be more exact. The word *quasi* does not
necessarily mean 'as if'. In Jn 1: 14, vidimus gloriam eius
gloriam *quasi* unigeniti a patre, and in 1 Peter 1: 14, *quasi*
filii obedientiae, non configurati prioribus ignorantiae
vestrae desideriis, the Revised Standard Version translates
the *quasi* by 'as': 'glory *as* of the only Son from the Father',
and '*as* obedient children, etc.'. Hence the translation

seems justified: 'they seek God in the Scriptures themselves as speaking to them in Christ'. As, then, Christ is really the Son of the Father, and as the Christians really should be obedient children, so too the *quasi sibi loquentem* can be taken as meaning that God really does speak in Scripture.

A good deal of ink has been spilt over this passage, but I do not think it worth while discussing the various interpretations which have been given of the emendation.

(19) No. 22, par. 2, the first sentence read: 'the full reality of the Eucharistic Mystery', and this was changed to read: 'the authentic and full reality of the Eucharistic Mystery'.

APPENDIX II

(Promulgated 21st November 1964): Chapter I, no. 15:
'The Church recognizes that in many ways she is linked with those who, being baptized, are honoured with the name of Christian, though they do not profess the Faith in its entirety or do not preserve unity of communion with the Successor of Peter. For there are many who honour Sacred Scripture, taking it as a norm of belief and a pattern of life, and who show a true apostolic zeal. They lovingly believe in God the Father Almighty and in Christ the Son of God and Saviour. They are consecrated by baptism, in which they are united with Christ. They also recognize and accept other sacraments within their own churches or ecclesiastical communities. Many of them rejoice in the episcopate, celebrate the Holy Eucharist and cultivate devotion towards the Virgin Mother of God. They also share with us in prayer and other spiritual benefits. Likewise we can say that in some real way they are joined with us in the Holy Spirit, for to them too he gives his gifts and graces whereby he is operative among them with his sanctifying power. Some indeed he has strengthened to the extent of the shedding of their blood. In all of Christ's disciples the Spirit arouses the desire to be peacefully united, in the manner determined by Christ, as one flock under one shepherd, and he prompts them to pursue this end. Mother Church never ceases to pray, hope and work that this may come about. She exhorts her children to purification and renewal that the sign of Christ may shine more brightly over the face of the earth.'

APPENDIX III

24. Those Eastern Churches which are in communion with the Apostolic Roman See have a particular responsibility for promoting unity among all, especially Eastern Christians, according to the principles laid down by the Decree '*On Ecumenism*' of this Holy Synod. This is done by prayer first of all, by personal example, by religious faithfulness to ancient Eastern traditions, and by better acquaintance-ship, co-operation and fraternal appreciation of each other's ways and outlooks.[1]

25. When separated Eastern Christians are drawn by the grace of the Holy Spirit to catholic unity, nothing more should be demanded of them than what is required by a plain profession of catholic faith. And since the authentic priesthood has been preserved among them, Eastern clerics who come to catholic unity may exercise their own Order, according to the norms laid down by competent Authority.[2]

26. The law of God forbids any such sharing in worship (*communicatio in sacris*) as contradicts the unity of the Church, or such as involves formal adherence to error, or endangers purity of faith, or gives rise to scandal or indifferentism.[3] But pastoral experience shows that, as regards Eastern brethren, there are various circumstances of particular individuals that can and should be taken into account, in which the unity of the Church is not affected and those dangers are absent, while the salvation and good of their souls are pressing needs. For this reason, the Catholic Church, according to the different circumstances of time,

---

[1] From the tenor of the Bulls of union of particular Eastern Catholic Churches.
[2] A synodal obligation regarding separated Eastern brothers and all Orders of every degree either of divine or ecclesiastical law.
[3] This teaching is held also by separated Churches.

place and persons, has often adopted and now adopts a course of action that is less rigid, offering to all the means of salvation and the witness of inter-Christian charity, by a sharing in the sacraments and in other sacred functions and practices. With this in mind, the Holy Synod, 'not wishing by any severe judgement to create obstacles for those on the way to salvation',[1] but rather to promote greater unity with the Eastern Churches that are separated from us, has resolved to adopt the following measures.

27. According to the principles laid down, the sacraments of Penance, the Eucharist and the Anointing of the Sick can be conferred on those Eastern Christians who in good faith are separated from the Catholic Church, if of their own accord they ask for them and are rightly disposed. Moreover, catholics may seek the same sacraments from those non-catholic ministers in whose Church the sacraments are considered to be valid, whenever there is need or real spiritual benefit, and access to a catholic priest is physically or morally impossible.[2]

28. Similarly, in accordance with the same principles, a sharing in sacred functions, services and places is for a just cause allowed between catholics and separated Eastern brothers.[3]

29. The application of this milder regulation regarding a sharing in worship (*communicatio in sacris*) with brothers of the separated Eastern Churches is entrusted to the care and direction of the local hierarchies. They should take counsel among themselves, and on due occasions confer with the hierarchies of separated Churches, and so direct the relationship of Christians through fitting and effective precepts and guidance.

[1] St Basil the Great: *Canonical Epistle to Amphilochius*, PG32 669B.

[2] The following points are to be taken into account as a basis for mitigation: (1) the validity of the sacraments; (2) good faith and disposition; (3) the necessity of eternal salvation; (4) the absence of one's own priest; (5) the exclusion of objectionable dangers and of formal adherence to error.

[3] Here there is reference to the so-called 'extra-sacramental share in holy things' (*communicatio in sacris extrasacramentalis*). It is the Council which permits this mitigation, *servatis servandis*.

APPENDIX IV

CITATIONS FROM VARIOUS ADDRESSES OF POPE JOHN XXIII

In his first public address, 29th October 1958, Pope John said:
'We embrace the whole Church, Western and Eastern, with warm fatherly love. We open our loving heart and extend our outstretched arms to all who are separated from the Apostolic See, where Peter lives in his successors 'even to the consummation of the world' (Mt 28: 20) and fulfills Christ's command to bind and loose on earth (cf. Mt 16: 19) and to feed the Lord's entire flock (cf. Jn 21: 15–17).

'We long for their return to the house of common Father and repeat the words of the Divine Redeemer: 'Holy Father, keep in Thy name those whom thou hast given me, that they may be one even as we are" (Jn 17: 11). For thus "there shall be one fold and one shepherd" (Jn 10: 16). We pray that they might all return freely and gladly; may this come to pass through the inspiration and assistance of God's grace. They will not find it a strange house, but one that is truly their own, a house which has from time immemorial been enlightened by the teachings and adorned by the virtues of their forefathers.'

Shortly after his announcement (on 25th January 1959) that he intended to call an Ecumenical Council, on 1st February 1959, the *Osservatore Romano* quoted him as having said:
'The faults from which we Catholics are not, alas, free, lie in our not having prayed enough to God to smooth the ways that converge on Christ's Church; in not having felt charity to the full; in not having always practiced it toward our separated brethren, preferring the rigour of learned, logical, incontrovertible arguments, to forbearing and patient love, which has its own compelling power of persuasion; in having preferred the philosophical rigidity of the lecture room to the friendly serenity of the *Controversies* of St Francis of Sales.'

In June 1959, an Anglican, Canon Rea, reported that the Holy Father had remarked to him: 'In working for reunion, it is necessary first to be very meek and humble; second, to be patient and know how to await God's hour; and third, to avoid discussions that may hurt the virtue of charity, leaving aside for the moment those elements on which we differ.'

'THE UNITY OF THE CHURCH'

In his Encyclical on the Unity of the Church, 20th June 1959, he spoke of his hopes for that unity of all Christians:

The Unity Christ Prayed For

'We must now speak of that unity which is our special concern, and which is intimately linked with the very pastoral office divinely committed to our charge: the unity of the Church.

'As is well known, our Divine Redeemer founded this society to be *one* to the end of time: "Behold I am with you all days, even to the consummation of the world" (Mt 28: 20). He prayed earnestly for this unity, and clearly His prayer was acceptable to God; 'He was heard for his reverence' (Heb 5: 7). This prayer of Christ "that they may all be one, as thou, Father in me and I in thee, that they may be one in us" (Jn 17: 21), is the source and guarantee of our cherished confidence that eventually all the sheep that are not of this fold will find their way back to it, and, as our Divine Redeemer promised, "there will be one fold and one shepherd" (Jn 10: 16).

'This irresistible assurance was the compelling motive which led us to announce publicly our resolve to call an Oecumenical Council. Bishops will come together there from every corner of the world to discuss important matters of religion. But the most pressing topics will be those which concern the spread of the Catholic faith, the revival of Christian standards of morality, and the bringing of ecclesiastical discipline into closer accord with the needs and conditions of our times. This in itself will provide an outstanding example of sincerity, concord and charity. May those who are separated from the Apostolic See, beholding this manifestation of unity, derive from it the inspiration to seek out that unity which Jesus Christ prayed for so ardently from His heavenly Father.'

The movement towards unity among separated Christians

'In recent years among a number of Communions separated from the See of Peter there has been a wider movement towards Catholic faith and practice, and considerable respect for this Apostolic See. We know this, and the knowledge is a source of great consolation to us. It is a movement which is increasing daily as zeal for the truth overrides past prejudices. Though separated from us and divided amongst themselves, they yet rejoice in the name of Christian, and we know of the several congresses and councils they have held in an effort to tighten the bonds which join them together. Here is proof indeed that they are consumed with the desire for unity, at least for some measure of unity.'

A father's call to unity

'May this striking evidence of the unity which characterizes the Catholic Church as unique, may the desires and prayers by which she implores from God the same unity for all mankind, exert a saving influence upon your minds and hearts—yes, *your* minds, for we are speaking now of those of you who are separated from this Apostolic See.

'Allow us to express our affection for you, and to call you sons and brothers. Permit that in our fatherly and loving heart we cherish the hope for your return. Once, when unhappy schism rent the seamless garment of the Church, Theophilus, the Bishop of Alexandria, implored his own "sons and brothers" in these words which we, fired with that same pastoral zeal, desire now to speak to you: "Most dear ones, sharers of a heavenly calling, let us do all in our power to imitate Jesus, the Guide and Author of our salvation. Let us embrace that humility and love which carries us aloft and joins us to God, and that sincere faith in the divine mysteries. Flee disunion, shun discord. Cherish mutual love. Listen to the words of Christ: 'In this all men will know that you are my disciples, if you have love for one another.'"[1]

'Observe, we beg of you, that when we lovingly invite you to

[1] Cf. *Hom. in mysticam caenam*; P.G. LXXVII, 1027.

the unity of the Church, we are inviting you not to the home of a stranger, but to your own, your Father's, house. It belongs to you all. We long for you "in the bowels of Jesus Christ" (Phil 1 : 8), permit then that we appeal to you to remember your fathers "who have spoken the word of God to you; consider the outcome of their life and imitate their faith" (Heb 13: 7). We seem to see the illustrious company of the saints in heaven inviting you by the example of their lives to this same unity. Your own nations sent them on before you into heaven. Many of them bequeathed to you in their writings an authentic and lucid explanation of the teaching of Jesus Christ. They invite you once more to union with this Apostolic See, with which for many centuries your Christian communities were once happily united.

'We address you, then, as brothers, even though you are separated from us. For as St Augustine said: "Whether they like it or not, they are our brothers. They will once cease to be our brothers when they cease to say: Our Father."[1] "Let us love the Lord our God, let us love his Church. The one as a Father, the other as a Mother; the one as Lord, the other as his handmaid, for we are the sons of this handmaid. And this marriage is cemented by a great love. No one offends the one, and is well-pleasing to the other. . . . What does it profit you not to have offended your father, if you have offended your mother? . . . Hold fast, therefore, dearest ones, all of you with one mind, to God your Father, and the Church your Mother." '[2]

The need for special prayer

'We therefore direct our suppliant prayers to God, the giver of heavenly light and of all that is good, of his great kindness to protect the Church's unity and extend Christ's fold and kingdom, and we urge everyone of our brethren and dearest children in Christ likewise to pray earnestly for this intention. For the success of the coming Oecumenical Council will depend more on the great ardour of their concerted prayers, vying, as it were, with each other in holy rivalry, than on any human

[1] Ps. 32, *Enarr.* II, 29, Migne, P.L. XXXVI, 299.
[2] Ps. 82, *Enarr.* II, 14; Migne, P.L., XXXVII, 1140.

efforts, care and industry. And we extend also a warm invitation to those who are not of this fold, yet who reverence and worship God and strive in all sincerity to obey his commandments; may they too join in this prayerful appeal to God.

'May the divine prayer of Christ increase in us this hope, these desires, and bring them to fulfilment: "Holy Father, keep them in Thy name whom thou hast given me; that they may be one, as we also are. . . . Sanctify them in truth. Thy word is truth. . . . And not for them only do I pray, but for them also who through their word shall believe in me . . . that they may be perfect in one." ' (Jn 17: 11, 17, 20, 21, 23).

Peace and joy, the fruits of harmony

'We, and the Catholic world united with us, recite this suppliant prayer again and again. It is not just our ardent love for all peoples that impels us, we are moved too by the spirit of Christian humility. We are well aware of our own inadequacy. It was not any merits of ours, but God's inscrutable designs, that raised us to the eminence of the Supreme Pastorate. To all our sons and brothers, therefore, who are separated from this See of Peter, we take up these words: "I am your brother Joseph" (Gen 45: 4). Come, then, "receive us" (2 Cor 7: 2). We desire, we long for, we beg God for nothing else but your salvation and your eternal happiness. Come; out of this yearned-for unity in harmony, nurtured and fostered by a father's love, may there spring forth a great peace which "surpasseth all understanding" (Phil 4: 7), for its origin is in heaven—the peace which Christ proclaimed to men of good-will when herald angels sang above his cradle (cf. Lk 2: 14); the peace which after instituting the sacrament and sacrifice of the Eucharist he bestowed with the words: "Peace I leave you, my peace I give unto you; not as the world giveth, do I give unto you" (Jn 14: 27). Peace and joy; yes, joy too, for those who are really and effectively joined to Christ's mystical body, the Catholic Church, share in the life that flows from the divine Head through all the members; and in virtue of this life, those who faithfully obey all the commandments and precepts of our Redeemer are enabled, even in this mortal life, to enjoy that happiness which is herald and harbinger of the eternal joys of heaven.'

On the 7th May 1960, at the close of an address to missionaries, 'the Holy Father appealed for a real understanding of those brethren who, while bearing the name of Christian on their foreheads and indeed in their hearts, are yet separated from the Catholic Church. We must bestir ourselves and not rest until we have overcome our old habits of thought, our prejudices and the use of expressions that are anything but courteous, as so to create a climate favourable to the reconciliation we look forward to, and so in every way to co-operate with the work of grace. Thus to one and all will be thrown wide open the gates to the unity of the Church of our Lord and Saviour Jesus Christ.'[1]

In June 1960, Pope John set up a special Secretariat for Promoting the Unity of Christians, and said he did so 'as a token of our affection and good will towards those who bear the name Christian but yet are separated from this Apostolic See.'[2]

On 14th November 1960, Pope John spoke in the Basilica of St Peter's about preparation for the Council, and referred to our separated brethren in these terms:

'The fact that the first reports about the Council, that were circulated to the world at large, should have aroused attention and respect even "beyond the bounds of the Catholic Church" on the part of separated brethren is especially consoling to us, and it furnished us with a foretaste of the joy of the unity of all believers in Christ—in his longing and in his very own prayer to his Father: "That they all may be one, that you may sanctify them in truth."

'But the Council, as everyone knows, and as has been announced repeatedly, has limits of its own, like a "city on a hill", and it will devote itself exclusively in the beginning to matters that have to do with our mother, the Catholic Church, and its present internal organization.

' "The spirit of the Lord has filled the earth and that which holds all things together knows what is said." These magnificent words from the first chapter of the Book of Wisdom are, like the

[1] *Osservatore*, 11th May 1960.   [2] *A.A.S.* 52 (1960), p. 436.

whole of that book, stupendous and very moving. With regard to those who do not share our full profession of the Catholic faith, and yet honestly and sincerely desire information on the work of the Council, we hope that they will not feel it impolite or suffer any inconvenience if we ask them to wait until the Fathers and qualified consultors who have been assigned to the individual commissions have completed their work and everything is set and properly prepared for loftier contacts: intellect, heart, and vision of the supernatural upon which the *Spiritus Domini* can settle to the glory and love of Christ Jesus who has founded his Church holy and glorious.

'Besides, it is well known that we have rounded out the official framework of the ten commissions among whom the work of the Council has been divided by providing for the institution of a special Secretariat, among others, that can reply to matters referred to it by all our brothers (who deserve every respect even though they are, as we are accustomed to say, separated) who may want to follow the work of the Council in the light of truth, and with a measure of wisdom and of friendly discretion.'[1]

In his address at the first session of the Council, 11th October 1962, his reference to Christian unity was brief but weighty:

'The Church's solicitude to forward and defend truth derives from the fact that, according to the plan of God, "who wishes all men to be saved and to come to the knowledge of the truth" (1 Tim 2: 4), men without the assistance of the whole of revealed doctrine cannot reach a complete and firm unity of minds, with which are associated true peace and eternal salvation.

'Unfortunately, the entire Christian family has not yet fully attained this visible unity in truth.

'The Catholic Church, therefore, considers it her duty to work actively so that there may be fulfilled the great mystery of that unity, which Jesus Christ invoked with fervent prayer from his heavenly Father on the eve of his sacrifice. She rejoices in peace, knowing well that she is intimately associated with that prayer, and then exults greatly at seeing that invocation extend its efficacy with salutary fruit even among those who are outside her fold.'

[1] *A.A.S.* 52 (1960), p. 1009–10.

His address to the delegated observers two days later, 13th October 1962, was disarming in its simplicity:

'Today's most welcome meeting is to be simple and friendly, respectful and brief. The first word which rises up in my heart is the prayer taken from the 67th Psalm, which has a lesson for all, "Blessed day by day be the Lord, who bears our burdens; God, who is our Salvation" (Ps 67: 20).

'When in 1952, Pope Pius XII most unexpectedly asked me to become the Patriarch of Venice, I told him that I did not need to reflect very long before accepting the appointment. For in the undertaking there was nothing at all of my own seeking; there was no desire in my heart of being appointed to one office or ministry rather than to another. My episcopal motto fitly provided my answer—"*Obedientia et Pax*" (Obedience and Peace).

'And so when after thirty years in the direct service of the Holy See I prepared myself to begin a new kind of life and found myself shepherd of the flock of Venice, which I was to tend for the next six years, I reflected and meditated upon those words of the Psalm: "The Lord who bears our burdens;" he carries us, what we are and what we possess; with his treasure in us and with our miseries.

'This same thought was present to me when I accepted, four years ago, the succession of St Peter, and it has been so in what has followed right up to the announcement and the preparation of the Council.

'In so far as it concerns my humble person, I would not like to claim any special inspiration. I content myself with the sound doctrine which teaches that everything comes from God. In this sense I have considered this idea of the council which began on 11th October to be a heavenly inspiration. I confess to you that it was for me a day of great emotion.

'On that providential and historic occasion, I devoted all my attention to my immediate duty of preserving my recollection, of praying and giving thanks to God. But from time to time my eye ranged over the multitude of sons and brothers and suddenly, as my glance rested upon your group, on each of you personally, I drew a special comfort from your presence.

'I will not say more about that at the moment, but will content myself with recording the fact. "Blessed day by day be the Lord." Yet, if you could read my heart, you would perhaps understand much more than words can say.

'Can I ever forget the ten years passed at Sofia, or the ten more at Istanbul and Athens? They were twenty years of happy and delightful acquaintance with persons I revere and with young people filled with generosity upon whom I looked with affection, even though my work as representative of the Holy Father in the Near East was not explicitly concerned with them.

'Then again at Paris, which is one of the crossroads of the world, and was especially so immediately after the end of the last war, I had frequent meetings with Christians of many different denominations.

'I cannot remember any occasion on which we were divided on principle nor that there was ever any disagreement on the plane of charity in the common work of helping those in need, which the circumstances of our time made necessary. We did not haggle, we talked together; we did not have arguments, but we bore each other good will.

'One day long ago I gave to a venerable and aged prelate of an oriental church, not in communion with Rome, a medal of the pontificate of Pius XI. This gesture was meant to be, and was, a simple act of friendly courtesy. Not long after, the old man, on the point of closing his eyes on the things of this earth, requested that, when he was dead, the medal of the Pope should be put on his breast. I saw it myself and the memory of it still moves me. I have mentioned this episode deliberately because in its simplicity and innocence, it is like a flower of the field which the return of spring allows one to pluck and offer. May the Lord always thus accompany our steps with his grace.

'Your welcome presence here and the emotion of our priestly heart (the heart of a bishop of the Church of God, as we said yesterday before the assembled council), the emotion of my beloved fellow workers and, I am certain of it, your own emotion too, combine to show you that there burns in my heart the intention of working and suffering to hasten the hour when for all men the prayer of Jesus at the Last Supper will have reached its fulfilment.

'But the Christian virtue of patience is not out of harmony

with the equally fundamental virtue of prudence. And so I say again: "Blessed day by day be the Lord." For today let that suffice.

'It is now the task of the Catholic Church to bend herself to her work with calmness and generosity; your task is to observe her with renewed and friendly attention. May the inspiration of heavenly grace which moves hearts and rewards good works be upon all of you and all that is yours.'

Three days before he died, on Friday, 31st May 1963, he said: 'In my vigils at night, I have always kept before me Jesus Christ with his arms outstretched to receive the whole world. It is the role of the Catholic and apostolic Church, of the Roman Church, to work for the realization of the prayers of the divine Master: *Ut unum, ut unum sint*.[1]

On 11th May 1963 Pope John XXIII wrote 'an apostolic letter' to the Bishops of the Slav nations in communion with the Holy See on the occasion of the eleventh centenary of the arrival of Saints Cyril and Methodius in Greater Moravia; in it occurs the following passage:

'You know, Venerable Brethren, that with fervent desire we have striven and laboured so that the Orientals who glory in the name of Christian separated from the communion of the Apostolic See may be zealous towards re-establishing it and that by gradually fulfilling the prayer of Christ, the unity of one flock and one shepherd may be realized.

'The desires of the Second Ecumenical Council of the Vatican, at which—bringing pleasure to the heart and the promise of fair hope—even delegated observers of the separated churches have been present, reach out towards the same end.

'The voice of the times is the voice of God. By more than one indication and by arguments which are not few nor insignificant, it seems to urge and impel towards the desired restoration of this communion and peace.

'In the most noble and useful cause of re-establishing harmonious bonds in the unity of integral faith, from which there will undoubtedly be born a new order of happiness in the Christian world, the things which unite both sides are much

[1] Quoted by Henri Fesquet, in *Wit and Wisdom of Good Pope John*, London, 1964, p. 154.

greater than those which separate them. Now both must prepare the roads which will be of solid construction and which, if
there will be mutual understanding and fraternal charity, will
lead to the desired success. This eagerness to fulfil the Will of
God strengthens all things, hopes all things, sustains all things.

'What a great contribution has been made towards this end
by the association founded by Antony Martin Slomsek, Bishop
of Maribor, and developed by Antony Cyril Stojan, Archbishop
of Olomouc, to which the name of Apostolate of Saints Cyril
and Methodius was given! How effective were the congresses
which were held at Velehrad, near the sacred relics of Saint
Methodius! The noteworthy and gratifying results which thus
developed for a common gain strongly accentuate the fervent
wish for better circumstances which will make easier the resump-
tion and promotion of a work so happily begun.

'We remember that in 1927, when we held the office of
Apostolic Delegate in Bulgaria, we wrote to the president of the
Congress of Velehrad: "It is my desire that a joyful voice coming out of Bulgaria may reach you and, through you, may be
spread among all those assembled in Velehrad where a solemn
convocation is being held in commemoration of Saints Cyril and
Methodius. This voice bears testimony to the fact that Catholics
here share in the prayers, studies, deliberations, and petitions
which Slav Catholics express and manifest for the union of the
churches. Truly we seem to be the grains of wheat scattered upon
the mountains, according to the beautiful image of the ancient
Christian prayer, grains which indeed unite together to form
delicious bread. Through the intercession of Saints Cyril and
Methodius, may God bless your fraternal union of spirits, and
may heavenly grace grant it a visible sign."[1]

'It was at that time that we began the practice of praying to
God not only for the beloved Bulgarian people but also for all
the peoples who made the name of Christ shine forth in the
heart of Europe. It was this impulse of fraternal love that
moved us each day during the years that followed to pour out
confident prayers to God in a spirit of tender reverence. In
these prayers it has been our custom to join to the Blessed
Mother of Jesus, Saints Cyril and Methodius and all the other

[1] *Acta V. Conv. Velehr.*, p. 61.

Saints of East and West so that by their ever powerful patronage they might beg of God the fulfilment of that brotherhood and peace so much desired.

'Certainly, for this sublime aim of unity strenuous efforts will be necessary, but as means to carry them out with alacrity, we have the exhortations, the encouragement and the patronage of Saints Cyril and Methodius who, like two heavenly stars illuminate the road upon which we are to travel. Surely, these two holy pillars of unity are praying much for the holy city which is the Church and for the peoples entrusted to their care: Cyril and Methodius, two olive trees, two candelabra, two anointed sons who stand before the Lord of the whole earth.[1]

'How opportune, how moving, and how fitting for present circumstances is the prayer which Saint Cyril, dying in Rome, uttered to ask great heavenly graces for his people: "O Lord God, who hast created all the orders of angels and spiritual powers, who hast stretched forth the heavens and established the earth . . . make thy Church grow in numbers, and gather all together in unity; establish all thy chosen ones in the harmony of thy true faith and thy right confession and inspire in their hearts the word of thy revelation . . . so that they may gird themselves to do what is good and pleasing to thee."[2]

'On the occasion of the commemoration of this happy event, with the greatest reverence should thanks be rendered to God for the indescribable benefit which was conferred on the Christian community by the auspicious coming of Saints Cyril and Methodius. For through them directly, or through their disciples, the Christian faith and civilization were brought to the Slavic nations. Thus there flourished, under the influence of the grace of the Gospel, those gifts happily implanted by nature which are the ornament of these nations: a vivid sense of the divine, a generous character, a rich and diversified talent, a sense of refinement, a copious disposition towards the fine arts, a genuine hospitality, all of which offers confident hopes for their future.

'Unhappily, in many of their regions, these heavenly blessings, the gifts received from their ancestors, and the noble name

---

[1] Cf. 2 Mach 11: 14; Rev 11: 4; Zach 4: 11–44.
[2] *Slavic Life of Constantine*, ch. XVIII.

of Christian are looked down upon. Heaven grant that repentance may be felt for despising what should be esteemed and loved and that, by a change in the attitude of their rulers—which we trust will come about—the tempest will be transformed into a pleasant breeze.

'In order that the Christian religion, that treasure of inestimable value handed down from their ancestors, may be preserved intact for your people, we urge you this year to intensify supplications to God, prayers, holy sacrifices, tears, and the fruit of good works, possessing the mystery of faith in a pure conscience (1 Tim 3: 9). The Ruler and Director of all things and times, having been appeased, as is our prayerful hope, will turn afflictions and sadness into better things and will prepare consolations for those who trust in his aid and protection so that the joy will be all the greater as less expected.

'We have learned that the celebration of this eleventh centenary is being commemorated by certain significant efforts to perpetuate it for the adornment and profit of religion. For example, studies on the history of Sts Cyril and Methodius and their teaching will be published, and pilgrimages will be organized.

'We urge you to add to these other undertakings so that by zealous efforts these two Apostles may in some way return to honour among your people and the torch which they brought may burn more brightly and be raised on high.'

APPENDIX V

At the opening of the Second Session of Vatican Council II, Pope Paul VI spoke as follows about ecumenism:

The Council has a third object, one which in the order of spiritual realities is most grave. This too was put before us by Pope John XXIII. It concerns 'the other Christians'—those who believe in Christ but whom we cannot happily number among ourselves in the perfect unity of Christ which only the Catholic Church can offer them.

This unity, objectively speaking, should be theirs by baptism. It is something which, virtually at least, they already desire. For recent movements, at present in full development in bodies of Christians separated from us, show clearly two things. The first is that the Church of Christ is one alone and therefore must be unique. The second is that this mystic and visible union cannot be attained except in identity of faith, and by participation in the same sacraments and in the organic harmony of a single ecclesiastical direction, even though this allows for a great variety of verbal expressions, movements, lawful institutions and preference with regard to modes of acting.

There can be no doubt about the attitude of the Council with regard to these great numbers of separated brethren and of the possibility of multiplicity in the unity of the Church. This too is one of the characteristics of the Council.

The Council aims at complete and universal ecumenicity. That is at least what it desires, what it prays and prepares for. Today it does so in hope that tomorrow it may see the reality. This Council, while calling and counting its own those sheep who belong to the fold of Christ in the fullest and truest sense, opens the door and calls out, too, in anxious expectation to the many sheep of Christ who are not present within the unique fold.

It is a Council, therefore, of invitation, of expectation, of confidence, looking forward toward a more widespread, more fraternal participation in its authentic ecumenicity.

We speak now to the representatives of the Christian denominations separated from the Catholic Church, who have nevertheless been invited to take part as observers in this solemn assembly. We greet them from our heart. We thank them for their participation. We transmit through them our message—as father and brother—to the venerable christian communities they represent.

Our voice trembles and our heart beats the faster both because of the inexpressible consolation and reasonable hope that their presence stirs up within us, as well as because of the deep sadness we feel at their prolonged separation.

If we are in any way to blame for that separation, we humbly beg God's forgiveness. And we ask pardon too of our brethren who feel themselves to have been injured by us. For our part, we willingly forgive the injuries which the Catholic Church has suffered, and forget the grief endured during the long series of dissensions and separations. May the heavenly Father deign to hear our prayers and grant us true brotherly peace.

We are aware that serious and complicated questions remain to be studied, treated and resolved. We would wish that this could be done immediately on account of the love of Christ that 'urges us on'. But we also realize that these problems require many conditions before satisfactory solutions can be reached—conditions which are as yet premature. Hence we are not afraid to await patiently the blessed hour of perfect reconciliation.

Meanwhile we wish to affirm before the observers here present some points in our attitude toward reunion with our separated brethren, with a view that they may communicate them to their respective christian communities.

May our voice also reach those other venerable christian communities separated from us, that did not accept the invitation freely extended to them to attend the Council. We believe these points are well known, but it is useful to repeat them here.

Our manner of speaking towards them is friendly, completely sincere and loyal. We lay no snares. We are not motivated by temporal interests. We owe our Faith—which we believe to be divine—the most candid and firm attachment.

But at the same time we are convinced that this does not constitute an obstacle to the desired understanding with our separated brethren, precisely because it is the truth of the Lord and therefore the principle of union, not of distinction or separation. At any rate we do not wish to make of our Faith an occasion for polemics.

Secondly, we look with reverence upon the true religious patrimony we share in common, which has been preserved and in part even well developed among our separated brethren. We are pleased to note the study made by those who seek sincerely to make known and to honour the treasures of truth and of genuine spirituality, in order to improve our relations with them.

We hope that just as they are desirous to know more about our history and our religious life, that they would also wish to make a closer study of our doctrine and its logical derivation from the deposit of divine Revelation.

Moreover we are aware of the enormous difficulties still in the way of this desired union. We humbly put our trust in God. We shall continue to pray. We shall try to give better proof of our efforts of leading genuine christian lives and practising fraternal charity. And should historical reality tend to weaken our hopes, we shall try to recall the comforting words of Christ: 'Things that are impossible with men are possible with God' (Lk 18:27).

In his address at Bethlehem, January 1964, Pope Paul VI used the following significant language:

We are living at the historic hour when the Church of Christ must live its deep and visible unity. It is the hour for us to answer the wish of Jesus Christ: 'That they may become perfectly one, so that the world may know that thou hast sent me.' To the internal unity of the Church corresponds externally its apologetic and missionary strength. We must pursue our Ecumenical Council to its conclusion. We must give the life of the Church new attitudes of mind, new aims, new standards of behaviour, make it rediscover a spiritual beauty in all its aspects: in the sphere of thought and word, in prayer and methods of education, in art and canon law. A unanimous effort is needed in which all groups must offer their co-operation. May everyone hear the call which Christ is making to him through our voice.

This is our message to the Catholics who already belong to Christ's sheepfold. But we are unable not to extend the same invitation to our Christian brothers who are not in complete communion with us. From now on it is clear to all that one cannot avoid the problem of unity. Today this desire of Christ thrusts itself on our minds and forces us to undertake, with wisdom and charity, everything that is possible in order to allow all Christians to enjoy the great blessing and supreme honour of the unity of the Church.

Even in the very special circumstances in which we find ourselves today, we must say that such an outcome cannot be obtained at the expense of the truths of the faith. We cannot be unfaithful to this patrimony of Christ; it is not ours but his, and we are only its depositaries and interpreters. But, we declare once again, we are ready to take into consideration every reasonable means capable of smoothing the roads of dialogue, in respect and in charity, with the aim of a future meeting— please God it may be near—with our Christian brothers who are still separated from us. The gate of the sheepfold is open. Everyone's hopes are loyal and sincere. Desire is strong and patient. The place available is broad and spacious. The step to be taken is awaited with all our affection: it can be made with honour and in honour and in mutual joy. We will refrain from asking for steps that would not be made freely and with full conviction, that is to say moved by the Spirit of the Lord, who bloweth when and where he listeth. We will wait for this blessed time. For the moment all we ask of our very dear separated brethren is what we ask of ourselves: that the love of Christ and of the Church may inspire every eventual step towards rapprochement and meeting. We will see to it that the desire for understanding and union remains living and unchanged; we will put our trust in prayer. Even if it is not yet in common, it can at least be said simultaneously and rise, parallel from our hearts, as from the hearts of the separated Christians, to join together at the feet of the Most High, the God of unity.

Meanwhile, we greet with great respect and affection the illustrious and venerable heads of Churches separated from ours but gathered here: we thank them sincerely for their participation in our pilgrimage, we pay homage to the share they possess of the authentic treasure of the Christian tradition, and to them we express our desire for an agreement in the faith, in the love and in the discipline of the one Church of Christ. We send our wishes for peace and prosperity to all the pastors, priests, religious and faithful of these Churches: on all we invoke the light and the grace of the Holy Ghost.

In a letter to the Catholic Bishops of the world on the occasion of the January Octave of Prayer for Christian Unity, Pope Paul VI spoke as follows about the Octave:

More especially we wish to recommend the Octave of Prayer for the unity of Christians which will begin in a few days and which yearly brings together Christians of every denomination in a single surge of intercession for the unity desired by Christ for all those who bear his name.

We are glad to recall that it was precisely on 25th January 1959, at the end of this octave of prayers, that our venerated predecessor John XXIII gave the first announcement of the ecumenical council with a view to the renewal of the Church and the unity of Christians, and who in his first encyclical, *Ad Petri Cathedram*, was pleased to call all Christians his most beloved brothers, inviting them all without exception to pray for unity.

We ourselves who, on acceding to the pontificate chose the name of the Apostle Paul, have always attached great importance to this octave in the course of the various stages of the ministry to which the Lord called us, and every year we have joyfully celebrated its conclusion on the day when the Roman liturgy commemorates the conversion of St Paul.

We know that innumerable persons in the various Christian denominations devote themselves to this sublime cause, and that in prayer and penitence, in Christian unity with us, they raise to God their humble and fervent intercession that God's will be done.

Let it not come to pass, Venerable Brothers, that the sons of the Catholic Church, because they already possess the fullness of truth as the gratuitous gift of divine Providence, should show themselves less zealous regarding so holy a cause. On the contrary, may a holy emulation inspire them, together with their non-Catholic brothers, and may it lead them to show themselves all the more generous in prayer and penitence since God has already granted them the inestimable gift of full membership in his Church.

Under the guidance of the sacred shepherds who showed during the ecumenical council how much they had the cause of union at heart, may the prayer of the faithful become more ardent than in the past, to ask from the Lord the realization of the unity of Christians by means of the grace of his Holy Spirit.

On Holy Thursday, 1964, Pope Paul VI celebrated in St John Lateran, the parish church of Rome, the Mass commemorating the institution of the Holy Eucharist. His sermon of that occasion dealt with the Eucharist and unity. It reads as follows:

We personally chose to celebrate this rite of Holy Thursday, being led to do so by the invitation and the encouragement of the recent constitution of the Ecumenical Council on the sacred liturgy. The particular aim of this constitution, in effect, is that of bringing the hierarchical and communal forms of the Church as close as possible in the exercise of worship, in the celebration, the understanding, and the appreciation of the sacred mysteries expressed, nay, contained in the official and sacramental prayer of the Church.

If every priest, as the leader of a group of the faithful, if every bishop, conscious of being the active and sanctifying head of a church, desires, when it is possible for him, to celebrate personally the Mass of Holy Thursday, the memorable day on which the holy Mass was instituted and celebrated for the first time by Christ himself, in order that it should then be repeated by those chosen to exercise his priesthood, should not the Pope, glad of the opportunity, carry out the rite himself on the occasion of this yearly remembrance which brings to mind the origin of this institution, which leads us to meditate upon it, which exalts with simplicity, yet with every interior disposition, its ineffable, most holy significance, and which worships the hidden but assured presence of Christ sacrificing himself for our salvation?

If we wished to add other reasons for this decision of ours (to celebrate personally), we should have no difficulty in finding many and excellent ones. Two of these motives, particularly, can help to render our present celebration more pious and more auspicious. The first is suggested to us by the many-sided movement within our contemporary society which is manifesting itself under so many different forms and which is leading this society, be it willing or not, towards expressions that at first are uniform and then unitary. Human thought, culture, activity, politics, social life—and even economic life with its singular preoccupation with the interests that divide and oppose the parties concerned—are all tending towards unification. Progress at once demands it and depends upon it. In it there is peace, and peace has need of it.

Now, the mystery which we are celebrating this evening is a mystery of unification, of a mystic and human unity, as we well know. And though it is unfolding itself in a sphere other than a purely temporal one, it does not prescind from nor overlook the social character of mankind. The Eucharistic mystery, which with good reason we term 'communion', presupposes, cultivates, affirms, and sublimates this social character by uniting us in an ineffable manner to Christ, and by Him to God, to our brethren, depending, however, on whether or not they participate at the table which gathers us together, in the faith which unifies our souls, and in the charity which draws us together into a single body, the Mystical Body of Christ.

The second motive concerns, as we said before, every priest, every bishop; but it concerns us principally, our mission and our person, whom Christ has placed at the heart of the unity of the whole Catholic Church, which at the dawn of her existence was said by one of the Fathers to be the 'president of charity'. We feel that we have the great and serious obligation of recapitulating here all of human history, linked, as to its source of enlightenment and salvation, to the sacrifice of Jesus, a sacrifice which is here reflected and renewed in an unbloody manner. It is for us to prepare a table in this place to which all the bishops, priests and faithful of the earth are mystically invited. That which is being celebrated here is the fraternity of all the children of the Catholic Church. Here, indeed, is the very fount of Christian society; it is here that it finds those transcendent principles that make it up; this is the source of its buoyant energy that is fed not by earthly interests, which are always ambiguous, not by political calculations that are ever ephemeral, not by imperialist ambitions nor by levelings forcibly imposed, nor even by the noble and ideal dream of universal concord which man can at most formulate, but which he is unable to realize or maintain. It is nourished, rather, by a superior and divine current, by the current of charity that urges us on, that charity which Christ obtained for us from God which he infuses in us to help us to 'be one' as he himself is one with his Father.

My brethren and my children, the time would not suffice for us to describe the fullness of this moment, and mere words are inadequate: here we have the celebration of the one and of the many; here we find the school of the higher love of individuals for others, the profession of mutual esteem, of engagement in fraternal co-operation and gratuitous service, the motivation for a wise tolerance; here we discover the precept of mutual forgiveness, the source of joy for the good fortune of others and of sorrow for the misfortune of others, the inspiration of preferring to give rather than to receive, the source of true friendship, the art of governing by serving and of cheerful obedience, the formation of sincere and courteous relations among men, the respect and veneration of the human person, the harmony of free and docile minds, the communion of souls—in a word, charity.

Just a few days ago we read these depressing words of a contemporary writer, the prophet of a world without love, of a world of egoism, proclaimed to be a liberating one: 'I do not want a communion of souls. . . .' Christianity is diametrically opposed to this attitude. It is our desire, instead, to build up, with the help of Christ, a community of souls, one with the widest possible dimensions.

This is why we priests, above all, proclaim those sacrosanct words of Holy Thursday: 'Let us love one another as Christ loved us.' Where could we ever find a greater, a simpler, or more appropriate programme for the renewal of our Church's life?

To you of the faithful, who are gathered about this altar, and to all of you, members of the Holy Church of God, we would propose still another saying, also uttered by Jesus on Holy Thursday: 'By this shall all men know that you are my disciples, if you have love one for another.'

To all those to whom the echo of this celebration of the Easter Supper may reach, we say, in the faith of Christ and in his charity: 'Love the brotherhood' (1 Peter 2, 17).

It is for this reason, as well, that we confirm our intention, which we have placed in the hands of our Lord Jesus Christ, of leading the Ecumenical Council to a successful conclusion, as a great manifestation of charity in the Church; and of giving to the collegiality of bishops the significance and value which Christ intended to confer on his apostles, in communion with and with respect for the first among them, Peter; and of favouring every project aimed at increasing charity, collaboration, and trust in the Church of God.

And it is still with these sentiments of charity that we greet from this basilica, 'the head and mother of all churches', all our Christian brethren, who are still unfortunately separated from us, but who are engaged in seeking the unity desired by Christ for his one Church. We send our best wishes and Easter greetings, the first perhaps, on an occasion as sacred as this, to the Eastern Churches, now separated from us, but already so close to us in the faith. Our greetings and Easter peace go to the Ecumenical Patriarch Athenagoras, whom we embraced at Jerusalem on the Latin feast of the Epiphany; may peace and greetings go to the other patriarchs whom we met on the same occasion. Greetings of peace, as well, to the other heads of those ancient and venerable Churches which have sent their representatives to the Vatican Ecumenical Council; and also to all those whom we are trustingly awaiting to meet one day in the embrace of Christ.

Greetings and peace to the whole Anglican Church, while with sincere charity and hope we look forward to see it one day honourably take up its place in the one and only fold of Christ.

Greetings and peace to all the other Christian communities

born of the Reformation in the sixteenth century which has separated them from us. May the virtue of Christ's Easter show us the right, and perhaps long, road for us to follow towards perfect communion. Meanwhile, let us now, with mutual respect and with reciprocal esteem, search for ways of shortening the distances between us and of practising the charity which we hope to see one day victorious.

With grateful remembrance, we likewise greet warmly all the believers in God belonging to one or the other non-Christian religions, who greeted our pilgrimage to the Holy Land with joyous respect. Finally, at this moment, we are thinking of the whole of humanity. Impelled by the charity of him who so loved the world that he gave his life for it, our heart assumes the dimensions of the world, as though it possessed the infinite dimensions of the heart of Christ.

And you, brethren and faithful children, who are here present, you are indeed one with us in celebrating this Holy Thursday, the day of Christ's love, consumed and perpetuated for our salvation.

In his Encyclical on the Church, 6th August 1964, Pope Paul VI spoke of the 'dialogue' of the Church with the world, with unbelievers, with non-Christian religions, with separated Christian brethren and, lastly, within the Church itself.

In general: adaptability to the concrete situation yet faithfulness to the teaching of Christ

Many, indeed, are the forms that the dialogue of salvation can take. It adapts itself to the needs of a concrete situation, it chooses the appropriate means, it does not bind itself to ineffectual theories and does not cling to hard and fast forms when these have lost their power to speak to men and move them. The question is of great importance, for it concerns the relation of the Church's mission to the lives of men in a given time and place, in a given culture and social setting.

To what extent should the Church adapt itself to the historic and local circumstances in which its mission is exercised? How should it guard against the danger of a relativism which would falsify its moral and dogmatic truth? And yet, at the same time, how can it fit itself to approach all men so as to save all, according to the example of the Apostle: 'I became all things to all men that I might save all' (1 Cor 9: 22)? The world cannot be saved from the outside. As the Word of God became man, so must a man to a certain degree identify himself with the forms of life of those to whom he wishes to bring the message of Christ. Without invoking privileges which would but widen the separation, without employing unintelligible terminology, he must share the common way of life—provided that it is human and honourable—especially of the most humble, if he wishes to be listened to and understood. And before speaking, it is necessary to listen, not only to a man's voice but to his heart. A man must first be understood; and, where he merits it, agreed with. In the very act of trying to make ourselves pastors, fathers and teachers of men, we must make ourselves their brothers. The spirit of dialogue is friendship and, even more, is service. All this we must remember and strive to put into practice according to the example and commandment that Christ left to us (cf. Jn 13: 14–17).

But the danger remains. The apostle's art is a risky one. The desire to come together as brothers must not lead to a watering-down or subtracting from the truth. Our dialogue must not weaken our attachment to our faith. In our apostolate we cannot make vague compromises about the principles of faith and action on which our profession of Christianity is based. An immoderate desire to make peace and sink differences at all costs is, fundamentally, a kind of scepticism about the power and content of the Word of God which we desire to preach. Only the man who is completely faithful to the teaching of Christ can be an apostle. And only he who lives his christian life to the full can remain uncontaminated by the errors with which he comes into contact.

We believe that the Council, when it comes to deal with questions on the Church's activity in the modern world, will indicate a number of theoretical and practical norms for the guidance of our dialogue with men of the present-day. We believe, too, that in matters concerning the apostolic mission of the Church, on the one hand, and, on the other, the diverse and changing circumstances in which that mission is exercised, it will be for the wise, attentive government of the Church to determine, from time to time, the limits and forms and paths to be followed in maintaining and furthering a living and fruitful dialogue.

The ministry of the word

Accordingly, let us leave this aspect of the subject and confine ourselves to stressing once again the supreme importance which christian preaching maintains, an importance which grows greater daily, for the Catholic apostolate and specifically for the dialogue. No other form of communication can take its place; not even the enormously powerful technical means of press, radio and television. In a sense, the apostolate and preaching are the same. Preaching is the primary apostolate. Our apostolate, Venerable Brothers, is above all the ministry of the Word. We know this very well, but it seems good to remind ourselves of it now, so as to direct our pastoral activities aright. We must go back to the study, not of human eloquence or empty rhetoric, but of the genuine art of the sacred word.

We must search for the laws of its simplicity and clarity, for its power and authority, so as to overcome our natural lack of skill in the use of the great and mysterious spiritual instrument of speech and to enable us worthily to compete with those who today exert so much influence through their words by having access to the organs of public opinion. We must beg the Lord for the great and uplifting gift of speech (cf. Jer 1 : 6), to be able to confer on faith its practical and efficacious principle (cf. Rom 10: 17), and to enable our words to reach out to the ends of the earth (cf. Ps 18: 5 and Rom 10: 18). May we carry out the prescriptions of the Council's Constitution on Sacred Liturgy with zeal and ability. And may the catechetical teaching of the faith to the christian people, and to as many others as possible, be marked by the aptness of its language, the wisdom of its method, the zeal of its exercise supported by the evidence of real virtues, and may it strive ardently to lead its hearers to the security of the faith, to a realization of the intimate connection between the divine Word and life, and to the illumination of the living God.

We must, finally, refer to those to whom our dialogue is directed. But, even on this point, we do not intend to forestall the Council, which, please God, will soon make its voice heard.

The message of truth, justice, freedom, progress, peace and civilization

Speaking in general on the role of a partner in dialogue, a role which the Catholic Church must take up with renewed fervour today, we should like merely to observe that the Church must be ever ready to carry on the dialogue with all men of good will, within and without its own sphere. There is no one who is a stranger to its heart, no one in whom its ministry has no interest. It has no enemies, except those who wish to be such. Its name of catholic is not an idle title. Not in vain has it received the commission to foster in the world, unity, love and peace.

The Church is not unaware of the formidable dimensions of such a mission; it knows the disproportion in numbers between those who are its members and those who are not; it knows the limitations of its power; it knows, likewise, its own human weaknesses and failings. It recognizes, too, that the acceptance of the Gospel depends, ultimately, not upon any apostolic effort of its own nor upon any favourable temporal conditions, for faith is a gift of God and God alone defines in the world the times and limits of salvation. But the Church knows that it is the seed, the leaven, the salt and light of the world. It sees clearly enough the astounding newness of modern times, but with frank confidence it stands upon the paths of history and says to men: 'I have that for which you search, that which you lack.' It does not thereby promise earthly felicity, but it does offer something—its light and its grace—which makes the attainment as easy as possible; and then it speaks to men of their transcendent destiny. In doing this it speaks to them of truth, justice, freedom, progress, concord, peace and civilization. These are words whose secret is known to the Church, for Christ has entrusted the secret to its keeping. And so the Church has a message for every category of humanity: for children, for youth, for men of science and learning, for the world of labour and for every social class, for artists, for statesmen and for rulers. Most of all, the Church has words for the poor, the outcasts, the suffering and the dying; for all men.

Dialogue with the whole of mankind: solidarity with all men

In speaking in this way, we may seem to be allowing ourselves to be carried away in the contemplation of our mission and to be out of touch with reality as regards the actual relations of mankind with the Catholic Church. But that is not so. We see the concrete situation quite clearly. To give a brief idea of it, we think it can be described as consisting of a series of concentric circles around the central point in which God has placed us.

The first of these circles is immense. Its limits stretch beyond our sight and merge with the horizon. It is that of mankind as such, the world. We gauge the distance that lies between us and the world; yet we do not consider the world a stranger. All things human are our concern. We share with the whole of mankind a common nature: human life with all its gifts and problems. In this primary universal reality we are ready to play our part, to acknowledge the deep-seated claims of its fundamental needs, to applaud the new, and sometimes sublime, expressions of its genius. We possess, too, vital moral truths, to be brought to men's notice and to be corroborated by their conscience, to the benefit of all. Wherever men are trying to understand themselves and the world, we can communicate with them. Wherever the councils of nations come together to establish the rights and duties of man, we are honoured when they allow us to take our seat among them. If there exists in men 'a soul naturally Christian', we desire to show it our respect and to enter into conversation with it. Our attitude in this, as we remind ourselves and everyone else, is, on the one hand, entirely disinterested: we have no temporal or political aim whatever, and on the other hand, its purpose is to raise up and elevate to a supernatural and Christian level every real human value in the world. We are not civilization, but we promote it.

The irreligious and the atheist

We realize, however, that in this limitless circle there are many, very many unfortunately, who profess no religion; and we are aware also that there are many who profess themselves, in various ways, to be atheists. We know that some of them proclaim their godlessness openly and uphold it as a programme of human education and political conduct, in the ingenuous but fatal belief that they are setting men free from false and outworn notions about life and the world and are, they claim, putting in their place a scientific conception that is in conformity with the needs of modern progress.

This is the most serious problem of our time. We are firmly convinced that the theory on which the denial of God is based is utterly erroneous. This theory is not in keeping with the basic, undeniable requirements of thought; it deprives the reasonable order of the world of its genuine foundation; this theory does not provide human life with a liberating formula but with a blind dogma which degrades and saddens it; this theory destroys, at the root, any social system which attempts to base itself upon it. It does not bring freedom; it is a sham, attempting to quench the light of the living God. We shall, therefore, resist with all our strength the assaults of this denial. This we do in the supreme cause of truth and in virtue of our sacred duty to profess Christ and his Gospel, moved by deep, unshakable love for men and in the invincible hope that modern man will come again to discover, in the religious ideals that Catholicism sets before him, his vocation to the civilization that does not die, but ever tends to the natural and supernatural perfection of the human spirit, and in which the grace of God enables man to possess his temporal goods in peace and honour, and to live in hope of attaining eternal goods.

These are the reasons which compel us, as they compelled our predecessors and, with them, everyone who has religious values at heart, to condemn the ideological systems which deny God and oppress the Church, systems which are often identified with economic, social and political régimes, amongst which atheistic communism is the chief. It could be said that it is not so much that we condemn these systems and régimes as that they express their radical opposition to us in thought and deed. Our regret is, in reality, more sorrow for a victim than the sentence of a judge.

Denial of freedom

Dialogue in such conditions is very difficult, not to say impossible, although, even today, we have no preconceived intention of excluding the persons who profess these systems and belong to these régimes. For the lover of truth discussion is always possible. The difficulties are enormously increased by obstacles of the moral order; by the absence of sufficient freedom of thought and action and by the perversion of discussion so that the latter is not made use of to seek and express objective truth but to serve predetermined utilitarian ends.

This is what puts an end to dialogue. The Church of Silence, for example, speaks only by her sufferings, and with her speaks also the suffering of an oppressed and degraded society, in which the rights of the spirit are crushed by those who control its fate. If we begin to speak in such a state of affairs, how can we offer dialogue, when we cannot be anything more than a 'voice crying in the wilderness' (Mk 1 : 3)? Silence, groaning, patience and always love, in such conditions, are the witness that the Church can still offer, and not even death can silence it.

Noble motives even of atheists

But though we must speak firmly and clearly in declaring and defending religion and the human values which it proclaims and upholds, we are moved by our pastoral office to seek in the heart of the modern atheist the motives of his turmoil and denial. His motives are many and complex, so that we must examine them with care if we are to answer them effectively. Some of them arise from the demand that divine things be presented in a worthier and purer way than is, perhaps, the case in certain imperfect forms of language and worship, which we ought to try to purify so that they express as perfectly and clearly as possible the sacred reality of which they are the sign. We see these men full of yearning, prompted sometimes by passion and desire for the unattainable, but often also by great-hearted dreams of justice and progress. In such dreams noble social aims are set up in the place of the Absolute and Necessary God, testifying thereby to the ineradicable need for the Divine

Source and End of all things, whose transcendence and immanence it is the task of our teaching office to reveal with patience and wisdom.

Again, we see them, sometimes with ingenuous enthusiasm, having recourse to human reason, with the intention of arriving at a scientific explanation of the universe. This procedure is all the less reprehensible in that it is often based upon laws of logical thought not unlike those of our classical school. It is a procedure which leads in a direction quite contrary to the will of those who use it, thinking to find in it an unanswerable proof of their atheism and its own intrinsic validity, for it leads them onward towards the new and final metaphysical and logical assertion of the existence of the supreme God. In this cogent process of reasoning the atheistic politico-scientist stops short wilfully at a certain point and so extinguishes the sovereign light of the intelligibility of the universe. Is there no one among us who could help him to reason on to a realization of the objective reality of the cosmic universe, a realization which restores to man the sense of the divine presence and bring to his lips the humble, halting words of a consoling prayer?

Sometimes, too, the atheist is spurred on by noble sentiments and by impatience with the mediocrity and self-seeking of so many contemporary social settings. He knows well how to borrow from our Gospel modes and expressions of solidarity and human compassion. Shall we not be able to lead him back one day to the christian source of such manifestations of moral worth?

Hope of future dialogue

Accordingly, bearing in mind the words of our predecessor of venerable memory, Pope John XXIII, in his Encyclical *Pacem in Terris* to the effect that the doctrines of such movements, once elaborated and defined, remain always the same, whereas the movements themselves cannot help but evolve and undergo changes, even of a profound nature, we do not despair that they may one day be able to enter into a more positive dialogue with the Church than the present one which we now of necessity deplore and lament.

But we cannot turn our gaze away from the contemporary world without expressing a cherished desire, namely that our intention of developing and perfecting our dialogue in the varied and changing facets which it presents, may assist the cause of peace between men, by providing a method which seeks to order human relationships in the sublime light of the language of reason and sincerity, and by making a contribution of experience and wisdom which can stir up all men to the consideration of the supreme values. The opening of a dialogue, such as ours would be, disinterested, objective and sincere, is in itself a decision in favour of a free and honourable peace. It excludes pretence, rivalry, deceit and betrayal. It cannot do other than condemn, as a crime and destruction, wars of aggression, conquest or domination. It cannot confine itself to relationships with the heads of nations but must set them up also with the body of the nation and with its foundations, whether social, family or individual, so as to diffuse in every institution and in every soul the understanding, the relish and the duty of peace.

Dialogue with non-Christian religions

Then we see another circle around us. This, too, is vast in its extent, yet it is not so far away from us. It is made up of the men who above all adore the one, supreme God whom we too adore. We refer to the children, worthy of our affection and respect, of the Hebrew people, faithful to the religion which we call that of the Old Testament. Then to the adorers of God according to the conception of monotheism, the Moslem religion especially, deserving of our admiration for all that is true and good in their worship of God. And also to the followers of the great Afro-Asiatic religions. Obviously we cannot share in these various forms of religion nor can we remain indifferent to the fact that each of them, in its own way, should regard itself as being the equal of any other and should authorize its followers not to seek to discover whether God has revealed the perfect and definitive form, free from all error, in which he wishes to be known, loved and served. Indeed, honesty compels us to declare openly our conviction that there is but one true religion, the religion of Christianity. It is our hope that all who seek God and adore him may come to acknowledge its truth.

But we do, nevertheless, recognize and respect the moral and spiritual values of the various non-Christian religions, and we desire to join with them in promoting and defending common ideals of religious liberty, human brotherhood, good culture, social welfare and civil order. For our part, we are ready to enter into discussion on these common ideals, and will not fail to take the initiative wherever our offer of discussion in genuine, mutual respect, would be well received.

With separated Christian brethren, stress what unites, not what divides

And so we come to the circle which is nearest to us, the circle of Christianity. In this field the dialogue, which has come to be called ecumenical, has already begun, and in some areas is making real headway. There is much to be said on this complex and delicate subject and our discourse only begins and does not end here. For the moment we limit ourselves to a few considerations—none of them new. The principle that we are happy to make our own is this: Let us stress what we have in common rather than what divides us. This provides a sound and fruitful subject for our dialogue. We are ready to carry it out wholeheartedly. We will say more: on many points of difference regarding tradition, forms of devotion, canon law, and worship, we are most ready to study how we can satisfy the legitimate desires of our christian brothers, still separated from us. It is our dearest wish to embrace them in a perfect union of faith and charity. But we must add that it is not in our power to compromise with the integrity of the faith or the requirements of charity. We foresee that this will cause misgiving and opposition among some, but now that the Catholic Church has deliberately committed herself to the recovery of unity in the one fold of Christ, it will not fail either in conscientious sincerity or consideration for others. It will not cease to affirm that the special claims which keep the separated brothers at a distance, are not the fruits of historic ambition or of tenuous theological speculation, but derive from the will of Christ and that, rightly understood, they are for the good of all and make for common unity, common freedom and the common welfare of christian life. The Catholic Church will not cease, by prayer and penance, to prepare herself to be worthy of the longed-for reconciliation.

The papacy

In reflecting on this subject, it distresses us to see how we, the promoter of such reconciliation, are regarded by many of the separated brethren as being its stumbling-block, because of the primacy of honour and jurisdiction which Christ bestowed upon the Apostle Peter, and which we have inherited from him. Do not some of them say that if it were not for the primacy of the Pope, the reunion of the separated Churches with the Catholic Church would be easy? We beg the separated brethren to consider whether this position is well founded. Without the Pope the Catholic Church would no longer be Catholic, and without the supreme, efficacious and decisive pastoral office of Peter the unity of the Church of Christ would utterly collapse. It would be vain to look for other principles of unity in place of the one established by Christ himself. As Saint Jerome justly wrote: 'There would arise in the Church as many sects as there are priests.'[1] We should also like to observe that this fundamental principle of Holy Church is not a supremacy of spiritual pride and human domination. It is a primacy of service, of ministration, of love. It is not empty rhetoric which confers upon the Vicar of Christ the title of 'servant of the servants of God'.

Consequently, our dialogue, before entering into fraternal conversation, speaks in prayer and hope with the heavenly Father.

Gratitude, respect and hope

We must observe, Venerable Brethren, with joy and confidence, that the vast and varied circle of separated Christians feels a certain spiritual compulsion which seems to promise consoling developments in regard to the reunion of all Christians in the one Church of Christ. We pray that the Holy Spirit will continue to breathe upon the 'ecumenical movement', and

[1] *Dial. contra Luciferianos*, n. 9.

we recall the emotion and joy we felt at Jerusalem in our meeting, full of charity and new hope, with the Patriarch Athenagoras. We wish to greet with gratitude and respect the participation of so many representatives of separated Churches in the Second Vatican Ecumenical Council. We want to give our assurance, once again, that we have an attentive, reverent interest in the spiritual movements connected with the problem of unity, which are stirring up vital and noble religious convictions in various individuals, groups and communities. With love and reverence we greet all these Christians, in hope that we may promote together, even more effectively, the cause of Christ and the unity which he desired for his Church, in the dialogue of sincerity and love.

Within the household, charity and loyal obedience

And lastly we turn to speak with the children of the house of God, the one, holy, catholic and apostolic Church, of which this Roman Church is 'mother and head'. It is our ardent desire that this conversation with our own children should be full of faith, of charity, of good works, should be intimate and familiar. We would have it responsive to all truth and virtue and to all the realities of our doctrinal and spiritual inheritance. Sincere and sensitive in genuine spirituality, ever ready to give ear to the manifold voice of the contemporary world, ever more capable of making Catholics truly good men, men wise, free, serene and strong; that is what we earnestly desire our family conversation to be.

This desire to impress upon the internal relationships of the Church the character of a dialogue between members of a body, whose constitutive principle is charity, does not do away with the exercise of the virtue of obedience where the right order necessary in all well constructed societies and, above all, the hierarchic constitution of the Church requires that, on the one side, authority should be exercised according to its proper function and that, on the other side, there should be submission. The Church's authority is instituted by Christ; it is, indeed, representative of him; it is the authorized channel of his word; it is the expression of his pastoral charity. Obedience, therefore, is motivated by faith, developes into a school of evangelical humility, and links the obedient man to the wisdom, unity, constructiveness and charity by which the body of the Church is sustained. It confers upon him who imposes it and upon him who conforms himself to it the merit of being like Christ who was 'made obedient unto death' (Phil 2: 8).

By obedience, therefore, in the context of dialogue, we mean the exercise of authority in the full awareness of its being a service and ministry of truth and charity, and we mean the observance of canonical regulations and respect for the government of legitimate superiors in the spirit of untroubled readiness as becomes free and loving children. The spirit of independence, of criticism, of rebellion ill accords with the charity which gives life to the Church's solidarity, concord and peace, and easily transforms the dialogue into argument, dispute and disagreement. This most regrettable attitude, so easy, alas, to produce, is condemned by the Apostle Paul in his admonition: 'Let there be no divisions among you' (1 Cor 1: 10).

New fervour, new themes, new speakers

It is, therefore, our ardent desire that the dialogue within the Church should take on new fervour, new themes and speakers, so that the holiness and vitality of the mystical body of Christ on earth may be increased. Anything that makes known the teachings of which the Church is both custodian and dispenser receives our approbation. We have already mentioned the liturgy, the interior life and preaching. We could add also: schools, the press, the social apostolate, the missions, the exercise of charity. All these are themes to which the Council will direct our attention. And we bless and encourage all those who, under the guidance of the competent authority, take part in the life-giving dialogue of the Church, priests especially and religious, and our well-loved laity, dedicated to Christ in Catholic Action and in so many other associations and activities.

It is a cause of joy and comfort for us to see that such a dialogue is already in existence in the Church and in the areas which surround it. The Church today is more than ever alive. But it seems good to consider that everything still remains to be done; the work begins today and never comes to an end. This is the law of our temporal, earthly pilgrimage. This is the ordinary task, Venerable Brothers, of our ministry, which everything today stimulates us to renew and to make more devoted and intense.

Father and brother

As for ourselves, in speaking to you of these things, we are pleased to trust in your co-operation and offer you our own in return. This union of aims and labour we ask for and offer not long after our elevation to the chair of the Apostle Peter, bearing the name and sharing, please God, something of the spirit of the Apostle of the Gentiles. And so celebrating the unity of Christ among us, we send to you with this, our first letter, in the name of the Lord, our blessing as brother and father, a blessing which we gladly extend to the whole Church and to all mankind.

From the Vatican, 6th August 1964, on the Feast of the Transfiguration of Our Lord Jesus Christ.

PAULUS PP. VI

APPENDIX VI

The Hierarchy of England and Wales gives its ready approval to the Constitution '*De Oecumenismo*' which it receives with joy. I say 'with joy' because the document shows us the mind of the Church and gives guidance for the future. We have all awaited this guidance from the supreme authority of the Church. Without it our ecumenical work cannot make progress.

There are those who have thought that the Catholics of England are indifferent to the ecumenical movement. Indeed some of our separated brethren in England have turned to Catholics outside our country in search of ecumenical dialogue. We obviously have no wish in any way to restrict their freedom to attend international ecumenical gatherings in any part of the world. We do feel, however, that it is of the greatest importance for this Council to recommend that normally, and as a general rule, the dialogue between Catholics and other Christians should take place in the country where they live. It should recommend, moreover, that so far as the Catholic side is concerned, the dialogue should come under the authority of the local hierarchy.

We have two reasons for our proposals:

(*a*) It is fitting for the dialogue to be held against the background of those local conditions under which the Catholics and other Christians concerned live at home.

(*b*) If eventually unity is reached, all these Christians will have to learn to live with each other.

For our part we promise our separated brethren that we shall cordially promote the ecumenical dialogue in England and Wales.

Gladly we proclaim our belief in the help and inspiration toward visible union given by the Holy Spirit to all Christians of goodwill. Without God's help ecumenical activity could not have started, nor could it continue. The Holy Spirit, and, indeed, Christian good sense assure us that all who rejoice in the name of Christ (if I may use the words of Pope John) should be united amongst themselves. They should have regard for the greatness of our common heritage and should forget past injuries. Thus charity may be in control and the spirit of dissension cast out. This union is more than ever necessary today since so many enemies of Christ are now seeking to destroy his kingdom.

At the beginning of the second session, Pope Paul declared that everyone, Catholics and separated brethren alike, should sincerely seek unity with humble and contrite heart. The document rightly says that the first step toward union must be a renewal of the spiritual life of the individual. Union will not be achieved through argument: it will be won by virtuous living.

In this spirit of charity and humility, and without in any way wishing to be obstructive, we must frankly outline to the Fathers of the Council a certain difficulty. The nature of ecumenical activity is not yet sufficiently clear and its objectives have not yet been fully explored. It is necessary for our aims and motives in the ecumenical dialogue to be made plain to all. Both the immediate and the ultimate objectives must be quite definitely stated.

Let me speak first of the immediate objective. The ecumenical dialogue is not undertaken with individual souls in mind, nor in order to gain the better of an argument. The dialogue has to be a sincere attempt to understand the beliefs of our separated brethren. It must also present and explain Catholic teaching to them. It is a coming together of brothers not an encounter of enemies. It takes place mainly between communities, that is, between the Catholic Church and non-Catholic Christian churches or communities. It is rooted in mutual trust and complete charity. On neither side is it an attempt to win an argument.

The final aim of ecumenical activity is, of course, the visible union of all Christians in the one Church of Christ. The immediate objective, however, is mutual understanding and love amongst those who are united by baptism but divided by doctrine. At the moment we must work for the first objective—the ultimate aim is not within our power.

It is right to praise the ecumenical dialogue. It seems to us, however, that we should also take note of our obligation to preach the whole truth to all men. That obligation arises from Christ's command to his Apostles and it must be carried out firmly, gently and with great humility by those to whom by God's grace the fullness of Christ's teaching has been given.

We should therefore like this document clearly to state *both* the necessity of the ecumenical dialogue *and* the obligation, imposed by Christ, of preaching the whole truth. Our separated brethren will not resent such preaching, for it comes from a good and honest conscience and shows our desire to follow Christ's command. In this way the demands of both charity and Christian truth are satisfied. If such a declaration were added to this document, the whole cause of ecumenism would be helped. For there are Catholics who are doubtful about all this ecumenical activity. They wonder if any good will come of it. They are greatly concerned about the dangers arising from ecumenism. They are willing enough to co-operate with other Christians in the social field and to combine with them in works of charity. But, as we know, this is simply not good enough. The renewal of the Church requires a true religious dialogue. The Chief Shepherd calls for this; the Church herself deserves it.

Christians living in England can still remember the days when bitter strife divided them, and when social life was soured by acrimony. Catholics and Protestants both regarded themselves as being in a state of war and sought each other's defeat. We give heartfelt thanks to God for the friendship and goodwill now flourishing between Christians. In the name of the whole hierarchy of England and Wales, we readily declare our intention of doing everything, short of denying our faith, to bring about the union of Christians. We wish to undertake a fuller and more frequent dialogue with all Christians, of whatever denomination.

At the Last Supper, in the final hours of his life on earth, Christ prayed to the Father that all his disciples should be one. The prayer of Christ cannot be in vain. Let all, therefore, both the Catholics and the separated brethren, so dear to us, strive that under the protection of Mary the Mother of God, the coming of the kingdom of Christ in the unity of the Church may soon be brought nearer.

JOHN CARMEL HEENAN (now Cardinal)
Archbishop of Westminster, England

APPENDIX VII

Regarding the 'hierarchy of truths' of which the Decree speaks (cf. p. 11), Archbishop Andrea Pangrazio, of Gorizia, Italy, in the Council said this:

A third remark: to arrive at a fair estimate of both the unity which now exists among Christians and the diversity which still remains, it seems very important to me to pay close attention to the *hierarchical order* of revealed truths which express the mystery of Christ and those elements which make up the Church.

Although all the truths revealed by divine faith are to be believed with the same divine faith and all those elements which make up the Church must be kept with equal fidelity, not all of them are of equal importance.

Some truths are *on the level of our final goal*, such as the mystery of the Blessed Trinity, the Incarnation and Redemption, God's love and mercy toward sinful humanity, eternal life in the perfect kingdom of God, and others.

Other truths are *on the level of means towards salvation*, such as that there are seven sacraments, truth concerning the hierarchical structure of the Church, the apostolic succession, and others. These truths concern the means which are given by Christ to the Church for her pilgrim journey here on earth; when this journey comes to an end, so also do these means.

Now doctrinal differences among Christians have less to do with these primary truths on the level of our final goal, and deal mostly with truths on the level of means, which are certainly subordinate to those other primary truths.

But we can say that the unity of Christians consists in a common faith and belief in those truths which concern our final goal.

If we explicitly make these distinctions in conformity with the hierarchy of truths and elements, I think the existing unity among all Christians will be seen more clearly, and it will become evident that all Christians are already a family united in the primary truths of the Christian religion.

APPENDIX VIII

Archbishop Eugene D'Souza, of Bhopal, India, spoke in the second session of the Council of our need for intellectual humility:

'A number of other missionary bishops have endorsed the remarks I am about to make.

'We warmly congratulate those who have drawn up the schema for having given us a text which is solid, beautiful, deeply Christian, a text which we hope will definitely fix the new orientation which has taken place in the Church in recent years. I speak of the fact that the Catholic Church as a Church has finally learned humility.

'The Sovereign Pontiff himself humbly begged pardon of God and of the separated brothers themselves at the beginning of this session, and the schema urges us to inner renewal and conversion of heart. I want to take a closer look at this last point.

'We confess that in this matter the law of progress has had more influence than the law of continuity. For after the famous confession which Pope Adrian VI ordered his legate in Germany to make at the start of the Reformation, such statements were very rarely made in the succeeding centuries. It is right for the Catholic Church to say that she has received the fullness of truth and of the means of grace, but it seemed that from this the false conclusion was drawn that she was practically guiltless.

'Confessions have become more frequent in recent decades. But what was confessed, at least by members of the hierarchy, remained limited—limited to moral life and the practice of christian virtues. The structures of the Church and the way of presenting doctrine were almost never mentioned.

'A few days ago other speakers eloquently demonstrated that, quite apart from the need to show a more attractive "face of the

Church" to our separated brothers, there is an urgent need to extend inner renewal to the various structures and methods of governing the Church. And there was no effective refutation of this demonstration. So I will speak only about renewal in presentation of doctrine.

"It is altogether certain that only the Catholic Church has integrally preserved the deposit of faith; and in the presence of our separated brothers we humbly bear witness to this fact in the Lord. In no official document, indeed never in the exercise of her ordinary teaching office, has she denied any revealed truth or taught error. But when asked whether she has always kept the proper balance, whether she has explained everything appropriately, whether Catholic theology and spiritual teaching has always given the proper emphasis, an objective observer would have to answer that she has not.

'The reasons for this are varied. Unrestrained emotion, for instance, or a subjective approach could confuse the issues. The deposit of faith is so complex that everyone can find something there which suits him, something which he can use, as the psychologists say, to "rationalize" his own individual or national character, his tendencies, even his will to power. He will gladly expound such a point, even if as a prelate or a theologian he has authority, and thus he will put forth a teaching which at the very least is one-sided.

'So it is a very good thing, even from this point of view, that the schema urges self-denial and humility, and consequently conversion of mind; for the mind cannot be separated from the heart.

'Another source of deviation is argumentative debate with a will to win. In controversy, when one side states a thesis the adversary usually states the antithesis, although often what should be proposed is a synthesis. When a particular truth is denied, Catholic theology usually takes a dogmatic definition as a starting point, often develops it in such a way that it becomes exaggerated, and finally yields a total image which is inadequate. And who will dare to claim that classical Catholic theology (in ecclesiology, Mariology, grace, revelation) has yet freed itself sufficiently from this polemical heritage?

'Here too, Brothers, we need humility. Let us with sincere

and truthful hearts direct our attention to those complementary truths which, as one of us has well said, our separated brothers sometimes emphasize better than we do.

'I want to insist on this point. Just as love is not perfect unless it is universal and total, so humility too should be total and should include what I will call intellectual humility, or even doctrinal humility.

'In recent days we have often heard "We must propose the whole of the Catholic truth to our separated brothers." Pardon me if I admit that I sometimes seem to read between the lines these words: "Although we are sinners, we Catholics possess the whole truth; and this is our great superiority."

'It is true that we Catholics need not cultivate an inferiority complex. But the time is long overdue for us to get rid of any superiority complex. And we must certainly do our best to root out that oversimplification: "We possess the truth; the others say the same thing as we do or they are in error; therefore we need not listen to them except to refute them."

'Horace said: "To learn from the enemy is legitimate"—*a fortiori* from brothers in Christ. For "catholic" means "universal". Just as Christ took to himself everything human, sin alone excepted, so Catholicism which is true to its name should take to itself everything which is Christian, leaving out negations. In actual fact, for the principal first fruits of renewal we are heavily indebted to others—for the biblical movement to the Protestants and for the liturgical movement to the Orthodox. Relying on their help, let us abandon those traditions which belong only to a particular school of theology or national character or religious order and which we have repeatedly confused with Tradition with a capital "T". Or let us make certain superficial and peripheral devotions give way to what is deep and central. All this can help us to grasp more perfectly the mystery of Christ and the Church.

'In this way ecumenism will contribute to the doctrinal *aggiornamento* of the Church. Obviously it is not a question of omitting or watering down certain dogmas out of opportunism or false irenicism. But the questions which are put to us will make us more alert to the full implications of the synthesis we seek. This will be true if we know how to listen with sincerity of heart, to "listen to one another" in the full sense, as the Sovereign Pontiff said in his talk to the Observers. But this presupposes that we are "not self-complacent, but humble-minded" (Rom 12: 16).

'Venerable Brothers, successors of the Apostles, let us often meditate on these words of the Apostle: "God forbid that I should boast of anything but the cross of our Lord Jesus Christ" (Gal 6: 14); or these others: "If I am to boast . . . I delight to boast of the weaknesses which humiliate me, and then the power of Christ will come and rest upon me" (2 Cor 12: 1–9).'

APPENDIX IX

My Dear Brothers and Sisters in Jesus Christ,

The other day a young Scottish missionary, not a Catholic, died in the Congo along with the friend he had been nursing. He could have gone free and saved his own life. He chose rather to stay with the sick man.

'Greater love than this no man hath that a man should lay down his life for his friend' (Jn 15: 13). Such heroic love only comes through the grace of Jesus Christ. We should all thank Our Lord from our hearts that He gave this great grace to this young Protestant.

This, I think, is a good beginning for the thoughts I want to share with you. These thoughts are concerned with Christian men and women, not Catholics, who bear Christ's name with joy, who live according to His teaching as they know it, and who clearly receive His grace.

There are two reasons why I want to share my thoughts about them: (1) In the last Session of the Vatican Council a Decree on Ecumenism was passed, which requires bishops to lead their preists and people in new approaches towards other Christians. (2) Tomorrow, Monday, January 18th, a special Octave begins in which other Christians are praying that Our Lord will remove differences and divisions among us. We are with our brethren in keeping this Octave of prayer.

One of the remarkable developments in these our times is the great desire on the part of all Christians to be one and so fulfil the prayer Our Lord made the night before He suffered. If you read Chapter 17 of the Gospel of St John you will see that He approached His Sacred Passion with this prayer on His lips: 'That they all may be one, as Thou Father in Me and I in Thee; that they also may be one in us' (Jn 17: 21).

The words 'ecumenism', and 'ecumenical' need not frighten us. In general, they mean all that Christians are now doing to fulfil this desire of Our Lord.

I need not tell you what harm the divisions among Christian people have done and still do to the preaching of the Gospel throughout the whole world. This is not a time to apportion blame. In many ways we are all guilty and must bear together the burden of this scandal. Our Holy Father, Pope Paul, on many occasions, has given us a vivid example of humility. He has begged pardon for the faults on our side and offered full forgiveness for any wrongs that have been done to us.

This note of sorrow must sound with the same depth of sincerity on both sides. We must all deplore our separation and long for the day when we shall be one.

It is not easy to change the habits and attitudes that history has forced upon us and maintained for hundreds of years. But the time has come when we must make the change.

Let me say, first of all, what this change does not mean. It does not mean that we lose any of our conviction about the one true Church of Christ. We know that the Church is founded on a rock and the rock is Peter. Through no merits of ours, Our Lord has given us the grace of full membership in the Church over which Peter's successor is Supreme Shepherd.

The change does not mean, again, that differences in doctrine or in worship no longer matter. They matter very much. The truth given by Our Lord is divine. We owe complete surrender to divine truth. Our Lord's teaching is guaranteed to us by Our Holy Mother the Church. She is the pillar and the ground of truth (1 Tim 3: 15).

What does the change mean, then? First of all grateful recognition that we are still united in important basic realities. The Reformation did not reverse everything. For instance Baptism and belief in the Blessed Trinity, the Incarnation and Redemption still unite us. Baptism makes all who receive it, children of God, brothers and sisters of Jesus Christ, and members of the Church. Of course baptism is a gateway, a beginning of life. Circumstances may interfere with later progress. It is not at all the fault of our brethren that they are not with us now at the Holy Sacrifice of the Mass, or at Holy Communion. Basically they have the right to everything through Holy Baptism, if they have received it validly.

There are other great Christian realities which our brethren share with us. They love and revere God's written word in the Holy Scriptures. Even when they differ from us in their understanding of the Gospel, they make their decisions and lead their lives in the conviction that they are fulfilling the word of God. We know how often they are selfless and dedicated in works of charity, in their efforts to deal with the ignorance, poverty and distress which afflict mankind. I began this letter with the supreme example of that heroic missionary who the other day gave his life for his friend in the Congo.

The change we are to make then is this. We are to look now at the big things which unite us in Our Lord and cultivate them diligently. There is no make-believe here. These are genuine realities—Baptism, the Holy Scriptures, Christian prayers and devotions, active works of charity in the name of Christ. Through these genuine realities our brethren do share with us in the good things Our Lord has given His Church. Unhappily we do not possess full communion together in the one true Church. We are nonetheless brothers and sisters in Christ.

I want you to pray very much during these days from to-morrow, January 18th until January 25th. All of us should make a special effort to go to Mass and Holy Communion in this Octave of prayer for the unity of Christians.

I want you to pray first of all for ourselves. We find it hard to change attitudes which may have been necessary in the past but are no longer permissible. It is the new grace moving all Christians to seek unity which has made old attitudes completely out of date. We are now to look not only at what divides us, but at what unites us.

Gently but firmly we must go on to draw the right practical conclusions. We shall be glad to meet our brethren who are not with us yet in full Christian unity; to meet them, to come to know and appreciate them, to share with them in common efforts for the good of the community in which we live and for the development and peace of those parts of the world which above all need Christian charity.

It is right that we should learn to pray with these brethren of ours. 'Where two or three are gathered together in My name there am I in the midst' (Mt 18: 20). Prayer for Christian unity, made by us together, could be a powerful means of hastening the great day of complete reconciliation.

For the time being it is not appropriate for us to meet together in one anothers' churches. This could give the impression that all is now happily settled, and whatever may still divide us of no importance.

To cultivate common religious studies with our brethren is right where, on our side, there is sound competence in explaining Catholic Faith; and a genuine effort to progress with the Church in Liturgical and Biblical Studies. Anything less than complete, frank loyalty to the whole teaching of the Church would be disastrous in any Catholic who seeks to play his part in work for Christian unity. Anything which aims merely at publicity or looks for surface success, is unworthy of this great cause and could do it real harm.

Really the best contribution we can make, as a beginning, is to renew our own Christian lives in the spirit of the Gospel. Pope John was very clear and explicit about this. He called the Council in order to purify and invigorate the Church. The Council is concerned primarily, he said, with our own reformation and renewal. But this very thing will be our greatest initial effort for unity among all Christians. If we simplify and concentrate our lives, the image of the Church will stand out clear. Our brethren will know us for what we are; we shall know them.

Here then are some simple ways of sharing in the Ecumenical Movement:

(1) Grow in love for Our Lord. Always, among ourselves and with other Christians, live His lesson of meekness and humility of heart (Mt 11: 29). This is the very soul of all ecumenical effort. Without it the rest will be window-dressing.

(2) Grow in love for the Church which is His body. Be alert to developments in the Liturgy and other departments of Christian life. If we are sensitively in touch with the Church's renewal, we are preparing for the approach to our brethren and may take a worthy part.

(3) Pray a lot for Christians to be one. Be ready to pray with

other Christians for this great cause. When it is authorised by those who hold authority, be ready to pray publicly with our brethren.

(4) Be ready to join with other Christians in promoting justice and charity, here and abroad. Here again, our authorities will not be slow to give the lead. Support them gladly.

(5) Meetings for common study with our brethren and other activities in which we may be called upon to speak as representing the Catholic Church, should normally be undertaken only with permission. I hope the ecumenical spirit will lead many of us to seek to be better qualified as Catholics, so that we may deserve to help in this work.

As I come to know you better, and also as I become friends with other Christian leaders, I hope to indicate from time to time other practical ways in which we can fulfil the Council's Decree on Ecumenism.

Today I would commend above all what the Council calls Spiritual Ecumenism: our duty to renew ourselves in grace and truth; our duty to pray for the right attitude of mind.

Let us begin then in the name of the Lord, and with the help of Our Lady!

Your loving Bishop,

✠ THOMAS.

Given at Wardley Hall on the Feast of the Epiphany, 6th January, 1965, and appointed to be read in all the churches and chapels of the diocese on Sunday, 17th January.

APPENDIX X

COMMENT ON THE DECREE ON ECUMENISM BY THE
RT REV OLIVER TOMKINS, ANGLICAN BISHOP OF BRISTOL

Behind the decree on Ecumenism lies the Constitution on the Church. It is an epoch-making document, taking its place in the expositions already delivered. As such, it is presumably to be understood as the most recent teaching on the subject, in light of which previous documents may now be construed and subsidiary statements (such as *de oecumenismo*) are to be interpreted.

As such, I personally and on first brief acquaintance, welcome it (in spite of some qualifications) for the following features: (1) the serious attention to Scriptural exegesis, especially in chapters 1 and 2; (2) the wider context in which the doctrine of papacy is set by chapter 3, especially in the collegiality of bishops, even though the claims still made for papacy go further than can be justified either by Scripture or by universal tradition; (3) the inclusion of a chapter (4) on the laity goes some way towards redressing the balance of an excessively 'clerical' view of the Church: any criticisms may well be tempered by the reflection that neither in theory nor practice do the rest of us manage much better; (4) the chapter on holiness, though stilted and remote in style, yet recalls us all to that level upon which the Church transcends argument and speaks with the authentic finality of simply *being* Christlike; (5) the 'eschatological nature of the pilgrim church' (chapter 7) opens a dialogue on the scriptural understanding of the Church's *limitations* for which there has been little encouragement before; (6) finally, the fact that chapter 8 on the Blessed Virgin is firmly set in a decree on the *Church* preserves the possibility of keeping the proportions of the faith. Unhappily, the Pope's proclamation of the Blessed

Virgin Mary as 'Mother of the Church' seemed to indicate some nervousness, lest it should appear that the Mariological doctrine is not after all a doctrine in its own right, as it were, capable of being developed independently of Christology and ecclesiology. But however much one may regret this action, the decree itself bears witness that ecclesiology (in its turn dependent on Christology) is the right setting for Mariology.

These are aspects of the Constitution *de ecclesia* which I find to be cause for thanksgiving as one considers the decree on Ecumenism which defines the relationship of the rest of us to 'the Church' as understood in the Constitution.

(1) Again, 'the principles on Ecumenism' seek true 'catholicity' by their appeal to the common ground of Scripture. In paragraph 2 I find little (beyond a claim for Petrine supremacy) which I cannot gladly echo with only the difference of meaning which I must attach to the word 'Church'.

(2) In paragraph 3 the wider context for 'all who have been justified by faith in baptism' as members of Christ's body, extends to a new recognition that we are not simply isolated individuals. In the 'Communities or Churches' to which we belong, we are formed by corporate and institutional realities in which the grace of God is acknowledged to have been at work, and may indeed serve to remind Catholics of their need for 'edification' in Christ. These implications are spelt out in more detail in chapter 3, which contains phrases for which Anglicans in particular may well be grateful.

(3) 'The Practice of Ecumenism' in chapter 2 is based upon explicit recognition that 'Christ summons the Church to continual reformation'. Although addressed to Catholics, it contains many golden maxims which we, not of the Roman obedience, equally need to observe in our dealings with them and with each other.

It would have been naïve to expect these documents *not* to be clearly and explicity 'Roman Catholic'. They come from Rome, but from a process of struggle. I should like to know more about the true significance of some of the last-minute changes (e.g. in the references to reading the Scriptures in paragraph 21). But I thankfully acknowledge the justice of describing the Council as 'a miracle'—if by this we understand that we confront an event inexplicable apart from a direct overruling by the power of God. To him all things are possible—and therein lies our hope.

OLIVER BRISTOL

APPENDIX XI

Ecumenical Patriarchate of Constantinople

Very Rev Archimandrite Panteleimon RODOPOULOS, Rector of the Greek Orthodox Theological School, Boston (U.S.A.).

Very Rev John ROMANIDES, Professor of Theology at the same Theological School.

Very Rev Archimandrite Andrew SCRIMA, Rector of the Greek Orthodox Church in Rome, representative of His Holiness Patriarch Athenagoras.

Russian Orthodox Church (Patriarchate of Moscow)

Very Rev Protoierei Vitali BOROVOI, Professor at the Theological Academy of Leningrad, president of the delegation of the Russian Orthodox Church to the World Council of Churches (Geneva).

Very Rev Protoierei Livery VORONOV, Professor at the Theological Academy of Leningrad.

The Orthodox Church of Georgia

Very Rev Protoierei Vitali BOROVOI (proxy).

Coptic Orthodox Church of Egypt

His Excellency the Rt Rev Amba SAMUIL, bishop in charge of Social Affairs of the Patriarchate.

Rev Morcos Elias Abdel MESSIH, pastor of the Coptic Orthodox in the United States and Canada.

Syrian Orthodox Church

Very Rev Ramban Saliba SHAMOON, Secretary of His Beatitude the Patriarch.

Syrian Orthodox Church of India

Very Rev Korepiscopa T. S. ABRAHAM, Vicar St Thomas

Church, Ayroor (India) member of the Diocesan Council of
Thumpamon.

Apostolic Armenian Church (Catholicosate of Etchmiadzin)
Right Rev Bishop Parkev KEVORKIAN, Delegate of the Catho-
licos of Etchmiadzin in Moscow, Bishop of the Armenians in
Moscow.
Mr Krikor BEKMEZIAN, theologian, member of the Supreme
Spiritual Council of Holy Etchmiadzin.

Greek Orthodox Patriarchate of Alexandria
Very Rev Archimandrite Cyril Konkoulakis of the patriarchal
clergy.
Dr Theodore Mosconas, Archivist and Librarian of the
Patriarchate.

Apostolic Armenian Church (Catholicosate of Cilicia)
His Excellency the Right Rev Karekin SARKISSIAN, superior of
the Patriarchal Seminary.
His Excellency the Right Rev Ardavazt TERTERIAN, Bishop of
the Armenians of Southern France.

Catholicosate Patriarchate of the East (Assyrians)
Rev Quashisha Isaac REHANA, Rector, St Thomas Church,
New Britain, Conn. (U.S.A.).
Mr George W. LAMSA, Doctor of Theology, Lecturer in Sacred
Scripture (U.S.A.).

Russian Orthodox Church Outside of Russia
Very Rev Archpriest Igor TROYANOFF, Director of the Russian
Orthodox Churches of Lausanne and Vevey (Switzerland).
Very Rev Archimandrite Dr Ambrose POGODIN, Rector of the
Russian Orthodox Church in Rome.
Substitute: Prof Dr Serge GROTOFF, of the University of Rome.

Old Catholic Church (Union of Utrecht)
Very Rev Canon Peter John MAAN, Professor of New Testa-
ment at the Old Catholic Seminary of Amersfoort and Vicar
of the Cathedral Church of Utrecht (The Netherlands).
Substitute: Rev Dr Herwig ALDENHOVEN, Pastor in Wallbach,
Aargau (Switzerland).

Mar Thoma Syrian Church of Malabar (India)
Most Rev Philipose Mar CHRYSOSTOM, missionary bishop, Kerala (South India).

Anglican Communion
Right Rev Dr John MOORMAN, Bishop of Ripon (England).
Rev Dr Eugene R. FAIRWEATHER, Professor of Divinity, Trinity College, University of Toronto (Canada).
Rev Ernest JOHN, of the Brotherhood of the Ascension, vicar of the Cathedral Church of the Redemption, New Delhi (India).
Substitutes: Rev Prof Howard ROOT, Fellow and Dean of Emmanuel College, Cambridge, and Lecturer in Divinity, University of Cambridge (England).
Rev Dr Massey Hamilton SHEPHERD, Jr, Professor of Liturgics, The Church Divinity School of the Pacific, Berkeley, California (U.S.A.).
Rev Canon Bernard PAWLEY, Canon-treasurer of Ely Cathedral, representative of the Anglican Archbishops of Canterbury and York.

Lutheran World Federation
Rev Prof Kristen E. SKYDSGAARD, Professor of Systematic Theology, The University of Copenhagen (Denmark).
Rev Prof Warren A. QUANBECK, Lutheran Theological Seminary, St Paul, Minnesota (U.S.A.).
Right Rev Dr Sven SILEN, Bishop of Västeras (Sweden).
Substitutes: Prof George LINDBECK, Associate Professor of Historical Theology, Yale University Divinity School, New Haven, Connecticut (U.S.A.).
Rev Dr Vilmos VAJTA, Director of the Theological Department of the Lutheran World Federation, Geneva.

World Alliance of Reformed and Presbyterian Churches
Rev Prof Vittorio SUBILIA, Dean of the Theological Faculty of the Waldensian Church, Rome.
Rev Dr A. Allan MCARTHUR, of the Church of Scotland, Minister of Pollokshield-Titwood Parish Church, Glasgow (Scotland).
Rev Prof John Newton THOMAS, of the United Presbyterian

Church, Professor of Systematic Theology, Union Theological Seminary in Virginia, Richmond (U.S.A.).

Evangelical Church in Germany
Prof Dr Edmund SCHLINK, Professor of Dogmatics at the University of Heidelberg (Germany).

Substitute: Rev Dr Wolfgang DIETZFELBINGER, Pastor in Erbendorf (Germany).

World Methodist Council
Rev Prof Harold ROBERTS, Principal at the Divinity School, Richmond College, Richmond (England).
Rev Prof Walter G. MUELDER, Dean and Professor of Social Ethics, Boston University School of Theology, Boston (U.S.A.).
Rev Prof Albert C. OUTLER, Professor of Theology, Southern Methodist University, Dallas, Texas.

Substitutes: Rev Prof William R. CANNON, Dean of the Candler School of Theology, Emory University, Atlanta, Georgia (U.S.A.).
Rev Prof Robert E. CUSHMAN, Dean of Duke University Divinity School, Durham, North Carolina (U.S.A.).
Rev Dr Philip POTTER, member of the Methodist Missionary Society, London (England).
Rev David Alan KEIGHLEY, representative in Italy of the British Methodist Church of the United Kingdom and of the Methodist Missionary Society, Rome.
Rev Max WOODWARD, Secretary of the World Methodist Council, London (England).
Rev Prof Franklin H. LITTELL, Professor at the Chicago Theological Seminary, Chicago (U.S.A.).

International Congregational Council
Rev Dr Douglas HORTON, former Moderator of the International Congregational Council, Randolph, New Hampshire (U.S.A.).
Rev Prof George B. CAIRD, Senior Tutor at Mansfield College, Oxford (England).

Substitutes: Rev Prof Bard THOMPSON, Professor of Ecclesiastical

History, Lancaster Theological Seminary, Lancaster, Pennsylvania (U.S.A.).

Rev Prof John R. VON ROHR, Professor of Historical Theology, Pacific School of Religion, Berkeley, California (U.S.A.).

Rev Prof Heiko A. OBERMAN, Professor of Church History, Harvard University Divinity School, Cambridge, Massachusetts (U.S.A.).

Friends World Committee for Consultation
Prof Douglas V. STEERE, Professor at Haverford College, Haverford, Penns. (U.S.A.).

Dr A. Burns CHALMERS, Director of Davis House, and Secretary of Education, American Friends Service Committee, Washington, D.C. (U.S.A.).

World Convention of Churches of Christ (Disciples)
Dr William George BAKER, Lecturer in Practical Theology, Scottish Congregational College, Edinburgh (Scotland).

Dr William B. BLAKEMORE, Dean of Disciples Divinity House, University of Chicago, Chicago (U.S.A.).

Substitute: Rev Dr Howard E. SHORT, Editor of *The Christian*, St Louis (U.S.A.).

International Association for Liberal Christianity
Prof L. J. VAN HOLK, Professor at the University of Leiden (The Netherlands).

Church of South India
Right Rev A. H. LEGG, Moderator of the Church of South India Synod, Trivandrum (South India).

World Council of Churches (Geneva)
Rev Dr Lukas VISCHER, Research Secretary in the Department of Faith and Order of the World Council of Churches, Geneva.

Dr Nikos A. NISSIOTIS, Associate Director of the Ecumenical Institute of the World Council of Churches, Bossey (Switzerland).

Dr Z. K. MATTHEWS, on the Staff of the Division of Inter-

Church Aid, World Service and Refugees of the World Council of Churches, Geneva.

Rev Dr Jerald C. BRAUER, Dean of the Divinity School, University of Chicago (U.S.A.).

Guests of the Secretariat for Promoting Christian Unity

Most Rev Bishop CASSIEN, Director of the Orthodox Theological Institute St Serge, Paris (France).

Rev Pastor Marc BOEGNER, of the French Academy, Honorary President of the Protestant Federation of France, Paris (France).

Prof Dr Theodore MOSCONAS, Secretary of the Council of Churches of Alexandria, Archivist and Librarian of the Library of the Greek Orthodox Patriarchate of Alexandria (Egypt).

Rev Prof G. C. BERKOUWER, Professor at the Free Protestant University of Amsterdam (The Netherlands).

Rev Prof Oscar CULLMANN, Professor at the Universities of Basle and Paris.

Prof Masatoshi DOI, United Church of Christ in Japan (Nippon Kirisuto Kyodan), Professor of Systematic Theology and Ecumenics, Doshisha University, Kyoto (Japan).

Dr David DU PLESSIS, Pentecostal minister, South Africa and California (U.S.A.).

Dr Oswald C. J. HOFFMANN, of the Lutheran Church-Missouri Synod, St Louis (U.S.A.).

Rev Pastor Wilhelm SCHMIDT, Vicar of the 'Evangelische Michaelsbruderschaft', Bremen-Horn (Germany).

Rev Dr William A. NORGREN, Director of Faith and Order Studies, National Council of Churches of Christ in the U.S.A., New York City (U.S.A.).

Rev Pastor Roger SCHUTZ, Prior of Taizé Community (France).

Rev Pastor Max THURIAN, Sub-prior of the same community.

INDEX

Abbott, W. M., 124 n
Afanassiev, N., 95 n
Agatho, Pope, 195
aggiornamento, 31
Alcuin, 195
Alexis, Patriarch, 177
Allchin, D., 228 n
Altaner, B., 192 n
Ambrose, St, 185, 190, 192
'Ambrosiaster', 185
Andrews, T., 159 n
Anglican(s), 35-7, 44-5, 49, 69, 70-1, 75-6, 79-80, 84, 86, 92, 105, 227-9 *et passim*
Anson, P. F., 207 n
Antony, Abbot, 199-200
Antony, St, 192-3
Apostle(s):
  Creed, 99
  episcope of, 93
  and N.T., 242
  and the Transfiguration, 199
  and sacraments, 3
Apostolic:
  mission of the Church, 93
  origin of Church, 3
  — Roman See, 24
  succession, 3, 149
Aquinas, T., St, 89, 192, 199 n, 201 n
Armstrong, A. H., and Fry, E. J. B., editors of *Rediscovering Eastern Christendom*, 20 n, 159 n, 178 n
Arseniev, N., 179 n, 199
Assumption of B.V.M., 152, 197, 243

'Athanasian Creed', 196
Athanasius, St, 190-2, 196, 202
Athenagoras, Patriarch of Constantinople, 162
Attwater, D., 156 n, 159 n, 160 n, 162 n, 174 n, 175 n, 177, 179 n, 202 n, 205 n
Augsburg Confession, 43
Augustine, St, 4 n, 91, 128, 189, 191, 195, 203
Authority of the Decree, 28-30

Baëta, C. G., 62 n
Baillie, D. M., and Smith Lieper, H., 56 n
Baptism, 17, 72, 91, 99, 234
Baptist(s), 37, 40, 44, 51, 105
baptized into Jesus Christ, 67
Bardy, G., 184 n, 185 n, 189 n, 190 n, 205 n
Barrett, C. R., 72 n
Barth, K., 77 n, 111 n, 145
Basil, St, 190-3
Bate, H. N., editor of *Proceedings of the World Conference of Faith and Order at Lausanne*, 34 n
Bates, M. S., 112 n
Baum, G., 19 n, 53, 66 n, 109 n, 225 n, 226 n, 249 n
Bayer, C., 217 n
Bayne, S. J., Jnr., 48 n, 69 n
Bea, Cardinal, 30, 51 n, 82, 88 n, 94, 99 n, 106, 109, 110 n, 115 n, 118, 143, 147 n, 182, 211, 215, 216, 219, 222, 232 n, 233, 237, 241, 249

319